HX   More, Thomas
811   Sir Thomas More's Utopia
1516
M66

DEC 2 1 2002

SIR THOMAS MORE'S UTOPIA

EDITED, WITH INTRODUCTION AND NOTES, BY

J. CHURTON COLLINS

Talent Corps Library

OXFORD
AT THE CLARENDON PRESS

Oxford University Press, Amen House, London E.C.4

GLASGOW NEW YORK TORONTO MELBOURNE WELLINGTON
BOMBAY CALCUTTA MADRAS KARACHI LAHORE DACCA
CAPE TOWN SALISBURY NAIROBI IBADAN ACCRA
KUALA LUMPUR HONG KONG

FIRST PUBLISHED 1904
REPRINTED 1909, 1914, 1920, 1926, 1930, 1936, 1949, 1952, 1961 1963
1964

PRINTED IN GREAT BRITAIN

PREFACE

THE present edition of the *Utopia* of More has been undertaken with a double object; to encourage and assist the study of a work which deserves to take a far more prominent place than it has hitherto held in our curricula of advanced education, and to supply a want which no preceding edition has aimed at supplying. Few works have so many claims to attention. Though not originally written in our own language it is, through the versions of Robynson and Bishop Burnet, one of the most famous works in English literature, and to every student with any pretension to a competent knowledge of that literature an acquaintance with it is indispensable. As a romance and work of art it ranks, if not in vogue at least in celebrity, with the *Pilgrim's Progress*, with *Robinson Crusoe*, and with *Gulliver's Travels*. To the student of moral and political philosophy or of the theory of education it is of equal importance, and it well deserves a place, as a subject of study, beside the *Republic* and *Laws* of Plato and the *Politics* of Aristotle; while the light which it throws on the state of Europe, and more particularly on that of England, at one of the most critical periods in their annals, would alone entitle it to be regarded as a textbook in the study of the social and political history of the sixteenth century.

Of preceding editions two only are known to me which have any claim to consideration, and neither supplies what it is the aim of the present edition to supply. Of Dr. Lupton's edition of the Latin text and

of Robynson's translation it is scarcely possible to speak
too highly. If Dr. Lupton had designed his work for
the class of students to which this edition appeals, for
circulation—that is to say, in schools and ordinary
educational institutes—the present edition would have
been a mere work of supererogation. But his work is
addressed to mature scholars; it is not designed to
include such information as junior students necessarily
require, or to become a popular textbook. My indebted
ness to Dr. Lupton I have, I hope, always acknowledged whenever it has been direct, but indirectly it
has been more considerable than my frequent acknow-
ledgements of it indicate. I have often been able to
add to his illustrations and to explain what he,
studying succinctness, has no doubt purposely left
unexplained, by resorting to sources of information
to which he has himself guided me. And this applies
both to the General Introduction and to the Notes.

Of Dr. Lumby's edition it becomes me to say no more
than that a comparison with the present will show that
he approaches the work from a very different point of
view to that from which it is approached here; that
his notes almost entirely confine themselves to elucidat-
ing the language of Robynson's text, with the addition
of a few explanations of the more obvious historical
and biographical allusions.

My own endeavour has been, both in the General
Introduction and in the Notes, to meet the probable
needs of those students who approach the work on its
various sides of interest and importance, namely, those
junior students who require elementary philological instruction, and those more advanced students who will be
concerned chiefly with its relation to philosophy and his-

PREFACE

tory. I have thus attempted to expand and supplement Dr. Lupton's more succinct treatment of these subjects, and to supply at the same time that more rudimentary information which did not come within the scope of his work. My fear is that I may have attempted too much, and that the voluminous annotation which this double purpose has rendered necessary may prove to be confusing. But a judicious student, whether pupil or teacher, will easily discriminate between what is needed for his particular purpose and what is not.

The text is practically that of the first edition of Robynson's translation, but I have corrected obvious misprints, and have not hesitated to adopt the text of the second edition where it is undoubtedly an improvement on that of the first. These deviations from the first edition have been recorded in the Notes.

To Dr. Lupton I have already acknowledged my obligations. I have also been indebted, both in the General Introduction and in the Notes, to Sir James Mackintosh's *Life of More*, to Father Bridgett's *Life and Writings of Sir Thomas More*, to Durand de Laur's *Érasme*, to Mr. Frederick Seebohm's *Oxford Reformers*, to Professor Arber's Bibliography in his reprint of the *Utopia*, to Dr. F. J. Furnivall's *Ballads from Manuscripts* (especially to the Introduction), to Mr. Cooper's edition of the *Dialogue between Pole and Lupset* in the Early English Text Society's Publications, and to other tracts in the same collection. I have also to thank Mr. Cannan for directing my attention to some interesting parallels with the *Germania* of Tacitus.

For the excellent Glossarial Index I am indebted to Miss Hilda M. R. Murray of the Royal Holloway College.

CONTENTS

INTRODUCTION   PAGE
    Life of More . . . . . vii–xxx
    Origin and Inspiration of the *Utopia* . xxx–xxxvi
    Framework and Models of the *Utopia* . xxxvi–xli
    The Plot . . . . . . xlii–xlvi
    Purpose of the Work . . . xlvi–xlviii
    Early Editions and Translations . . xlix–lii

TEXT OF *UTOPIA* 1–144

NOTES TO *UTOPIA* 145–245

APPENDIX 247–254

GLOSSARIAL INDEX 255–283

INTRODUCTION

I. LIFE OF MORE

The *Utopia* is so closely bound up with the personal life and character of More, and with the social and political movements and events immediately preceding and contemporary with its composition, that a sketch of both is a necessary prelude to its study. Thomas More, the second child and eldest son of John More, successively (1503) serjeant of law, (1518) judge in the Court of Common Pleas, and (1520) of the King's Bench; and of Agnes, daughter of Thomas Graunger, was born February 7, 1478, in Milk Street, London. Of the history of his mother we know nothing. His father, 'of gentle but not noble blood,' is described by his son as 'courteous, affable, innocent, gentle, merciful, just and uncorrupted'; he was also a man of much shrewdness and humour, and all these qualities he bequeathed to his son. Young More received his early education at the school attached to St. Anthony's Hospital in Threadneedle Street, then under the rule of Nicholas Holt, a very competent scholar. But he was removed from school, to be transferred to the household of Cardinal Morton, Archbishop of Canterbury and Lord Chancellor, before Holt could have done much more for him than to ground him in Latin. When he entered Morton's household he was little more than a child. But while there, he probably received impressions from the conversation of that eminent statesman and ecclesiastic, which were among the moulding influences of his life. What he thought of Morton, and what perhaps by implication he owed to him, he has himself described in the words which he places in the mouth of Hythlodaye, in the first book of the *Utopia*. What Morton thought of him is recorded by Roper; 'This child,' he said more than once, 'whoever shall live to see it, will prove a marvellous man.' Perhaps even in these early days he may have heard much from Morton, which many years later he wove into the history of Richard III, and which gave it its colour.

At Morton's recommendation he proceeded to Oxford, probably in 1492, when he was in his fifteenth year. We know comparatively little about his residence there, and that little is uncertain. One tradition places him at Canterbury Hall, a foundation the site of which is now occupied by the Canterbury Quadrangle of Christ Church; another at St. Mary's Hall, another in lodgings at both places. In any case he remained at Oxford 'not fully two years.' He pursued his studies with diligence and enthusiasm, 'wonderfully profiting' says Harpsfield, 'in the Latin and Greek tongues.'

His residence at Oxford was the initiation of his intellectual life, and brought him into contact with that movement which was to transform the England of Mediaevalism into the England of the Renaissance and of the Reformation. Of all the agencies by which that transformation was accomplished the most potent was the New Learning, the revival of the study of Greek, and the substitution of an intelligent study of the great, for an unintelligent study of the inferior Latin Classics. Since the fall of

Constantinople in 1453, the ardour for the New Learning in Italy had kindled into fanaticism, Scholars were burning lamps before the bust of Plato, and refusing to study the New Testament lest it should spoil their Greek. Devout and sober Christians were labouring to reconcile Platonism with the teachings of St. John and of St. Paul. The Platonic Academy had been established. The press of Aldus was beginning to pour out the volumes which brought the new treasures within the reach of all. Soon the enthusiasm spread to England. Before 1488, William Grocyn had placed himself under the tuition of Demetrius Chalcondylas at Florence, and had, some two years later, returned to Oxford to lecture on Greek. Thomas Linacre had followed his example, and it was Linacre who was More's Oxford tutor in Greek. Two others who were before long to be numbered among More's most intimate and influential friends—John Colet and William Lilly—also visited Italy for the same purpose and with the same object, to acquire that they might impart.

More left Oxford perfected in Latin and a zealous student of Greek. His practical father, who designed him for the Law, did not, it seems, approve of these studies, and withdrew him prematurely from the University to enter him as a student at New Inn. From New Inn he was removed to Lincoln's Inn, where he was admitted on February 12, 1496; and here he continued with a very small allowance from his stern old father till his call to the Bar in 1500. That father was not a man to be trifled with, and the most dutiful of sons was little likely to provoke him. But though More pursued his legal studies with industry, and no doubt subordinated them to the pursuits to which his tastes led him, those pursuits were by no means neglected.

Two years after his entry into Lincoln's Inn, he made the acquaintance of a man in whom he must have recognized almost a second self; the same mingled playfulness and earnestness, the same enthusiasm for letters, the same delicate humour, the same shrewd insight into life and men. This was Erasmus. Erasmus was then about thirty years of age, and though as yet he had produced nothing of importance he had been the author of many brilliant trifles both in verse and prose, and was no doubt meditating his *Adagia*. Erasmus was in raptures with his young friend. 'Did nature ever frame a character more gentle, more endearing and happy than Thomas More?' ('Thomae Mori ingenio quid unquam finxit natura vel mollius vel dulcius vel felicius?') he wrote to his friend Robert Fisher. From the day of this meeting the two men were as brothers; and in the history of literary friendships there is nothing more interesting and more touching than the correspondence which, extending to the close of their arduous and troubled lives, records their mutual affection, sympathy and respect.

In 1501, just after his call to the Bar, More was appointed Reader at Furnival's Inn, and while holding this post, he delivered a course of lectures in the Church of St. Laurence, Old Jewry, of which his friend Grocyn was rector, on St. Augustine's *De Civitate Dei*. They were attended, Roper tells us, not only by Grocyn himself but 'by all the chief learned in the city of London.'

In the spring of 1504, when in his twenty-sixth year, More was returned to Parliament, but for what borough cannot now be ascertained. Shortly after taking his seat he made himself conspicuous by the courage with which he resisted the iniquitous rapacity of Henry VII.

The story which Roper tells, and which has till lately been accepted without question, cannot, as Bishop Stubbs has shown, be reconciled with facts. But whatever difficulty there may be about the precise details, it is quite clear that More imperilled his prospects and even his personal liberty by opposing an unconstitutional and exorbitant demand on the part of the king's ministers. 'God was with you,' said Dudley some years afterwards when More visited him in prison, 'that you confessed no fault against the king; had you done so you would have paid the penalty with your head.' As it was, More had to retire from public life, and the King characteristically revenged himself by seeking a pretext to fine John More £100, and by keeping him in the Tower till it was paid.

This was a critical period in More's life. For some time he buried himself in his lodgings near the Charterhouse and seriously thought of joining the Carthusian brotherhood. His life had always been plain and simple, it now became austerely ascetic. He daily passed long hours in prayer. His body he mortified by fasting and by wearing next his skin a shirt of the sharpest and roughest hair; the naked boards of his chamber were his bed, a log of wood his pillow. Everything indeed seemed to indicate that he had done with the world and with worldly ambition. But More fortunately had wise friends, and healthy instincts. His old tutor Linacre had left Oxford and had settled in London; Grocyn lived within a stone's throw of him, and Colet had recently come into residence as Dean of St. Paul's. They soon recalled him to old studies and to larger and saner conceptions of religion and duty than the ideals of the cloister. Nor was he affected only by living friends. Among the moulding influences of More's early life a very prominent place must be given to a writer whose works were at that time seldom out of his hands. This was Pico della Mirandola, in whom met morally and in some degree intellectually all that was most characteristic of Savonarola, and all that was most characteristic of Colet, in other words what was most characteristic of the Renaissance on its best side and of the Reformation on its sanest and most sober side. More, as a man, was essentially sympathetic and receptive, and though later he was to receive impressions from the most varied studies, it would not be too much to say that at this period of his life he was more powerfully affected by the personal influence of Colet and by the fascination exercised on him by the character and writings of Pico than by anything else. 'You are,' he said to Colet, 'the director of my life.' And that Pico might be to others what he had been to him he translated about this time Gherascho's Life of him, together with four of his Epistles, his Commentary on the sixteenth Psalm and some minor pieces in prose and verse, which were published in 1510.

It was by Colet's advice that he took the step which finally severed him from a monastic life. In 1505 he married Jane the eldest daughter of John Colt, a country gentleman of New Hall in Essex. There is a tradition that he preferred her younger sister, but thinking that such a choice would seem a slight on the elder, very considerately and, it may be added, characteristically, made Jane his bride. He had probably no reason to regret his choice. He appears to have been very happy with her during the six years that she was spared to him. She bore him four children, among them Margaret, afterwards the wife of William Roper, 'likest her father as well in favour as in wit,' and destined to be his chief solace and comfort when he sorely needed both. After his marriage he took a house in Bucklersbury, St. Stephen's, Walbrook. Erasmus has left a very charming picture of More's household at Bucklersbury when he visited him both in 1505 and in 1510.

During the remainder of the reign of Henry VII, More chiefly occupied himself with his legal studies, with his translation of Pico, with his versions from Lucian's *Dialogues*—and the choice he made was significant, the *Cynicus*, the *Menippus* and the *Philopseudes*—and generally with classics and theology. It would seem also that he visited the Continent and made some inquiries into the educational studies and methods of the Universities of Paris and Louvain.

The accession of Henry VIII, to whom he addressed, and whom he welcomed in the longest and most important of his poems, the *Carmen Gratulatorium*, removed all impediments from his path, and More rapidly rose to distinction. He was made a Bencher of his Inn, and in September 1510 Under-sheriff of London, in those days a judicial office of great responsibility and honour. In addition to this his private practice as a barrister became so extensive that in a short time he was making an income estimated in our money at about £5,000 a year. Distinguished alike by his eminent abilities, his untiring industry, his integrity, his tact and the extraordinary charm of his manners, his temper and his conversation, he not only became generally one of the most popular men of his time, but was soon singled out as one peculiarly qualified for the nicest offices of negotiation and diplomacy. His connexion with the City had always been a close one; his courageous resistance to the subsidy of 1504 had been gratefully remembered by those who would have most smarted from it, and it seems that as early as 1508 he had been made free of the Mercers' Company.

He had not long to wait for a flattering testimony to the high opinion which had been formed of his abilities by the City authorities. In 1514 the breaking off of the proposed marriage between Prince Charles, the son of Philip, Archduke of Austria, and Mary, the sister of Henry VIII, had not only led to unpleasantly strained relations between England and Castile and the Netherlands, but had provoked the English Government to take a step which most seriously affected the wool-trade. Wool was then the staple commodity of our merchandise, Flanders the chief centre of cloth manufacturing. As those manufactures were freely admitted into England, it was of great importance that our wool should be as freely admitted into Flanders. Henry, however, piqued and irritated by the step which Prince Charles's advisers had taken, had retorted by prohibiting the exportation of wool to Holland and Zealand, in the hope of injuring Charles's subjects by causing a wool-famine in the Netherlands. But before this there had been, both in London and in

Antwerp, continual friction between the Flemish and English merchants on matters connected with the staple. As it was not at this time desirable that there should be any rupture between Castile and England, and as both Henry and Wolsey were anxious to reestablish friendly relations, it was decided in the spring of 1515 to send an Embassy to the Netherlands 'for the continuance of the treaties of intercourse between the late Kings of England and Castile.' At the head of the Embassy was Cuthbert Tunstall, then Archdeacon of Chester and shortly to become Master of the Rolls, and with him were joined Richard Sampson, Vicar-General of Tournay, and Sir Thomas Spinelly. On hearing of the proposed Embassy the London merchants petitioned that their grievances should also be considered, that they should be specially represented, and that More should represent them. Accordingly, with the King's consent, More was attached to the Embassy, with one John Clifford as his assistant. It appears that More's duties were strictly confined to the mercantile arrangements, which he found exceedingly troublesome. He arrived at Bruges on May 18, 1515, where he remained about four months. As the deputies appointed to confer with the Embassy could not agree on all points, they withdrew to Brussels 'to know their Prince's pleasure'; and More went on to Antwerp, where he made the acquaintance of Peter Giles, and employed his leisure time in writing the second book of the *Utopia*.

He returned to England towards the end of the year, after an absence of some seven months, by no means in love with a foreign Ambassador's position, but thankful, he says, for having had the privilege of living in intimacy with Tunstall, and for having made the acquaintance of Peter Giles. He had been so successful as a negotiator that both the King and Wolsey were anxious that he should give up his practice and devote himself to public life. But More had little faith either in kings as masters, or in the prospects of their servants. If he was too courteous and prudent even to hint—for he was at this time engaged on the first book of the *Utopia*—what he was putting into the mouth of Hythlodaye, there can be no doubt that it represented his real opinions. But he had only staved off the unwelcome moment when greatness was to be thrust upon him. An accident soon turned the scale. It chanced that a vessel belonging to the Pope had been seized at Southampton and claimed as forfeit to the Crown. Campeggio the Papal Envoy demanded counsel to defend the right of his master. It was an important suit, and More was selected to represent the Pope. The King, himself an accomplished casuist who delighted in such displays, was present when More argued the case. He was so struck with More's ability as a lawyer and a logician that he importuned him to reconsider his former decision. There can only be one end to the importunities of kings under such circumstances, and in March 1517 we find Erasmus writing to Tunstall that More had been 'dragged to Court.' In one of his conversations with the King on this subject, Henry, probably in reply to some objection of More, said solemnly, 'First look up to God and after God to me,' words of which some eighteen years later More had occasion to remind him.

It is not difficult to understand More's unwillingness to change his position. A philosopher and a scholar to whom above all things the humanities and everything that pertained to them was dear, with as little worldly ambition as St. Francis or as his friend Erasmus, of the simplest tastes, blest and delighting in the communion of men of like temper with himself, contented with the fulfilment of his daily professional duties, happy in his simple home, of the strongest domestic affections—no man had so little to gain by what so many less happily tempered would have coveted so eagerly. It is moreover not unlikely that if he did not foresee the tragedy of the future in its terrible details he apprehended it generally. His life as a private man had been a very full one. Though his official and professional duties had kept him incessantly occupied he had taken the greatest interest in the foundation of his friend Colet's School, St. Paul's, which was opened in 1510, and in the regulation of its studies. He had more than once championed him against the opposition and calumnies of the Obscurantists, who were as active in England as they were in Germany. With letters and with men of letters he had been in daily communion. In 1510 Erasmus had been his guest at Bucklersbury, and had delighted his host by reading to him the inimitable *Encomium Moriae* composed under his roof. Nor had his own pen been idle. In addition to the *Utopia* he had found time to compose his Latin epigrams on the French War, and what was of more importance, his epoch-marking *History of Richard III*—'the first example,' according to Hallam, 'of good English language, pure and perspicuous, well chosen, without vulgarisms and pedantry.'

In 1510 a great sorrow had befallen him, for, in that year, he had lost his first wife, who had left him with four helpless children, the eldest of whom was only six years of age. If before the year had run out he had brought home a second bride, this is to be attributed, not to any want of respect or affection for the wife whom he had lost, but to the necessity of finding a kindly and trustworthy guardian for his children. This lady, who was a widow seven years older than her husband, reminds us occasionally, it must be admitted, of Xantippe, and we have it on the authority of her husband that she was *nec bella nec puella*, as he more than once playfully observed to her; but she proved a good housekeeper and was kind to his children. Shortly after his second marriage he is said to have left his house at Bucklersbury and settled at Crosby Place, Bishopsgate.

His entrance into public life was the turning-point in his career. Honours and preferments quickly followed. In 1518 he was Master of the Requests, a month afterwards sworn of the Privy Council. In 1520 he attended the King to the Field of the Cloth of Gold. In 1521 he was knighted and made Under-Treasurer. In April 1523 he was chosen Speaker of the House of Commons, probably at the King's request. In 1526 he succeeded Sir Richard Wingfield as Chancellor of the Duchy of Lancaster, and in the same year held an office—one of a committee of three appointed to confer daily with the King—which brought him into close communion with Henry and led to the affectionate intimacy of which Roper speaks. The extraordinary success with which in the summer of 1529 he conducted the negotiations at the Treaty of Cambray—'procuring,' says Roper, 'far more benefits unto his realm than at that time by the King and Council was possible to be compassed'—led immediately to the climax of his honours. On October the 19th of that year the Great Seal was taken from Wolsey, and on the 25th transferred to More.

Over the chief events of More's Chancellorship, namely his attitude to the Reformation and his persecution of the Reformers, as well as on what led to his fall and death, we must pause.

Few incidents in history have been so little understood and so much misrepresented as the part he played in the great schism. It seems indeed to involve inexplicable contradictions. The mildest, the kindliest, the most benevolent of men appears suddenly transformed into the harshest and austerest of fanatics, and undoubtedly connived at many cruel actions. A man who in theory was not only the advocate of religious toleration, but upheld as an ideal a religion so liberal and catholic that it differed in no respect from that of Plato and Cicero, becomes in practice the stern and uncompromising champion of mere and rigid dogma. Many of the charges against him, it is true, fall to the ground on investigation, for some, perversion and exaggeration are responsible. But there can be no doubt that when he described himself in his epitaph as *furibus homicidis haereticisque molestus* he interpreted both his temper and his attitude. He may not have been responsible for the law which he administered when he sent Bilney, Tewkesbury, Bayfield and Bainham to their terrible death, but there can be no doubt that he approved of it, and would have been the last to consent to its repeal. It is clear from his *Apology* that he submitted many, if not to the torture of the rack, to the severest corporal punishment, and it is abundantly clear from his writings and cor respondence generally that he thought no measures too stringent for the extirpation of heresy. His controversial works, particularly the *Vindicatio Henrici VIII* published under the pseudonym of Gulielmus Rosseus, and his *Dialogue* against heresies, are written with an intemperance, a coarseness and an acrimony which must amaze every one who knows him as he appears in his other writings and in the other passages of his life.

But this is easily explained and as easily reconciled with all that we love and all that we honour in the man who in temper and character most nearly realizes the Socrates of the *Apology*, *Crito* and *Phaedo*. To More, from his boyhood upwards, nothing was so sacred and so dear as the Church of his fathers. Its ritual, its ceremony, its doctrines, its authority were to him what the Ark of the Covenant was to the ancient Israelites. Like Savonarola, like his friends Colet and Erasmus, he denounced the ignorance, the worldliness, the vices, the corruption generally of its unworthy servants, and he allowed himself—for wit and humour are difficult to restrain—a licence in satire which might, like Swift's *Tale of a Tub*, seem at times to involve more than was intended. But heresy he regarded with horror. In orthodoxy, and in orthodoxy alone, was salvation. He had no more notion that what he had written about the religion and the religious tolerance of the Utopians would be taken to indicate his real opinions than that what he had written about communism would be taken to indicate what as a statesman he was prepared to put in practice. It was as pure an extravaganza as the *Ecclesiazusae* and the Abbey of the Thelemites.

When, therefore, in 1520 Luther, bursting the bonds of reformation in the sense of the term in which More understood it and was himself contributing to further it, initiated heresy in his *De Captivitate Babylonica*, More at once became alarmed. He was drawn into the controversy against his will, thinking at first that Luther's book would carry in itself its own condemnation. But he soon found that he was mistaken and must gird up his loins for the battle. By the time he had become Chancellor the Pope had not only been denounced as Antichrist, but was in prison; Rome had been sacked, and some forty thousand Christians, so it was said, massacred in her streets; the Peasant Wars had deluged Germany with blood; the Anabaptist insurrection had let loose every element of lawlessness and horror, More's correspondent Cochlaeus assuring him that for all this Lutheranism, and Lutheranism alone, was responsible. Tyndale's Bible and many other publications were spreading the heresy throughout England, and even into his own household it had made its way. 'Friend Roper,' he had sadly said, while as yet the cloud was but a speck upon the horizon, 'I pray God that some of us, high as we seem to sit upon the mountains, treading heretics under our feet like ants, live not to see the day when we gladly would wish to be at league with them, to let them have their churches quietly to themselves, so that they would be contented to let us have ours quietly to ourselves.' What, in More's opinion, was at stake was the whole fabric of society and government, the temporal and eternal salvation of Christendom. He was in truth witnessing the breaking-up of the life and work of ten centuries, the dissolution of an old, the initiation of a new world. He stood in a similar position to the position of Burke two centuries and a half later. Both were mistaken, both were in the right; mistaken, for they were not seers and could not discern the future; in the right, for they read correctly what was directly involved in what they saw and what the immediate consequences would be. Both were in panic, for in both alarm had been intensified by acute sensibility, by imaginations easily impressed and kindled, and by misinformation. When More accepted the Seals the course which his fears, his connexions and his conscience had, as a private man, directed him to take, he was now, as the chief official of the Crown, compelled by oath to take: for a part of the oath administered to him as Lord Chancellor was an assurance that he would 'use of his power to destroy all manner of heresies.' What is supposed to be the greatest blot on his memory—the execution of Bilney, Bayfield, Tewkesbury and Bainham—he has himself justified on grounds the sufficiency of which is, from his point of view, indisputable. Their lives were taken that many other lives might be saved. Examples were necessary that frenzy might not become epidemic. Admitting, then, without reserve that More was a persecutor of the Protestants, that in practice he was party to many very cruel actions, and that as a controversialist he employed all the legitimate weapons of indignation and contempt, it may yet be contended, that there was nothing incompatible in this with the gentleness and benevolence which in all the other actions of his life he displays. In this connexion it would be unjust to him to omit an anecdote which Harpsfield relates. When Roper, seduced by some of Luther's books, had taken up with the new heresy, his father-in-law reasoned with him and endeavoured to bring him back to orthodoxy, but in vain. Meeting shortly afterward with his daughter Margaret, he said, 'Meg, I have borne a long time with thy husband. I have reasoned and argued a long time with him and still given him my poor fatherly counsel; but I perceive none of all this can call him home again. And, therefore, Meg, I will no longer dispute with him, nor yet will I give him over; but I will go another way to work, and get me to God and pray for him.' And of one thing we may be very sure, that this was neither the first nor the last time that he thus tempered controversy and persecution.

But to turn to More in another capacity. As Lord Chancellor his industry, his integrity, and his incorruption when corruption was universal, have been admitted even by his enemies. When he took office there were, says Stapleton, causes which had remained undecided for twenty years; but 'he presided so dexterously and so successfully that once, after taking his seat, and deciding a case, when the next case was called there was no second case for trial, such a thing is said never to have happened before or since.' As a rule, every afternoon he sat in his open hall that all who had suits or complaints might have free access to him. Many stories are told of his refusal to accept from suitors what his predecessors had come to regard as the perquisites of their office, and of the scrupulous impartiality of his administration of justice. 'If,' he once said to one of his sons-in-law who had, on the grounds of kinship, expected to be favoured, ' my father whom I dearly love were on one side and the devil whom I sincerely hate were on the other, the devil should have his rights.' The two and a half years during which More occupied the Woolsack are certainly to be numbered among its brightest annals.

Till the spring of 1532 there had been no cloud on the intimate and even affectionate relations which existed between More and the King. The King had frequently visited him at Chelsea, wandering about the garden with his arm round his favourite's neck; and it had been at Henry's urgent request that More had accepted the Chancellorship. But the two men were soon to stand in very different relations. As early as September 1527 Henry had informed him of the scruples which were beginning to trouble him about the legitimacy of his marriage with Catherine. More promised to study the question. He did so, and satisfied himself that there was nothing to justify the dissolution of the marriage. This he frankly acknowledged to the King, and it appears to have been agreed between them that until More could arrive at a different conclusion he should be silent on the subject and confine himself to his ordinary duties. He became Chancellor against his will, being probably well aware of the King's motives in conferring the honour upon him, but remained silent. The King then became importunate—Was his friend still of the same opinion, was he still unable to serve him? Then More wrote: 'It is grievous in my heart that I am not able to serve your Grace in this matter . . . . but I ever bear in my mind the words which your Highness spoke to me on my first coming into your noble service, bidding me first look up to God and after God to you.'

Meanwhile the events which preceded the divorce

and the rupture with Rome took place, and More, finding his position increasingly embarrassing, resigned the Seals. Then came the rupture, the divorce, and the marriage with Anne Boleyn. On all these subjects More expressed publicly no opinion; he avoided the Court and absented himself from the Coronation of the new Queen. Next ensued the affair of the Maid of Kent. The King was furious. Fisher, Bishop of Rochester, was accused of misprision of treason, convicted, imprisoned and ruinously fined. More, who had been suspected of complicity, was examined; but as the only evidence against him was that he had written a letter to the Maid advising her to attend to her devotions and not meddle in the affairs of princes, his name was struck out of the Bill of Attainder, and the King contented himself with depriving him of his salary. 'Master More,' said the Duke of Norfolk, 'it is perilous striving with Princes; the revenge of Princes is death.' 'Is that all, my Lord?' replied More, with a smile; 'then, in good faith, the difference between your Grace and me is, that I shall die to-day and you to-morrow.'

But the long struggle in which More endeavoured to reconcile his loyalty as a subject to his sovereign and his loyalty as a Christian to his conscience was soon to cease. In March 1534 the Act of Succession was passed. It limited the succession to the issue of the King and of Anne Boleyn, but to it was appended a formula declaring the Princess Mary to be illegitimate, and forbidding obedience to any foreign potentate. More had no difficulty in expressing on oath his assent to the settlement of the Crown on the offspring of the new marriage; but assent to the Bill involved assent to what the formula implied, the illegality of the marriage with Catherine and the repudiation of the Pope as head of the Church. Such was the oath which More was required to take, or, at his peril, to refuse. He received a summons to appear at Lambeth. He knew his hour had come. 'Son Roper,' he said to his daughter Margaret's husband, 'I thank our Lord the field is won.' As he left his house for the last time he would not allow his wife and children to follow him, as they were accustomed to do, to the boat, for he usually went as then he did by river, but 'pulled the wicket after him and shut them from him.' That evening he was in the custody of the Abbot of Westminster, and four days afterwards in the Tower.

Nearly fifteen months intervened between his arrival at his prison and the final scene. The history of that time is written in his own correspondence, and in the biographies of Roper, of Stapleton and of Cresacre More; and no story, with one obvious exception, so noble and so pathetic has ever been told of man since Plato related how Socrates addressed his judges, refuted Crito, and passed his last hours on earth.

When More left his house at Chelsea, he no doubt saw that there could be only one end to the course which he was taking; but what removed him from the pale of jurisdiction which affected only his liberty and property and brought him within reach of the law which inflicted the death sentence was the Act of Supremacy. He could now no longer reply to questions intended to incriminate him as he replied to Cromwell, 'I am the King's faithful subject and daily bedesman. I say no harm, I think no harm.' For the new Act provided that it was not only high treason to deny the King's title to supremacy over the Church, but to refuse to acknowledge it. On the first of July 1534, after many harassing examinations, he stood at the Bar in Westminster Hall, before the Lord Chancellor and nine other judges. In the indictment was included much which was false and much which was irrelevant, and More pleaded not guilty. But as before, so now, he would not acknowledge the title of the King to Supremacy over the Church. On the same day the jury returned a verdict of guilty; sentence of death was passed upon him, and what one of his successors on the Woolsack has described as 'the blackest crime that ever has been perpetrated in England under the form of law' had been committed by that jury and by those judges.

He was led out of court, for he was very feeble, by his old friend Sir William Kingston, Constable of the Tower, who accompanied him as far as the Swan Inn, near London Bridge, where the guards in charge and the throng of people paused. There Kingston had to leave him, and More, seeing the tears running down his friend's cheeks, tried to comfort him, promising that he would pray for him—would pray that they might meet and be 'merry together' in heaven. On the way, probably as he approached the Tower, his son John threw himself at his feet and implored his blessing. Calmly it was given, more calmly than it was received. The procession moved on. He had now arrived at the Tower Wharf, where his daughter Margaret was awaiting him. On seeing her father she rushed forward, 'pressing in,' writes Roper, who witnessed the scene, 'amongst the midst of the throng and company of the guard that with halberts and bills went round about him, hastily ran to him, and there openly, in sight of them all, embraced him and took him about the neck and kissed him.' The frenzy of her grief was such that she could only utter the words, 'Oh, my father! Oh, my father!' Then she kneeled that she might receive his benediction. 'Take patience, Margaret,' he said with composure, after giving it, 'and do not grieve. God has willed it so. For many years didst thou know the secret of my heart.' She rose and left him, but again she returned, 'as one that had forgotten herself,' throwing her arms round his neck and covering his face with kisses. It was a scene which brought tears into the eyes of all who witnessed it, the very guards themselves, we are told, were weeping. At last she withdrew, and for More the bitterness of death had passed.

The few days that remained to him he spent not in preparation for what his whole life had been a preparation, but in endeavouring to cheer and console those who loved him, in assuring those who did not that he had no intention of saving his life by recantation, in sending little remembrances of himself to those who would treasure them, and in cheery and often humorous conversation with the officials of the Tower. On Sir Thomas Pope informing him, early in the morning of the day fixed for his execution, that it was the King's will that it should take place at nine o'clock, he replied, 'I am bounden to his Highness that it pleaseth him so shortly to rid me from the miseries of this wretched world; and there will I not fail earnestly to pray for his Grace, both here and also in the world to come.' He also expressed his gratitude to the King for consenting to his request that his daughter Margaret should be present at his burial. As he left the Tower-gate on his way to the scaffold, a poor woman came from her house and offered him a cup of wine. He courteously thanked her, but declined it, saying, 'Christ at His Passion drank no wine, but gall and vinegar.' The scaffold, which had been hurriedly erected, was very unsteady, and shook as he placed his foot on the ladder. Turning to the lieutenant who was standing by he said 'merrily,' 'I pray thee see me safe up, and for my coming down let me shift for myself.' In accordance with custom the executioner begged his forgiveness. More turned to him, kissed him and said, 'Thou wilt do me this day a greater benefit than ever any mortal man can be able to do me'; and then, as he probably saw that there was some danger of the man's nerve failing him, added, 'Pluck up thy spirits, man, and be not afraid to do thine office. My neck is very short; take heed therefore that thou strike not awry for saving of thine honesty.' He then laid his head on the block, but suddenly raising it, said in a low voice, 'Stay till I have moved my beard; that at least has not committed treason'—a touch of humour equally characteristic, but not so pointed as the last inimitable request which Socrates uncovered his face to utter.

The axe fell; and the blood of the wisest, the noblest and most faithful of his servants was on the head of a brutal and stupid tyrant. When the Emperor Charles V heard of More's death from the English ambassador the comment he made on it was: 'Well, this we will say, if *we* had been the master of such a servant *we* would rather have lost the best city of our dominions than have lost such a counsellor.'

More is the English Socrates, and if we except what may be called the accidents of his career, the facts, namely that he inherited narrowing superstitions which he could not cast off, and that in high office he served his country, and was thus involved in transactions and controversies little becoming a philosopher, the parallel is so close that nothing is wanting to complete it.

II. ORIGIN AND INSPIRATION OF THE *UTOPIA*

WHERE and under what circumstances the *Utopia* was composed we have already seen. As it is, whether regarded as a work of art, as a satire, or in relation to its didactic purpose a mirror of the age which witnessed its composition, on the general characteristics of that age a few words are necessary. When More took up his pen the knell of the Mediaeval World had sounded. The World of the Renaissance, which had fully developed itself in Italy, was beginning to assume definition in England. On all sides the horizons of intelligence and experience were being enlarged. The study of Greek had been introduced into our Universities and into two or three of our schools, and was being pursued with enthusiasm by influential men. A regular communication had been opened with the most eminent scholars of the Continent, some of whom had been our visitors. The Greek Testament and *Novum Instrumentum* of Erasmus had made an era not merely in Theology but in theological thought, practically revolutionizing both. With the Christian Scriptures had been associated the Platonic writings, and the philosophy and literature generally of ancient Greece and Rome were beginning curiously and reverently to be studied. And to all this the invention

ORIGIN AND INSPIRATION OF 'UTOPIA'

of moveable types had given wings. The great astronomical discovery of Copernicus, and the geographical discoveries associated with the names of Dias, of Cabo, of Columbus, of Vespucci had opened out new vistas and new paths to speculation and enterprise. The *Intercursus Magnus* had laid the foundations of International Law. Social life was being slowly transformed, the old Feudalism was dying; the old Chivalry was all but dead. The Church was still unchanged; but already the distant murmur of the Reformation was beginning to be heard. In a word, what were at work everywhere, in different stages of definition and in different degrees of activity, were the forces which dissolved the world of the Middle Ages and constructed the world of the Renaissance and of the Reformation.

We have seen how More lived in intimate communion with the apostles of the New Learning, how closely he was in touch with the Humanists and with all that pertained to the humanities, how devoted a student of the Greek and Roman Classics. But he was much more than a student and a humanist: he was a lawyer, a churchman in his instincts, and a politician, keenly interested in legal, ecclesiastical and political questions. Singularly observant of all that passed before his eyes, of acute sensibility, most sympathetic, and of infinite benevolence, he was eminently a philanthropist. With this temper, with these tastes and with these accomplishments, he surveyed the world which was passing round him, both at home and on the Continent. That world he has painted in the first book of the *Utopia*. Let us glance at it.

On the Papal Chair sat indeed a Pope (Leo X) who

was mild and humane, and who preferred peace to war, but two years before it had been filled by Julius II, whose pontificate had been one long and bloody struggle to extend his dominions and aggrandize his family. The restoration of Hungary and Bohemia, the annexation of the Netherlands, of Franche Compté, of Artois, and of Castile and Aragon, by marriage, by intrigue or by war, may be said to sum up the aims of the Emperor Maximilian. In France the 'most Christian King' Louis XII, who had sacrificed thousands of lives, and had been prepared to sacrifice thousands more, in a most un-Christian attempt to possess himself of Milan and the two Sicilies, had just been succeeded by Francis I, who was about to enter on a vaster course of rapacious conquest; Ferdinand of Aragon, whose whole career had been little else than an ignoble record of rapacity and fraud, was scheming to wrest Navarre from France. To come nearer home, Henry VIII, burning for military glory, had twice invaded France, to find on the first occasion that he had been made the dupe of his greedy father-in-law and the laughingstock of Europe. To retrieve this disaster, a second expedition, with himself at the head of it, had, at a vast expense, been fitted out. The result had been a series of blunders, a futile victory won by an accident, and the capture of two unimportant towns, Terouenne and Tournay; Henry returning in ridiculous pomp to concert with Wolsey a third expedition. Animated by the same spirit as his more conspicuous brethren, James IV, the King of Scotland, had invaded England, to pay the penalty of his mingled ambition, perfidy and recklessness with his own life and with the lives of ten thousand of his countrymen. Of the entire indifference of the sovereigns of that day to the interests of their subjects, or indeed to everything but the gratification of their own tastes and pleasures, whether at ruinous expense in pomps and tournaments and every form of profligate expenditure, or in the pursuit at any cost of misery and blood to their kingdoms and dependants,—of this the literature of those times is full. (For illustrations see the Notes.) The internal condition of England was deplorable. Agriculture had been almost destroyed by the wholesale conversion of arable into pasture land for the purpose of breeding sheep to obtain wool. Hundreds of miles of country, once occupied by thriving hamlets and villages, had been enclosed and converted into sheepwalks. The effects of this had been to turn thousands of able-bodied men and their families adrift on the roads and in the towns, to become beggars and thieves. While the peasant and labourer were either starving or swinging on the gibbet—for they were hanged in hundreds for petty larcenies—the nobility, capitalists and abbots were revelling in the wealth which had been acquired by the infliction of this misery. (For illustrations of all this see the Notes.) Well might More make Hythlodaye say that in Christian Commonwealths he 'could see nothing but a certain conspiracy of rich men procuring their own commodities under the name and title of the Commonwealth.' Nor were there wanting other sources of distress and evil. In London and in the towns the administration of justice was conducted with merciless severity. The punishment for larceny was death; and each year many hundreds, sometimes twenty at a time, perished on the gallows. Sanitary regulations were unknown. The poor lived like pigs, their habits being too loathsome to describe. Many of the streets of the city were little better than open sewers, and even the Strand is described in an Act of Parliament passed in 1523 as 'very noyous, foul and jeopardous.' The consequence was the periodical visitation of decimating epidemics, while fever and diseases of all kinds were generally busy. Public hospitals, with the exception of St. Bartholomew's, there were none; and it was not till two years after the *Utopia* was written, till the foundation, that is to say, of the Royal College of Physicians in 1518 by More's friend Linacre, that any attempt was made to organize medical science. Such was the world the elements of which, whether as inspiration or theme, entered into the composition of the *Utopia*.

The work had probably been in More's mind some years before its inception; at all events, it is certain that some of the subjects with which it deals had occupied his attention. Dr. Lupton remarks that in his *Epigrammata*, written probably as early as 1500, More had dwelt on the subject of greed, public and private, and on the difference between a lawful king and a tyrant (see the Epigrams 'In avarum,' the titles 'Dives avarus pauper est sibi,' the 'Sola Mors Tyrannicida est,' 'Quid inter Tyrannum et Principem,' 'Bonum Principem esse Patrem non Dominum,' 'Regem non satellitium sed virtus reddit tutum,' and, most remarkable of all, 'Populus consentiens regnum dat et aufert,' 'Quis optimus reipublicae status'). In the *Carmen Gratulatorium*, addressed on his accession to Henry VIII, he had ventured to hint a contrast between the 'end of bondage' and 'the beginning of freedom,' between the time 'when public offices were sold' and the time when they 'would be freely bestowed on the good.' His studies, too, of the *De Civitate Dei* must have familiarized him with the notion of an ideal republic.

But the work was probably suggested and inspired by Erasmus. We have only to turn to the *Adagia* and to the *Encomium Moriae* to see how much there was in common between what Erasmus had already expressed and what More was about to express. In these works will not, indeed, be found any hint either for the framework or for the method and tone adopted and assumed by More. But there is the same analysis of the maladies under which the political communities of those times were labouring; the same attribution to the same causes, the ignorance, the selfishness, the rapacity, the ambition of princes; the same contempt for priests and lawyers; the same exposure of the mischief and misery caused by the employment of mercenary troops; the same pity for the poor; the same indignation at oppression and undue severity in the administration of justice. And, what is still more striking, we find Erasmus expressing sympathy with Communism, and acknowledging that it would be a remedy for the greater part of the evils then prevalent. In commenting on the proverb 'Amicorum communia omnia' he says: 'Quod quidem si tam esset fixum in hominum animis, quam nulli non est in ore, profecto maxima malorum parte vita nostra levaretur . . . . Sed dictu mirum quam non placeat, immo quam lapidetur a Christianis Platonis illa communitas, cum nihil unquam ab ethnico philosopho dictum sit magis ex Christi sententia.' *Adagia*, Ed. 1606, p. 109, *sub cap.* 'Amicorum communia omnia.' Nor must we forget the inspiring influence of his friend Colet, who, in a public sermon preached at Easter, 1513, before the King, had had the courage to inform him that wars were seldom undertaken 'except from hatred and ambition,' and that, instead of imitating the examples of Caesars and Alexanders, it much more became a Christian prince to imitate the example of Christ.'

III. FRAMEWORK AND MODELS

THE notion of an ideal commonwealth, as the expression in a fable of what would at once be a standard and touchstone for social and political regulations—a counsel of perfection, and a satire by implication on existing conditions and institutions—was not new. More had several precedents, and, for his details, laid many works under contribution. The references of Hythlodaye to Plato indicate the first and most important of More's models. To the *Republic* he was indebted generally for the idea of a pattern commonwealth based on Communism, and to it and to Plato's other dialogues for the suggestion of the dramatic setting and dialectic of the first book: the many details which he has borrowed from it have been pointed out in the notes. But his indebtedness to the *Timaeus* and *Critias* was almost equally great. In Atlantis he found the archetype, in the physical description of Atlantis a model for the physical description of *Utopia*. And he found more. He learned from the artist of these dialogues the art of making fiction assume a form almost indistinguishable from truth, the art of 'noble lying.' But a subtler influence is to be traced to Plato, the influence of the Platonic Socrates, with his delicate play of irony, his jest and seriousness so finely and bafflingly mingled that no wit not of kinship with his own can distinguish them. To the Romance which comes next in order, and which, though written with the same object as More's, has in its framework nothing in common, the *Cyropaedia* of Xenophon, he is under no obligation. Of Cicero's *De Republica* he could of course have made no use. But Plutarch's *Instituta Laconica* he had certainly studied, and has borrowed some details from it which are pointed out in the Notes. It is possible, it is indeed not improbable, that he may have been influenced by a work which at first sight appears to have nothing in common with his own, the *Germania* of Tacitus. There can be little doubt that under the guise of an ethnographical and historical treatise Tacitus was, like More, satirizing by implication the morals and institutions of his own nation and countrymen; that his object was to contrast the characters, habits and polity of his virtuous savages with those of the degenerate Romans, just as More contrasts the Europeans of his own time with the Utopians. The structure and method of the *Germania* and of the second book of the *Utopia* are closely analogous. Both begin with a description of the physical features of the country described in them; both proceed to an account in detail of all those peculiarities in public and private, in agricultural and political life which stand in the sharpest contrast to what obtained in civilized Europe, and in each many of the peculiarities most emphasized are curiously similar. (For some of the most striking of these parallels see the Notes.)

As his acquaintance with Saint Augustine's *De Civitate Dei* was very intimate, we naturally look for traces of its influence on his work. Dr. Lupton discerns it 'in the conception of a perfect order as it prevailed in the city of God: in the due subordination of every member of the society, each being glad to do his own work and fall into his own place: in the community of goods, and in the use and limitation of bond-service.'

But what furnished More, not with the notion, but with the actual framework of the *Utopia* was something very different from any of these works. In September 1507 appeared, printed at St. Dié in the Vosges, as an appendix to a little book entitled *Cosmographiae Introductio*, to which was appended a Latin translation of Amerigo Vespucci's four voyages as described by himself—*Quatuor Americi Vesputii Navigationes*. In this tract Vespucci describes how, on his second voyage, he sailed from Lisbon on May the 14th, 1501, passed the Canary Islands to Cape Verde, and explored 'those regions.' He there found a people leading a life very similar in many respects to More's Utopians. They had no property, but held all things in common, living according to nature. They had no king, no sovereignty, and every one was his own master. They had a great quantity of gold but regarded it of no account. Of pearls, jewels, and all such things as Europeans prize, they thought nothing. More's use of this is obvious.

But it is on the description of the fourth voyage that More founds his fable. Vespucci here relates how, again setting sail in May 1503 with six ships, they crossed the line, and in August sighted an island, now identified as Fernando Noronha; how the chief vessel was here wrecked; how, getting separated from the other ships, he fell in with one of them after eight days; how they then both made for Bahia, and, after a stay of seventeen days there, proceeded southwards till they arrived at a harbour (Cape Frio); how, after freighting their ships with Brazil wood, they returned to Lisbon, leaving behind at Cape Frio a small garrison or factory, 'castellum,' of twenty-four men with arms, and provisions: 'Relictis in castello prefato Christicolis xxiiij, et, cum illis, xiij machinis ac aliis pluribus armis, una cum provisione pro sex mensibus sufficiente, necnon pacata nobiscum telluris illius gente .... introivimus' (that is, reached home). Before leaving, Vespucci and his comrades had penetrated some forty leagues inland, presumably to ascertain, among other things, the disposition of the inhabitants previous to the establishment of the factory. More represents Hythlodaye as one of the twenty-four men who had been left by Vespucci in the factory. To Hythlodaye's assertion, that he went travelling about through many countries with five of the twenty-four men who had been left in the factory after Vespucci's departure, there is nothing to correspond in Vespucci's narrative.

More has, with great art, completely baffled all attempts to localize or identify Utopia. For, he represents Hythlodaye as Vespucci's companion, not merely on his last voyage, but on his last three voyages; so that we do not know whether Utopia lay among the 'townes and cities and weale publiques full of people, governed by good and holsome lawes,' which he visited with his five companions after leaving the 'castellum,' or whether it was one of the communities described above, as having been visited in the second voyage.

The mystification was kept up with much humour

in two letters, one written by Peter Giles to Busleyden, and one written by More himself to Giles, prefixed to the work when it was printed. Giles tells Busleyden that More had been reproaching himself for not having ascertained from Hythlodaye where Utopia was situated. Hythlodaye had, indeed, said something on the subject, but it unfortunately happened that, when Hythlodaye was speaking, More's attention had been diverted by the entrance of a servant who whispered in his ear. And Giles himself had been equally unlucky; for, though he was listening, one of the company who had caught a cold chanced to cough so loudly, just at the critical moment, that it drowned what Hythlodaye said. However, he would do his best, he adds, to get the information, if Hythlodaye could be found, which was doubtful; for some reported that he had died on his journey home, others that he had gone back to Utopia. More also writes, humorously importuning Giles to get this information from Hythlodaye, for he felt ashamed to have written so elaborately about a place of which he did not even know the site. And he had another reason, he says, for repairing this great and most unfortunate omission: he had heard that a devout and godly man, a Professor of Divinity, had expressed a wish to go out to Utopia, as a missionary, and spread still further the Christianity which some of the Utopians had adopted; indeed, he indulged the hope of becoming Bishop of Utopia. And if, added More, you do see Hythlodaye, have the goodness to ask him if the bridge of Amaurote is five hundred paces? for 'my boy John Clement says that two hundred of those paces must be plucked away, for that the river contains there not above three hundred paces in breadth.' The matter in itself was a trifle, he continues, but scrupulous accuracy had been his aim, and this would be a test of the fidelity of his memory. 'For I will take good hede that there be in my book nothynge false.' This elaborate mystification probably had another purpose than a merely artistic one.

More must have known the peril he incurred by the publication of such a book, and he was no doubt anxious to find some loophole for escape should awkward questions be asked. He wished, therefore, to emphasize its purely fictitious character—the fact that it was a mere work of art, a fantastical and ingenious fable. By connecting Hythlodaye with Vespucci he gave it an air of reality which could deceive no one. and at the same time left it open to him to say that it was a mere parody of travellers' tales, a satire on one of the most popular forms of literary fraud. To scholars, of course, the very nomenclature employed would betray its origin. Utopia is 'Nusquamia,' ' no-place land '; its founder, Utopus, 'no-place one'; its capital, Amaurote, 'a phantom city'; its river, the Anyder, 'a river which is no water'; the Anemolians, ' people of the wind'; the Polylerites, 'babblers of much nonsense'; Achoriens, 'those who have no place on earth'; the very name of the hero, Hythlodaye, signifies 'skilled in babble,' or possibly 'a distributor of babble.' But More's own comments, and especially the closing paragraph, would be a sufficient apology for him, should any one propose to take him seriously. Certainly, as an artist, he was the master of De Foe and Swift, and neither has excelled him in 'the art of feigning.'

IV. THE PLOT

THE dramatic opening and setting were evidently suggested by Plato's *Republic*, while in the report of the conversation at Morton's table, we are still more closely reminded of Plato's Dialogue, Morton corresponding to Cephalus, Hythlodaye to Socrates, and the lawyer to Thrasymachus. But the framework is artfully linked with the facts of More's own life. He relates how, when on the embassy with Tunstall to the Low Countries, as he was one morning leaving the Cathedral Church at Antwerp after hearing Mass, he saw his friend Peter Giles in conversation with a stranger. To that stranger, whose name was Raphael Hythlodaye, Giles introduced him, telling him that Hythlodaye was a most interesting man, an accomplished classical scholar, and one who had been a great traveller. The three then go on together to More's house and sit down on a bench in the garden. Hythlodaye begins to talk of his adventures, and to describe how in the course of them he had come across many interesting communities, among them the commonwealth of the Utopians, whose customs and laws might well serve as examples to European countries. The conversation of the traveller is so entertaining, his learning and wisdom so apparent, that Giles expresses surprise that he had not made his way into some king's court, for he was sure that there was no prince living who would not welcome a man from whom he could learn so much, and whose counsel would be so useful to him. But Hythlodaye replies that he has no taste for anything that a king or court could give him, to say nothing of the fact that princes are too much occupied with their own vain pleasures and greedy ambition to listen to such counsel as he could give them, that there is no place in courts for any but flatterers and parasites, as ignorant as they are envious. Even in England he had 'chaunced upon such prowde, lewede, overthwarte and waywarde judgementes.' Interested to hear that he had been in England, More elicits from him that he had resided there some four or five months, and had received much kindness from Cardinal Morton, of whose character Hythlodaye speaks with enthusiastic admiration. He then goes on to relate a conversation in which he once took part at Morton's table. One of the guests, a certain lawyer, had been expressing his approval of the law which punished thieves with death, and his wonder at the fact that it had had so little effect in diminishing the crime. Upon this Hythlodaye took courage to say that it was a most cruel law, a punishment which greatly exceeded the offence—that the poor fellows stole that they might live, and that the true remedy for thieving was not to hang them, but to provide them with the means of getting an honest livelihood. 'But,' retorted the lawyer, 'there are handycrafts, there is husbandry, ample opportunities for working, if they would avail themselves of them.' This Hythlodaye denied. The country was full, he went on to say, of disbanded soldiers, either unfitted by their wounds or too old to learn trades, and of idle retainers and serving-men, who had lost or been turned adrift by their masters, and who, being accustomed to expensive habits and to swaggering about with swords and bucklers, would not condescend to ply a spade and mattock for poor wages. 'Why these,' replied the lawyer, 'are just the men we want to maintain our glory in war.' This turns the question on to war and its ruinous social effects, on which Hythlodaye proceeded to enlarge. 'But,' he added, there are other reasons for the poverty, misery and crime which prevailed, namely, the selfishness of the landlords in enclosing and turning arable land into pasture': and on this, as well as on what it necessarily involved, he dilated at length. 'Remove these grievances,' he said, 'forbid enclosures, restore agriculture, put some restraint on the means by which the rich are able to aggrandize themselves at the expense of the poor, and you will have fewer thieves.'

The Cardinal, interrupting the lawyer, who was about to reply at length, then turned to Hythlodaye and said he should be glad to hear his reasons for thinking that theft should not be punished by death. These reasons Hythlodaye proceeded to give. In the course of his remarks, he referred to the customs of a certain Persian community which he had visited in his travels, namely, the Polylerites, as worthy of imitation in the use to which they put felons and serving-men. After a suggestion of the Cardinal's with respect to the treatment of vagabonds, the conversation was interrupted by a lively passage of arms between a certain Fool who happened to be standing by and a Friar. The Fool humorously suggested that beggars who through infirmity could not work should be quartered on religious houses, the men to become lay brethren and the women nuns. 'And what,' said the Friar, 'is to be done with us'? 'You,' replied the Fool, 'have been already provided for, when it was suggested that vagabonds should be kept in restraint and compelled to work.' This so enraged the Friar, and the altercation between

THE PLOT

insulter and insulted grew so hot, that the Cardinal deemed it expedient to nod to the Fool to withdraw.

Hythlodaye having finished his account of his experiences in England, the conversation then turns to Giles's former suggestion, that Hythlodaye should enter some prince's court, More insisting that for the Commonwealth's sake he ought to do so. Had not Plato said that realms could never prosper till their rulers were philosophers? and how could those rulers become philosophers till philosophers advised them? Again Hythlodaye points out the futility of such a plan, and we have an account of the occupations and characters of the princes of those days. Then occurs a passage which it is surprising that More could at that time have ventured to publish, in which he makes Hythlodaye—citing the example of the salutary decrees passed by the Achorians, 'a people situate over against the Island of Utopia'—enlarge on the uselessness and ruinous folly of Henry VIII's French wars. He then proceeds to depict the advisers and means by which princes are encouraged and supported in their evil courses, comparing the wise provisions made by the Macariens, 'a people not far distant from Utopia,' limiting the power of their kings. At last he comes to the contrast presented by the wise and goodly ordinances of the Utopians to what obtained in Europe, and to these in his subsequent remarks he continually refers. These repeated references to Utopia and the Utopians excite More's curiosity about them, and he begs Hythlodaye to give him a full and precise account of this wonderful place and those wonderful people. This, he says, he will gladly do; but it will take some time. More proposes that they should first have dinner, and then return into the garden. Dinner over, the three sit on the same bench on which they had been sitting before, and Hythlodaye begins his narrative. This occupies the whole of the second book, being uninterrupted by any remarks on the part of the listeners. The narrative concluded, the three friends go in to supper. Of some things Hythlodaye had said More could not approve; but he resolved, for the present at least, to keep this to himself, partly because Hythlodaye was weary, and partly because he was not sure whether he would like to be opposed.

Such is the plot—a masterpiece of dramatic skill and propriety.

V. PURPOSE OF THE WORK

THE purpose of the *Utopia* was, as Erasmus said at the time, to point out where and from what causes the European Commonwealths, and more especially the English, with which More was most familiar, were at fault. And he deals with the subject politically, socially and economically, his method being threefold—first, by placing in the mouth of Hythlodaye direct comments on the evils and miseries prevalent in England and Europe, with an analysis of their causes and suggestions for their remedies; secondly, by describing the regulations, habits and institutions of the Utopians for his readers to draw their own conclusions, rejecting or accepting as exemplary what they please; and thirdly, by holding up the mirror to the vices and defects of existing commonwealths, by presenting them in contrast with their perfected correction in an ideal commonwealth. As examples of the first we have Hythlodaye's picture of the state

PURPOSE OF THE WORK

of England and of the characters of princes, in the first book; his bitterly sarcastic remarks on leagues and treaties, in the seventh chapter of the second book; his delineation of the habits and characters of mercenary troops, in the eighth chapter; and his indignant protest against the tyranny of the rich over the poor, in the ninth. Examples of the second would be afforded by the numerous paradoxes and semi-serious suggestions in which the work abounds, such as the institution of a purely elective monarchy and the defence and adoption of Communism by the Utopians: their theory of the right of civilized states to the soil of waste countries; the limitation of labour to six hours a day for every citizen by the compulsory imposition of it on all citizens; the gratuitous presentation to the poor of every nation with which they are trading to the seventh part of all the goods exported; their mode of conducting war by the assassination of the leaders and by bribing the subjects of the enemy to commit treason; their contempt for military glory; their contempt for titles and ancestry; the horror with which they regard hunting—'the loweste, vyleste and most abjecte part of bocherye'; their detestation of priests and lawyers; their religion, and the extent to which religious toleration was carried; their employment of women as priests; the ceremonies before marriage; the regulations for the education of women; the encouragement of suicide in cases of painful and hopeless disease; and their mode of regarding death and conducting burials. Examples of the third would be the description of Amaurote, which is plainly contrasted with London, as the model of what a city should be, both architecturally and in relation to sanitary provisions; the description of the importance attached to study and culture, and the objects with which they are pursued; the account given of their domestic life—a life, it may be observed, realized by More in his own household; and the illustration generally of a polity in which the true ends and aims of legislation and government, as well as the mutual happiness of all classes of citizens, had been attained.

To inquire how far More was in earnest, or rather where he is in earnest, and where he is jesting in his Romance, is not altogether an idle question. Erasmus tells us, that even members of More's own family were sometimes puzzled to gather from his look or tone, whether he was speaking seriously, or whether he was joking. Like Socrates he moved in an atmosphere of irony. But no one who is acquainted with More's character and with the circumstances under which the work was written can doubt that, however much licence he may have allowed himself in giving the reins to his humour, his purpose was essentially a serious one. Perhaps the question could not be put better than it has been put by Sir James Mackintosh:

'The true notion of *Utopia* is, that it intimates a variety of doctrines, and exhibits a multiplicity of projects which the writer regards with almost every possible degree of approbation and shade of assent: from the frontiers of serious and entire belief, through gradations of descending plausibility, where the lowest are scarcely more than the exercises of ingenuity, and to which some wild paradoxes are appended, either as a vehicle, or as an easy means (if necessary) of disavowing the serious intention of the whole of this Platonic fiction.'—*Life of More*, 'Miscellaneous Works,' Vol. I. p. 423.

And side by side with this may be placed the remarks of Brewer:

'Though the *Utopia* was not to be literally followed — was no more than an abstraction at which no one would have laughed more heartily than More himself, if interpreted too strictly—Utopia might serve to show a corrupt Christendom what good could be effected by the natural instincts of men, when following the dictates of natural prudence and justice. If kings could never be elective in Europe, Utopia might show the advantage to a nation where kings were responsible to some other will than their own. If property could never be common, Utopia might teach men how great was the benefit to society, when the state regarded itself as created for the wellbeing of all, and not of a class or a favoured few. Literally, property could never be common except in Utopia; but it might be so in effect in Christian communities when capital and property were more widely diffused, when the enormous disproportion between the poor and the rich, the noble and the serf, was modified by social improvements, and the statute-book disencumbered of obsolete and unintelligible Acts, too often put in force to catch the unwary, and made an instrument of oppression by the crown lawyers.'—*Reign of Henry VIII*, Vol. II. pp. 290-1.

Indeed the student of the *Utopia* could not be admonished better than by the words of Chaucer's Nun's Priest:

'Taketh the fruyt and let the chaf be stille.'

VI. EARLY EDITIONS AND THE TRANSLATIONS

THE first edition of the *Utopia*, in Latin, was printed at Louvain by Thierry Martin, towards the end of

1516. To it was prefixed the letter of Peter Giles to Busleyden, dated Nov. 1, 1516; a letter of Ioannes Paludanus Cassiletensis to Peter Giles, with a set of ten elegiac verses, both of which were suppressed in the edition of 1518; some Latin verses by Gerardus Noviomagus and Cornelius Grapheus; the letter of Busleyden to More; and More's prefatory letter to Peter Giles; together with a representation of the Utopian alphabet, and a metre of four verses in the Utopian language. A second edition was printed by Gilles de Gourmont, at Paris, about the end of 1517. To it were added a letter addressed by Budé to Lupset acknowledging a presentation copy of the first edition, and expressing the delight with which he had read the work, and a second letter of More to Giles. This had been hurried out prematurely, without any corrections of the author, from Budé's wish to popularize the work by a smaller and more handy edition. Then appeared, in 1518, in two issues, one in March and another in November, the third edition, printed by Froben at Basle, embodying More's corrections. In 1519 the work was issued from the Juntine Press at Venice, and in the following year it is said to have been reprinted in quarto at Basle. This was, so far as is known, the last edition published in More's lifetime.

Of the translations Ralph Robynson's was the first, and it was published by Abraham Vele, at the sign of the 'Lambe' in St. Paul's Churchyard, in 1551, with a dedication to Cecil, afterwards Lord Burleigh. The letter of More to Peter Giles is all of the preliminary matter which he translated. But in 1556 appeared a second edition, carefully corrected and with many alterations, omitting the dedication to Cecil, but

EARLY EDITIONS AND TRANSLATIONS li

adding versions of Giles's letter to Busleyden, and the 'meter of iiij verses.' A third edition appeared in 1597, and a fourth in 1624. Since then it has been reprinted several times—by Dibdin, in 1808; by Professor Arber, in 1869; by Dr. Lumby, in 1879; by Robert Roberts, at Boston, in 1887; and by William Morris, at the Kelmscott Press, in 1893. All these are reprints of the second edition, Dr. Lupton being the first to reprint the *editio princeps*.

Till 1684 Robynson's was the only English version, but in that year appeared a new translation by the celebrated Gilbert Burnet, afterwards Bishop of Salisbury. It is closer to the Latin and more accurate than Robynson's, but it has not the charm of Robynson's racy and picturesque English. A work so characteristic of the English Renaissance finds much more appropriate expression in the diction and tone of that time, and what it loses in exact scholarship—though Burnet himself is by no means impeccable—it gains in affinity. The version of Arthur Cayly, which appeared in 1808, though it purported to be a new one, merely modified Burnet.

Of Ralph Robynson very little is known. He was born in Lincolnshire, in 1521, and received his early education at the Grantham and Stamford grammar schools, and was at both a schoolfellow of William Cecil, afterwards Lord Burleigh. He entered Corpus Christi College, Oxford, in 1536, at the age of fifteen, of which College he became, in June 1542, a Fellow. Leaving Oxford, he settled in London, where he obtained the livery of the Goldsmiths' Company, and some employment in the service of Cecil. He came of a numerous and poor family, whose difficulties appear to have hampered him, and two appeals to Cecil for assistance are extant; but whether he responded to them does not appear. The withdrawal of the dedicatory epistle to his old schoolfellow from the second edition of his translation seems significant. That he was alive, and in poverty, in 1572 is certain from Cecil's endorsement to his second appeal; but beyond that nothing more of him is known.

Robynson's version of the *Utopia* is an excellent specimen of that style of translation which found its expression not in the simple and musical English of the versions of the Bible, but of that style of expression which was afterwards adopted in the Tudor versions of the Greek and Roman Classics, the characteristic excellences of which are vigour and dignity, the characteristic defects, diffuseness and cumbrousness. He had by no means an easy task with his original, for More's Latin is often very involved and sometimes obscure. As a translator, though he is occasionally guilty of strange lapses, he is, as a rule, fairly trustworthy, and seldom fails to give the general sense correctly; at times indeed he is exceedingly felicitous, improving the original. His chief fault lies in his diffuseness and in an over-done accumulation of synonyms, which however has, at least sometimes, a not unpleasing effect. In addition to its delightful quaintness, its raciness, picturesqueness and vigour, the version is an important monument of the English of the first part of the sixteenth century.

It has not been thought necessary to print and annotate the preliminary matter in the *Utopia*; but, as Peter Giles's letter to Busleyden, and More's to Peter Giles may almost be regarded as a part of the machinery of the fiction, they have been printed in an Appendix.

⁋ The fyrste

boke of the communyca

cion of Raphaell hythlodaye concernynge the best state of a commen
wealthe.

The moste vyctoryous and tryumphante Kynge of Englande, Henry theight of that name, in all royal vertues Prince moste peerlesse, hadde of late in contra-uersie with the right hyghe and myghtie king of Castell weightye matters, and of greate importaunce; for the debatement and final determination wherof the kinges Maieste sent me Ambassadour into flaunders, ioined in commission with cuthebert Tunstall, a man doubteles owte of comparison, and whom the kinges maiestie of late, to the greate reioysyng of all men, did preferre to the office of maister of the Rolles. But of thys mans prayses I will saye nothynge; not bycause I do feare that small credence shalbe geuen to the testymony that commyth owt of a frindes mouthe, but bicause hys vertue and lernyng be greater and of more excellencye, than that I am able to prayse them; and also in all places so famous, and so perfectlye well knowne, that they nede not nor ought not of me to be praysed, onles I wolde seme to shew and set furth the brightenes of the sonne wyth a candell, as the Prouerbe sayth.

There met vs at Bruges (for thus yt was before agreed) they whome theire prince hadde for that matter appoynted commyssyoners, excellente men all. The chiefe and the head of them was the Marcgraue (as they cal him) of Bruges, a right honorable man: but the wisest and tho best spoken of them was George

Temsice, prouoste of Casselles; a man not onlye by lernyng but also by nature of singuler eloquence, and in the lawes profoundelye lerned; but in reasonynge, and debatynge of matters, what by his naturall witte, and what by daylye exercise, suerlye he hadde fewe fellowes. After that we hadde ones or twise mette, and vpon certeyne poyntes or artycles could not fully and throughlye agre; they for a certeyne space toke their leaue of vs, and departed to Bruxelle, there to knowe theire princes pleasure. I in the meane tyme (for so my busynes laye) wente streyghte thens to Antwerpe.

Whyles I was there abydinge, often tymes amonge other, but whyche to me was more welcome then annye other, dyd vysite me one Peter Gyles, a Citisien of Antwerpe; a man there in hys contrey of honest reputatyon, and also preferred to hyghe promotyons, worthye truelye of the highest. For it is harde to saye whether the yong man be in lernynge or in honestye more excellent. For he is bothe of wonderfull vertuous condytyons, and also singulerlye well lerned, and towardes all sortes of people excedynge gentyl; but towardes hys fryndes so kynde harted, so louynge, so faythfull, so trustye, and of so earneste affectyon, that yt were verye harde in any place to fynd a man, that wyth hym in all poyntes of frendshyppe maye be compared. No man can be more lowlye or courteys. No man vsithe lesse symulatyon or dyssymulatyon; in no man ys more prudente symplycytye. Besydes this, he is in his talke and communycatyon so merye and pleasaunte, yea, and that wythout harme, that, throughe hys gentyll intertaynement and hys swete and delectable communycatyon, in me was greatlye abated and dymynyshed the feruent desyre that I hadde to see my natyue contreye, my wyffe and my chyldren; whome then I dyd muche longe and couett to see, bicause that at that tyme I hadde byn more then .iiii. monythes from them.

OF UTOPIA

Upon a certeyne daye when I hadde herde the deuyne seruyce in our ladies churche, whyche is the fayrest, the moste gorgious and curyous churche of buyldynge in all the cytye, and also moste frequented of people, and the seruice beynge done, was readye to goo home to my lodgyng, I chaunced to espie thys forsayde Peter talkynge wyth a certeyne straunger, a man well stryken in age, wyth a blake sonne burned face, a longe bearde, and a cloke caste homely aboute hys shoulders; whom by hys fauour and apparrel forthwythe I iudged to be a maryner. But when thys Peter sawe me, he cummythe to me and saluteth me. And as I was abowte to answere hym: 'see you thys man?' sayeth he (and therwyth he poynted to the man that I sawe hym talkynge wyth before). 'I was mynded,' quod he, 'to brynge hym streyghte home to you.' 'He should haue bene verye welcome to me,' sayd I, 'for your sake.' 'Naye' (quod he) 'for hys owne sake, if you knewe hym; for there ys no man this daye lyuynge that can tell you of so manye strange and vnknowne peoples and contreis as this man can. And I know well that you be verye desyrous to heare of suche newes.' 'Than I coniectured not farre a mysse' (quod I) 'for euen at the fyrste syghte I iudged hym to be a maryner.' 'Naye' (quod he) 'there ye were greatlye deceaued. He hayth sayled indede, not as the maryner Palynure, but as the experte and prudent prince Ulisses; yea, rather as the auncyent and sage Philosopher Plato.

'For thys same Raphaell Hythlodaye (for thys ys hys name) is verye well lerned in the Latyne tonge; but profounde and excellent in the greke tonge, wherein he euer bestowed more studye than in the lattyne, because he had geuen hym selfe holye to the studye of Phylosophy. Wherof he knewe that there ys nothynge extante in the lattyne tonge, that is to anny purpose, sauynge a few of Senecaes and Ciceroes doinges. His patrymonye that he was borne vnto he lefte to his

bretherne (for he is a Portugalle borne); and for the
desyre that he hadde to see and knowe the farre
contreys of the worlde, he joyned him selfe in companye wyth Amerike vespuce, and in the .iii. laste
voyages of thoes .iiii., that be nowe in prynte and
abrode in euerye mans handes, he contynued styll in
hys companye; sauynge that in the laste voyage
he came not home again wyth hym. For he made
suche meanes and shyfte, what by intreataunce and
what by importune sute, that he gotte lycence of
mayster Amerycke (thoughe it were sore agaynst his
will) to be one of the .xxiiii. whyche in the ende of
the last voyage were lefte in the contrye of Gulike.
He was therfore lefte behynde for hys mindes sake, as
one that toke more thoughte and care for trauaylyng
then dyinge; hauynge customablye in hys mouthe
theis sayinges: He that hathe no graue ys couered
wyth the skie; and, The way to heauen owte of all
places is of like lenghth and distance. Which fantasye
of his (if God had not bene his better frende) he hadde
suerlye bought full deere.

'But after the departynge of Mayster vespuce, when
he hadde trauayled thoroughe and abowte manye contreis, with v. of his companyons Gulykyans, at the
laste by maruelous chaunce he arryued in Taprobane,
from whens he wente to Calyquit, where he chaunced
to fynde certeyne of hys contrey shyppes, wherin he
retorned again into hys countreye, nothynge lesse then
lokyd for.'

All thys when Peter hadde tolde me, I thankyd hym
for his gentyll kyndnes, that he hadde vouchesaufed to
brynge me to the speche of that man. whose communication he thought sholde be to me pleasaunte and acceptable. And there wyth I turned me to Raphaell; and
when we hadde haylsede thone thother, and hadde
spoken thies comen wordes, that be customably spoken
at the fyrste metynge and acquentaunce of straungers,
we wente thens to my house, and there in my gardeyne,

OF UTOPIA

vpon a benche coueryd wyth grene torues, we satte downe talking togethers.

There he tolde vs howe that, after the departynge of vespuce, he and hys fellowes, that tarryed behynde in Gulyke, beganne by lytle and lytle, thoroughe fayre and gentle speche, to winne the loue and fauour of the people of that contreye; in so muche that within shorte space, theye dydde dwell amonges them not onlye harmelese, but also occupyed wyth them verye famylyerly. He tolde vs also that they were in hyghe reputatyon and fauoure wyth a certeyne greate man (whose name and contreye ys nowe quyte owte of my remembraunce), which of hys mere lyberalytye dyd beare the costes and charges of hym and his fyue companions, and besydes that gaue them a trustye guyde, to conducte them in theyre iorney (whyche by water was in botys and by lande in wagains), and to bring them to other princes withe verye frindlye commendatyons. Thus after manye dayes iourneis, he sayd they found townys and cytyes, and weale publyques full of people, gouerned by good and holsom lawes.

For vnder the lyne equynoctyall and of bothe sydes of the same, as farre as the sonne doth extend hys course, lyeth (quod he) greate and wyde desertes and wyldernesses, parched, burned and dryed vppe with continuall and intollerable heate. All thynges be hydeous, terryble, lothesome, and vnpleasaunte to be holde; all thynges owte of fasshyon and comylynes, inhabyted wyth wylde beastes and serpentes, or at the leaste wyse wyth people that be no lesse sauage, wylde, and noysome then the verye beastes themselfes be. But a lytle farther beyonde that all thynges begyn by lytle and lytle to waxe pleasaunte; the ayre softe, temperate, and gentle; the ground couered wyth grene grasse; less wildnes in the beastes. At the laste shall ye come again to people, cities, and townes, wherin is contynuall entercourse and occupyinge of marchandyse and chaffare, not onelye amonge them selfes and wyth theyre borderers, but also wyth marchauntes of farre contreys bothe by lande and water.

'Ther I had occasion' (sayde he), 'to go to manye contreys of euery syde. For there was no shyppe reddye to anye voyage or iorney, but I and my fellowes were into it verye gladlye receauyde. The shyppes that they founde fyrste were made playne, flatte, and broade in the botome, troughewyse. The sayles were made of greate russhes, or of wyckers, and in some places of lether. Afterwarde they founde shyppes wyth rydged kyeles, and sayles of canuas; yea, and shortelye after hauynge all thynges lyke owers; the shyppemen also verye experte and connynge both in the sea and in the wether.'

But he sayde that he founde greate fauour and fryndeshyppe amonge them for teachynge them the feate and vse of the lode stone, whych to them before that tyme was vnknowne; and therefore they were wonte to be verye tymerous and fearefull vpon the sea, nor to venter vpon it, but onlye in the somer time. But nowe they haue such a confidence in that stone, that they feare not stormy wynter; in so doynge, ferther frome care then ieopardye. In so muche that it is greatlye to be doubtyd, leste that thynge, thoroughe theyre owne folyshe hardynes, shall tourne them to euyll and harme, whyche at the fyrste was supposyde shoulde be to them good and commodyous.

But what he tolde vs that he sawe, in euerye contrey wheare he came, it were verye longe to declare. Nother it is my purpose at this time to make rehersall therof. But peraduenture in an other place, I wyll speake of yt; chyefelye suche thynges as shalbe profytable to be knowne; as in specyall be thoese decrees and ordinaunces that he marked to be well and wyselye prouyded and enacted amonge suche peoples as do lyue to gethere in a cyuyle pollycye and good ordre. For of suche thynges dyd we busilie enquyre and demaunde of hym, and he lyke wise verye wyllynglye tolde vs

of the same. But as for monsters, because they be
no newes, of them we were nothynge inquysitiue.
For nothynge is more easye to be founde, then be
barking Scyllaes, rauenyng Celenes, and Lestrygones
deuowerers of people, and suche lyke greate and vn-
credyble monsters; but to fynde cytyzyns ruled by
good and holsome lawes, that ys an excedynge rare
and harde thynge.

But as he markyd manye fonde and folyshe lawes
in thoose newe founde lands, so he rehersyde manye
actes and constytutyons wherby thies our cytyes,
nations, contreys, and Kyngdomes maye take ensample, to amende theyre faultes, enormytyes and
errors; wherof in another place, as I sayde, I wyll
intreate. Now at thys tyme I am determyned to
reherse onlye that he tolde vs of the maners, customes,
lawes, and ordinaunces of the vtopians. But fyrste
I wyll repete our former communycatyon; by thocca-
syon, and, as I myghte saye, the dryfte wherof he
was browghte into the mentyon of that weale publyque.

For when Raphaell hadde verye prudently touched
dyuers thynges that be amysse, sume here and sume
there; yea, verye manye of bothe partes; and agayne
hadde spoken of suche wyse and prudent lawes and
decrees as be establyshed and vsyde bothe here amonge
vs and also there emonge them; as a man so connynge
and experte in the lawes and customes of euery seueral
countreye, as though into what place soeuer he came
geaste wyse, there he had lede al his life: then
Peter, much meruellyng at the man: 'Surely mayster
Raphaell' (quod he), 'I wondere greatlye whie you
gette you not into some Kinges courte; for I am
sewre there is no prynce lyuynge that wolde not
be very gladde of yowe; as a man not onlye able
hygholye to delyte hym wyth youre profounde lernynge, and thys youre knowledge of contreis and
peoples, but also are meat to instructe him with
examples, and helpe hym wyth counsell. And thus

doynge yowe shal bring yowre selfe in a verye good case, and also be in habylytye to helpe all youre frindes and kynsfolke.'

'As concernyng my fryndes and kynsfolke' (quod he), 'I passe not greatly for them: for I think I haue suffycyentlye done my parte towardes them all readye. For thies thinges that other men doo not depart from vntyll they be olde and sicke. yea, which they be then verye lothe to leaue when they can no lenger kepe, those verye same thynges dyd I, beynge not onlye lustye and in good helth, but also in the flowere of my youthe, deuyde among my fryndes and kynsfolkes; which I think wyth thys my liberalytye owghte to holde them contentyd, and not to requyre nor to looke that besydes thys I shoulde for theyre sakes gyue my selfe in bondage to kynges.'

'Naye god forbedde' (quod peter), 'it is not my mynd that you shoulde be in bondage to kynges, but as a retaynoure to them at youre pleasure; whyche sewrelye I thynke ys the nygheste waye that you can deuyse, howe to bestowe youre tyme frutefullye, not onlye for the pryuate commoditye of your fryndes and for the general proffytte of all sortes of people, but also for the auauncemente of your selfe to a muche welthier state and condytyon then you be nowe in.'

'To a welthyer condition' (quod Raphael), 'by that meanes that my mynde standethe cleane agaynst? Nowe I lyue at lybertye, after myn owne mynde and pleasure; whiche I thynke verye fewe of thes greate states and peeres of realmes can saye. Yea, and there be ynowe of them that sike for greate mens frindeshippes; and therfore thynke it no great hurte, if they haue not me, nor .ii. or .iii. suche other as I am.'

'Well, I perceyue plainlye, frind Raphaell' (quod I), 'that yowe be desierous nother of riches nor of powre. And truly I haue in no lesse reuerence and estimacyon a man that is of your mind, then anny of them al that be so high in pour and aucthoritie. But you shall

doo as it becommith yow, yea, and accordinge to this
wisedome and thys highe and free couraghe of youres.
yf yowe can fynde in youre harte so to appoynte and
dyspose your selfe, that you maie apply your wytte
and delygence to the proffyt of the weale publyque,
though it be sume what to youre owne payne and
hyndraunce. And thys shall yow neuer so well doo,
nor wyth so greate proffitte perfourme, as yf yowe be
of sum great prynces councell, and put into his heade
(as I doubte not but you wyll) honeste opynyons, and
vertuous persuasyons. For from the prynce, as from
a perpetuall well sprynge, cummythe amonge the
people the floode of all that is good or euell. But
in yowe is so perfitte lernynge, that wythowte anye
experience; and agayne so greate experyence, that
wythoute anye lernynge; yowe maye well be anny
kinges councellour.'

'Yow be twyse deceaued, maister More' (quod he),
'fyrste in me, and agayne in the thing it selfe. For
nother is in me that habilitye that yowe force vpon
me; and yf it were neuer so muche, yet in dysquieting
myne owne quietnes I should nothing further the
weale publique. For, fyrst of all, the moste parte of
all princes haue more delyte in warlike matters and
feates of cheualrie (the knowlege wherof I nother
haue nor desire), than in the good feates of peace;
and employe muche more study howe by right or by
wrong to enlarge their dominions, than howe well and
peaceablie to rule and gouerne that they haue all redie.
Moreouer, they that be counsellours to kinges, euery
one of them eyther is of him selfe so wyse in dede,
that he nede not, or elles he thinketh him self so
wise, that he will not allowe an other mans councell;
sauing that they do shamefully and flatteringly geue
assent to the fond and folishe sayinges of certeyn
greate men, whose fauours, bicause they be in high
aucthoritie with their prince, by assentacion and
flatteringe they labor to opteyne. And verily it is

naturally geuen to all men to esteame their owne
inuentyons best. So both the rauen and the ape
thincke their owne yong ones fayrest.

'Than if a man in such a company, where some
disdayne and haue despite at other mens inuentions; and some cownte their owne best; if among suche men, I saye, a man shoulde bringe furth any thinge that he hayth redde done in tymes paste, or that he hathe sene done in other places, there the hearers fare as thoughe the hole existimacion of theyr wisdome were in ieopardy to be ouerthrowen, and that euer after they should be counted for very diserdes, onles they colde in other mens inuentions pycke out matter to reprehende and find fawt at. If all other pore helpes faile, then this is their extreame refuge: " Thies thinges" (say they) "pleased oure forefathers and auncetours: wolde god wee coulde be so wise as they were." And as though they had wittely concluded the matter, and with this answere stoppid euery mans mouthe, they sitt downe agayn. As who should saye it were a very daungerous matter, if a man in any pointe should be founde wiser then his forefathers were. And yet be we content to suffer the best and wittiest of their decrees to lye vnexecuted; but if in any thinge a better ordre mighte haue bene taken, than by them was, theare we take faste holde, and finde many fawtes. Many times haue I chaunced vpon suche prowde, lewde, ouerthwarte, and waywarde Judgementes; yea, and ones in Englande.'

'I praye yow, Syre' (quod I), 'haue yow bene in owr contrey?' 'Yea forsothe' (quod he), 'and their I tarried for the space of iiii. or v. monythes together, not longe after the insurreccion, that the westerne Englishe men made agaynst their kynge; whych by their owne myserable and pitefull slaughter was suppressed and endyd. In the meane season I was much bounde and beholden to the righte reuerende father Jhon Morton. Archebishop, and cardenall of Canter-

OF UTOPIA

burye, and at that tyme also Lord chauncellour of England; a man, maister Peter (for maister More knoweth all reddy that I wyll saye), not more honorable for his aucthority, then for his prudence and vertue. He was of a meane stature, and though streken in age yet bare he his body vpryght. In his face did shine such an amiable reuerence, as was pleasaunte to beholde. Gentell in communycatyon, yet earneste and sage. He had greate delyte manye tymes wyth roughe speche to hys sewters to proue, but wythowte harme, what prompte wytte and what bolde sprite were in euery man. In the which, as in a vertue much agreinge with his nature, so that therewyth were not ioyned impudency, he toke greate delectatyon; and the same person, as apte and mete to haue an administratyon in the weale publique, he dyd louingly enbrace. In hys speche he was fyne, eloquent, and pythye. In the lawe he had profounde knowledge; in witte he was incomparable; and in memory wonderfull excellent. Thies qualytyes, whych in hym were by nature synguler, he by learnynge and vse had made perfytte.

'The Kynge putt muche truste in hys councell: the weale publyque also in a maner leaned vnto hym, when I was there. For euen in the chiefe of hys youth he was taken from schole into the Courte, and there passyd all hys tyme in muche trouble and busynes, and was contynually tumbled and tossed in the waues of dyuers mysfortunes and aduersytyes. And so by many and greate daungers he lerned the experience of the worlde, whyche so beynge learned can not easely be forgotten.

'It chaunced on a certayne daye, when I sate at hys table, there was also a certayne laye man, cunnynge in the lawes of yowre Realme. Whyche, I can not tel wherof takyng occasyon, began dyligently and busily to prayse that strayte and rygorous iustice, which at that tyme was there executed upon fellones, who, as he sayde, were for the moste part ᴠᴠ hanged together vpon one gallowes. And, seyng so fewe escapyd punyshement, he sayd he coulde not chewse but greatly wonder and maruell, howe and by what euill lucke it should so cum to passe, that theues neuertheles were in euery place so ryffe and ranke. "Naye, Syr," quod I (for I durst boldely speake my mind before the Cardynall), "maruell nothing herat; for thys punyshement of theues passeth the limites ⟨of⟩ Justyce, and is also very hurtefull to the weale publyque. For it is to extreame and crewell a punishement for thefte, and yet not sufficient to refrayne men from thefte. For simple thefte is not so greate an offence, that it owght to be punished with death. Nother there is any punishmente so horrible, that it can kepe them from stealynge whych haue no other crafte wherby to get their liuing. Therefore in this poynte, not yow only, but also the moste part of the worlde, be lyke euyll scholemasters, whych be readyare to beate then to teache their scholers. For great and horryble punyshementes be appoynted for theues; whereas muche rather prouysyon should haue bene made, that there were some meanes wherby they might gett theyr lyuynge, so that no man should be dreuen to thys extreame necessitie, fyrst to steale, and then to dye." "Yes" (quod he), "this matter is well ynoughe prouyded for all ready. There be handy craftes, there is husbandry, to gett their liuinge by, if they wolde not wyllingely be nowght." "Nay" (quod I), "you shall not skape so; for, fyrste of all, I wyll speake nothynge of them that come home owte of warre maymede and lame, as not longe ago owte of blacke heath filde, and a lityll before that owt of the warres in Fraunce: suche (I say) as put their lyues in ieopardy for the weale publiques or the kinges sake, and by the reason of weakenes and lamenes be not able to occupy their olde craftes, and be to aged to lerne newe: of them I wyll speake nothinge, because warre lyke the tyde ebbeth and floweth. But let vs consydere those thinges that chaunce dayly before our eyes.

'"Fyrste, there is a great number of gentilmen, which can not be content to lyue ydle them selfes, like dorres, of that whiche other haue laboryd for: their tenauntes I meane, whom they polle and shaue to the quycke by reysing their rentes (for this only poynte of frugalitye do they vse, men els thoroughe their lauasse and prodigall spendynge able to bringe them selfes to very beggery): thies gentilmen (I say) do not only liue in ydilnes them selfes, but also carry about with them at their tayles a greate flocke or trayne of ydell and loytrynge seruynge men, whyche neuer learned any crafte wherby to get their liuinges. Thies men, as sone as theyr mayster is dead, or be sicke them selfes, be incontinent thruste owte of doores. For gentlemen had rather kepe ydil persones then sycke men; and many times the dead mans heyr is not able to mainteyne so great a howse, and kepe so many seruinge men, as his father dydde. Then in the meane season they that be thus destytute of seruice other starue for honger, or manfully playe the theaues. For what wolde yow haue them to do? When they haue wandred abrode so longe, untyll they haue worne threde bare their apparell, and also appayred their health, then gentlemen, because of their pale and sicke faces and patched cotes, wyll not take them into seruyce. And husbandmen dare not sett them a worke, knowyng well ynough that he is nothynge mete to doo trewe and faythfull seruice to a poore man wyth a spade and a mattoke, for small wages and harde fare, whyche, beynge deyntely and tenderly pampered vp in ydilnes and pleasure, was wont with a sworde and a buckeler by hys syde to iette through the strete with a bragging looke, and to thynke hym selfe to good to be any mans mate."

'"Naye by saynt Marie, ser" (quod the lawier) "not so, for this kinde of men muste we make moot of. For in them, as men of stowter stomackes, bolder spyrytes, and manlyer currages, then handy craftes men and plowe men be, doth consyste the hole powre, strengthe, and puisaunce of oure hoste, when we muste fight in battaill."

' "Forsothe, ser, aswel yowe myghte saye" (quod I) "that for warres sake you must cheryshe theues. For sewerly yow shal neuer lacke theues whyles yowe haue them. No, nor theues be not the most false and faynt harted soldiers, nor souldiours be not the cowardliste theues: so well thees .ii. craftes agree together. But this fawte, though it be muche vsed among yow, yet is it not peculiar to yow only, but commen also almost to all natyons. Yet Fraunce, besydes thys, is troubled and infected wyth a muche sorer plage. The hole realme is fylled and besieged wyth hierede soldiours in peace tyme, yf that be peace; whyche be brought in under the same coloure and pretence, that haith persuaded yow to kype thies ydell seruynge men. For thies wisefooles and very archedoltes thought the wealth of the hole contrey herin to consist, yf there were euer in a readynes a stronge and a sewer garrison, specyallye of olde practysed soldyours; for they put no truste at all in men vnexercysed. And therfore they must be fayne to seke for warre, to thende they maye euer haue practysed souldyours and cunnynge mansleers; leaste that (as it is pretilie sayde of Saluste) their handes and their myndes thoroughe ydylnes or lacke of exercyse shoulde waxe dull.

' "But howe pernycyous and pestylente a thynge it is to maynteyne suche beastes, the Frenche men by there owne harmes haue learned; and the examples of the Romaynes, Carthaginiens, Siriens and of many other contreys, do manyfestly declare. For not only the empire, but also the fieldys and cityes of all thies, by diuers occasyons haue bene ouerrunned and destroyed of their owne armies before hand had in a reddines.

OF UTOPIA

Now how vnnecessary a thynge thys is, hereby it maye appere: that the Frenche souldiours, whyche from their youthe haue byne practysed and inured in feates of armes, doo not cracke nor auaunce them selfes to haue verye often gotte the vpper-hande and masterye of your newe made and vnpractysed souldiours. But in thys poynte I wyll not vse manye wordes, leaste perchaunce I maye seme to flatter yow. No nor those same handy craft men of yours in cities, nor yet the rude and vplandishe ploughemen of the contrey, are not supposed to be greatly affraid of your gentilmens ydill seruing men, onles it be suche as be not of body or stature correspondent to theyr strenghte and currage; orels whose bolde stomackes be dyscourraged thoroughe pouertye. Thus yowe maye see, that yt ys not to be feared leaste they shoulde be effemynatede yf they were broughte vppe in good craftes and laborsome wourkes, whereby to gett theyre lyuynge; whose stowte and sturdye bodyes (for gentlemen vouchesauffe to corrupte and spill none but picked and chosen men) nowe, other by reason of rest and ydilnes, be brought to weakenes, orels by to easy and womanlye exercises be made feble and vnable to endure hardenes. Trewly howe soeuer the case stondeth, thys me thinketh is nothyng avayleable to the weale publique, for warre sacke, whyche yowe neuer haue but when yow wyll your selfes, to kepe and mainteyn an vnnumerable flocke of that sort of men, that be so troblesome and noyous in peace; wherof yow owght to haue a thowsande times more regard then of warre.

'"But yet this is not onlye the necessary cause of stealing. There is an other which as I suppose is proper and peculiare to yow Englishe men alone." "What is that?" quod the Cardenall. "Forsoth" (quod I), "your shepe, that were wont to be so myke and tame, and so smal eaters, now, as I heare saie, be become so greate deuowerers, and so wylde, that they eate vp and swallow down the very men them selfes. They consume, destroy, and deuoure hole fieldes, howses, and cities. For looke in what partes of the realme doth growe the fynyst, and therfore dearist woll, there noble men and gentlemen, yea, and certeyn Abbottes, holy men god wote, not contenting them selfes with the yearely reuennues and profyttes that were wont to grow to theyr forefathers and predecessours of their landes, nor beynge content that they liue in rest and pleasure, nothyng profytyng, ye, muche noyinge the weale publique, leaue no grounde for tyllage; they enclose all in pastures; they throw downe houses; they plucke downe townes; and leaue nothing stondynge but only the churche, to make of it a shepehowse. And, as thoughe yow loste no small quantity of grounde by forestes, chases, laundes, and parkes; those good holy men turne all dwellinge places and all glebelande into desolation and wildernes.

'"Therfore, that one couetous and vnsatiable cormaraunte and verye plage of his natyue contrey may compasse abowte and inclose many thousand acres of grounde to gether within one pale or hedge, the husbandmen be thrust owte of their owne; orels other by coueyne or fraude, or by vyolent oppression, they be put besydes it, or by wronges and iniuries they be so weried that they be compelled to sell all. By one meanes therfore or by other, other by howke or crooke, they must nedes departe awaye, pore, sylie, wretched soules; men, women, husbandes, wyues, fatherles chyldren, widdowes, wofull mothers with their yonge babes, and their hole housholde smal in substaunce, and much in nombre, as husbandrie requireth many handes. Awaye they trudge, I say, out of their knowen and accustomed howses, fyndyng no places to rest in. All their housholde stuffe, whiche is verye lytle worth, though it myght well abyde the sale, yet beyng sodeynelye thrust out, they be constrayned to sell it for a thyng of nought. And when they haue, wanderynge about, sone spent that, what can they els do but steale, and then iustelye, God wote, behanged, or els go about a beggyng? And yet then also they be cast in prison as vagaboundes, because they go about and worke not; whom no man will set a worke, though they neuer so willingly offer them selfes therto. For one shepherde or heard man is ynough to eate vp that grounde with cattel, to the occupying wherof about husbandrye many handes were requysyte.

'"And this is also the cause that victualles be nowe in many places dearer. Yea, besydes this the pryce of wolle is so rysen that poore folkes, whiche were wont to worke it and make cloth of it, be nowe able to bye none at all. And by thys meanes verye manye be fayne to forsake worke, and to gyue them selfes to ydelnes. For after that so muche grounde was inclosed for pasture, an infinite multitude of shepe died of the rotte, suche vengaunce God toke of their inordinate and vnsaciable couetuousnes, sendyng amonge the shepe that pestiferous morreyn, which much more iustely should haue fallen on the shepemasters owne heades. And though the numbre of shepe increase neuer so fast, yet the pryce falleth not one myte, because there be so fewe sellers. For they be almoste all commen into a fewe riche mens handes, whome no neade driueth to sell before they lust; and they luste not before they may sell as deare as they lust. Now the same cause bryngeth in licke dearth of the other kindes of cattell; yea, and that so much the more, bycause that after farmes pluckyd downe, and husbandry decayed, ther is no man that passyth for the breadyng of yonge stoore. For thees ryche men brynge not vp the yonge ones of greate cattell as they do lambes. But first they bye them abrode very chepe, and aftorward, when they be fattede in their pastures, they sell them agayne excedyng deare. And therfor (as I suppose) the hole incommoditie herof is not yet felte. For yet they make dearth only in those places where they sell. But when they shall fetche them awaye from thens wheare they be bredde, faster then they can be brought vp, then shall there also be felte great dearth, when stoore begynnyth to fayle their whear the ware ys bought.

'"Thus the vnreasonable couetousnes of a fewe hath turned that thyng to the vtter vndoyng of your Ilande, in the whiche thyng the chiefe felicitie of your realme dyd consist. For this great dearth of victualles causeth euery man to kepe as lytle houses and as small hospitalitie as he possible maye, and to put awaye their seruauntes: whether, I praye you, but a beggynge? or els, whiche thies gentle bloodis and stoute stomakes wyll soner set theyr myndes vnto, a stealinge?

'"Nowe, to amende the matters, to this wretched beggerye and myserable pouertie is ioyned great wantonnes, importunate superfluytie, and excessiue ryote. For not only gentle mens seruauntes, but also handy craft men, yea, and almoste the ploughemen of the countrey, with all other sortes of people, vse muche straunge and prowde newe fanglenes in their apparrell, and to muche prodigal riotte and sumptuous fare at their table. Nowe bawdes, qweynes, hoores, harlottes, strumpettes, brothelhouses, stewes, and yet an other stewes, wine tauernes, ale houses, and tipling houses, with so many noughty lewde and vnlawfull games, as dice, cardes, tables tennyes, bolles, coytes, do not al thys sende the haunters of them streyght a stealynge when theyr money is gone?

'"Caste out thies pernycious abomynacyons; make a lawe that they whyche plucked downe fermes and townes of husbandrye, shall buylde them vp agayne or els yelde and vprender the possessyon of them to suche as wyll goo to the coste of buyldynge them anewe. Suffer not thies ryche men to bye vp all, to ingrosse and forstalle, and with theyr monopolye to kepe the market alone as please them. Let not so

OF UTOPIA

manye be brought vp in ydlenes; lett husbandrye and tyllage be restored agayne; let clothe workynge be renewed; that there maye be honest labours for thys ydell sorte to passe theyre tyme in profytablye, whyche hytherto other pouertye hathe caused to be theues, or elles nowe be other vagabondes, or ydell seruynge men, and shortelye wylbe theues. Dowteles, oneles yowe fynde a remedye for thyes enormytyes, yowe shall in vayne auuance your selfes of executinge iustice vpon fellones. For this iustice is more beautyfull then iuste or profytable. For by sufferynge your youthe wantonlye and viciouslye to be brought vp, and to be infected euen from theyr tender age by lytle and lytle wyth vyce; than a goddes name to be punyshed, when they commytte the same faultes after they be commen to mannes state, whiche frome ther youthe they were euer lyke to doo: in thys pointe, I praye yowe, what other thynge doo yowe, then make theues, and then punyshe them?"

'Nowe as I was thus speakynge, the Lawier beganne to make hym selfe readye to aunswere, and was determyned wyth hym selfe to vse the common fassyon and trade of disputers, whyche be more dylygent in rehersynge then aunswerynge, as thynking the memorye worthye of the chiefe prayse. "In dede syr" (quod he) "yow haue sayd well, beinge but a straunger, and one that myght rather here somme thynge of thyes matters, then haue anye exacte or perfecte knowledge of the same, as I will incontinent by open proffe make manifest and playn. For firste I wyll reherse in ordre all that yow haue sayde; then I wyll declare in what thynge yowe be deceaued, through lacke of knowledge, in all our fassions, maners and customes; and laste of all I wyll aunswere to your argumentes, and confute them euery one. Fyrste therfore I wyll begynne where I promysed. Foure thynges yowe semed to me"—"Hold your peace" (quod the Cardynall), "for by lyke yowe wyll make no shorte aunswere, whiche make such a begynnyng; wherfore at thys tyme yowe shall not take the paynes to make youre aunswere, but kepe it to youre nexte meatynge, whiche I would be ryght gladde that it myght be euen to morrowe nexte (onles other yowe or mayster Raphaell haue any earnest lette).

'"But now, maister Raphaell, I woulde very gladly heare of yow, whie yow thynke thefte not worthy to be punished with death: or what other punyshment yow can deuyse more expedient to the weale publique. For I am sewer yowe are not of that mynde, that yowe woulde haue thefte escape vnpunyshed. For if now the extreme punishment of death cannot cause them to leaue stealynge, then if ruffians and rubbers shoulde be sewer of their lyues, what violence, what feare were able to holde their handes from robbynge, whiche would take the mitigacion of the punishment as a verye peruocation to the mischiefe?"

'"Suerly my lorde" (quod I) "I thynke it no right nor iustice that the losse of money should cause the losse of mans lyfe. For myne opinion is that all the goodes in the worlde are not able to counteruayle mans lyfe. But if they wold thus say: that the breaking of iustice, and the transgression of the lawes is recompensed with this punishment, and not the losse of the money; then why maye not thys extreame iustice wel be called extreme iniurie? For neither so cruel gouernaunce, so streyte rules, and vnmercyfull lawes be allowable, that if a small offence be commytted, by and by the sworde shoulde be drawen; nor so stoycall ordinaunces are to be borne wythall, as to counte all offences of suche equalitie, that the kyllynge of a man, or the takynge of hys money from hym, were bothe a matter; and the one no more heynous offence then the other: betwene the whyche two, yf we haue annye respecte to equitie, no symylytude or equalytie consysteth. God commaundeth vs that we shall not kyll. And be we then so hastie to kyll a man for takynge a lytle money? And yf annye man woulde vnderstande kyllynge, by this commaundement of GOD, to bee forbydden after no larger wyse then mans constitucions defyneth kyllynge to be lawfull, then whye maye it not lykewyse, by mannes constitutions, be determyned after what sorte hooredome, fornication, and periurye maye be lawfull? For where as by the permission of GOD no man hathe power to kyll nother hym selfe, nor yet annye other man; then yf a lawe made by the consente of men concernynge slaughter of men oughte to be of suche strengthe, force, and vertue, that they whyche contrarye to the commaundement of GOD haue kylled those, whome thys constitucion of man commaunded to be kylled, be cleane quyte and exempte owte of the bondes and daunger of Goddes commaundemente; shall it not then by thys reason followe that the powre of Goddes commaundement shall extende no further then mannes lawe dothe defyne and permytte? And so shall it come to passe, that in lyke manner mans constitucions in al thynges shal determyne howe farre the obseruation of all Goddes commaundementes shall extende. To be shorte, Moyses lawe, thoughe it were vngentle and sharpe, as a lawe that was gyuen to bondmen; yea, and them verye obstinate, stubborne, and styf necked; yet it punnyshed thefte by the purse, and not wyth deathe. And let vs not thynke that GOD in the newe lawe of clemencie and mercie, vnder the whiche he ruleth vs with fatherlie gentlenesse, as his dere chyldren, hath geuen vs greater scoupe and license to execute crueltie one vpon an other.

'"Now ye haue hard the reasons, whereby I am perswaded that this punishment is vnlawful. Furthermore I thinke there is no body that knoweth not, how vnreasonable, yea how pernitious a thynge it is to the weale publique, that a thefe, and a homicide or morderer, shuld suffer equall and lyke punyshment. For the thefe, seing that man that is condempned for thefte in no lesse ieoperdie, nor iudged to no lesse punishment, then hym that is conuict of manslaughter; through thys cogitacion onlye he is stronglye and forcybly prouoked, and in a maner constreyned, to kyl him, whom els he would haue but robbed. For, the murder ones done, he is in lesse care, and in more hope that the dede shall not be bewrayed or knowen, seynge the partye is now deade and rydde out of the waye, whyche onely myght haue vttered and disclosed it. But if he chaunce to be taken and discriued, yet he is in no more daunger and ieopardie then yf he had commytted but single fellonye. Therfore whyles we goo about wyth suche crueltye to make theues aferd, we prouoke them to kyll good men.

'"Now as touchyng this question, what punysshe- mente were more commodyous and better; that trulye in my iudgement is easyer to be founde, than what punysshement were wurse. For whie should we dowt that to be a good and a profytable waye for the punysshemente of offendours, whyche we knowe dydde in tymes paste so longe please the Romaynes; men in thadmynystratyon of a weale publyque moste experte, polytyque, and cunnyng? Such as amonge them weare conuycte of great and heynous trespaces, them they condempned into ston quarris, and in to myenes to dygge mettalle, there to be kepte in cheynes all the dayes of theyr lyfe.

'"But as concernyng this matter, I allow the ordenaunce of no nation so well as that I sawe (whyles I trauayled a brode abowt the wordle) vsed in Persia, amonge the people that commenlye be called the polylerytes; whose lande is bothe large and ample, and also well and wyttelye gouerned; and the people in all conditions free and ruled by their owne lawes, sauing that they paye a yerely tribute to the great king of Persia. But bicause they be farre from the sea, compassed and closed in almoste rounde abowte wyth hygh mountaynes, and do content them

selfes wyth the frutes of theyr owne lande, whyche
is of yt selfe verye fertyle and frutefull: for thys cause
nother they goo to other cowntreys, nor other comme
to them. And accordynge to the olde custome of the
lande, they desyre not to enlarge the bowndes of theyr
domynyons; and those that they haue by reason of
the hyghe hylles be easelye defended; and the trybute
whyche they paye to their chiefe lord and kinge settethe them quyete and free from warfare. Thus theyre
lyffe ys commodyous rather then gallawnte, and maye
better be callede happye or luckye, then notable or
famous. For they be not knowne asmuche as by
name, I suppose, sauynge onlye to theyr nexte neyghbours and borderours.

'"They that in thys lande be attayntede and conuycte of felonye, make restitutyon of that they stoole
to the ryghte owner, and not (as they doo in other
landes) to the Kynge; whome they thynke to haue
no more ryghte to the thefe stolen thynge than the
thieffe himselfe hath. But if the thynge be loste or
made awaye, then the value of yt is paide of the
goodes of such offendours, whyche elles remayneth
all hole to theire wyffes and chyldrene. And they
them selfes be condempned to be common laborers;
and, onles the thefte be verye heynous, they be nother
locked in pryson, nor fettered in gyues, but be vntyed
and goo at large, laborynge in the common workes.
They that refuse labour, or goo slowly and slacly to
there woorke, be not only tied in cheynes, but also
pricked forward with stripes. They that be diligent
about their woorke liue without checke or rebuke.
Euery nyghte they be called in by name, and be
locked in theyr chambers. Besyde their dayly labour,
their lyffe is nothyng harde or incommodyous. Their
fare is indyfferent good, borne at the chardges of the
wealo publyque, bycause they be commen seruauntes
to the commen wealth. But their charges in all places
of the land is not borne a lyke. For in some partes

that is bestowed vpon them is gathered of almes.
And though that waye be vncerteyn, yet the people
be so full of mercye and pytie, that none is fownde
more profytable or plentyfull. In some places certeyn
landis be appoynted here vnto; of the reuenewes
wherof they be mainteined. And in some places euery
man geuyth a certeyne trybute for the same vse and
purpose. Agayne in some partes of the lande thies
seruyng men (for so be thies damned persons called),
do no common worke; but, as euery priuate man
nedeth laborours, so he cometh into the markette
place, and there hiereth some of them for meate and
drynke, and a certeyne limityd wayges by the daye,
sumwhat cheper then he shoulde hire a free man.
It is also lawfull for them to chastyce the slowth of
thies seruynge men wyth strypes.

'"By thys meanes they neuer lacke woorke; and
besydes their meate and dryncke euery one of them
bryngeth dayly sum thynge into the common treasoury.
All and euery one of them be apparrayled in one
colour. Their heddys be not polled or shauen, but
rownded a lytle aboue the eeres; and the typpe of the
one eare is cut of. Euery one of them may take meat
and drincke of their frindes, and also a cote of their
owne collour; but to receyve monye is deathe, as
well to the geuer as to the receyuour. And no lesse
ieopardie it is for a free man to receyue moneye of
a seruynge man, for any manner of cause; and lykewyse for seruynge men to touche weapons. The
seruyng men of euery seuerall shyere be dystyncte
and knowen from other by their seuerall and dystyncte badges; whyche to caste away is death: as it
is also to be seene owte of the precyncte of their owne
sheire, or to talke wyth a seruynge man of another
shyere. And it is no lesse daunger to them for to
intende to runne awaye, then to do yt in dede. Yea,
and to concele suche an enterpryes in a seruynge man
yt is deathe; in a free man seruytude. Of the con-

trarye parte, to hym that openeth and vttereth suche cownselles be decreyde large giftes: to a free man a great somme of moneye; to a seruynge man freedome; and to them bothe forgeuynes and pardone of that they were of councell in that pretence. So that yt can neuer be so good for them to goo forwarde in theyre euyll purpose, as by repentaunce to turne backe.

'"Thys is the lawe and ordre in thys behalfe, as I haue shewed yow. Wherin what humanytye is vsede, howe farre yt is frome crueltye, and howe commodyous yt is, yow doo playnlye perceue: for asmuche as the ende of their wrath and punyshemente intendeth nothyng elles but the distructyon of vyces and sauynge of men; wyth so vsynge and orderynge them, that theye can not chuse but be good; and what harme so euer theye dyd before, in the resydewe of theyre lyffe to make amendys for the same.

'"Moreouer yt is so lytle feared, that they shoulde torne agayne to theyre vycyous condytyons, that wayefarynge men wyll for theyre sauegarde chuse them to theyre guydes before annye other, in euerye sheyre chaungynge and takynge newe. For yf they wolde commytte robberye, theye haue nothynge abowte them meate for that purpose. They maye towche no weapons: moneye fownde abowte them shoulde betraye the robberye. They shoulde be no soner taken wyth the maner, but furthwyth they shoulde be punysshed. Nother theye can haue annye hoope at all to skape awaye by flyenge. For howe shoulde a man, that in no parte of hys apparrell is lyke other men, flye preuelye and vnknowen, oneles he wolde runne awaye naked? Howe be yt, so also flyinge, he shoulde be dyscryued by hys rounding and his eare marke. But yt is a thynge to be dowted, that they will lay their heddes togither, and conspire agaynst the weale publyque. No, no, I warraunte you. For the seruyng men of one shere alone could neuer hoope to brynge to passe suche an enterpryse, wythowte sollycytynge, entysynge, and allurynge the seruynge men of many other shyeres to take their partes. Whych thynge is to them so impossyble, that they may not asmuche as speake or talke togethers, or salute one an other. No, it is not to be thought that they wold make their owne countrey men and companyons of their cownsell in such a matter, whych they knowe well shoulde be ieopardye to the concelour therof, and greate commodytye and goodnes to the openner of the same: where as on the other parte, ther is none of them al hoopeles or in dyspayre to recouer agayne hys freedome, by humble obedience, by pacyent suffrynge, and by geauyng good tokens and lyklyhode of hymself, that he wyll euer after that liue lyke a trewe and an honeste man. For euery yeare dyuers be restoryd agayne to their freedome, throughe the commendatyon of their patience."

'Whan I had thus spoken, saynge moreouer that I coulde see no cause whie this ordre might not be had in England, with much more proffyte then the Justyce which the lawier so highly praised: "Naye" (quod the lawier), "this could neuer be so stablished in England, but that it must neades bringe the weale publique into great ieopardie and hasarde." And as he was thus saying, he shaked his heade, and made a wrie mouth, and so held his peace. And all that were ther present, with one assent agreid to his saying.

' "Well" (quod the Cardinall), "yet it were hard to iudge withowte a proffe whether this order wold doo well here or no. But when the sentence of deathe is geuen, if than the king should commaunde execution to be differryd and spared, and wold proue this order and fassion; taking away the priuileges of all saintuaries; if then the proffe wold declare the thing to be good and profitable, than it were well done that it were stablisshed. Els the condempned and repriued

OF UTOPIA

parsons may aswell and as iustly be put to death after this proffe, as when they were first cast. Nother any ioperdye can in the meane space growe here of. Yea, and me thinketh that thies vagaboundes may very well be ordered after the same fassion, against whome we haue hitherto made so many lawes, and so litle preuailed."

'When the Cardinal had thus said, than euery man gaue greate praise to my sayinges, which a litle before they had disallowed. But most of all was estemed that which was spoken of vagaboundes, bicause it was the cardinalles owne addition.

'I can not tell whether it were best to reherse the communication that followed, for it was not very sad. But yet you shal here it: for ther was no euell in it; and partly it parteined to the matter before said.

'Ther chaunsed to stond by a certein iesting parasite, or scoffer, which wold seme to resemble and cownterfeit the foole. But he did in such wise counterfeyt, that he was almost the very same in dead that he labored to represent. He so studied with wordes and saynges, brought furth so out of time and place, to make sporte and moue laughter, that he himself was oftener laughed at then his iestes were. Yet the foolish fellow brought out now and then such indifferent and reasonable stuffe, that he made the prouerbe trew, which sayeth: he that shoteth oft, at the last shal hit the marke. So that when one of the company said that thorough my communication a good ordre was found for theues, and that the Cardinall also had wel prouided for vagaboundes; so that only remained some good prouision to be made for them that through siknes and age were fallen into pouerty, and were become so impotente and vnweldye, that they were not able to woorke for their liuing: "Tush" (quod he) "let me alon with them; you shall see me do well ynough with them. For I had rather then anye good that this kind of people were dreuen sumwhether out of my sighte: they haue so sore troubled me many times and oft, when they haue with their lamentable teares begged money of me; and yet thei could neuer to mi mind so tune theire song, that therby they euer got of me one farthynge. For euer more the one of thies two chaunced: eyther that I wolde not, or elles that I could not, bicause I had it not. Therefore nowe they be waxed wyse. When they see me goo bye, bycause they wyll not leese theyr laboure, they lette me go, and saye not one worde to me. So they looke for nothing of me; no, in good sothe, no more then if I were a priest. But I will make a law, that all thies beggers shalbe distribute and bestowed into houses of religion. The men shalbe made laye bretherne, as they call them, and the women nunnes." Here at the Cardenall smiled, and allowed it in iest; yea, and all the residue in good earnest.

'But a certeyne freare, graduate in diuinitie, toke such pleasur and delite in this ieste of priestes and monkes, that he also, beinge elles a man of grislye and sterne grauitye, beganne merilye and wantonlye to ieste and taunt. "Nay" (quod he), "you shal not so be ridde and dispatched of beggers, oneles you make some prouision also for us frears." "Whie" (quod the iester) "that is doon all redy. For mi lord him selfe set a very good ordre for yow, when he decreed that vagaboundes should be kept strayt, and set to worke; for yow be the greatest and veriest vagaboundes that be."

'This iest also, when they saw the Cardinal not disproue it, euery man tooke it gladly, sauing only the Frear. For he (and that no marueil) when he was thus towchyd one the quicke, and hit on the gawl, so fret, so fumed and chafid at it, and was in such a rage, that he could not refrayn himselfe from chiding, skolding, railing, and reuiling. He called the fellow ribbald, villayn, iauell, backbiter, sclaunderer, and the sonne of perdition; citing therwith

OF UTOPIA

terrible threatening out of holy scriptur. Then the iesting skoffer began to play the scoffer indede, and verily he was good at yt, for he could play a part in that play, no man better. "Patient iourself, good maister Freare" (quod he), "and be not angry; for scriptur saith: *in your patience you shal saue your sowles.*" Then the Freare (for I wil rehearse his oune very woordes): "No, gallous wretche, I am not angry" (quod he); "or at the leaste wise I do not synne: for the psalmiste saith, *be you angry and sinne not.*"

'Then the Cardinal spake gently to the Freare, and desiered him to quyete hymself. "No, my lord" (quod he), "I speake not but of a good zeal as I ought; for holly men had a good zeale. Wherfor it is said; *the zeale of thy house hath eaten me.* And it is song in the church: *The skorners of Helizeus, whiles he went vp into the house of god, felt the zcale of the bald*; as peraduentur this skorning villain ribauld shal feel." "You do it" (quod the cardinall) "perchaunce of a good mind and affection. But me thinketh you should do, I can not tel whether more holily, certes more wisely, if you wold not set your wit to a fooles witte, and with a foole take in hand a foolish contention." "No, forsoeth, my lorde" (quod he), "I should not doo more wiselye. For Salomon the wise sayeth: *Answer a foole according to his folishnes*; like as I do now, and do shew him the pit that he shall fall into, if he take not hede. For if many skorners of Helizeus, which was but one bald man, felt the zeal of the balde, howe much more shall one skorner of many frears feele, amonge whom be many bald men? And we haue also the popes bulles, wherby all that mock and skorno us be excommunicate, suspended, and acursed." The cardinal seing that none end wold be made, sent away the iester by a preuy beck, and turned the communication to an other matter. Shortly after, when he was risen from the table, he went to heare his sueters, and so dimissed vo.

F

'Loke, mayster More, with how long and tedious a tale I haue kept you, which suerly I wolde haue bene ashamed to haue done, but that you so earnestly desiered me, and did after suche a sort geue eare vnto hit, as though you wolde not that any parcell of that communication should be left out; which though I haue doone sumwhat briefely, yet coulde I not chuse but rehearse it, for the iudgement of them, which, when they had improued and disallowed my sayinges, yet incontinent hearinge the Cardinall allowe them, dyd themselfes also approue the same; so impudently flattering him, that they were nothinge ashamed to admit, yea, almost in good earnest, his iesters folish inuentions; bicause that he him selfe, by smylynge at them, did seme not to disproue them. So that hereby you may right well perceaue, how litle the courtiers wold regard and esteme me and my sayinges.'

'I ensure you, maister Raphael' (quod I), 'I toke great delectation in hearing you: all thinges that yow sayde were spoken so wittily and so pleasauntly. And me thought my self to be in the meane time not only at home in my countrey, but also, throughe the pleasaunt remembraunce of the Cardinall, in whose housse I was brought vp of a child, to waxe a childe agayne. And, frend Raphaell, though I did beare verye greate loue towardes you before, yet seynge yow do so earnestly fauour thys man, yow wyll not beleue howe muche my loue towardes yow is nowe increased. But yet, all this notwithstanding, I can by no meanes chaunge my mind, but that I must needys beleue that you, if you be disposed, and can find in youre harte to followe some prynces courte, shall with your good cownselles greatly healpe and further the commen wealthe. Wherefore there is nothynge more apperteynynge to your dewty; that is to say, to the dewty of a good man. For where as youre Plato Judgethe that weale publyques shall by this meanes attayne perfecte felicitie, other if phylosophers be kynges, or els if kynges giue them selfes to the study of Philosophie; how farre, I praye yowe, shall commen wealthes then be from thys felicitie, if phylosophers wyll ⟨not⟩ vouchesaufe to instructe kynges with their good counsell?' 'They be not so vnkind' (quod he), 'but they would gladlye do it; yea, manye haue done it all readie in bookes that they haue put furth, if kynges and princes would be wyllyng and readie to folowe good counsell. But Plato doubteles dyd well forsee, oneles kynges themselfes would applye their myndes to the studye of philosophie, that elles they would neuer thoroughlye allowe the counsell of philosophers; beyng themselfes before euen from their tender age infectyd and corrupt with peruerse and euyll opinions. Whiche thynge Plato hymselfe prouyd trewe in kynge Dionise. If I should propose to any kynge holsome decrees, doinge my endeuour to pluck out of hys mynde the pernitious originall causes of vice and noughtenes, thynke you not that I shoulde furthe with other be dryuen awaye, or elles made a laughynge stocke?

'Goo to, suppose that I were with the Frenche kynge, and there syttynge in hys counsell, whyles that in that moste secrete consultation, the kyng hym self there beynge present in hys owne persone, they beat their braynes, and serche the verye bottomes of theyr wittes to discusse by what crafte and meanes the kyng maye styll kepe Myllayne and drawe to hym agayne fugatyue Naples; and then howe to conquere the Venetians, and howe to bryng vnder his Iurisdiction all Italye; then howe to wynne the dominion of Flaunders, Brabant, and of all Burgundie, with dyuers other landes, whose kyngdomes he hath longe a goo in mynde and purpose inuaded. Here, whyles one counselleth to conclude a leage of peace with the Venetians, whiche shal so longe endure, as shalbo thought mete and expedient for theire purpose, and to make them also of their counsell, yea, and besydes that to gyue them parte of the praye, whyche afterwarde, when they haue brought theyr purpose abowte after theyr owne myndes they maye requyre and claym agayne. An other thynketh beste to hyere the Germaneynes. An other would haue the fauoure of the Swychers wonne with money. An others aduyse is to appease the puyssaunte powre of the emperours maiestie with golde, as with a moste pleasaunt and acceptable sacrifice. Whyles an other gyueth counsell to make peace wyth the kynge of Arragone, and to restore vnto hym hys owne kyngdome of Nauarra, as a full assuraunce of peace. An other cummeth in wyth his .v. egges, and aduyseth to howke in the kynge of Castell with somme hope of affynytie or allyaunce, and to brynge to theyr parte certeyne peers of hys courte for greate pensions: whyles they all staye at the chyefeste dowte of all, what to doo in the meane tyme with England, and yet agree al in this to make peace with the englishmen, and with moste suere and strong bondes to bind that weake and feable frendshyppe, so that they must be called frendes, and hadde in suspicion as enemies; and that therfore the skottes must be hadde in a reddines, as it were in a standing reddie at all occasions, in aunters the Englyshe men should sturre neuer so litle, incontinent to set vpon them; and moreouer preuilie and secretly, for openly it maye not be doone by the truce that is taken; pryuelye therfore, I saye, to make muche of some peere of Englande, that is bannyshed his countrey, whiche must cleyme title to the crown of the realme, and affirme hym selfe iuste inheritoure therof; that by thys subtyll meanes they maye holde to them the kynge, in whom elles they haue but small truste and affiaunce.

'Here, I saye, where so great and high matters be in consultation, where so manye noble and wyse men counsell their kyng only to warre; here, if I, sely man, should ryse vp and wylle them to turne ouer the leafe,

and learne a newe lesson; sayng that my counsell is
not to medle with Italy, but to tarrye styll at home,
and that the kyngdome of fraunce alone is all moste
greater, then that it maye well be gouerned of one
man; so that the kyng shoulde not nede to studye
howe to gett more: and then shoulde propose vnto
them the decrees of the people that be called the
Achoriens, whiche be situate ouer agaynst the Ilande
of Vtopia on the sowtheaste syde. Thies Achoriens
ones made warre in their kinges quarrel, for to gette
him an other kyngdom, whiche he layde clayme vnto,
and auaunced hymself righte inheritoure to the crowne
therof, by the title of an olde aliaunce. At the last,
when they had gotten it, an sawe that they hadde euen
as muche vexation and trouble in keping it, as they
had in gettyng it; and that other there newe conquered subiectes by sondrye occasions were makynge
dayly insurrections to rebell agaynste them, or els that
other countreys were contynually with diuers inrodes
and forraginges inuadinge them; so that they were
euer fyghtinge other for them, or agaynste them, and
neuer coulde breke vp their campes: seynge them
selfes in the meane season pylled and impoueryshed;
their money carryed owt of the Realme; theyr owne
men kylled to mayntayne the glory of an other nation;
when they had no warre, peace nothynge better then
warre, by reason that their people in warre had inured
themselfes to corrupte and wycked maners; that they
hadde taken a delycte and pleasure in robbynge and
stealyng; that through manslaughter they had gathered
boldenes to mischiefe; that their lawes were hadde in
contempte, and nothynge set by or regarded; that
their kynge, beynge troubled with the chardge and
gouernaunce of two kingdomes, coulde not nor was not
able perfectly to discharge his office towardes them
bothe; seynge agayne that all thies euelles and troubles
were endeles: at the last laid there heades together;
and, lyke faithful and louinge subiectes, gaue to their

kynge free choyse and libertie to kepe still the one of
this .ii. kingdomes, whether he would ; allegyng that
he was not able to kepe both, and that they were mo
then might wel be gouerned of half a king ; for asmuche as no man would be content to take hym for
his mulettour that kepeth an other mans moyles
besides his. So this good prince was constreyned to
be content with his olde kyngdome, and to gyue ouer
the newe to one of his frendes ; whiche shortelie after
was violentlie dreuen out. Furthermore if I should
declare vnto them, that all this busy preparaunce to
warre, wherby so many nations for hys sake shuld be
brought into a troublesom hurley-burley, when all hys
coffers were emptied, his treasures wasted and his
people destroyed, should at the length through som
mischaunce be in vaine and to none effect ; and that
therfore it were best for him to content him selfe with
his owne Kingdom of fraunce, as his forfathers and
predecessours did before him ; to make much of it, to
enriche it, and to make it as flourisshing as he could ;
to endeuoure himself to loue his subiects, and again to
be beloued of them ; willingly to liue with them,
peaceably to gouerne them ; and with other kyngdomes not to medle, seinge that whiche he hath all
reddy is euen ynough for hym, yea, and more then he
can well turne hym to ; thys myne aduyse, maister
More, how thynke you it would be harde and taken ?'
'So God helpe me, not very thankefully' (quod I).

'Wel, let vs procede then' (quod he). 'Suppose
that some kyng and his counsell were together
whettinge their wittes, and deuisinge what subtell
crafte they myght inuente to enryche the king with
greate treasures of money. First one councelleth to
rayse and enhaunce the valuacion of money, when the
king must paye any ; and agayne to calle downe the
value of coyne to lesse then it is worthe, when he must
receiue or gather any : for thus great sommes shalbe
payde with a lytyll money, and where lytle is due

OF UTOPIA

muche shalbe receaued. An other counselleth to fayne warre, that when vnder this coloure and pretence the kyng hath gathered great aboundaunce of money, he maye, when it shall please hym, make peace wyth great solempnitie and holye ceremonies, to blynde the eyes of the poore communaltie, as taking pitie and compassion Gode wote vpon mans bloude, lyke a louing and a mercifull prince.

'An other putteth the kyng in remembraunce of certeyn olde and moughte-eaten lawes, that of long tyme haue not bene put in execution; whiche, because no man can remembre that they were made, euerie man hath transgressed. The fynes of thies lawes he counselleth the kynge to require: for there is no waye so proffytable, nor more honorable; as the whiche hath a shewe and coloure of iustice. An other aduyseth hym to forbidde manye thynges vnder great penalties and fines, specially suche thynges as is for the peoples profit not be vsed; and afterward to dispence for money with them, which by this prohibicion susteyne losse and dammage. For by this meanes the fauour of the people is wonne, and proffite riseth two wayes: first by takyng forfaytes of them whom couetousnes of gaynes hath brought in daunger of thys statute; and also by sellynge preuyleges and licences; whiche the better that the prynce is forsothe, the deerer he selleth them; as one that is lothe to graunte to any pryuate persone any thyng that is agaynste the proffyt of hys people; and therfore maye sell none but at an exceding dere pryce.

'An other giueth the kynge counsell to endaunger vnto hys grace the iudges of the Reyalme, that he maye haue them euer on hys syde; whyche muste in euerye matter despute and reason for the kynges rygth. And they muste be called into the kynges palace, and be desired to argue and discusse his matters in his owne presence. So there shalbe no matter of his, so openlyo wronge and uniuste, wherin one or other of them, other because he wyll haue sumthyng to allege and obiecte, or that he is ashamed to saye that whiche is sayde already, or else to pike a thanke with his prince, wyll not fynde som hole open to set a snare in, wherewith to take the contrarie parte in a trippe. Thus whiles the iudges cannot agree amonges themselfes, reasoning and arguing of that which is playne enough, and bringing the manifest trewthe in dowte, in the meane season the kyng may take a fyt occasion to vnderstand the lawe as shal most make for his aduauntage; wher vnto al other for shame or for feare wil agree. Then the Judges maye be bolde to pronounce of the kynges side. For he that geueth sentence for the kyng cannot be without a good excuse. For it shalbe sufficient for hym to haue equitie of his part, or the bare wordes of the lawe, or a wrythen and wrested vnderstandynge of the same, or els, whiche with good and iust Judges is of greater force then all lawes be, the kynges indisputable prerogatiue. To conclude, al the counsellours agre and consent together with the riche Crassus, that no abundance of gold can be sufficient for a prince, which muste kepe and maynteyne an armie: furthermore that a kynge, thoughe he would, can do nothynge uniustly; for all that all men haue, yea also the men them selfes, be all his; and that euery man hath so much of his owne as the kynges gentilnes hath not taken from hym; and that it shalbe moste for the kynges aduauntage that his subiectes haue very lytle or nothing in their possession; as whose sauegarde dothe herein consiste, that his people do not waxe wanton and wealthie through riches and libertie; because, where thies thinges be, there men be not wonte patientlye to obeye harde, vniuste, and vnlawfull commaundementes; where as, on the other part, neade and pouertie doth holde downe and kepe vnder stowte courages, and maketh them patient perforce, takyng from them bolde and rebellynge stomakes.

'Here agayne if I should ryse vp, and boldelye affirme that all thies counselles be to the kyng dishonoure and reproche, whoes honoure and sauitie is more and rather supported and vpholden by the wealth and ryches of his people, then by hys owne treasures; and if I shuld declare that the comminaltie chueseth their king for their owne sake and not for his sake; for this intent that through his labour and studie they might al liue wealthily, sauffe from wronges and iniuries; and that therfore the kynge ought to take more care for the wealthe of his people, then for his owne wealthe, euen as the office and dewtie of a shephearde is, in that he is a shepherd, to feade his shepe rather then hymself. For as towchynge this, that they thinke the defence and mayntenaunce of peace to consiste in the pouertie of the people, the thyng it solf sheweth that they be farre owt of the way. For where shall a man finde more wrangling, quarelling, brawling, and chiding, then among beggers? Who be more disierous of newe mutations and alterations, then they that be not content with the present state of their lyfe? Or, finally, who be bolder stomaked to brynge all in hurlieburlie (therby trustyng to get sum wyndfall), then they that haue nowe nothing to leese? And if so be that there were any kyng, that were so smallye regarded, or so behated of his subiectes, that other wayes he coulde not kepe them in awe, but onlie by open wronges, by pollinge and shauinge, and by brynginge them to beggerie; sewerly it were better for hym to forsake hys kyngdome, then to holde it by this meanes; whereby, though the name of a kyng be kept, yet the maiestie is lost. For it is against the dignitie of a kynge to haue rule ouer beggers, but rather ouer ryche and welthio men. Of thys mynde was the hardie and couragius Fabrice, when he sayde that he had rather be a ruler of ryche men then be ryche hymselfe. And verelye one man to lyue in pleasure and wealth, whyles all other wepe and smarte for it, that is the parte not of a kynge but of a iayler.

'To be shorte, as he is a folyshe phisition, that cannot cure his patientes disease, onles he caste hym in an other syckenes; so he that cannot amend the liues of his subiectes, but be taking from them the wealth and commoditie of lyfe, he must nedes graunte that he knoweth not the feate howe to gouerne fre men. But let hym rather amende hys owne lyfe, renounce vnhonest pleasures, and forsake pride. For thies be the chiefe vices that cause hym to runne in the contempt or hatered of his people. Let him lyue of hys owne, hurtinge no man. Let him do coste not aboue his power. Let hym restreyne wyckednes. Let hym preuente vices, and take a waye the occasions of offences be well orderyng his subiectes, and not by sufferyng wickednes to increase, afterward to be punyshed. Let hym not be to hastie in callynge agayne lawes, whiche a custome hathe abrogated; speciallye suche as haue bene long forgotten and neuer lacked nor neaded. And let hym neuer vnder the cloke and pretence of transgression take suche fynes and forfaytes, as no Iudge wyll suffre a priuate persone to take, as uniuste and ful of gile.

'Here if I should brynge furth before them the lawe of the Macariens, whiche be not farre distaunt from Vtopia; whose kynge, the daye of hys coronacion, is bounde by a solempne othe, that he shall neuer at anye tyme haue in hys treasure aboue a thousande pounde of golde or syluer. They saye a verye good kynge, whiche toke more care for the wealthe and commoditie of hys countrey, then for thenrychinge of himself, made this lawe to be a stop and a barre to kynges for heaping and hording vp so muche money as might impoueryshe their people. For he forsawe that this som of treasure woulde suffice to supporte the kynge in battail against his owne people, if they shuld chaunce to rebell; and also to maintein his

OF UTOPIA

warres against the inuasions of hys forreyn enemies.
Againe he perceiued the same stocke of money to be
to litle, and vnsufficient to encourage and able hym
wrongfullye to take a waye other mens goodes; whyche
was the chiefe cause whie the lawe was made. An
other cause was this. He thought that by thys
prouision his people shuld not lacke money wherewith
to maynteyne their dayly occupieng and chaffayre.
And seynge the kynge coulde not chewse but laye
owt and bestowe all that came in aboue the prescript
some of his stocke, he thought he woulde seke no
occasions to doo hys subiectes iniurie. Suche a kynge
shalbe feared of euell men, and loued of good men.
Thies and suche other informatyons yf I should vse
emonge men holy enclined and geuen to the contrarye part, how deaffe hearers, thyncke you, should
I haue?'

'Deaffe hearers douteles' (quod I), 'and in good
faith no marueyle. And to speake as I thynke, truelye
I can not a lowe that such communicatyon shall be
vsed, or suche cownsell geuen, as you be suere shall
neuer be regarded nor receaued. For how can so
straunge informations be profitable, or how can they
be beaten into their headdes, whose myndes be all
reddye preuented with cleane contrarye persuasyons?
Thys schole philosophie is not vnpleasaunte emonge
fryndes in famylier communication; but in the counselles of kynges, where greate matters be debated and
reasoned wyth great aucthorytye, thies thynges haue
no place.'

'That is yt whyche I mente' (quod he), 'when I said
phylosophye hadde no place amonge kinges.' 'In
dede' (quod I) 'this schole philosophie hath not;
whiche thinketh all thynges mete for euery place. But
ther is an other philosophye more cyuyle, whyche
knoweth as ye wolde saye her owne stage, and there-
after orderynge and behauynge herselfe in the playe
that she hathe in hande, playethe her parte accordyng-

lye wyth comlynes, vtteringe nothynge owte of dewe
ordre and fassyon. And thys ys the phylosophye that
yowe muste vse. Orels, whyles a commodye of Plautus
is playinge, and the vyle bondemen skoffynge and
tryffelynge amonge them selfes, yf yowe shoulde
sodenlye come vpon the stage in a philosophers apparrell, and reherse owte of Octauia the place wherin
Seneca dysputeth with Nero ; had it not bene better
for yowe to haue played the domme persone, then by
rehersynge that, which serued nother for the tyme nor
place, to haue made suche a tragycall comedye or
gallymalfreye? For by bryngynge in other stuffe that
nothynge apperteyneth to the presente matter, yowe
must nedys marre and peruert the play that ys in
hande, thoughe the stuffe that yowe brynge be muche
better. What parte soeuer yowe haue taken vpon
yowe, playe that as well as yowe canne, and make the
beste of yt; and doo not therefore dysturbe and brynge
owte of ordre the hole matter, bycause that an othere,
whyche is meryere and bettere, cummethe to yowre
remembraunce.

'So the case stondethe in a common wealthe; and
so yt ys in the consultatyons of Kynges and prynces.
Yf euell opynyons and noughty persuasions can not be
vtterly and quyte pluckede owte of their hartes ; if
you can not euen as you wold remedye vyces, whiche
vse and custome hath confirmed ; yet for this cause
yow must not leaue and forsake the common wealth ;
yow must not forsake the shippe in a tempeste, bycause
yowe can not rule and kepe downe the wyndes. No,
nor yow muste not laboure to dryue into their heades
newe and straunge informatyons, whyche yow knowe
well shalbe nothynge regarded wyth them that be of
cleane contrary mindes. But you must with a crafty
wile and a subtell trayne studye and endeuoure your
selfe, asmuch as in yow lyethe, to handle the matter
wyttelye and handsomelye for the purpose; and that
whyche yowe can not turne to good, so to ordre it that

it be not very badde. For it is not possible for all
thynges to be well, onles all men were good: which I
thynke wil not be yet thys good many yeares.'

'By thys meanes' (quod he) 'nothynge elles wyll be
broughte to passe, but, whyles that I goo abowte to
remedy the madnes of others, I should be euen as
madde as they. For if I wolde speake thynges that
be trewe, I muste neades speake suche thinges. But
as for to speake false thinges, whether that be a philosophers part, or no, I can not tell; truely it is not my
part. Howebeit thys communicatyon of myne, thoughe
peraduenture it maye seme vnplesaunte to them, yett
can I not see whie it should seme straunge, or
foolisshelye newfangled. If so be that I shoulde
speake those thynges that Plato fayneth in his weale
publique, or that the vtopians do in theires; thies
thinges thoughe they were (as they be in dede)
better, yet they myghte seme spoken owt of place; for
as much as here amonges us, euerye man hath hys
possessyons seuerall to hymselfe, and there all thinges
be common.

'But what was in my communication conteyned,
that mighte not and oughte not in anye place to be
spoken? sauynge that to them whyche haue throughlye
decreed and determined with them selfes to rome
hedlonges the contrary waye, it can not be acceptable
and plesaunt; bicause it calleth them backe, and
sheweth them the ieopardies. Verilye yf all thynges
that euell and vitiouse maners haue caused to seme
inconueniente and noughte should be refused, as thinges
vnmete and reprochefull, then we must emong Christen
people wyncke at the most parte of all those thynges
whyche Christe taughte vs, and so streytlye forbadde
them to be wyncked at, that those thinges also whyche
he whispered in the eares of hys dyscyples, he commaunded to be proclaymed in open howses. And yet
the most parte of them is moore dissident from the
maners of the worlde nowe a dayes then my com-

municatyon was. But preachers, slye and wilie men, followynge your cownsell (as I suppose), bicause they saw men euel willing to frame theyr manners to Christes rule, they haue wrested and wriede hys doctryne, and lyke a rule of leade haue applyed yt to mennys maners; that by some meanes at the leaste waye they myghte agree to gether. Wherby I can not see what good they haue doone, but that men may more sickerlye be euell. And I truelye shoulde preuaile euen asmuche in kinges counselles. For other I muste saye other wayes then they saye, and then I were as good to saye nothynge; or els I muste saye thesame that they saye, and (as Mitio saieth in Terence) helpe to further their madnes. For that craftye wyle and subtill traine of yours, I can not perceaue to what purpose it serueth; wherewyth yow wolde haue me to studdy and endeuoure my selfe, yf all thynges can not be made good, yet to handle them wittily and handsomely for the purpose; that, as farre furth as is possible, they maye not be very euell. For there is no place to dissemble in nor to wincke in. Noughtye cownselles must be openlye allowed, and verye pestylent decrees muste be approued. He shalbe cowntede worse then a spye, yea almoste as euell as a traytoure, that wyth a faynte harte doth prayse euell and noyesome decrees.

'Moreouer a man canne haue no occasyon too doo good, chauncynge into the companye of them, whyche wyll sonere make noughte a good man, then be made good themselfes; throughe whose euell companye he shalbe marred, or els yf he remayne good and innocent, yett the wyckednes and folysshenes of others shalbe imputed to hym, and layde in hys necke. So that yt is impossyble wyth that craftye wyele and subtell trayne to turne anny thing to better.

'Wherfore Plato by a goodly simylitude declareth whie wise men refreyn to medle in the common wealth. For when they see the people swarm in to

OF UTOPIA

the stretes, and dailie wett to the skin wyth rayne, and yet can not persuade them to goo owt of the rayne, and to take their houses; knowynge well that if they shoulde goo owte to them, they shoulde nothynge preuayle, nor wynne ought by it, but be wett also in the rain; they do kepe them selfes within their howses; beynge content that they be saffe them selfes, seynge they can not remedye the follye of the people.

'Howe be it dowteles, mayster Moore (to speke truelye as my mynde geueth me), where soeuer possessyons be pryuate, where moneye beareth all the stroke, it is hard and almoste impossyble that there the weale publyque maye iustelye be gouerned and prosperouslye floryshe. Onles you thynke thus: that Iustyce is there executed, wher all thynges come into the handes of euell men; or that prosperytye their floryssheth, where all is deuyded amonge a fewe; whyche fewe neuerthelesse do not leade their lyues very wealthely, and the resydewe lyue myserablye, wretchedlye, and beggerlye.

'Wherefore when I consyder wyth my selfe, and weye in my mynde, the wyse and godlye ordynaunces of the Vtopyans, amonge whome wyth verye fewe lawes all thynges be so well and wealthelye ordered, that vertue is had in pryce and estimatyon; and yet, all thynges beynge ther common, euerye man hath abundaunce of euery thynge: agayne, on the other part, when I compare wyth them so manye natyons euer makyng new lawes, yet none of them all well and suffycyentlye furnysshed wyth lawes; where euery man calleth that he hath gotten hys owne proper and pryuate goodes; where so many newe lawes daylye made be not suffycyente for euerye man to enioye, defend, and knowe from an other mans that whych he calleth his owne; which thyng the infinyte controuersies in the lawe, that daylye ryse neuer to be ended, playnly declare to be trewe: thies thynges (I say) when I consider with me selfe, I holde well with

Plato, and doo no thynge marueyll that he wolde make no lawes for them that refused those lawes, wherby all men shoulde haue and enioye equall portions of welthes and commodities. For the wise man dyd easely forsee, that thys is the one and onlye waye to the wealthe of a communaltye, yf equaltye of all thynges sholde be broughte in and stablyshed. Whyche I thynke is not possible to be obserued, where euerye mans gooddes be proper and peculyare to him selfe. For where euerye man vnder certeyne tytles and pretences draweth and plucketh to himselfe asmuch as he can, and so a fewe deuide amonge themselfes all the riches that there is, be there neuer so muche abundaunce and stoore, there to the resydewe is lefte lacke and pouertye. And for the moste parte yt chaunceth that thys latter sort is more worthye to enioye that state of wealth, then the other be; bycause the rych men be couetous, craftye, and vnprofytable: on the other parte, the poore be lowlye, symple, and by their daily labour more profytable to the common welthe then to them selfes.

'Thus I doo fullye persuade me selfe, that no equall and iuste distrybutyon of thynges can be made; nor that perfecte wealthe shall euer be among men; onles this propriety be exiled and bannished. But so long as it shal contynew, so long shal remayn among the most and best part of men the heuy and ineuitable burden of pouerty and wretchednes. Which, as I graunt that it may be sumwhat eased, so I vtterly deny that it can holy be taken away. For if ther wer a statute made, that no man should possesse aboue a certein measure of ground, and that no man should haue in his stocke aboue a prescripte and appointed some of money; if it were by certein lawes decreed that nother the king should be of to greate powre, nother the people to prowd and wealthye; and that offices shold not be obteined by inordinate suyte or by brybes and giftes; that they should nother be bought

OF UTOPIA

nor sold, nor that it sholde be nedeful for the officers to be at any cost or charge in their offices: for so occasion is geuen to the officers by fraud and rauin to gather vp their money again, and by reason of giftes and bribes the offices be geuen to rich men, which shoulde rather haue bene executed of wise men; by such lawes, I say, like as sicke bodies that be desperat and past cure, be wonte with continual good cherissing to be kept vp, so thies euelles also might be lightened and mytygated. But that they may be perfectlye cured and brought to a good and vpryght state, it is not to be hoped for, whiles euery man is maister of his owne to hym selfe. Yea, and whyles yow goo abowt to do your cure of one part, yow shall make bygger the sore of an other parte: so the healpe of one causeth anothers harme, for as much as nothynge can be geuen to annye man, onles that be taken from an other.'

'But I am of a contrary opinion' (quod I) 'for me thynketh that men shal neuer there lyue wealthelye, where all thynges be commen. For how can there be abundaunce of gooddes, or of any thing, where euery man with draweth his hande from labour? whome the regarde of his owne gaines driueth not to woorke, and the hoope that he hath in other mens trauayles maketh hym slowthfull. Then when they be prycked with pouertye, and yet no man can by any law or right defend that for his owne, which he hath gotten wyth the laboure of his owne handes, shall not ther of necessitie be continuall sedition and bloodshede? specially the aucthoritie and reuerende of magistrates being taken away; which what place it maye haue wyth suche men, amonge whome is no difference, I can not deuise.' 'I maruell not' (quod he) 'that you be of this opinion. For you conceaue in your mynde other none at all, or els a very false ymage and symylitude of thys thynge. But yf yow hadde bene wyth me in Vtopia, and hadde presently sene their fasshions and

lawes, as I dyd, whiche liued ther .v. yeares and moore,
and wolde neuer haue commen thence, but only to
make that new lande knowen here; then dowteles you
wold graunt, that you neuer sawe people well ordered,
but only there.'

'Surely' (quod maister Peter), 'it shalbe harde for
you to make me beleue, that ther is better order in
that newe lande, then is here in thies countreys that
wee knowe. For good wyttes be aswell here as there;
and I thynke owr commen wealthes be auncienter than
theires: wherin long vse and experience hath fownde
owt many thinges commodious for mannes life, besides
that many thinges here amonge vs haue bene founde
by chaunce, whych no wytte colde euer haue deuysed.'

'As towchynge the auncyetnes' (quod he) 'of common
wealthes, than you might better iudge, if you had red
the histories and chronicles of that lande; which if
wee may beleue, cities were there, before there were
men here. Now what thinge soeuer hitherto by witte
hath bene deuised, or found by chaunce, that myghte
be aswell there as here. But I thinke verily, though
it were so that we did passe them in witte, yet in
studye and laboursome endeuoure they farre passe vs.
For (as there Cronicles testifie) before our arriuall ther
they neuer harde any thinge of vs, whome they call
the ultraequinoctialles; sauinge that ones about .M.CC.
yeares ago, a certein shyppe was loste by the Ile of
Vtopia whiche was driuen thither by tempest. Certeyn
Romayns and Egyptyans were caste on lande, whyche
after that neuer wente thence.

'Marke nowe what profite they tooke of thys one
occasion, through delygence and earneste trauaile.
There was no craft nor scyence within the impery of
Rome, wher of any proffite could rise, but they other
lerned it of thies straungers, or els, of them taking
occasion to searche for yt, fownde it owte. So great
proffyte was it to them that euer annye wente thyther
from hence. But yf annye lyke chaunce before thys

hath brought any man from thence hether, that is as
quyte out of remembraunce, as this also perchaunce in
time to come shalbe forgotten that euer I was there.
And like as they quickelye, almoste at the first meting,
made their owne, what so euer is among vs wealthely 5
deuysed ; so I suppose it wolde be longe befor we wolde
receaue any thing that amonge them is better instytuted then amonge vs. And thys I suppose is the
chiefe cause whie theyr common wealthes be wyselyere
gouerned, and do florysh in more wealth then ours ; 10
though wee nother in wytte nor in ryches be ther
inferiours.'

'Therfore, gentle maister Raphaell' (quod I) 'I praye
you and beseche yow descrybe vnto vs the Iland. And
study not to be shorte; but declare largely in order 15
their groundes, there ryuers, their cities, theire people,
theire manners, their ordenaunces, ther lawes, and, to
be short, al thinges that you shal thinke vs desierous
to knowe. And you shal thinke vs desierous to know
what soeuer we knowe not yet.' 'There is nothing' 20
(quod he) 'that I will do gladlier. For all these
thinges I haue freshe in mind. But the matter requireth leasure.' 'Let vs go in therfor' (quod I) 'to
dinner: afterward we will bestowe the time at our
pleasure.' 'Content' (quod he) 'be it.' So we went 25
in and dyned.

When diner was done, we came into the same place
again, and sate vs downe vpon the same benche, com-
maunding oure seruauntes that no man should trowble
vs. Then I and maister Peter Giles desiered maister 30
Raphaell to performe his promise. He therfore seinge
vs desierous and willinge to harken to him, when he
had sit still and paused a litle while, musing and
bethinkynge hymselfe, thus he began to speake.

The ende of tho ffyrste boke. 35

[CHAPTER I]

The second
Boke of the communication
of Raphael Hythlodaye, concernyng
the best state of a common wealthe : con-
teynyng the discription of Vtopia,
with a large declaration of the
Godly gouernement, and of
all the good lawes and
orders of the same
Ilande.

The Ilande of Vtopia conteyneth in breadthe in the myddell part of it (for there it is brodest) CC. miles. Whiche bredthe continueth through the moste parte of the lande, sauyng that by lytle and lytle it commeth in and waxeth narrower towardes both the endes. Whiche fetchynge about a circuite or compasse of .v.c. myles, do fassion the hole Ilande lyke to the newe mone. Betwene thys two corners the sea runneth in, diuydyng them a sonder by the distaunce of .xi. miles or there aboutes, and there surmounteth into a large and wyde sea, which, by reason that the lande of euery syde compasseth it about, and shiltreth it from the windes, is not rough nor mountith not with great waues, but almost floweth quietlye, not muche vnlike a great standing powle; and maketh almoste al the space within the bellye of the lande in maner of a hauen; and to the great commoditie of the Inhabitauntes receaueth in shyppes towardes euery parte of the lande. The forefrontes or frontiers of the .ii.

THE SECOND BOKE OF UTOPIA

corners, what wythe fordys and shelues, and what with rockes, be very ieoperdous and daungerous. In the middel distaunce betwene them both standeth vp aboue the water a great rocke, which therfore is nothing perillous bicause it is in sight. Vpon the top of this rocke is a faire and a strong towre builded, which thei holde with a garison of men. Other rockes ther be, that lye hidde vnder the water, and therefore be daungerous. The channelles be knowen onely to themselfes. And therfore it seldome chaunceth that any straunger, oneles he be guided by a Vtopian, can come in to this hauen. In so muche that they themselfes could skaselie entre without ieoperdie, but that their way is directed and ruled by certaine lande markes standing on the shore. By turning, translatynge, and remouinge this markes into other places, they maye destroye their enemies nauies, be thei neuer so many. The out side of the lande is also full of hauens; but the landing is so suerly defenced, what by nature and what by workmanshyp of mans hande, that a fewe defenders maye dryue backe many armies.

Howebeit, as they saye, and as the fassion of the place it selfe doth partely shewe, it was not euer compassed about with the sea. But kyng Vtopus, whose name as conquerour the Iland beereth (for before that tyme it was called Abraxa), which also brought the rude and wild people to that excellent perfection, in al good fassions, humanitie, and ciuile gentilnes, wherin they now go beyond al the people of the world; euen at his first arriuinge and enteringe vpon the lande, furth with obteynynge the victory caused .xv. myles space of vplandyshe grounde, where the sea had no passage, to be cut and dygged vp; and so brought the sea rounde aboute the lande. He set to thys worke not only the inhabitauntes of the Ilande (because they should not thynke it done in contumelye and despyte), but also all hys owne soldiours. Thus the worke, beyng diuyded into so great a numbre of workemen, was with exceding maruelous spede dyspatched. In so muche that the borderers, whiche at the fyrst began to mocke and to gieste at thys vayne enterpryse, then turned theyr laughter to marueyle at the successe, and to feare.

There be in the Ilande .liiii. large and faire cities or shiere townes, agreyng all together in one tonge, in lyke maners, institucions, and lawes. They be all set and situate a lyke, and in all poyntes fashioned a lyke, as farfurth as the place or plotte suffereth. Of thies cyties they that be nighest together be xxiiii. myles a sonder. Again there is none of them distaunt from the next aboue one dayes iorneye a fote.

There cum yearly to Amaurote out of euery cytie .iii. olde men, wyse and well experienced, there to entreate and debate of the common matters of the lande. For thys cytie (because it standeth iust in the myddes of the Ilande, and is therfore moste mete for the embassadours of all partes of the realme) is taken for the chiefe and head cytie. The precinctes and boundes of the shieres be so commodiously appoynted out, and set furth for the cyties, that neuer a one of them all hath of anye syde lesse then xx. myles of grounde, and of som syde also muche more, as of that part where the cyties be of farther distaunce a sonder. None of the cities desire to enlarge the boundes and lymites of their shieres. For they count them selfes rather the good husbandes, then the owners of their landes.

They haue in the countrey in all partes of the shiere howses or fermes buylded, wel appointed and furnyshed with all sortes of instrumentes and tooles belongyng to husbandrie. Thies houses be inhabited of the cytezens, whiche cum thyther to dwel by course. No howsholde or ferme in the countrey hath fewer then .xl. persones, men and women, besydes two bonden men, whiche be all vnder the rule and order of the good man and the good wyfe of the house, beynge bothe very sage and discrete persones. And euery .xxx. fermes or famelies

OF UTOPIA

haue one heade ruler, whiche is called a Phylarche, being as it were a hed baylyffe. Out of euery one of thies famelies or fermes cummeth euery yeare into the cytie .xx. persones whiche haue contynewed .ii. yeres before in the countrey. In their place so manye freshe be sent thither out of the citie, whiche of them that haue bene there a yeare all ready, and be therfore expert and conninge in husbandry, shalbe instructed and taught; and they the next yeare shall teache other. This order is vsed, for feare that other skarsenes of victualles or some other like incommoditie shuld chaunce through lacke of knowledge, yf they should be al together newe and fresh and vnexperte in husbandrie. This maner and fassion of yearlye chaunginge and renewinge the occupiers of husbandrie, though it be solempne and customablie vsed, to thintent that no man shall be constrayned against his wil to contynewe longe in that harde and sharpe kynde of lyfe, yet manye of them haue suche a pleasure and delete in husbandrye, that they obteyne a longer space of yeares. Thies husbandmen plowe and till the grounde, and bryde vp cattell, and make readye woode, whiche they carrye to the cytie, other by lande or by water, as they maye moste conuenyently. They brynge vp a greate multytude of pulleyne, and that by a meruelous policie. For the hennes doo not syt vpon the egges: but by kepynge them in a certayne equall heate, they brynge lyfe into them, and hatche them. The chykens, assone as they be come owte of the shell, followe men and women in steade of the hennes.

They bryng vp very fewe horses; nor non, but very fearce ones; and for none other vse or purpose, but only to exercyse their youthe in rydynge and feates of armes. For oxen be put to all the labour of plowynge and drawyng. Whiche they graunte to be not so good as horses at a sodeyne brunt, and (as we saye) at a dead lifte; but yet they holde opinion, that they wyll abyde and suffre much more laboure and payne then horses

wyl. And they thinke that they be not in daunger
and subiecte vnto so manye dysseases, and that they
bee kepte and maynteyned wyth muche lesse coste and
charge ; and fynally that they be good for meate when
they be past labour.

They sowe corne onlye for bread. For their drynke
is other wyne made of grapes, or els of apples or peares,
or els it is cleane water ; and many tymes methe made
of honey or liqueresse sodde in water, for therof they
haue great store. And though they knowe certeynlye
(for they knowe it perfectly in dede), how much
victayles the cytie with the hole countrey or shiere
rounde a boute it dothe spende ; yet they sowe much
more corne, and bryed vp muche more cattell, then
serueth for their own vse. And the ouerplus they
parte amonge their borderers. What soeuer necessary
thynges be lackynge in the countrey, all suche stuffe
they fetche out of the citie; where without anye exchaunge they easelye obteyne it of the magistrates of
the citie. For euerye moneth manye of them goo into
the cytie on the hollye daye. When theyr haruest
daye draweth nere and is at hande, then the Philarches,
whiche be the hed officers and bayliffes of husbandrye,
sende woorde to the magistrates of the citie, what
numbre of haruest men is nedefull to bee sente to them
out of the cytie. The

      whiche companye of haruest men,
        beyng there readye at the daye
          appoynted, almoste in one
            fayre daye dispatcheth
              all the haruest
                woorke.
                (∴)

OF UTOPIA

[CHAPTER II]

Of the cy=

ties and namely of Amaurote.

As for their Cyties, he that knoweth one of them knoweth them all: they be all so lyke one to an other, as ferfurth as the nature of the place permytteth. I wyll descrybe therfore to yowe one or other of them, for it skylleth not greatly whych; but which rather then Amaurote? Of them all this is the worthiest and of moste dignitie. For the resydwe knowledge it for the head Cytie, because there is the councell house. Nor to me any of them al is better beloued, as wherin I lyued fyue hole yeares together.

The cytie of Amaurote standeth vpon the syde of a low hill, in fashion almoste four square. For the bredeth of it begynneth a litle benethe the toppe of the hyll, and styll contyneweth by the space of twoo miles vntyll it cum to the ryuer of Anyder. The lenghte of it whiche lyeth by the ryuers syde is sumwhat more.

The ryuere of Anyder rysethe .xxiiii. myles aboue Amaurote owte of a lytle sprynge. But beynge increasede by other small floodes and broukes that runne into yt, and amonge othere .ii. sumwhat bygge ons, before the cytye yt ys halfe a myle brode, and farther broder. And .lx. myles beyonde the citye yt falleth into the Ocean sea. By al that space that lyethe betwene the sea and the cytye, and a good sorte of myles also aboue the Cytye, the water ebbethe and flowethe .vi. houres togethere wyth a swyfte tyde. Whan the sea flowethe in for the lenghte of xxx. myles, yt fyllethe all the Anydor wyth salte water, and dryuethe backe the fresshe water of the ryuer.

And sumwhat furthere yt chaungethe the swetenes of the freshe water wyth saltnes. But a letell beyonde that, the ryuer waxeth swet, and runneth forby the city fresh and pleisaunt. And when the sea ebbeth, and goyth backe agayn, the freshe water followeth yt almoste euen to the verye falle in to the sea.

There goeth a brydge ouer the ryuer made not of pyles or of tymber, but of stonewarke, with gorgious and substanciall archeis at that parte of the cytye that is farthest from the sea; to the intent that shyppes maye goo alonge forbie all the syde of the cytie without lette. They haue also an other ryuere, whiche in dede is not very great. But it runneth gentelly and pleasauntlye. For it ryseth euen out of the same hyll that the cytie standeth vpon, and runneth downe a slope through the myddes of the citie into Anyder. And bicause it ryseth a lytle without the cytie, the Amaurotians haue inclosed the head sprynge of it with stronge fences and bulwarkes, and so haue ioyned it to the cytie. Thys is done to the intente that the water should not be stopped, nor turned a waye, or poysoned, if their enemyes should chaunce to come vpon them. From thence the water is deryued and brought downe in cannellis of brycke dyuers wayes into the lower partes of the cytie. Where that cannot be done, by reason that the place wyll not suffer it, there they gather the rayne water in greate cisternes, which doth them as good seruice.

The cytie is compassed aboute wyth a highe and thycke walle, full of turrettes and bulwarkes. A drye dyche, but deape and brode and overgrowen with busshes, briers, and thornes, goeth about .iii. sydes or quarters of the cytie. To the fowrth syde the ryuer it selfe serueth for a dytche. The stretes be appoynted and set forth verye commodious and handsome, bothe for carriage and also agaynst the wyndes. The houses be of fayre and gorgious buyldyng, and in the streete syde they stonde ioyned together in a longe rowe throughe the hole streate without anye partition or separacion. The stretes be twenty fote brode. On the backe syde of the houses, through the hole lengthe of the strete, lye large gardeynes, whyche be closed in rounde about with the backe parte of the stretes. Euery house hath two doores; one into the strete, and a posternne doore on the backsyde into the gardyne. Thyes doores be made with two leaues, neuer locked nor bolted, so easye to be opened that they wil followe the least drawing of a fynger and shutte agayne by themselfes. Euerye man that wyll maye goo yn, for there is nothynge wythin the howses that ys pryuate, or annye mannes owne. And euerye .x. yeare they chaunge their howses by lotte.

They sett great stoore be theyr gardeins. In them they haue vyneyardes, all manner of frute, herbes, and flowres, so pleisaunte, so well furnished, and so fynelye kepte, that I neuer sawe thynge more frutefull nor better trymmed in anny place. Their studye and delygence herin cummeth not only of pleasure, but also of a certeyne stryffe and contentyon that is betwene strete and strete, concernynge the trymmynge, husbanding, and furnyshyng of their gardeyns, euery man for hys owne part. And verily yow shall not lyghtly fynde in all the citye annye thynge that is more commodyous, other for the proffyte of the citizins, or for pleasure. And therfore it may seme that the first fownder of the city mynded nothynge so muche as he dyd thies gardeyns.

For they say that kyng Vtopus himself, euen at the first begenning, appointed and drew furth the platte fourme of the city into this fasion and figure that it hath nowe; but the gallaunt garnishing, and the bewtiful setting furth of it, wherunto he sawe that one mans age wold not suffice, that he left to his posterity. For their Cronicles, which they kepe written with al deligent circumspection, conteining the history of m.viio.lx. years, euen from the fyrste conquest of the Iland, recorde and witnesse that the howses in the beginning were verye lowe, and lyke homelye cotages, or poore shepparde howses, made at all aduentures of euerye rude pyece of woode that came fyrste to handes, wyth mudde walles, and rydged rooftes thatched ouer with straw. But nowe the houses be curiously builded, after a gorgiouse and gallaunt sort, with .iii. storries one ouer another. The owte sydes of the walles be made other of harde Flynte or of plauster, or elles of brycke; and the ynner sydes be well strengthened with tymber woorke. The rooffes be playne and flatte, couered with a certayne kinde of plaster, that is of no coste, and yet so tempered that no fyre can hurte or peryshe it, and withstandeth the violence of the weether better then anye leade. They kepe the wynde out of their windowes with glasse, for it is there much vsed; and sumwhere also with fyne lynnen clothe dipped in oyle or ambre; and that for twoo commodities. For by thys meanes more lyght cummeth in, and the wynde is better kept out.

[Chapter III]

Of the Ma=
gystrates.

Euerye thyrty families or fermes chewse them yearlye an offycer, whyche in their olde language is called the Syphograunte, and by a newer name the Phylarche. Euerye tenne Syphoagrauntes, with all their 300 families, bee vnder an offycer whyche was ones called the Tranibore, now the chiefe Phylarche.

Moreouer, as concerninge the electyon of the Prynce, all the Syphoagrauntes, which be in number 200, first be sworne to chewse him whome they thynke moste mete and expedyente. Then by a secrete electyon they name prynce one of those .iiii. whome the people before named vnto them. For owte of the .iiii. quarters of the citie there be .iiii. chosen, owte of euerye quarter one, to stande for the election, whiche be put vp to the counsell. The princes office contineweth all his liffe time, onles he be deposed or put downe for suspition of tirannye. They chewse the tranibores yearlye, but lightlye they chaunge them not. All the other offices be but for one yeare. The Tranibores euerye thyrde daye, and sumtymes, if neade be, oftener, come into the councell howse with the prynce. Theire councell is concernynge the common wealth. Yf there be annye controuersyes amonge the commoners, whyche be very fewe, they dyspatche and ende them by and by. They take euer ii. Siphograntes to them in cowncell, and euerye daye a newe coupel. And that ys prouydedo that no thynge towchynge the common wealthe shalbe confyrmed and ratifyed, on les yt haue bene reasonede of and debatede iii. dayes in the cowncell, before yt be decreed. It is deathe to haue annye consultatyon for the common wealthe owte of the cownsell, or the place of the common electyon. Thys statute, they saye, was made to thentente, that the prynce and Tranibores myghte not easely conspire together to oppresse the people by tyrannye, and to chaunge the state of the weale publique. Therfore matters of greate weyghte and importaunce be brought to the electyon house of the syphograuntes, whyche open the matter to their familyes; and afterwarde, when they haue consulted among them selfes, they shewe their deuyse to the cowncell. Sumtyme the matter is brought before the cowncell of the hole Ilande.

Furthermore thys custome also the cowncell vseth, to dyspute or reason of no matter the same daye that it ys fyrste proposed or putt furthe, but to dyfferre it to the nexte syttynge of the cownsell. Bycause that no man when he hathe rasshelye there spoken that cummeth fyrste to hys tonges ende, shalt then afterwarde rather studye for reasons wherewyth to defende and confyrme hys fyrste folyshe sentence, than for the commodytye of the common wealthe; as one rather wyllynge the harme or hynderaunce of the weale publyque, then annye losse or dymynutyon of hys owne existymatyon; and as one that wolde not for shame (which is a verye folyshe shame) be cowntede annye thynge ouerseen in the matter at the fyrste; who at the fyrste owghte to haue spoken rather wysely then hastely or rashelye.

[CHAPTER IV]

Of scyences
Craftes and Occupatyons.

Husbandrye is a scyence common to them all ingenerall, both men and women, wherin they be all experte and cunnynge. In thys they be all instructe euen from their youth; partely in scholes with traditions and preceptes, and partely in the contrey nighe the cytye, brought vp as it wer in playing, not onlye beholdynge the vse of it, but by occasyon of exercisinge their bodies practising it also.

Besides husbandry, which (as I sayde) is common to them all, euery one of them learneth one or other seuerall and particuler science, as hys owne proper crafte. That is most commonly other clothe-workinge in wolle or flaxe, or masonrie, or the smythes crafte, or the carpentes scyence. For there is none other occupacyon that anye numbre to speke of doth vse there. For their garmentes, whyche through owte all the Ilande be of one fassion, (sauynge that there is a difference betwene the mans garmente and the womans, betwene the maried and the unmaryed), and this one continueth for euer more unchaunged, semely and comely to the eye, no let to the mouynge and weldynge of the bodie, also fitte bothe for winter and summer; as for thies garmentes (I saye), euery familye maketh theire owne. But of the other foreseyde craftes euerye man learneth one; and not only the men, but also the women. But the women, as the weaker sorte, be put to the easere craftes. They worke wull and flaxe. The other more laborsome sciences be committed to the men. For the moste parte euerye man is brought vp in his fathers craft. For moste commonly they be naturally therto bente and inclined. But yf a mans minde stonde to anny other, he is by adoption put into a famelye of that occupation which he doth most fantasy. Whome not only his father, but also the magistrates do diligently looke to, that he be putt to a discrete and an honest housholder. Yea and if anny person, when he hath lerned one crafte, be desierous to lerne also another, he ys lykewyse suffrede and permytted. When he hathe learned bothe, he occupyethe whether he wyll; onles the cytye haue more neade of the one then of the other.

The chyefe and almoste the onelye offyce of the Syphograuntes ys to see and take hede that no man sytte ydle, but that euerye one applye hys owne crafte wyth earneste delygence; and yet for all that not to be weryed from earlye in the mornynge to late in the euennynge wyth contynuall woorke, lyke laborynge and toylynge beastes. For thys ys worse then the myserable and wretced condytyon of bondemen; whyche neuer the lesse is almoste euery where the lyffe of woorkemen and artyfycers, sauynge in vtopia. For they, dyuydinge the daye and the nyghte into xxiiii. iust houres, appoynte and assygne only vi. of those houres to woorke; iii. before none, vpon the whyche they goo streyghte to dyner; and after dyner, when they haue rested ii houres, then they woorke iii.; and vpon that they goo to supper. Aboute viii. of the clocke in the euenynge (cowntynge one of the clocke at the fyrste houre after none) they go to bedde. viii. houres they giue to sleape. All the voide time, that is betwene the houres of woorke, slepe, and meate, that they be suffered to bestowe, euerye man as he lyketh beste hym selfe: not to thyntente they shoulde myspende thys tyme in ryote, or slough-fullenes; but, beynge then lycensed from the laboure of theyr owne occupacyons, to bestowe the time wel and thriftely vpon some other good science, as shall

OF UTOPIA

please them. For yt ys a solempne custome there, to haue lectures daylye earlye in the morning; wher to be present they onlye be constreined that be namelye chosen and appoynted to learnynge. Howe be yt a greate multytude of euerye sorte of people, bothe men and women, goo to heare lectures; some one and some an other, as euerye mans nature is inclyned. Yet, this notwithstonding, yf any man had rathere bestowe thys tyme vpon hys owne occupatyon (as yt chaunceth in manye, whose myndes ryse not in the contemplatyon of annye scyence lyberal), he is not letted nor prohibited, but is also praysed and commended, as profitable to the common wealthe.

After supper they bestowe one houre in playe; in somer in their gardeynes, in winter in their commen halles, where they dyne and suppe. There they exercise them selfes in musyke, or els in honeste and holsome communicacion. Diceplaye, and suche other folish and pernicious games, they knowe not; but they vse .ii. games not muche vnlike the chesse. The one is the battell of nombers, wherin one numbre stealethe awaye another. The other is wherin vices fyghte wyth vertues, as it were in battell array, or a set fyld. In the which game is verye properlye shewed bothe the striffe and discorde that vices haue amonge themselfes, and agayne theire unitye and concorde againste vertues; and also what vices be repugnaunt to what vertues; with what powre and strenght they assaile them openlye; by what wieles and subteltye they assaute them secretelye; with what helpe and aide the vertues resiste, and ouercome the puissaunce of the vices; by what craft they frustate their purposes; and finally by what sleight or meanes the one getteth the victory.

But here, lease you be deceaued, one thinge you muste looke more narrowly vpon. For seinge they bestowe but vi. houres in woork, perchaunce you maye thinke that the lacke of some necessarye thinges herof

may ensewe. But this is nothinge so. For that small
time is not only inough, but also to muche, for the
stoore and abundaunce of all thinges that be requisite,
other for the necessitie or commoditie of liffe. The
whiche thing yow also shall perceaue, if you weye and
consider with your selfes how great a parte of the
people in other contreis lyueth ydle. First, almoost
all women, which be the halfe of the hole numbre;
or els, if the women be annye where occupied, their
most comonlye in their steade the men be ydle.
Besydes thys, how great, and howe ydle a companye
ys theyr of prystes, and relygyous men, as they call
them? Put there to all ryche men, speciallye all
landed men, whyche comonly be called gentylmen,
and noble men. Take into this numbre also their
seruauntes; I meane, all that flocke of stout, bragging,
russhe bucklers. Ioyne to them also sturdy and
valiaunt beggers, clokinge their idle leffe vnder the
colour of some disease or sickenes. And truely you
shall find them much fewer then you thought, by
whose labour all these thynges be gotten, that men
vse and lyue bye. Nowe consyder wyth youre selfe,
of thies fewe that do woorke, how few be occupied in
necessary woorkes. For where money beareth all the
swing, ther many vayne and superfluous occupations
must nedys be vsed, to serue only for ryotous superfluyte and vnhonest pleasure. For the same multytude
that now is occupied in woorke, if they were deuided
into so few occupations as the necessary vse of nature
requyreth, in so greate plentye of thinges, as then of
necessity wolde ensue, doubtles the prices wolde be to
lytle for the artifycers to maynteyne theyre lyuynges.
But yf all thyes, that be nowe bisiede about vnprofitable occupations, with all the hole flocke of them that
lyue ydellye and slouthfullye, whyche consume and
waste euerye one of them more of thies thinges that
come by other mens laboure, then ii. of the work men
themselfes doo; yf all thyes (I saye) were sette to

profytable occupatyons, yowe easelye perceaue howe
lytle tyme wolde be enoughe, yea and to muche, to
stoore vs wyth all thynges that maye be requysyte
other for necessytye, or for commodytye; yea, or for
pleasure, so that the same pleasure be trewe and
naturall.

And thys in Vtopia the thynge yt selfe maketh
manifeste and playne. For there in all the citye, wyth
the hole contreye or shyere adioynynge to yt, scaselye
500 persons of all the hole numbre of men and women,
that be nother to olde nor to weake to woorke, be
licensed from labour. Amonge them be the Siphograuntes, which (though they be by the lawes exempte
and pryuyleged from labour) yet they exempte not
themselfes; to the intent they maye the rather by
their example prouoke other to woorke. The same
vacation from labour do they also enioye, to whome
the people, persuaded by the commendation of the
priestes and secrete election of the Siphograntes, haue
geuen a perpetual licence from labour to learnyng.
But if anny one of them proue nott accordinge to the
expectation and hoope of him conceaued, he is furth
with plucked backe to the company of artificers. And
contrarye wise, often yt chaunceth that a handicraftes
man doth so earnestly bestowe hys vacaunte and spare
houres in learninge, and through dilygence so profytte
therin, that he is taken frome hys handy occupation,
and promoted to the company of the learned.

Owt of this ordre of the learned be chosen ambassadours, priestes, Tranibores, and finallye the prince him
selfe; whome they in their olde tonge call Barzanes,
and by a newer name, Ademus. The residewe of the
people being nother ydle, nother occupied about vnprofitable exercises, it may be easely iudged in how
fewe howres how much good woorke by them maye be
doone towardes those thinges that I haue spoken of.
This commodity they haue also aboue other, that in
the most part of necessary occupations they neade nott

so muche worke, as other nations doo. For firste of all the buildinge or repayring of houses asketh euery where so manye mens continuall labour, bicause that the vnth⟨r⟩yfty heyre suffreth the howses that hys father buylded in contynewaunce of tyme to fall in decay. So that which he myghte haue vpholden wyth lytle coste, hys successoure is constreynede to buylde yt agayne a newe, to hys greate chardge. Yea, manye tymes also the howse that stoode one man in muche moneye, anothere ys of so nyce and soo delycate a mynde that he settethe nothynge by yt. And yt beynge neglected, and therefore shortelye fallynge into ruyne, he buyldethe vppe anothere in an othere place wyth no lesse coste and chardge. But emonge the Vtopyans, where all thynges be sett in a good ordre, and the common wealthe in a good staye, yt very seldome chaunceth, that they chuse a new plotte to buylde an house vpon. And they doo not only finde spedy and quicke remedies for present fautes, but also preuente them that be like to fall. And by this meanes their houses continewe and laste very longe with litle labour and small reparacions; in so much that this kind of woorkemen sumtimes haue almost nothinge to doo; but that they be commaunded to hewe timbre at home, and to square and trime vp stones, to the intente that if annye woorke chaunce, it may the spedelier rise.

Now, Syre, in theire apparell marke, I praye yow, howe few woorkemen they neade. Fyrste of all, whyles they be at woorke, they be couered homely with leather or skinnes that will last .vii. yeares. When they go furthe a brode, they caste vpon them a cloke, whyche hydeth the other homelye apparell. Thyes clookes thoroughe owte the hole Ilande be all of one coloure, and that is the naturall colour of the wul. They therfor do not only spende muche lesse wullen clothe then is spente in othere contreys, but also the same standeth them in muche lesse coste.

But lynen clothe ys made wyth lesse laboure, and ys therefore hadde more in vse. But in lynen clothe onlye whytenese, in wullen onlye clenlynes, ys regardede. As for the smalnese or fynesse of the threde, that ys no thynge passed for. And thys ys the cause wherfore in other places .iiii. or v. clothe gownes of dyuers colours, and as manye sylke cootes, be not enoughe for one man. Yea, and yf he be of the delycate and nyse sorte, x. be to fewe ; where as there one garmente wyll serue a man mooste commenlye .ii. yeares. For whie shoulde he desyre moo ? seing if he had them, he should not be the better hapt or couered from colde, nother in his apparell any whyt the cumlyer.

Wherefore, seynge they be all exercysed in profytable occupatyons, and that fewe artyfycers in the same craftes be suffycyente, thys ys the cause that, plentye of all thynges beynge emonge them, they doo sumtymes bring furthe an innumerable companye of people to amende the hyghe wayes, yf annye be broken. Manye times also, when they haue no such woorke to be occupied about, an open proclamation is made that they shall bestowe fewer houres in woorke. For the magistrates do not exercise their citizens againste theire willes in vnneadfull laboures. For whie? in the institution of that weale publique this ende is onlye and chiefely pretended and mynded, that what time maye possibly be spared from the necessary occupations and affayres of the commen wealthe, all that the cytizeins sholde withdrawe from the bodely seruice to the free liberty of the mind and garnisshing of the same. For herin they suppose the felicity of this liffe to consist.

[Chapter V]

Of their ly=

uing and mutuall conuersation together.

But now will I declare how the citizens vse themselfes one towardes another; what familiar occupieng and enterteynement there is emong the people; and what fasion they vse in distributinge euery thynge. First, the city consisteth of families: the families most commonlie be made of kinredes. For the women, when they be maryed at a lawfull age, they goo into their husbandes houses. But the male chyldren, with al the hole male ofspring, continewe still in their owne familie, and be gouerned of the eldest and auncientest father, onles he dote for age; for then the next to hym in age is put in his rowme.

But to thintent the prescript numbre of the citezens shoulde nether decrease, nor aboue measure increase, it is ordeined that no famylie, whiche in euerye citie be vi. thousand in the hole, besydes them of the contrey, shall at ones haue fewer chyldren of the age of xiiii. yeares or there aboute then x., or mo then xvi.; for of chyldren vnder thys age no numbre can be appointed. This measure or numbre is easely obserued and kept, by puttinge them that in fuller families be aboue the numbre into families of smaller increase. But if chaunce be that in the hole citie the stoore encrease aboue the iust numbre, therewith they fyll vp the lacke of other cityes. But if so be that the multitude throughout the hole Ilande passe and excede the dew numbre, then they chewse out of euery citie certeyn cytezens, and buylde vp a towne vnder their owne lawes in the nexte lande where the inhabitauntes haue muche waste and vnoccupied

OF UTOPIA

grounde, receauinge also of the inhabitauntes to them, if they wil ioyne and dwel with them. They, thus ioyning and dwelling together, do easelye agre in one fassion of liuing, and that to the great wealth of both the peoples. For they so brynge the matter about by their lawes, that the grounde which before was nether good nor profitable for the one nor for the other, is nowe sufficiente and frutefull enough for them both. But if the inhabitauntes of that lande wyll not dwell with them, to be ordered by their lawes, then they dryue them out of those boundes, which they haue limited and apointed out for themselues. And if they resiste and rebell, then they make warre agaynst them. For they counte this the moste iust cause of warre, when any people holdeth a piece of grounde voyde and vacaunt to no good nor profitable vse, kepyng other from the vse and possession of it, whiche notwithstandyng by the lawe of nature ought thereof to be nowryshed and relieued. If any chaunce do so muche dimynishe the numbre of anye of their cyties, that it cannot be fylled vp agayne wythout the diminishynge of the iust numbre of the other cyties (whiche they say chaunced but twyse syns the begynnynge of the lande, through a greate pestilente plage), then they make vp the numbre with cytezens fetched out of their owne forreyne townes; for they hadde rather suffer theyr forreyn townes to decaye and peryshe, then annye cytie of their owne Ilande to be dimynyshed.

But nowe agayne to the conuersation of the cytezens amonge themselfes. The eldeste (as I sayde) rueleth the familie. The wyfes bee ministers to theyr husbandes, the chyldren to theyr parentes, and, to bee shorte, the yonger to theyr elders. Euerye Cytie is diuided into foure equall partes. In the myddes of euery quarter there is a market place of all maner of thynges. Thether the workes of euery familie be brought in to certeyne houses. And euery kynde of

thynge is layde vp seuerall in barnes or store houses.
From hence the father of euery famelie or euery
housholder fetcheth whatsoeuer he and hys haue neade
of, and carieth it awaye with hym without money,
without exchaunge, without annye gage or pledge. 5
For whye should anye thynge be denyed vnto hym;
seyng there is abundaunce of all thynges, and that
it is not to be feared lest anye man wyll aske more
then he neadeth ? For whie should it be thoughte
that that man would aske more then enough, which is 10
sewer neuer to lacke? Certeynly, in all kyndes of
lyuynge creatures, other fere of lacke doth cause
couetousnes and rauyne, or in man only pryde ; whiche
counteth it a gloryouse thynge to passe and excell
other in the superfluous and vayne ostentacion of 15
thynges. The whyche kynde of vice amonge the
Vtopians can haue no place.

Next to the market places that I spake of stonde
meate markettes, whether be brought not onlye all
sortes of herbes, and the fruites of trees with breade, 20
but also fishe, and all maner of iiii. footed beastes, and
wilde foule that be mans meate. But first the
fylthynes and ordure therof is clene washed awaye in
the runnynge ryuer, without the cytie, in places appoynted, mete for the same purpose. From thence 25
the beastes ⟨be⟩ brought in kylled, and cleane wasshed
by the handes of their bondemen. For they permytte
not their frie citezens to accustome there selfes to the
killing of beastes ; through the vse whereof they thinke
that clemencie, the genteleste affection of our nature, 30
doth by litle and litle decaye and peryshe. Nother
they suffer anye thynge that is fylthye, lothesome,
or vnclenlye, to be brought into the cytie ; least the
ayre, by the stenche therof infected and corrupte,
shoulde cause pestilente diseases. 35

Moreouer euerye strete hath certeyne great large
halles sett in equal distaunce one from an other,
euerye one knowne by a seuerall name. In thies

halles dwell the Syphograuntes. And to euery one of the same halles be apoynted xxx. families, of ether side xv. The stewardes of euery halle at a certayn houre come in to the meate markettes, where they receyue meate accordinge to the numbre of their halles.

But first and chieflie of all, respect is had to the sycke that be cured in the hospitalles. For in the circuite of the citie, a litle without the walles, they haue .iiii. hospitalles; so bygge, so wyde, so ample, and so lardge, that they may seme .iiii. litle townes; which were deuised of that bygnes, partely to thintent the sycke, be they neuer so many in numbre, shuld not lye to thronge or strayte, and therfore uneasely and incomodiously; and partely that they which were taken and holden with contagious diseases, suche as be wonte by infection to crepe from one to an other, myght be laid a part farre from the company of the residue. Thies hospitalles be so well apointed, and with al thynges necessary to health so furnished; and more ouer so diligent attendaunce through the continual presence of cunnyng phisitians is geuen, that though no man be sent thither against his will, yet notwithstandinge there is no sicke persone in all the citie, that had not rather lye there then at home in his owne house. When the stewarde of the sicke hath receiued suche meates as the phisitians haue prescribed, then the beste is equally deuided among the halles, according to the company of euery one, sauing that there is had a respect to the prince, the byshop, the tranibours, and to ambassadours, and all straungers, if there be any, whiche be verye fewe and seldome. But they also, when they be there, haue certeyne houses apointed and prepared for them.

To thies halles at the set houres of dinner and supper cummith all the hole Siphograuntie or wardo, warned by the noyse of a brasen trumpet; except such as be sicke in the hospitalles or els in their owne houses. Howe be it, no man is prohibited or forbid, after the halles be serued, to fetch home meate out of the market to his own house. For they knowe that no man wyl doo it without a cause resonable. For thoughe no man be prohibited to dyne at home, yet no man doth it willynglye, because it is counted a pointe of small honestie. And also it were a follye to take the payne to dresse a badde dyner at home, when they maye be welcome to good and fyne fare so nyghe hande at the hall. In this hal all vyle seruice, all slauerie and drudgerye, with all laboursome toyle and busines, is done by bondemen. But the women of euery famelie by course haue the office and charge of cokerye, for sethinge and dressynge the meate, and orderyng al thinges therto belonging. They syt at iii. tables or moo, accordyng to the numbre of their company. The men syt vpon the benche next the wall, and the women agaynst them on the other syde of the table; that, if anye sodeyne euell should chaunce to them, as many tymes happeneth to women with chylde, they maye ryse wythout trouble or disturbaunce of anye body, and go thence into the nurcerie.

The nourceis sitte seuerall alone with their yonge suckelinges in a certayne parloure apointed and deputed to the same purpose, neuer without fire and cleane water, nor yet without cradels; that when they wyll they maye laye downe the yong infauntes, and at their pleasure take them out of their swathynge clothes and holde them to the fyere, and refreshe them with playe. Euery mother is nource to her owne chylde, onles other death or syckenes be the let. When that chaunceth, the wyues of the Siphograuntes quyckelye prouyde a nource. And that is not harde to be done. For they that can doo it do proffer themselfes to no seruice so gladlye as to that. Because that there thys kynde of pitie is muche praysed; and the chylde that is nouryshed euer after taketh hys nource for his owne naturall mother. Also amonge the nourceis syt all

OF UTOPIA

the chyldren that be vnder the age of v. yeares. All
the other children of both kyndes, aswell boyes as
gyrles, that be vnder the age of marryage, doo other
serue at the tables, or els if they be to yonge therto,
yet they stande by with meruelous silence. That
whiche is giuen to them from the table they eate, and
other seuerall dynner tyme they haue none. The
Siphograunt and his wife sitteth in the middes of the
highe table, forasmuche as that is counted the honer-
ablest place, and because from thence al the hole
companye is in their syght. For that table standeth
ouer wharte the ouer ende of the halle. To them be
ioyned ii. of the anctientest and eldest. For at euery
table they syt iiii. at a meesse. But if there be a
church standing in that Siphograuntie, or warde, then
the priest and his wyfe sitteth with the Siphograunte,
as chiefe in the company. On both sydes of them
sytte yonge men, and nexte vnto them agayne olde
men. And thus throughe out all the house equall of
age be sette together, and yet be myxte with vnequall
ages. Thys they saye was ordeyned, to the intent
that the sage grauitie and reuerence of the elders
should kepe the yongers from wanton licence of wordes
and behauiour ; for as muche as nothyng can be so
secretly spoken or done at the table, but either they
that syt on the one syde or on the other must nedes
perceiue it. The disshes be not set downe in ordre
from the first place, but all the old men (whoes places
be marked with som speciall token to be knowen) be
first serued of there meate, and then the residue
equally. The old men deuide their dainties, as they
think best, to the yonger that sit of both sides them.
Thus the elders be not defrauded of their dewe
honoure, and neuerthelesse equall commoditie commeth
to euery one.

They begin euerye dynner and supper of reading
sumthing that perteineth to good maners and vertue.
But it is short, becawse no man shalbe greued therwith.

Here of thelders take occasion of honest communication, but nother sad nor vnpleasaunt. Howbeit, they do not spend all the hole dyner time themselfes with long and tedious talkes; but they gladly here also the yong men; yea and do purposly prouoke them to talke, to thentent that they maye haue a profe of euery mans wit and towardnes or disposition to vertue, which commonly in ye liberte of feasting doth shew and vtter it selfe. Theire dyners be verye short; but there suppers be sumwhat longer; because that after dynner followeth laboure; after supper sleape and naturall reste; whiche they thynke to be of no more strengthe and efficacy to holsome and healthfull digestion. No supper is passed without musicke; nor their bankettes lacke no conceytes nor ionckettes. They burne swete gummes and speces for perfumes and pleasaunt smelles, and sprincle about swete oyntmentes and waters; yea they leaue nothyng vndone that maketh for the cheryng of the company. For they be muche enclyned to this opinion: to thinke no kynde of pleasure forbidden, wherof cummeth no harme.

Thus therfore and after this sorte they lyue togethers in the citie; but in the contrey they that dwell alone, farre from anye neyghbours, do dyne and suppe at home in their own houses. For no famelie there lacketh anye kynde of victualles, as from whome cummeth all that the cytezens eate and lyue bye.

[Chapter VI]

¶ Of their

iourneyenge or trauaylynge a brode,
with dyuers other matters cun-
nyngly reasoned and witti-
lie discussed.

But if any be desierous to vysite other their fryndes that dwel in an other Cytie, or to see the place it selfe, they easelye obteyne lycence of their Siphograuntes and Tranibores, oneles there bee som profitable let. No man goeth out alone; but a companye is sente furth to gether with their princes letters, whiche do testifie that they haue licence to go that iorney, and prescribeth also the day of their retourne. They haue a wageyn geuen them, with a common bondman, whiche driueth the oxen and taketh charge of them. But onles they haue women in their company, they sende home the wageyn againe, as an impediment and a let. And though they carrye nothyng furth wit them, yet in all their iorney they lacke nothing. For whersoeuer they come they be at home. If they tary in a place longer then one day, than there euery one of them falleth to his own occupation, and be very gentilly enterteined of the workmen and companies of the same craftes. If any man of his owne head and without leaue walke out of his precinct and boundes, taken without the princes lettres, he is brought again for a fugitive or a runaway with great shame and rebuke, and is sharpely punished. If he be taken in that faulte agayne, he is punished with bondage.

If anye be desierous to walke a brode into the fieldes, or into the contrey that belongeth to the same citie that he dwelleth in, obteynyng the good will of his father, and the consent of his wife, he is not prohibited. But into what part of the contrey soeuer he cummeth, he hath no meat geuin him untill he haue wrought out his forenones taske, or els dispatched so muche worke as there is wonte to be wrought befor supper. Obseruing this lawe and condition, he may go whether he well within the boundes of his owne citie. For he shalbe no les profitable to the citie, then if he were within it.

Now yow see howe litle libertie they haue to loyter; how they can haue no cloke or pretence to ydelnes. There be nether wyn tauernes, nor ale houses, nor stewes, nor any occasion of uice or wickednes, no lurking corners, no places of wicked councelles or vnlawfull assembles; but they be in the present sight, and vnder the iyes of euery man; so that of necessitie they must other applie their accustomed labours, or else recreate themselfes with honest and laudable pastymes.

This fassion being vsed among the people, they must of necessitie haue store and plentie of all thinges. And seing they be al therof parteners equally, therfore cane no man there be poore or nedye. In the councel of Amaurot (whether, as I sayde, euery citie sendeth .iii. men a pece yearly), assone as it is perfectly knowen of what thynges there is in euery place plentie, and agayne what thynges be skant in anye place; incontinent the lacke of the one is performed and fylled vp with the aboundaunce of the other. And this they doo frelye without any benifite, takyng nothing agayn of them to whom the thinges is geuen; but those cyties that haue geuen of their store to anye other cytie that lacketh, requyrynge nothynge agayne of the same cytie, do take suche thinges as they lacke of an other cytie, to whome they gaue nothynge. So the hole Ilande is as it were one famelie or housholde.

But when they haue made sufficiente prouision of

OF UTOPIA

stoore for them selfes (whiche they thynke not doone untyll they haue prouyded for two yeares followynge, bicause of the vncertentie of the nexte yeares proffe), then of those thynges wherof they haue abundaunce they carry furthe into other contreis greate plenty; as grayne, honnye, wulle, flaxe, woode, madder, purple die felles, waxe, tallowe, lether, and liuyng beastes. And the seuenth part of all thies thynges they gyue franckely and frelye to the poore of that contrey. The resydewe they sell at a reasonable and meane price. By this trade of traffique or marchandise, they bring into their own contrey not only great plentie of golde and siluer, but also all suche thynges as they lacke at home, whych is almoste nothynge but Iron. And by reason they haue longe vsed thys trade, nowe they haue more abundaunce of thies thynges then any man wyll beleue. Nowe, therfore, they care not whether they sell for reddye moneye, or els vpon truste to be paide at a daye, and to haue the most part in debtes. But in so doyng they neuer followe the credence of pryuat men, but the assureaunce or warrauntise of the hole citye, by instrumentes and writinges made in that behalfe accordinglye. When the daye of paymente is come and expyred, the cytye gathereth vp the debte of the priuate dettours, and putteth it into the common boxe, and so long hath the vse and proffytte of it, vntyll the vtopians their creditours demaunde it. The mooste parte of it they neuer aske. For that thynge whyche is to them no proffyte, to take it from other to whom it is proffytable, they thinke it no righte nor conscience. But yf the case so stande, that they must lende parte of that money to an other people, then they requyre theyre debte; or when they haue warre. For tho whyche purpose onelye they keap at home al the treasure which they haue, to be holpen and socoured by yt other in extreame ieopardyes, or in suddeyne daungers; but especyallyo and chieflye to hiere therwyth, and that for vnreasonable greate wayges, straunge soldyours. For they hadde rather put straungers in ieopardye then theyre owne contreye men; knowinge that for moneye enoughe theire enemyes themselfes manye tymes may be bowghte and solde, or els throughe treason be sette togethers by the eares emonge themselfes. For thys cause they kype an inestymable treasure; but yet not as a treasure; but so they haue yt and vse yt as in good faythe I am ashamede to shewe, fearynge that my woordes shal not be beleued. And thys I haue more cause to feare, for that I knowe howe dyffucultlye and hardelye I meselfe wolde haue beleued an othere man tellynge the same, yf I hadde not presentlye seene yt wyth myne owne iyes. For yt muste nedes be, that howe farre a thing is dissonaunt and disagreinge from the guyse and trade of the hearers, so farre shall yt be owte of theyr beleffe. Howe be yt, a wyse and indyfferente estymer of thynges wyll not greatly marueil perchaunce, seing al theyre other lawes and customes doo so muche dyfferre from owres, yf the vse also of golde and syluer amonge them be applyed rather to theyr owne fassyons then to owers. I meane, in that they occupye not moneye themselfes, but kepe yt for that chaunce; whyche as yt maye happen, so yt maye be that yt shall neuer come to passe.

In the meane tyme golde and syluer, whereof moneye ys made, they doo soo vse, as none of them dothe more estyme yt, then the verye nature of the thynge deseruethe. And then who dothe not playnlye see howe farre yt ys vnder Iron? as wythoute the whyche men canne no better lyue then withowte fyere and water; whereas to golde and syluer nature hathe geuen no vse that we may not wel lacke, yf that the folly of men hadde not sette it in hygher estymacyon for the rarenes sake. But, of the contrary parte, nature, as a moste tender and louynge mother, hath placed the beste and moste necessarye thynges open

OF UTOPIA

a brode; as the ayere, the water, and the earth it selfe; and hath remoued and hydde farthest from vs vayne and vnprofytable thynges. Therfore yf thies metalles among them shoulde be fast locked vp in some tower, it myghte be suspected that the prynce and the cowncell (as the people is euer foolyshelye ymagininge) intended by some subtyltye to deceaue the commons, and to take some proffette of it to themselfes. Furthermore, if they should make therof plat and such other finely and cunningly wrought stuffe; yf at anye tyme they shoulde haue occasyon to breake it, and melte it agayne, and therwyth to paye their souldiours wages; they see and perceiue very well that men wolde be lothe to parte from those thynges that they ons begonne to haue pleasure and delyte in.

To remedye all thys, they haue fownde owt a meanes, which, as it is agreable to al their other lawes and customes, so it is from ours, where golde is so muche set by and so delygently kepte, very farre discrepant and repugnaunt; and therfore vncredible, but only to them that be wise. For where as they eate and drincke in earthen and glasse vessells, which in dede be curiously and properlie made, and yet be of very small value; of gold and siluer they make commonlye chamber pottes, and other like vessells that serue for moste vile vses, not only in their common halles, but in euery mans priuate house. Furthermore of the same mettalles they make greate cheynes with fetters and giues, wherin they tye their bondmen. Finally, who so euer for any offence be infamed, by their eares hange ringes of golde; vpon their fingers they were ringes of golde, and about their neckes chaynes of gold; and in conclusion their heades be tiode about with golde. Thus, by all meanes that may be, they procure to haue gold and siluer emong them in reproche and infamy. And therfore thies metalles, which other nations do as greuously and sorroufully forgo, as in a maner from their owne liues: if they should all togethers at ones be taken from the vtopians, no man there wold thinke that he had lost the worth of one farthing.

They gather also peerles by the sea side, and Diamondes and Carbuncles upon certein rockes; and yet they seke not for them; but by chaunce finding them they cutt and polish them. And therwith they decke their yonge infanntes. Which, like as in the first yeares of their childhod they make much and be fond and proud of such ornamentes, so when they be a litle more growen in yeares and discretion, perceiuing that none but children do were such toies and trifeles, they lay them awaye euen of theyre owne shamefastenes, wythowte annye biddyng of there parentes: euen as oure chyldren, when they waxe bygge, doo caste awaye nuttes, brouches, and puppettes. Therfore thyes lawes and customes, whych be so farre dyfferente from all othere natyons, howe diuers fanseys also and myndes they doo cause, dydde I neuer so playnlye perceaue, as in the Ambassadoures of the Anemolians.

Thyes Ambassadoures came to Amaurote whyles I was there. And bycause they came to entreat of greate and weighty matters, those .iii. citizeins a pece out of euery city were commen thether before them. But al the Ambassadours of the next contreis, which had bene there before, and knewe the fassions and maners of the Vtopians, amonge whome they perceaued no honoure geuen to sumptuous and costelye apparrell, silkes to be contemned, golde also to be enfamed and reprochefull, were wont to come thether in very homely and simple apparrell. But the Anemolianes, bicause they dwell farre thence, and had verye litle acquaintaunce with them, hearinge that they were al apparelled a like, and that verye rudelye and homelye, thynkynge them not to haue the thynges whyche they dydde not weare, beynge therefore more proud then wise, deter-

mined in the gorgiousnes of their apparel to represent
very goddes, and wyth the bright shynynge and
glisteringe of their gaye clothinge to dasell the eyes of
the silie poore vtopians. So ther came in iii. Ambassadours with C. seruauntes all apparelled in chaungeable colours; the moost of them in silkes; the Ambassadours themselfes (for at home in their owne countrey
they were noble men) in cloth of gold, with great
cheines of gold, with gold hanging at their eares, with
gold ringes vpon their fingers, with brouches and
aglettes of gold vpon their cappes, which glistered ful
of peerles and pretious stones; to be short, trimmed
and aduorned with al those thinges, which emong the
vtopians were other the punnishement of bondmen, or
the reproche of infamed persones, or elles trifels for
yonge children to playe with all. Therfore it wolde
haue done a man good at his harte to haue sene howe
proudelye they displeyed theire pecockes fethers; howe
muche they made of their paynted sheathes; and
howe loftely they sett forth and aduaunced them selfes,
when they compared their gallaunte apparrell with the
poore rayment of the vtopians. For al the people were
swarmed furth into the stretes. And on the other
side it was no lesse pleasure to consider howe muche
they were deceaued, and how farre they missed of their
purpose; being contrary wayes taken then they thought
they shoulde haue bene. For to the iyes of all the
vtopians, excepte very fewe, whiche had bene in other
contreys for some resonable cause, al that gorgeousnes
of apparrel semed shamefull and reprochefull; in so
much that they most reuerently saluted the vylest and
most abiect of them for lordes; passing ouer the Am-
passadours themselfes without any honour; iudging
them, be their wearing of golden cheynes, to be bondemen. Yea, you shuld haue sene children also that had
caste away their peerles and pretious stones, when
they sawe the like sticking vpon the Ambassadours
cappes, digge and pushe their mothers vnder the sides,

sayinge thus to them : 'Loke, mother, how great a
lubbor doth yet were peerles and pretious stoones, as
though he were a litel child still.' But the mother,
yea, and that also in good earnest : 'peace, sone,' saith
she ; 'I thynk he be some of the Ambassadours fooles.' 5
Some fownde fawte at theire golden cheynes, as to no
vse nor purpose ; beynge so small and weake, that
a bondeman myghte easelye breake them ; and agayne
so wyde and large, that, when it pleased him, he
myght cast them of, and runne awaye at lybertye 10
whether he wolde.

But when the Ambassadoures hadde bene there a
daye or .ii., and sawe so greate abundaunce of gold so
lyghtelye estymed, yea, in no lesse reproche then yt
was wyth them in honour ; and, besydes that, more 15
golde in the cheynes and gyues of one fugytyue bondeman, then all the costelye ornamentes of them .iii.
was worth ; they beganne to abate theyre currage, and
for verye shame layde awaye all that gorgyouse arraye
wherof theye were so prowde ; and specyallye when 20
they hadde talkede famylyerlye wyth the Vtopyans,
and hadde learnede all theyre fassyons and opynyons.
For they marueyle that annye men be soo folyshe as
to haue delyte and pleasure in the glysterynge of a
lytyll tryfelynge stone, whyche maye beholde annye 25
of the starres, or elles the soone yt selfe ; or that
annye man ys so madde as to counte him selfe the
nobler for the smaller or fyner threde of wolle, whyche
selfe same woll (be it nowe in neuere so fyne a sponne
threde) dyde ones a shepe weare ; and yet was she all 30
that time no other thing then a shepe.

They marueyle also that golde, whyche of the owne
nature is a thynge so vnprofytable, is nowe emonge
all people in soo hyghe estymatyon, that man hym
selfe, by whom, yea and for the vse of whome, yt ys 35
so muche sett by, ys in muche lesse estymatyon then
the golde yt selfe. In so muche that a lumpyshe
blockehedded churle, and whyche hathe no more wytte

then an asse, yea, and as full of noughtenes and
folyshenes, shall haue neuertheles many wyse and
good men in subiectyon and bondage, onlye for thys,
bycause he hathe a greate heape of golde. Whyche yf
yt should be taken from hyme by annye fortune, or
by some subtyll wyle of the lawe, (which no lesse then
fortune doth raise vp the lowe, and plucke downe the
high) and be geuen to the most vile slaue and abiect
dreuell of all his housholde, then shortely after he
shall goo into the seruice of his seruaunt, as an aug-
mentation or an ouerplus besyd his money. But they
much more marueill at and detest the madenes of
them, whyche to those riche men, in whose debte and
daunger they be not, do giue almoste diuine honowres,
for non other consideration, but bicause they be riche;
and yet knowing them to be suche nigeshe penny
fathers, that they be sure, as long as they liue, not the
worthe of one farthinge of that heape of gold shall
come to them.

Thies and such like opinions haue they conceaued,
partely by education, beinge brought vp in that
common wealth, whose lawes and customes be farre
different from thies kindes of folly, and partely by
good litterature and learning. For though ther be
not many in euery citye, whiche be exempte and discharged of all other laboures, and appointed only to
learninge; that is to saye, suche in whome euen from
theire very childhode they haue perceaued a singuler
towardnes, a fyne witte, and a minde apte to good
learning; yet all in their childhode be instructe in
learninge. And the better parte of the people, bothe
men and women, throughe owte all theire hole lyffe,
doo bestowe in learninge those spare howres, which
we sayde they haue vacante from bodelye laboures.
They be taughte learninge in theire owne natyue tonge.
For yt is bothe copious in woordes, and also pleasaunto
to the eare, and for the vtteraunce of a mans minde
verye perfecte and sure. The mooste parte of all that

syde of the wordle vseth the same langage ; sauinge that amonge the Vtopians yt is fyneste and puryste ; and accordynge to the dyuersytye of the contreys yt ys dyuerslye alterede.

Of all thyes Philosophers, whose names be here famous in thys parte of the wordle to vs knowen, before owre cummynge thether, nott as muche as the fame of annye of them was comen amonge them ; and yett in Musycke, Logycke, Arythmetyke, and Geometrye, they haue fownde owte in a manner all that oure auncyente Philosophers haue tawghte. But as they in all thynges be almoste equall to our olde auncyente clerkes, so our newe Logiciens in subtyll inuentyons haue farre passed and gone beyonde them. For they haue not deuysed one of all those rules of restryctyons, amplyfycatyons, and supposytyons, very wittelye inuented in the small Logycalles, whyche heare oure chyldren in euerye place do learne. Furthermore they were neuer yet able to fynde out the seconde intentyons ; in so muche that none of them all coulde euer see man hymselfe in commen, as they call hym ; thoughe he be (as yow knowe) bygger then euer was annye gyaunte, yea, and poynted to of vs euen wyth our fynger. But they be in the course of the starres, and the mouynges of the heauenlye spheres, verye expert and cunnynge. They haue also wyttelye excogytated and diuised instrumentes of diuers fassyons, wherin is exactly comprehended and conteyned the mouynges and sytuatyons of the sonne, the moone, and of all the other starres which appere in theyre horyzon. But as for the amityes and dissentyons of the planettes, and all that deceytefull diuynatyon by the starres, they neuer asmuch as dreamed therof. Raynes, windes, and other courses of tempestes they knowe before by certein tokens, which they haue learned by long vse and obseruation. But of the causes of all thies thinges, and of the ebbinge, flowinge, and saltenes of the sea, and fynallye of the orygynall begynnyng and nature of heauen and of the wordle, they holde partelye the same opynyons that our olde philosophers holde; and partelye, as our philosophers varye emonge themselfes, so they also, whiles they bringe new reasons of thynges, doo disagree from all them, and yet emonge themselfes in all poyntes they doo not accorde.

In that part of philosophie which intreateth of manners and vertue, theire reasons and opynyons agree wyth ours. They dyspute of the good qualytyes of the sowle, of the body, and of fortune; and whether the name of goodnes maye be applied to all thies, or onlie to the endowmentes and giftes of the sowle. They reason of vertue and pleasure. But the chiefe and principall question is in what thynge, be yt one or moo, the felycytye of man consisteth. But in thys poynte theye seme almooste to muche geuen and enclyned to the opinion of them whiche defende pleasure; wherin they determine other all or the chiefyste parte of mans felycytye to reste. And (whyche is more to bee marueled at) the defence of thys soo deyntye and delycate an opynyon they fetche euen from theyre graue, sharpe, bytter, and rygorous relygyon. For they neuer dyspute of felycytye or blessednes, but they ioyne to the reasons of Philosophye certeyne pryncyples taken owte of relygyon; wythoute the whyche, to the inuestygatyon of trewe felycytye, theye thynke reason of yt selfe weak and vnperfecte. Thoose pryncyples be thyes and suche lyke: That the sowle ys immortall, and by the bountifull goodnes of God ordeyned to felicitie: That to our vertues and good deades rewardes be apoynted after this lyfe, and to our euell deades punyshementes. Though thies be perteynyng to religion, yet they thynke it mete that they shoulde be beleued and graunted by profes of reason. But if thies prınciples were condempned and dysanulled, then without anye delaye they pronounce no man to be so folish, whiche woulde not do all hys

diligence and endeuoure to obteyne pleasure be ryght
or wronge, onlye auoydynge this inconuenience, that
the lesse pleasure should not be a let or hynderaunce
to the bygger; or that he laboured not for that pleasure whiche would bryng after it displeasure, greefe,
and sorrowe. For they iudge it extreame madnes to
folowe sharpe and peinful vertue, and not only to
bannyshe the pleasure of lyfe, but also wyllyngly
to suffre grief without any hope of proffyt thereof.
For what proffyt can there be, if a man, when he hath
passed ouer all hys lyfe vnpleasauntly, that is to say,
wretchedlye, shall haue no rewarde after hys death?
But now, syr, they thynke not felicitie to reste in all
pleasure, but onlye in that pleasure that is good and
honest; and that hereto, as to perfet blessednes, our
nature is allured and drawen euen of vertue; wherto
only they that be of the contrary opinion do attribute
felicitie. For they define vertue to be a life ordered
according to nature; and that we be hereunto ordeined
of god; and that he doth followe the course of nature,
which in desiering and refusyng thynges is ruled by
reason. Furthermore, that reason doth chiefelie and
pryncipallye kendle in men the loue and veneration of
the deuyne maiestie; of whoes goodnes it is that we be,
and that we be in possibilitie to attayne felicite. And
that, secondarely, it moueth and prouoketh vs to leade
our lyfe out of care in ioye and myrth, and to helpe all
other, in respecte of the sosiete of nature, to obteyne
the same. For there was neuer man so earnest and
paynefull a follower of vertue, and hater of pleasure,
that woulde so inioyne you laboures, watchinges, and
fastinges, but he would also exhort you to ease and
lighten to your powre the lacke and myserye of
others; praysyng the same as a dede of humanitie
and pitie. Then if it be a poynte of humanitie for man
to bryng health and comforte to man, and speciallye
(whiche is a vertue moste peculiarlye belongynge to
man) to mitigate and assuage the grief of others, and

OF UTOPIA

by takyng from them the sorowe and heuynes of lyfe, to restore them to ioye, that is to saye to pleasure; whye maye it not then be sayd that nature doth prouoke euerye man to doo the same to hymselfe?

For a ioyfull lyfe, that is to saye, a pleasaunt lyfe, is other euell; and if it be so, then thou shouldest not onlye helpe no man therto, but rather, as muche as in the lieth, helpe all men from it, as noysome and hurtefull; or els, if thou not onlye mayste, but also of dewtie art bounde to procure it to others, why not chiefely to theself, to whome thou art bound to shewe as muche fauour as to other? For when natur biddeth the to be good and gentle to other, she commaundeth the not to be cruell and vngentle to the selfe. Therfore euen very nature (saye they) prescribith to vs a ioyfull lyfe, that is to saye, pleasure, as the ende of all our operations. And they defyne vertue to be lyfe ordered accordyng to the prescrypt of nature. But in that that nature dothe allure and prouoke men one to healpe an other to lyue merilye (whiche suerlye she doth not without a good cause; for no man is so farre aboue the lot of mans state or condicion, that nature doth carke and care for hym only, whiche equallye fauoureth all that be comprehended vnder the communion of one shape, forme, and fassion), verely she commaundeth the to vse diligent circumspection, that thou do not so seke for thine owne commodities, that thou procure others incommodities.

Wherfore their opinion is, that not onlye coueunauntes and bargaynes made amonge priuate men ought to be well and faythfullye fulfylled, obserued, and kept, but also commen lawes; whiche other a good prince hath iustly publyshed, or els the people, nother oppressed with tyranny, nother deceaued by fraude and gyell, hath by their common consent constitute and ratifyed, concernyng the particion of the commodities of lyfe.—that is to say, the matter of pleasure.

Thies lawes not offendid, it is wysdome that thou looke to thyne own wealthe. And to do the same for the common wealth is no lesse then thy duetie, if thou bearest any reuerent loue or any naturall zeale and affection to thy natiue contrey. But to go about to let an other man of his pleasure, whiles thou procurest thyne owne, that is open wrong. Contrary wyse, to withdrawe somethynge from they selfe to geue to other, that is a pointe of humanitie and gentylnes; whiche neuer taketh a waye so muche commoditie, as it bryngeth agayne. For it is recompensed with the retourne of benefytes; and the conscience of the good dede, with the remembraunce of the thankefull loue and beneuolence of them to whom thou hast done it, doth brynge more pleasure to thy mynde, then that whiche thou hast withholden from thy selfe could haue brought to the bodye. Finallye (which to a godly disposed and a religious mind is easie to be persuaded), God recompenseth the gifte of a short and small pleasure with great and euerlastinge ioye. Therfore, the matter diligentlie wayde and considered, thus they thinke: that all our actions, and in them the vertues themselfes, be referred at the last to pleasure, as theire ende and felicitie.

Pleasure they call euery motion and state of the bodie or mynde, wherin man hath naturally delectation. Appetite they ioyne to nature, and that not without a good cause. For like as not only the senses, but also right reason, coueteth whatsoeuer is naturally pleasaunt; so that it may be gotten without wrong or iniurie, not letting or debarring a greater pleasur, nor causing painful labour; euen so those thinges that men by vaine ymagination, do fayne against nature to be pleasaunt (as though it lay in their powre to chaunge the thinges as they do the names of thinges), al suche pleasurs they beleue to be of so small helpe and furtheraunce to felicitie, that they counte them great let and hinderaunce; because

OF UTOPIA

that, in whom they haue ones taken place, all his mynde they possesse with a false opinion of pleasure; so that there is no place left for true and naturall delectacions. For there be manye thynges, whiche of their owne nature conteyne no plesauntnes; yea the moste part of them muche grief and sorrow; and yet, through the peruerse and malicious flickering inticementes of lewde and vnhoneste desyres, be taken not only for speciall and souereigne pleasures, but also be counted amonge the chiefe causes of life.

In this counterfeat kinde of pleasure they put them that I speake of before; which, the better gown they haue on, the better men they thynke themselfes. In the whiche thynge they doo twyse erre. For they be no lesse deceaued in that they thynke their gowne the better, than they be in that they thinke themselfes the better. For if you consider the profitable vse of the garmente, whye shoulde wulle of a fyner sponne threde be thought better, then the wul of a course sponne threde? Yet they, as though the one dyd passe the other by nature, and not by their mistakyng, auaunce themselfes and thinke the price of their owne persones therby greatly encreased. And therfore the honoure, whiche in a course gowne they durste not haue lokyd for, they require as it were of dewtie for their fyner gownes sake. And if they be passed by without reuerence, they take it angerlye and disdaynfully.

And agayne is it not a lyke madnes to take a pride in vayne and vnprofitable honoures? For what naturall or trewe pleasure doest thou take of an other mans bare hede or bowed knees? Will thys ease the payne of thy knees, or remedye the phrensie of thy heade? In this ymage of counterfeyte pleasure, they be of a maruelous madnes, which for the opinion of nobilitie reioyse muche in their owne conceite, because it was their fortune to come of suche auncetours, whoes stocke of longe tyme hath bene counted ryche (for nowe nobilitie is nothynge elles), specially ryche in landes. And though their auncetours left them not one fote of lande, or els they themselfes haue pyssed it agaynste the walles, yet they thynke themselfes not the lesse noble therefore of one heare.

In thys numbre also they counte them that take pleasure and delyte (as I saide) in gemmes and precious stones, and thynke themselues almoste goddes, if they chaunce to gette an excellent one ; speciallye of that kynde whyche in that tyme of their owne contreye men is had in hyghest estimation. For one kynde of stone kepeth not hys pryce styll in all contreis, and at all tymes. Nor they bye them not but taken out of the golde and bare ; no, nor so nother, before they haue made the seller to sweare that he wyll warraunte and assure it to be a trewe stone and no counterfeyt geme. Suche care they take lest a counterfet stone shoulde deceaue their eyes in the steade of a right stone. But whye shouldest thou not take euen as muche pleasure in beholdynge a counterfette stone, whiche thyne eye cannot discerne from a ryght stone ? They should both be of lyke value to the, euen as to a blynde man. What shall I saye of them that kepe superfluous ryches, to take delectacion only in the beholdynge, and not in the vse or occupyenge therof ? Do they take trewe pleasure, or els be they deceaued with false pleasure ? Or of them that be in a contrary vice, hydynge the golde whiche they shall neuer occupie, nor peraduenture neuer see more ; and, whiles they take care leaste they shall leese it, do leese it in dede ? For what is it elles, when they hyde it in the grounde, takynge it bothe from their owne vse, and perchaunce from all other mens also ? And yet thou, when thou haste hidde thye treasure, as one out of all care, hoppest for ioye. The whyche treasure if it shoulde chaunce to bee stoolen, and thou, ignoraunt of the thefte, shouldest dye tenne yeares after ; all that tenne yeares

OF UTOPIA

space that thou lyuedest, after thy money was stolen, what matter was it to the whether it hadde bene taken a waye, or els sauffe as thou lefteste it? Truelye bothe wayes lyke proffyt came to the.

To thyes so foolyshe pleasures they ioyne dycers, whose madnes they knowe by heare say and not by vse; hunters also, and hawkers. For what pleasure is there (saye they) in castynge the dice upon a table; which thu hast done so often, that if theire were anye pleasure in it, yet the ofte vse myghte make the werye therof? Or what delite can there be, and not rather dyspleasure, in hearynge the barkynge and howlynge of dogges? Or what greater pleasure is there to be felte, when a dogge followeth an hare, then when a dogge followeth a dogge? for one thynge is done in both; that is to saye, runninge; if thou haste pleasure therein. But if the hope of slaughter, and the expectation of tearynge in pieces the beaste dothe please the, thou shouldest rather be moued with pitie to see a seely innocent hare murdered of a dogge; the weake of the stronger; the fearefull of the fearce; the innocente of the cruell and vnmercyfull. Therefore all thys exercyse of huntynge, as a thynge vnworthye to be vsed of free men, the Vtopians haue reiected to their bochers; to the whiche crafte (as wee sayde before) they appointe ther bondmen. For they counte huntyng the loweste, vyleste, and moste abiecte parte of bocherye; and the other partes of it more profytable and more honeste, as whiche do brynge muche more commoditie; and doo kyll beastes onlye for necessytie. Where as the hunter seketh nothynge but pleasure of the seely and wofull beastes slaughter and murder. The whiche pleasure in beholdyng death they thynke dothe ryse in the very beastes, other of a cruell affection of myndo, or els to be chaunged in continuaunce of time into crueltie, by longe vse of so cruell a pleasure. Thies therfore and all suche lyke, which be innumerable, though the common sorte of people doth take them for pleasures, yet they, seyng there is no naturall pleasauntnes in them, do playnelye determine them to haue no affinitie with trewe and right pleasure. For as touchyng that they do commonlye moue the sence with delectacion (whiche semeth to be a worke of pleasure) thys doth nothing diminishe their opinion. For not the nature of the thynge, but there peruerse and lewde custome is the cause hereof; whiche causeth them to accepte bitter or sowre thinges for swete thinges; euen as women with childe, in their viciate and corrupt taste, thinke pitche and tallowe sweter then anye honney. Howbeit no mans iudgement, depraued and corrupte, other by sickenes or by custome, can chaunge the nature of pleasure, more then it can doo the natur of other thinges.

They make diuers kyndes of trew pleasures. For som they attribute to the soule, and som to the bodye. To the soule they gyue intellygence, and that delectation that cummeth of the contemplation of truthe. Here vnto is ioyned the pleasaunt remembraunce of the good lyfe past.

The pleasure of the bodye they deuide into ii. partes. The first is when delectation is sensibly felte and perceaued: whiche many times chaunceth by the renewing and refresshyng of thoes partes which owre naturall heate drieth vp: thys cummeth by meate and drynke: and sumtymes whyles those thynges be voided, wherof is in the body ouer great abundaunce. This pleasure is felte when wee doo our naturall easemente, or when we be doynge the acte of generatyon, or when the ytchynge of annye parte is eased with rubbynge or scratchynge. Sumtimes pleasure riseth, exhibitinge to any membre nothing that it desireth, nor taking from it any payne that it feeleth; which for all that tikleth and moueth our senses with a certein secrete efficacy, but with a manifest motion, and turneth them to it; as is that which cummeth of musicke.

The second part of bodely pleasure they say is that which consisteth and resteth in the quiete and vpright state of the body. And that truelye is euery mans owne propre health, entermyngled and dysturbed wyth no grieffe. For thys, yf yt be not letted nor assaulted with no greiffe, is delectable of yt selfe, thoughe yt be moued wyth no externall or outwarde pleasure. For though it be not so plain and manyfeste to the sense, as the gredye luste of eatynge and drynckynge, yet neuerthelesse manye take it for the chyefeste pleasure. All the Vtopyans graunte yt to be a ryghte greate pleasure, and as you wolde saye the foundatyon and grownde of all pleasures; as whyche euen alone ys able to make the state and condytyon of lyffe delectable and pleasaunte; and, yt beynge ones taken awaye, there ys no place lefte for annye pleasure. For to be wythowte greyffe, not hauinge health, that they call vnsensybylyte and not pleasure. The Vtopians haue longe agoo reiected and condempned the opynyon of them, whyche sayde that stedfaste and quyete healthe (for thys questyon also hath bene dylygentelye debated emonge them) owghte not therefore to be cownted a pleasure, bicause they saye yt can not be presentlye and sensyblye perceaued and felte by some owtwarde motion. But, of the contrarye parte, nowe they agree almoste all in thys, that healthe ys a moste souereygne pleasure. For seinge that in syckenes (saye they) is grieffe, which is a mortal ennemie to pleasure, euen as sicknes is to health, why shuld not then pleasure be in the quietnes of health? For they say it maketh nothing to thys matter, whether you saye that sickenes is a griefe, or that in sickenes is griefe; for all cummeth to one purpose. For whether health be a pleasure it selfe, or a necessary cause of pleasure, as fyer is of heate, truelye bothe wayes it foloweth, that they cannot be without pleasure that be in perfyt healthe. Furthermore, whyles we eate (saye they), then health, whiche began to be appayred, fygbteth by the helpe of foode against hunger. In the whych fighte whyles healthe by lytle and lytle getteth the vpper hande, that same procedyng, and (as ye would say) that onwardnes to the wonte strengthe mynistreth that pleasure, wherbye wee be so refresshed. Health therefore, whiche in the conflycte is ioyfull, shall it not bee merye when it hathe gotten the victory? But as sone as it hathe recouered thee pristynate strengthe, whyche thinge onelye in all the fyghte it coueted, shall it incontinent be astonied? Nor shall it not knowe nor imbrace the owne wealthe and goodnes? For that it is sayed healthe can not be felte, this, they thinke, is nothing trew. For what man wakynge, say they, feleth not hymselfe in health, but he that is not? Is there annye man so possessed wyth stonyshe insensibilitie, or with the sleping sicknes, that he wyll not graunt health to be acceptable to hym and delectable? But what other thing is delectation, than that whiche by an other name is called pleasure?

They imbrace chiefely the pleasures of the mind. For them they cownte the chiefist and most principall of all. The cheyfe parte of them they thinke doth come of the exercise of vertue, and conscience of good lyffe. Of thies pleasures that the boddye ministreth they geue the preemynence to helth. For the delyte of eating and drincking, and whatsoeuer hath anny like pleasauntnes, they determyne to be pleasures muche to be desiered, but no other wayes than for healthes sake. For suche thynges of theyre owne propre nature be not pleasaunte, but in that they resyste syckenes preuelye stealynge one. Therefore, lyke as yt ys a wyse mans parte rather to auoyde syckenes, then to wyshe for medycynes, and rather to dryue away and put to flyghte carefull greyffes, then to call for comforte; so yt ys much better not to neade thys kynde of pleasure, then in sealynge the contrarye greyffe to be eased of the same. The whyche kynde of pleasure

yf annye man take for hys felycytye, that man muste
nedes graunte, that then he shall be in mooste felycytye, yf he lyue that lyffe whyche ys ledde in contynuall honger, thurste, itchynge, eatynge, drynkynge,
scratchynge, and rubbynge. The whyche lyffe howe
not onlye foule yt is, but also myserable and wretched,
who perceauethe not? Thyes dowteles be the baseste
pleasures of all, as vnpure and vnperfecte. For they
neuer cum but accompanied wyth their contrary greiffes.
As with the pleasure of eatinge is ioyned hunger, and
that after no very egal sort. For of thies ii. the gryeffe
is bothe the more vehement, and also of longer continuaunce. For it rysethe before the pleasure, and
endeth not vntyll the pleasure dye wyth it.

Wherfore such pleasures they think not greatly to
be set by, but in that they be necessary. Howbeit
they haue delite also in thies, and thankfully knouledge
the tender loue of mother nature, which with most
plesaunt delectation allureth her children to that,
which of necessitye they be driuen often vse. For
how wretched and miserable should our liffe be, if
thies daily greiffes of hunger and thrust coulde not
be dreuen away, but with bitter potions, and sower
medicines; as the other deseases be, where with we
be seldomer trowbled? But bewtye, strengthe, nemble-
nes, thies, as peculiare and pleasaunte giftes of nature,
they make muche of. But those pleasures which be
receaued by the eares, the iyes, and the nose; which
nature willeth to be proper and peculiar to man (for no
other kind of liuing beastes doth behold the fayrenes
and the bewtie of the worlde, or is moued with anny
respect of sauours, but only for the diuersity of meates,
nother perceaueth the concordaunt and discordante
distaunces of soundes and tunes) thies pleasures (I say)
they accept and allowe, as certein pleasaunt reioysinges
of liffe. But in all thinges thys cautell they vse, that
a lesse pleasure hinder not a bigger, and that the
pleasur be no cause of dyspleasur; whych they thinke

K

to followe of necessytye, if the pleasure be vnhoneste.
But yet to dyspyse the comlynes of bewtye, to waste
the bodylye strengthe, to tourne nymblenes into
sloughishnes, to consume and make feble the boddye
wyth fastynge, to doo iniury to health, and to reiect
the other pleasaunte motyons of nature (ones a man
neglecte thies hys commodytyes, whyles he doth wyth
a feruent zeale procure the wealth of others, or the
commen proffytte, for the whyche pleasure forborne
he is in hope of a greater pleasure at Goddes hand):
els for a vayne shaddowe of vertue, for the wealthe
and proffette of no man, to punyshe hymselfe, or to the
intente he maye be able courragiouslye to suffre aduer-
sityes, whyche perchaunce shall neuer come to hym:
thys to doo they thynke it a poynte of extreame madnes, and a token of a man cruelly minded towardes
hymselfe, and vnkynd towarde nature, as one so dys-
daynynge to be in her daunger, that he renounceth
and refuseth all her benefytes.

Thys is theire sentence and opinion of vertue and
pleasure. And they beleue that by mans reason none
can be fownde trewer then this, onles annye godlyer be
inspyred into man from heauen. Wherin whether they
belyue well or no, nother the tyme dothe suffer us to
discusse, nother it ys nowe necessarye. For we haue
taken vpon vs to shewe and declare theyr lores and ordenaunces, and not to defende them.

But thys thynge I beleue verely: howe soeuer thies
decrees be, that their is in no place of the wordle nother
a more excellent people, nother a more flouryshynge
commen wealthe. They be lyghte and quycke of boddy,
full of actiuity and nymblenes, and of more strengthe
then a man wold iudge them by theyre stature, whyche
for all that ys not to lowe. And thoughe theyre soyle
be not verye frutefull, nor theyre ayer verye holsome,
yet agaynste the ayer they soo defende them wyth
temperate dyete, and soo order and husbande theyr
grounde wyth dylygente trauayle, that in no contreye

ys greatter increase, and plentye of corne and cattell, nor mens bodies of longer liffe, and subiect or apte to fewer deseases. There, therfore, a man maye see well and diligentlye exploited and furnished, not onlye those thinges whiche husbandmen doo commenly in other countreys; as by craft and cunning to remedy the barrennes of the grounde; but also a hole wood by the handes of the people plucked vp by the rotes in one place and sett agayne in an other place. Wherin was hadde regard and consideration not of plenty but of commodious carriage; that wood and tymber might be nigher to the sea, or the riuers, or the cities. For it is lesse laboure and busines to carrye grayne farre by lande then wood. The people be gentle, merye, quycke, and fyne wytted, delytynge in quyetnes, and, when nede requyreth, able to abyde and suffre muche bodelye laboure. Elles they be not greatelye desyerous and fonde of yt; but in the exercyse and studdye of the mynde they be neuer werye.

When they had harde me speake of the Greke lytter[ar]ature or learnynge (for in Latyne theyre was nothynge that I thougthe they wolde greatelye allowe, besydes hystoryens and Poetes), they made wonderfull earneste and importunate sute vnto me, that I wolde teache and instructe them in that tonge and learnynge. I beganne therefore to reade vnto them; at the fyrste, truelye, more bycause I wolde not seme to refuse the laboure, then that I hooped that they wolde annye thyng proffytte therin. But when I had gone forwarde a lytle, and perceaued incontynente by theyr dylygence that my labour should not be bestowed in vayne; for they beganne so easelye to fassyon theyre letters, so plainly to pronounce the woordes, so quyckely to learne by harte, and so suerly to rehearse the same, that I marueled at it; sauynge that the most parte of them were fyne and chosen wittes, and of rype age, pyked oute of the companye of the learned men, whyche not onlye of thoyr owne free and voluntarye wyll, but also

by the commaundemente of the cowncell, vndertoke
to learne thys langage. Therfore in lesse then iii. yeres
space their was nothing in the Greke tonge that they
lackede. They were able to reade good authors wythout
anny staye, if the booke were not false.

Thys kynde of learnynge, as I suppose, they toke
so muche the souner, bycause it is sumwhat allyaunte
to them. For I thynke that thys nation tooke their
beginninge of the Grekes, bycause their speche, which in
all other poyntes is not muche vnlyke the persian tonge,
kepeth dyuers signes and tookens of the greke langage
in the names of their cityes and of theire magystrates.
They haue of me (for, when I was determyned to entre
into my .iiii. voyage, I caste into the shippe in the steade
of marchandyse a pretye fardell of bookes, bycause I
intended to come agayne rather neuer than shortelye) the
mooste parte of Platoes woorkes; more of Aristotles;
also Theophrastus of Plantes, but in diuers places (which
I am sorye for) vnperfecte. For whyles wee were
saylynge, a mormosett chaunced vpon the booke, as yt
was neglygentlye layde by; whyche, wantonlye playinge
therewyth, plucked owte certeyne leaues, and toore
them in pieces. Of them that haue wrytten the grammer,
they haue onelye Lascaris. For Theodorus I caried
not wyth me; nor neuer a dyctyonarye, but Hesichius
and Dioscorides. They sett greate stoore by Plutarches
bookes. And they be delyted wyth Lucianes merye
conceytes and iestes. Of the Poettes they haue Aristophanes, Homer, Euripides, and Sophocles in Aldus
small prynte. Of the Historyans they haue Thucidides,
Herodotus, and Herodian. Also my companion, Tricius
Apinatus, caried with him phisick bokes, certein smal
woorkes of Hippocrates, and Galenes Microtechne; the
whyche boke they haue in greate estymatyon. For
thoughe there be almost no nation vnder heauen that
hath lesse nede of Phisick then they, yet, this notwithstandyng, Phisicke is no where in greater honour;
bycause they count the knowlegde of yt emonge the

goodlieste, and mooste profytable partes of Philosophie. For whyles they by the helpe of thys Philosophie searche owte the secrete mysteryes of nature, they thynke that they not onlye receaue therby wonderfull greate pleasur, but also obteyn great thankes and fauour of the auctoure and maker therof. Whome they thynke, accordynge to the fassyon of other artyfycers, to haue sett furthe the maruelous and gorgious frame of the worlde for man to beholde; whome onelye he hathe made of wytte and capacytye to consydre and vnderstand the excellencye of so greate a woorke. And therefore, saye they, dothe he beare more good wyll and loue to the curyous and diligent beholder and vewere of his woorke, and maruelour at the same, then he doth to him, whyche lyke a very beaste wythowte wytte and reason, or as one wythowte sense or mouynge, hath no regarde to soo greate and soo wonderfull a spectacle.

The wyttes therefore of the Vtopians, inurede and exercysed in learnynge, be maruelous quycke in the inuentyon of feates, helpynge annye thynge to the aduantage and wealthe of lyffe. Howebeyt, ii. feates theye maye thanke vs for; that is, the scyence of imprintyng, and the crafte of makynge paper: and yet not onelye vs but chyefelye and pryncypallye themselfes. For when wee shewede to them Aldus hys prynte in bookes of paper, and told them of the stuffe wher of paper is made, and of the feat of grauynge letters, speakynge sumwhat more then wee colde playnlye declare (for there was none of vs that knewe perfectlye other the one or the other), they furthwyth verye wyttelye coniectured the thynge. And where as before they wrote onelye in skynnes, in barkes of tryes, and in rides, now they haue attempted to make paper and to imprint letters. And thoughe at tho fyrste yt prouod not all of the beste, yet by often assayinge the same they shortelye gott the feate of bothe; and haue so broughte the matter abowte, that yf they had copyes of Grecko authores, they coulde lacke no bookes. But nowe they haue no moore then I rehearsed before ; sauynge that by pryntynge of bookes they haue multyplyed and increased the same into manye thowsande of copyes.

Who soeuer cummeth thether to see the lande, beynge excellente in annye gyfte of wytte, or throughe muche and longe iournyenge well experiensed and sene in the knowledge of manye countreys (for the whyche cause wee were verye welcome to them), hym they receyue and interteyne wonders gentyllye and louynglye; for they haue delyte to heare what ys done in euerye lande. Howebeyt, verye few marchaunte men come thythere. For what shoulde they brynge thither ? onles yt were Iron, or els golde and syluer ; whiche they hadde rathere carrye home agayne. Also suche thynges as arre to be caryed owte of their lande, they thynke yt more wysedome to carrye that geer furthe themselfes, then that othere shoulde come thether to fetche yt ; to thentente they maye the better knowe the owte landes of euerye syde them, and kepe in vre the feat and knouledge of saylinge.

[Chapter VII]

Of Bonde=

men, sicke persons, wedlocke, and dyuers
other matters.

They nother make bondemen of prysoners taken in battayll, oneles yt be in battaylle that the fowghte themselfes, nor bondemens chyldren, nor, to be shorte, annye man whome they canne gette owte of an othere countreye, thoughe he were theyre a bondeman; but other suche as amonge themselfes for heynous offences be punnyshed wyth bondage, or elles suche as in the Cytyes of other landes for greate trespasses be condempned to deathe. And of thys sorte of bondemen they haue mooste stoore. For manye of them they brynge home, sumtymes payinge very lytle for them; yea, mooste commonlye gettynge them for gramercye. Thyes sortes of bondemen they kepe not onelye in contynuall woorke and laboure, but alsoo in bandes. But theyre owne men they handle hardeste, whome they judge more desperate, and to haue deseruede greater punnysshemente; bycause they, beynge so godlye broughte vp to vertue, in soo excellente a common wealthe, cowlde not for all that be refreyned from mysdoynge.

An other kynde of bondemen they haue, when a vyle drudge, beynge a poore laborer in an other cowntreye, dothe chewse of hys owne free wyll to be a bondeman amonge them. Thyes they handle and ordor honestelye, and entertoyne almooste as gentyllye, as theyre owne free cytyzeyns; sauynge that they put them to a lytle more laboure, as thereto accustomede. Yf annye suche be dysposed to departe thenc (whyche seldome ys seene) they nother holde hym agaynste hys wyll, nother sende hym awaye wyth emptye handes.

The sycke (as I sayde) they see to wyth greate affectyon, and lette nothynge at all passe, concernynge other Physycke or good dyete, wherby they may be restored agayne to theyre healthe. Them that be sycke of incurable dyseases they comforte wyth syttynge by them, wyth talkynge wyth them, and, to be shorte, wyth all maner of helpes that maye be. But yf the dysease be not onelye vncurable, but also full of contynuall payne and anguyshe, then the priestes and the magistrates exhort the man, seynge he ys not able to doo annye dewtye of lyffe, and by ouerlyuing hys owne deathe is noysome and yrkesome to other, and greuous to hymself; that he wyll determyne with hymselfe no longer to cheryshe that pestilent and peynefull dysease: and, seynge hys lyfe ys to hym but a tourmente, that he wyll nott bee vnwyllynge too dye, but rather take a good hope to hym, and other dyspatche hymselfe owte of that paynfull lyffe, as owte of a pryson or a racke of tormente, or elles suffer hym selfe wyllynglye to be rydde owte of yt by other. And in so doynge they tell hym he shal doo wyselye, seynge by hys deathe he shall lyse no commodytye, but ende hys payne. And bycause in that acte he shall followe the cownsell of the pryestes, that is to saye of the interpreters of goddes wyll and pleasure, they shewe hym that he shall do lyke a godly and a vertuouse man. They that be thus persuaded fynyshe theyre lyues wyllynglye, othere wyth hunger, or elles dye in theyre sleape wythowte annye fealinge of deathe. But they cause none suche to dye agaynste hys wyll; nor they vse no lesse dilygence and attendaunce about hym; beleuynge thys to be an honorable deathe. Elles he that kylleth hym selfe before that the pryestes and the cownsell haue allowed the cause of hys deathe, hym, as vnworthy both of the earth and of fyer, they cast vnburied into some stinkyng marrish.

OF UTOPIA

The woman is not maried before she be xviii. yeres olde. The man is iiii. yeres elder before he mary. If other the man or the woman be proued to haue bodely offended, before their marriage, with an other, he or she whether it be is sharpely punyshed; and both the offenders be forbydden euer after in all their lyfe to marrye, oneles the faulte be forgeuen by the princes pardone. But bothe the good man and the good wyfe of the house where that offence was done, as beyng slacke and neglygent in lokyng to there chardge, be in daunger of great reproche and infamye. That offence is so sharpelye punyshed, bicause they perceaue, that onles they be diligentlye kept from the lybertie of this vice, fewe wyll ioyne together in the loue of marriage; wherin all the lyfe must be led with one, and also all the griefes and displeasures that come therewith must paciently be taken and borne.

Furthermore, in cheusyng wyfes and husbandes they obserue earnestly and straytelye a custome whiche semed to vs very fonde and folysh. For a sad and an honest matrone sheweth the woman, be she maide or widdowe, naked to the wower. And lykewyse a sage and discrete man exhibyteth the wowere naked to the woman. At this custome we laughed and disalowed it as foolyshe. But they on the other part doo greatlye wonder at the follye of all other nations, whyche in byinge a colte, where as a lytle money is in hassarde, be so charye and circumspecte, that though he be almoste all bare, yet they wyll not bye hym, oneles the saddel and all the harneys be taken of, leaste vnder those couerynges be hydde som galle or soore; and yet in chewsynge a wyfe, whyche shalbe other pleasure or dyspleasure to them all theire lyfe after, they be so recheles, that, all the resydewe of the wooman's bodye beinge couered wyth cloothes, they esteme here scaselye be one handebredeth (for they can se no more but her face); and so do ioyne her to them not without great ieoperdie of euell agreing together, if any thynge in her body afterwarde do offende and myslyke them. For all men be not so wyse as to haue respecte to the vertuous condicions of the partie; and the endowmentes of the bodye cause the vertues of the mynde more to be estemed and regarded, yea, euen in the mariages of wyse men. Verely so fowle deformitie may be hydde vnder thoes coueringes, that it maye quite alienate and take awaye the mans mynde from his wyfe, when it shal not be lawfull for their bodies to be seperate agayne. If suche deformitie happen by any chaunce after the mariage is consumate and finyshed; well, there is no remedie but patience. Euery man must take his fortune, well a worthe. But it were well done that a lawe were made, wherebye all suche deceytes myghte be eschewed and aduoyded before hand. And thys were they constreyned more earnestlye to looke vpon, because they onlye of the nations in that parte of the worlde bee contente euerye man wyth one wyfe a piece; and matrymoney is there neuer broken, but by death; excepte adulterye breake the bonde, or els the intollerable waiward maners of eyther partie. For if either of them fynde themselfe for any suche cause greued; they maye by the licence of the councell chaunge and take an other. But the other partie lyueth euer after in infamye and out of wedlocke. But for the husbande to put away his wyfe for no faulte, but for that some myshappe is fallen to her bodye, thys by no meanes they wyll suffre. For they iudge it a greate poynte of crueltie that any body in their moste nede of helpe and comforte, shoulde be cast of and forsaken; and that olde age, whych both bryngeth sycknes with it, and is a syckenes it selfe, should vnkyndlye and vnfaythfullye be delte withall. But nowe and then it chaunseth, where as the man and the woman cannot well agree betwene themselfes, bothe of them fyndynge other with whome they hope to lyue more quyetlye and meryly, that they by the full consent of them both be diuorsed a sonder and newe maried to other; but that not without the aucthoritie of the councell; which agreeth to no dyuorses, before they and their wyfes haue diligently tried and examyned the matter. Yea and then also they be loth to consent to it, bicause they knowe thys to be the nexte waye to breke loue betwene man and wyfe, to be in easye hope of a newe mariage.

Breakers of wedlocke be punyshed with moste greuous bondage. And if both the offenders were maried, then the partyes whiche in that behalfe haue suffered wronge be diuorsed from the auoutrers if they wyll, and be maried together, or els to whom they luste. But if eyther of them both do styll contynewe in loue towarde so vnkynde a bedfellowe, the vse of wedlocke is not to them forbydden, if the partie be disposed to followe in toylinge and drudgerye the person, which for that offence is condempned to bondage. And very ofte it chaunceth that the repentaunce of the one, and the earnest diligence of the other, dothe so moue the prince with pytie and compassion, that he restoreth the bonde persone from seruitude to libertie and fredom again. But if the same partie be taken eftsones in that faulte, there is no other way but death.

To other trespaces there is no prescript punyshment appoynted by anye lawe. But accordinge to the heynousenes of the offence, or contrarye, so the punyshemente is moderated by the discretion of the councell. The husbandes chastice theire wyfes; and the parentes theire chyldren; oneles they haue done anye so horryble an offence, that the open punyshemente thereof maketh muche for the aduauncemente of honeste maners. But moste commenlye the moste heynous faultes be punyshed with the incommoditie of bondage. For that they suppose to be to the offenders no lesse griefe, and to the common wealth more profitable, then if they should hastely put them to death, and make them out of the waye. For there cummeth more profite of theire laboure, then of theire

deathe ; and by theire example they feare other the
lenger from lyke offences. But if they, beinge thus
vsed, doo rebell and kicke agayne, then forsothe they
be slayne as desperate and wilde beastes, whom nother
pryson nor chayne could restraine and kepe vnder.
But they whiche take theire bondage patientlye be not
left all hopeles. For after they haue bene broken and
tamed with longe myseries, yf then they shewe suche
repentaunce, wherebye it maye be perceaued that they
be soryer for theire offence then for theire punyshemente, sumtymes by the Prynces prerogatyue, and
sumtymes by the voyce and consent of the people,
theire bondage other is mitigated, or els cleane re-
mytted and forgeuen. He that moueth to aduoutrye
is in no lesse daunger and ieoperdie, then yf he hadde
committed aduoutrye in dede. For in all offences
they counte the intente and pretensed purpose as euell
as the acte or dede it selfe. For they thynke that no
lette owghte to excuse hym, that dyd hys beste too
haue no lette.

They sette greate store by fooles. And as it is
greate reproche to do to annye of them hurte or iniury,
so they prohibite not to take pleasure of foolyshnes.
For that, they thynke, doth muche good to the fooles.
And if any man be so sadde and sterne, that he cannot
laughe nother at their wordes nor at their dedes, none
of them be commytted to his tuition ; for feare lest he
would not ordre them gentilly and fauorably enough,
to whom they should brynge no delectation (for other
goodnes in them is none); muche lesse any proffyt
shoulde they yelde hym.

To mocke a man for hys deformitie, or for that he
lacketh anye parte or lymme of hys bodye, is counted
greate dishonestie and reproche, not to hym that is
mocked, but to hym that mocketh ; which vnwysely
doth imbrayde any man of that as a vice, whiche was
not in his powre to eschewe. Also as they counte and
reken very lyttell wytte to be in hym that regardeth

OF UTOPIA

not naturall bewtie and comlines, so to helpe the same with payntinges is taken for a vayne and a wanton pryde, not without great infamye. For they knowe euen by verye experience, that no comelines of bewtie doth so hyghly commende and auaunce the wyues in the conceyte of there husbandes, as honest conditions and lowlines. For as loue is oftentimes wonne with bewtie, so it is not kept, preserued, and continued, but by vertue and obedience.

They do not only feare theire people from doinge euell by punyshmentes, but also allure them to vertue with rewardes of honoure. Therfore they set vp in the market place the ymages of notable men, and of such as haue bene great and bounteful benefactors to the common wealth, for the perpetual memorie of their good actes; and also that the glory and renowme of the auncetors may sturre and prouoke theire posteritie to vertue. He that inordinatlie and ambitiously desireth promotions, is lefte all hopeles for euer atteynyng any promotion as longe as he liueth. They lyue together louingly. For no magistrate is other hawte or ferefull. Fathers they be called, and lyke fathers they vse themselfes. The citezens (as it is their dewtie) do willingly exhibite vnto them dewe honoure, without any compulsion. Nor the prince hymselfe is not knowen from the other by his apparel, nor by a crown or diademe or cappe of maintenaunce, but by a littell sheffe of corne caried before hym. And so a taper of wax is borne befor the byshop, whereby onely he is knowen.

Thei haue but few lawes. For to people so instructe and institute very fewe do suffice. Yea this thynge they chieflye reproue amonge other nations, that innumerable bokes of lawes and expositions vpon the same be not sufficient. But they thinke it against al right and iustice, that men shuld be bound to thoes lawes, whiche other be in numbre mo then be able to be readde, or els blinder and darker, then that any man can well vnderstande them. Furthermore they vtterly exclude and bannyshe all proctours and sergeauntes at the lawe, which craftely handell matters, and subtelly dispute of the lawes. For they thinke it most mete, that euery man shuld pleade his owne matter, and tell the same tale before the iudge, that he would tel to his man of lawe. So shall there be lesse circumstaunce of wordes, and the trwth shal soner cum to light; whiles the iudge with a discrete iudgement doth waye the wordes of hym whom no lawier hath instruct with deceit; and whiles he helpeth and beareth out simple wittes agaynst the false and malicious circumuertions of craftie chyldren. This is harde to be obserued in other countreis, in so infinitie a numbre of blynd and intricate lawes. But in Vtopia euery man is a cunnyng lawier. For, as I sayde, they haue verye fewe lawes; and the playnner and grosser that anye interpretation is, that they allowe as most iuste. For all lawes (saye they) bee made and publysshed onelye to thenthente, that by them euerye man shoulde be put in remembraunce of hys dewtye. But the craftye and subtyll interpretation of them can put verye fewe in that remembraunce (for they be but fewe that do perceaue them); where as the simple, the plaine, and grosse meaning of the lawes is open to euerye man. Els as touchynge the vulgare sorte of the people, whiche be bothe moste in numbre, and haue moste neade to knowe theire dewties, were it not as good for them that no lawe were made at all, as, when it is made, to brynge so blynde an interpretacion vpon it, that without greate witte and longe arguynge no man can discusse it? to the findinge out whereof nother the grosse iudgement of the people can attayne, nother the hole lyfe of them that be occupied in woorkynge for theire lyuynges can suffyse therto.

Thies vertues of the Vtopians haue caused theire nexte neyghbours and borderers, whiche lyue fre and vnder no subiection (for the Vtopians longe agoo haue delyuered manye of them from tyrannye), to take magistrates of them, some for a yeare, and some for fyue yeares space. Whiche, when the tyme of theire office is expired, they brynge home agayn with honoure and prayse; and take newe ons agayne wyth them into theire countrey. Thies nations haue vndowtedlye verye well and holsomlye prouyded for theire common wealthes. For seynge that bothe the makyng and the marrynge of the weale publique doth depende and hange of the maners of the rulers and magistrates, what officers coulde they more wyselye haue chosen, then thoes whiche cannot be ledde from honestye by brybes (for to them that shortlye after shall departe thens into theyre owne countreye money shoulde be vnprofytable); nor yet be moued other with fauour or malyce towardes annye man, as beynge straungers and vnaquainted with the people? The which twoo vices of affection and auryce where they take place in iudgementes, incontynente they breake iustice, the strongeste and suereste bonde of a common wealthe. Thies peoples, whiche fetche theire officers and rulers from them, the Vtopians cal theire fellowes; and other, to whome they haue bene beneficiall, they call theire frendes.

As towchynge leages, which in other places betwene countrey and countrey be so ofte concluded, broken, and made agayne, they neuer make none with anye nacion. For to what purpose serue leagues? saye they; as though nature had not set sufficient loue betwene man and man. And who so regardeth not nature, thynke yowe that he wyll passe for wordes? They be brought into thys opinion chiefely bicause that in thoes parties of the wordle leagues betwene princes be wont to be kept and obserued very slenderly. For here in Europa, and especiallye in thies partes, where the faythe and religion of Christe reygneth, the maiestie of leagues is euerye where estemed holly and inuiolable; partlye through the iustice and goodnes of princes, and partelye through the reuerence of great byshoppes. Whyche, lyke as they make no promysse themselfes, but they doo verye religiouslye perfourme the same, so they exhorte all prynces in any wyse to abyde by theyre promisses; and them that refuse or denye so to do, by theire pontificall powre and aucthorytie they compell therto. And surely they thynke well that it myght seme a verye reprochefull thynge, yf in the leagues of them, whyche by a peculiare name be called faythfull, faythe shoulde haue no place.

But in that newefonnde parte of the worlde, whiche is scaselye so farre from vs beyonde the lyne equinoctiall, as owre lyfe and manners be dissidente from theirs, no truste nor confydence is in leagues. But the mo and holyer cerymonies the league is knytte vp with, the soner it is broken, by some cauillation founde in the woordes; whyche manye tymes of purpose be so craftelye put in and placed, that the bandes can neuer be so sure nor so stronge, but they wyll fynde some hole open to crepe owte at, and to breake bothe league and trewthe. The whiche crafty dealynge, yea, the whiche fraude and deceyte, yf they shoulde knowe it to bee practysed amonge pryuate men in theire bargaynes and contractes, they woulde incontinent crye owte at it with a sower countenaunce, as an offence most detestable, and worthie to be punnyshed with a shamefull death; yea, euen verye they that auaunce themselfes authours of like councel geuen to princes. Wherfore it maye well be thought other that all iustice is but a basse and a lowe vertue, and whiche aualeth it self farre vnder the hyghe dignitie of kynges; or, at the least wyse, that there be two iustices; the one mete for the inferioure sorte of the people, goinge a fote and crepynge by lowe on the grounde, and bounde downe on euery side with many bandes, because it shall not run at rouers: the other a pryncely vertue, whiche lyke as it is of muche hygher maiestie then the other poore iustice, so also

OF UTOPIA 109

it is of muche more lybertie, as to the whiche nothinge is vnlawful that it lusteth after.

Thies maners of princes (as I sayde) whiche be there so euyll kepers of leagues cause the Vtopians, as I suppose, to make no leagues at all: whiche perchaunce woulde chaunge theire mynde if they lyued here. Howebeit they thynke that thoughe leagues be neuer so faythfully obserued and kept, yet the custome of makinge leagues was verye euel begonne. For this causeth men (as though nations which be separate a sondre by the space of a lytle hyl or a ryuer, were coupled together by no societe or bonde of nature), to thynke them selfes borne aduersaryes and enemyes one to an other; and that it is lawfull for the one to seke the death and destruction of the other, if leagues were not; yea, and that, after the leagues be accorded, fryndeshyppe dothe not growe and encrease; but the lycence of robbynge and stealynge doth styll remayne, as farfurthe as, for lacke of forsight and aduisement in writinge the woordes of the league, anny sentence or clause to the contrary is not therin suffycyentlye comprehended. But they be of a contrary opinion: that is, that no man ought to be counted an enemy, whyche hath done no iniury; and that the felowshyppe of nature is a stronge league; and that men be better and more surely knitte togethers by loue and beneuolence, then by couenauntes of leagues; by hartie affection of minde, then by woordes.

L

[Chapter VIII]

Of warfare,

Warre or battel as a thinge very beastelye, and yet to no kynde of beastes in so muche vse as it is to man, they do detest and abhorre; and, contrarye to the custome almost of all other natyons, they cownte nothinge so much against glorie, as glory gotten in warre. And therefore, though they do daily practise and exercise themselfes in the discypline of warre, and that not only the men, but also the women, vpon certeyne appoynted dayes, leste they shoulde be to seke in the feat of armes yf nead should requyre; yet they neuer [to] goo to battayle, but other in the defence of their owne cowntreye, or to dryue owte of theyr frendes lande the enemyes that be comen in, or by their powre to deliuer from the yocke and bondage of tyrannye some people that be oppressed wyth tyranny. Whyche thynge they doo of meere pytye and compassion. Howebeit they sende healpe to theyre fryndes; not euer in theire defence, but sumtimes also to requyte and reuenge iniuries before to them done. But thys they do not, onles their counsell and aduise in the matter be asked, whyles yt ys yet newe and freshe. For yf they fynde the cause probable, and yf the contrarye parte wyll not restore agayne suche thynges as be of them iustelye demaunded, then they be the chyeffe auctores and makers of the warre. Whyche they do not onlye as ofte as by inrodes and inuasions of soldiours prayes and booties be dreuen away, but then also much more mortally, when their frindes marchauntes in any land, other vnder the pretence of vniust lawes, or els by the

OF UTOPIA

wresting and wronge vnderstonding of good lawes, do sustaine an vniust accusation vnder the colour of iustice. Nother the battel which the vtopians fowghte for the Nephelogetes against the Alaopolitanes, a lytle before oure time, was made for annye other cause, but that the Nephelogete marchaunte men, as the vtopians thought, suffred wrong of the Alaopolitanes, vnder the pretence of righte. But whether it were righte or wrong, it was with so cruell and mortal warre reuenged, the countreis round about ioyning their healpe and powre to the puysaunce and malice of bothe parties, that most florishing and wealthie peoples beyng some of them shrewedely shaken, and some of them sharpely beaten, the mischeues were not finished nor ended, untill the Alaopolitanes at the last were yelded vp as bondmen into the iurisdiction of the Nephelogetes. For the vtopians foughte not this warre for themselfes. And yet the Nephelogetes before the warre, when the Alaopolitanes flourished in wealth, were nothyng to be compared with them.

So egerly the Vtopians prosequute the iniuries done to ther frindes, yea, in money matters; and not their owne likewise. For if they by coueyne or gyle be wiped beside their gooddes, so that no violence be done to their bodies, they wreake their anger by absteining from occupieng with that nation, untill they haue made satisfaction. Not for bicause they set lesse stoore by their owne cytyzeyns, then by theire frindes; but that they take the losse of their fryndes money more heuely then the losse of theyr owne: bicause that their frindes marchaunte men, forasmuche as that they leise is their owne priuate gooddes, susteyne great damage by the losse; but their owne citizeyns leise nothing but of the commen gooddes, and of that which was at home plentifull and almost superfluous, elles hadde it not bene sent furth. Therfore no man feeleth the losse. And for this cause

they thynke it to cruell an acte to reuenge that losse
wyth the death of many; the incommoditie of the
whiche losse no man feeleth nother in his liffe, nother
in his liuinge. But if it chaunce that any of their
men in any other countreye be maymed or kylled, 5
whether it be done by a commen or a priuate councell;
knowing and trying out the treuth of the matter by
their ambassadours, onles the offenders be rendered
vnto them in recompence of the iniury, they will not
be appeased; but incontinent they proclayme warre 10
against them. The offenders yelded they punnishe
other with death or with bondage.

They be not only sorye, but also ashamed to atchieue
the victory with much bloodshed; cowntinge it greate
follye to bye pretyous wares to dere. They reioyse 15
and auaunte themselfes, yf they vaynquyshe and
oppresse theire enemyes by crafte and deceyt. And
for that act they make a generall tryumphe; and as
yf the matter were manfullye handeled, they sett vp
a pyller of stone in the place where they so van- 20
quysshed theyre ennemyes, in token of the vyctory.
For then they glorye, then they booste and cracke
that they haue plaied the men in dede, when they
haue so ouercommen, as no other lyuynge creature
but onely man coulde; that ys to saye, by the myghte 25
and pusyaunce of wytte. For wyth boddelye strengthe
(saye they) beares, lyons, boores, wulffes, dogges, and
other wylde beastes doo fyghte. And as the mooste
parte of them doo passe vs in strengthe and fyerce
courage, so in wytte and reason wee be muche stronger 30
then they all.

Theyre chyefe and princypall purpose in warre ys
to obteyne that thynge, whyche yf they had before
obteyned, they wolde not haue moued battayle. But
if that be not possible, they take so cruell vengeaunce 35
of them whych be in the fault, that euer after they be
aferde to doo the lyke. Thys ys theyre cheyffe and
pryncypall intente, whyche they immedyatelye and

OF UTOPIA

fyrste of all prosequute and sette forewarde; but yet so, that they be more cyrcumspecte in auoydynge and eschewynge ieopardyes, then they be desyerous of prayse and renowne. Therfore immediatly after that warre is ones solemply denounced, they procure manye proclamations, signed with their owne commen seale, to be sett up preuilie at one time in their ennemyes lande, in places mooste frequented. In thyes proclamatyons they promysse greate rewardes to hym that will kyll their enemies prince; and sumwhat lesse gyftes, but them verye greate also, for euerye heade of them, whose names be in the sayde proclamacions conteined. They be those whome they count their chieffe aduersaries, next vnto the prince. What soeuer is prescribed vnto him that killeth any of the proclamed persons, that is dobled to him that bringeth any of the same to them aliue: yea, and to the proclamed persones them selfes, if they wil chaunge their mindes and come into them, takinge their partes, they profer the same greate rewardes with pardon, and suerty of their liues.

Therfore it quickely cummeth to passe that they haue al other men in suspicion, and be vnfaithfull and mistrusting emong themselfes one to another; liuing in great feare and in no lese ieopardye. For it is well knowen that dyuers times the most part of them, and specially the prince him selfe, hath bene betraied of them in whome they put their most hoope and trust. So that there is no maner of acte nor dede, that giftes and rewardes do not enforce men vnto. And in rewardes they kepe no measure; but, remembring and considering into howe great hasard and ieopardie they call them, endeuoure themselfes to recompence the greatenes of the daunger with lyke great benefites. And therfore they promisse not only wonderfull greate abundaunce of golde, but also landes of greate reuenues, lyenge in moost sauffe placoo omongo thoiro fryndes And theyre promysses they perfourme faythfully, wythowte annye fraude or couyne.

Thys custome of byinge and sellynge aduersaryes amonge other people ys dysallowed, as a cruell acte of a basse and a cowardyshe mynde. But they in thys behalfe thynke themselfes muche prayse woorthye, as who lyke wyse men by thys meanes dyspatche greate warres wyth owte annye battell or skyrnyshe. Yea, they cownte yt also a dede of pyty and mercye, bycause that by the deathe of a fewe offenders the lyues of a greate numbre of ynnocentes, aswell of their own men as also of their enemies, be raunsomed and saued, which in fighting shoulde haue bene sleane. For they doo no lesse pytyo the basse and commen sorte of theyr enemyes people, then they doo theyre owne; knowynge that they be dryuen to warre agaynste theyre wylles by the furyous madnes of theyre prynces and heades.

Yf by none of thies meanes the matter go forwarde as they wolde haue yt, then they procure occasyons of debate and dyssentyon to be spredde emonge theyre enemyes; as by bryngynge the prynces brother, or some of the noble men, in hoope to obtayne the kyngedome. Yf thys way preuayle not, then they reyse vp the people that be nexte neygheboures and borderers to theyr enemyes, and them they sette in theyre neckes vnder the coloure of some olde tytle of ryghte, suche as kynges doo neuer lacke. To them they promysse theire helpe and ayde in theyre warre. And as for moneye they gyue them abundance; but of theyre owne cytyzeyns they sende to them fewe or none. Whome they make so much of, and loue so intyerlye, that they wolde not be willing to chaung anye of them for their aduersaries prince. But their gold and siluer, bycause they kepe yt all for thys only purpose, they laye it owte frankly and frely; as who shoulde lyue euen as wealthely, if they hadde bestowed it euerye pennye. Yea, and besydes theyre ryches,

OF UTOPIA

whyche they kepe at home, they haue also an infynyte treasure abrode, by reason that (as I sayde before) manye natyons be in their debte. Therefore they hyere soldyours oute of all countreys, and sende them to battayle; but cheiflye of the Zapoletes. Thys people is .500. myles from Vtopia eastewarde. They be hydeous, sauage, and fyerce, dwellynge in wild woodes and high mountaines, where they were bredde and brought vp. They be of an harde nature, able to abide and susteine heate, cold, and labour; abhorrynge from all delycate deyntyes, occupyenge no husbandrye nor tyllage of the ground, homelye and rude both in the buildinge of their houses and in their apparrell; geuen vnto no goodnes, but onelye to the breede and bringynge vp of cattell. The mooste parte of theire lyuynge is by huntynge and stealynge. They be borne onelye to warre, whyche they dylygentlye and earnestlye seke for. And when they haue gotten yt, they be wonders gladde therof. They goo furthe of theyre countreye in greate companyes together, and who soeuer lacketh souldyours, there they proffer theyre seruyce for small wages. Thys ys onely the crafte that they haue to gette theyre lyuynge by. They maynteyne theyr lyfe by sekyng theyre deathe. For them, whomewyth they be in wayges, they fyghte hardelye, fyerslye, and faythefullye. But they bynde themselfes for no certeyne tyme. But vpon thys condytion they entre into bondes, that the nexte daye they wyll take parte wyth the other syde for greatter wayges; and the nexte daye after that they wyll be readye to come backe agayne for a lytle more moneye. There be fewe warres there awaye, wherin is not a greate numbre of them in bothe partyes. Therefore yt daylye chauncethe that nye kynsefolke, whyche were hiered together on one parte, and there verye fryndelye and famylyerly vsed themselfes one wyth an other, shortely after, beynge separate into contrarye partes, runne one agaynste an other enuyouslye and fyercelye;

and forgettynge bothe kyndred and frendeshyp, thruste
theyre swordes one in another: and that for none
other cause, but that they be hyered of contrarye
pryncos for a lytle moneye. Whyche they doo so
hyghelye regarde and esteame, that they will easelye 5
be prouoked to chaunge partes for a halfpenye more
wayges by the daye. So quyckelye they haue taken
a smacke in couetesenes; whyche for all that ys to
them no proffyte. For, that they gette by fyghtynge,
ymmedyatelye they spende vnthryftelye and wretched- 10
lye in ryott.

Thys people fyghte for the Vtopyans agaynste all
natyons, bycause they giue them greatter wayges, then
annye other natyon wyll. For the Vtopians, lyke as
they seke good men to vse wel, so they seke thyes 15
euell and vycyous men to abuse. Whome, when neade
requyreth, wyth promisses of greate rewardes they
putt furthe into greate ieopardyes; from whens the
mooste part of them neuer cummeth againe to aske
their rewardes. But to them that remain on liue 20
they paye that which they promissed faithfully, that
they may be the more willinge to put themselfes in
like daungers another time. Nor the Vtopians passe
not how many of them they bring to distruction.
For they beleue that they should doo a very good 25
deade for all mankind, if they could ridde out of the
wordle all that fowle, stinkinge denne of that most
wicked and cursed people.

Next vnto thies they vse the soldiours of them
whom they fight for. And then the help of their 30
other frindes. And last of al they ioyne to their owne
citizeins. Emong whome they gyue to one of tried
vertue and prowes the rewle, goouernaunce, and conductyon of the hole armye. Vnder hym they appoynte
ii. other, whyche whyles he ys sauffe be bothe pryuate 35
and owte of offyce; but yf he be taken or slayne, the
one of the other .ii. succedeth hym, as yt were by
inherytaunce. And if the second miscarry, then the

OF UTOPIA

third taketh hys rowme; leaste that (as the chaunce
of battell ys vncerteyne and dowtefull), the yeopardye
or deathe of the capytayne shoulde brynge the hole
armye in hasarde. They chuse soldyers owte of
euerye cytye those whyche putt furthe themselfes
wyllynglye. For they thruste no man furthe into
warre agaynste hys wyll; bycause they beleue, yf
annye man be fearefull and faynte harted of nature,
he wyll not onelye doo no manfull and hardye act hym
selfe, but also be occasyon of cowardenes to hys
fellowes. But yf annye battell be made agaynste
theyre owne countreye, then they putt thyes cowardes,
so that they be stronge bodyed, in shyppes emonge
other bolde harted men. Or elles they dyspose them
vpon the walles, from whens they maye not flye. Thus,
what for shame that theyre ennemyes be at hande,
and what for bycause they be withowt hope of
runnynge awaye, they forgette all feere. And manye
tymes extreame necessytye turneth cowardnes into
prowes and manlynes.

But as none of them ys thrust forthe of his countrey
into warre agaynste hys wyll, so women that be
wyllynge to accompanye their husbandes in times
of warre be not prohybyted or stopped. Yea, they
prouoke and exhorte them to yt wyth prayses. And
in sett fylde the wyues doo stande euerye one by here
owne husbandes syde. Also euery man is compassed
nexte abowte wyth hys owne chyldren, kins folkes,
and alliaunce; that they, whom nature chiefelye
moueth to mutuall succoure, thus stondynge together,
maye helpe one an other. It is a great reproche and
dishonestie for the husbande to come home wythowte
hys wiffe, or the wiffe withoute her husband, or the
sonne without his father. And therfore, if the other
part sticke so harde by it, that the battell come to
their handes, it is fought with great slaughter and
bloodshed, euen to the vtter destruction of both partes.
For as they make all the meanes and shyftes that

maye be, to kepe themselfes from the necessitye of fyghtynge, so that they may dispatche the battell by their hiered soldyours, so, when there is no remedy but that they muste neades fyghte themselfes, then they do as corragiouslye fall to it, as before, whyles they myght, they dyd wyselye auoyde it. Nor they be not moste fierce at the fyrst bronte. But in continuaunce by litle and lytle theire fierce corrage encreaseth, with so stubborne and obstynate myndes, that they wyll rather die then gyue backe an ynche. For that suertye of lyuynge, whiche euery man hath at home, beynge ioyned with noo carefull anxietye or remembraunce how theire posteritie shall lyue after them (for this pensifenes oftentymes breaketh and abateth couragious stomakes) maketh them stowte and hardy, and dysdaynful to be conquered. Moreouer, theire knowledge in cheualrye and feates of armes putteth them in a good hope. Finally, the holsome and vertuous opinions, wherin they were brought vp euen from theire childhode, partely through learnyng, and partelye throughe the good ordenaunces and lawes of theire weale publique, augmente and encrease theire manfull currage. By reason whereof they nother set so litle store by theire liues, that they will rasshely and vnaduisedlye cast them away; nor they be not so farre in lewde and fond loue therewith, that they will shamefully couete to kepe them, when honestie biddeth leaue them.

When the battel is hottest and in al places most fierce and feruent, a bende of chosen and picked yong men, whiche be sworne to liue and dye togethers, take vpon them to destroye theire aduersaries capitaine. Hym they inuade, now with preuy wyeles, now by open strength. At hym they strike both nere and farre of. He is assayled with a long and a continewal assault; freshe men styll commyng in the weried mens places. And seldome it chaunceth (onles he

saue hymselfe by flying) that he is not other slayne,
or els taken prysoner, and yelded to his enemies alyue.
If they wynne the fyelde, they persecute not theire
enemies with the violent rage of slaughter. For they
had rather take them aliue then kyll them. Nother 5
they do so followe the chase and pursute of theire
enemies, but they leaue behynde them one parte of
theire hoste in battayl arraye vnder theire standardys.
In so muche that, if all theire hole armie be discum-
fetyd and ouercum, sauing the rerewarde, and that 10
they therewith achieue the victory, then they had
rather lette all theire enemies scape, then to followe
them owt of array. For they remembre it hath
chaunced vnto themselfes more then ones: the hole
powre and strength of theyre hoste being vanquished 15
and put to flight, whiles theire enemies, reioysing
in the victory, haue persecuted them flying, some
one way and some an other; fewe of theire men
lying in an ambusshe, there reddy at all occasions,
haue sodaynly rysen vpon them thus dispersed and 20
scattered owt of array, and through presumption of
safetye vnaduisedly pursuynge the chase, and haue
incontinent changed the fortune of the hole battayll;
and spyte of there tethes wrestynge owt of theire
handes the sure and vndowted victory, being a litle 25
before conquered, haue for theire parte conquired the
conquerers.

It is hard to say whether they be craftier in laynge
an ambusshe, or wittier in auoydynge the same.
Yowe woulde thynke they intende to flye, when they 30
meane nothing lesse. And contrary wise, when they
go about that purpose, yow wold beleue it were the
least part of their thoughte. For if they perceaue
themselfes other ouermatched in numbre, or closed in
to narrowe a place, then they remoue their campe 35
other in the nyght season with silence, or by some
pollicie they deceaue theire enemies; or in the daye
time they retiere backe so softely, that it is no lesse

ieoperdie to medle with them when they gyue backe then when they preese on. They fence and fortifie theire campe sewerlye with a deape and a brode trenche. The earth therof is cast inward. Nor they do not set drudgeis and slaues a worke about it. It is doone by the handes of the souldiours them selfes. All the hole armye worketh vpon it, except them that watche in harneis before the trenche for sodeyne auentures. Therefore, by the labour of so manye, a large trenche closinge in a great compasse of grounde is made in lesse tyme then any man wold beleue.

Theire armoure or harneis whiche they weare is sure and stronge to receaue strokes, and handsome for all mouinges and gestures of the bodye; in so muche that it is not vnweldy to swymme in. For in the discipline of theire warefare, amonge other feates thei lerne to swimme in harneis. Their weapons be arrowes afarre of, which they shote both strongely and suerly; not onelye fotemen but also horsemen. At hande strokes they vse not swordes but pollaxes, whiche be mortall, aswel in sharpenes as in weyghte, bothe for foynes and downe strokes. Engines for warre they deuyse and inuente wonders wittely. Whiche, when they be made, they kepe very secret; leaste if they should be knowen before neade requyre, they should be but laughed at, and serue to no purpose. But in makynge them, hereunto they haue chiefe respecte; that they be both easy to be caried, and handsome to be moued and turned about.

Truce taken with theire enemies for a shorte time they do so fermelye and faythfully keape, that they wyll not breake it; no not though they be theire vnto prouoked. They do not waste nor destroy there enemies lande with forraginges, nor they burne not vp theire corne. Yea, they saue it as muche as maye be from beinge ouerrune and troden downe, other

OF UTOPIA

with men or horses; thynkynge that it groweth for theire owne vse and proffyt. They hurt no man that is vnarmed, onles he be an espiall. All cities that be yelded vnto them, they defende. And suche as they wynne by force of assaute they nother dispoyle nor sacke; but them that withstode and dyswaded the yeldynge vp of the same they put to death; the other souldiours they punnyshe with bondage. All the weake multitude they leaue vntouched. If they knowe that anye cytezeins counselled to yelde and rendre vp the citie, to them they gyue parte of the condempned mens goodes. The resydewe they distribute and gyue frely amonge them, whose helpe they had in the same warre. For none of them selfes taketh anye portion of the praye.

But when the battayll is fynyshed and ended, they put theire frendes to neuer a penny coste of al the chardges that they were at, but laye it vpon theire neckes that be conquered. Them they burdeyne with the hole chardge of theire expenceis; which they demaunde of them partelye in money, to be kept for lyke vse of battayll, and partelye in landes of greate reuenues, to be payde vnto them yearlye for euer. Suche reuenues they haue nowe in manye countreis; whiche by litle and lytle rysyng, of dyuers and sondry causes, be encreased aboue vii. hundreth thousand ducates by the yere. Thither they sende furth some of their citezeins as Lieuetenauntes, to lyue theire sumptuously lyke men of honoure and renowne. And yet, this notwithstanding, muche money is saued, which commeth to the commen treasory; onles it so chaunce, that thei had rather truste the countrey with the money. Which many times thei do so long vntil they haue neade to occupie it. And it seldomo happeneth, that thei demaund al. Of thies landes thei assigne part vnto them, which at their request and exhortacion put themselfes in such ieoperdies as I spake of before. If anye prynce stirre vp warre agaynst them, intendyng

to inuade theire lande, they mete hym incontinent owt of theire owne borders with great powre and strengthe. For they neuer lyghtly make warre in their owne countreis. Nor
       they be neuer brought into so ex-
        treme necessitie, as to take
         helpe out of forreyne
          landes into thire
           owne Ilande.

[CHAPTER IX]

Of the reli=
gyons in Vtopia.

There be dyuers kyndes of religion, not only in sondry partes of the Ilande, but also in dyuers places of euerye citie. Some worshyp for God the sunne; some the mone; some some other of the planetes. There be that gyue worshyp to a man that was ones of excellente vertue or of famous glory, not only as God, but also as the chiefest and hyghest God. But the moste and the wysest parte (reiectynge all thies) beleue that there is a certayne Godlie powre unknowen, euerlastyng, incomprehensible, inexplicable, farre aboue the capacitie and retche of mans witte, dispersed through out all the worlde, not in bygnes, but in vertue and powre. Hym they call the father of all. To hym allone they attrybute the begynnynges, the encreasynges, the procedynges, the chaunges, and the endes of all thynges. Nother they gyue deuine honours to any other then to him.

Yea, all the other also, though they be in diuers opinions, yet in this pointe they agree all togethers with the wisest sort, in beleuynge that there is one chiefe and pryncipall God, the maker and ruler of the hole worlde; whome they all commonly in theire countrey language call Mythra. But in this they disagre, that amonge some he is counted one, and amonge some an other. For euery one of them, whatsoeuer that is whiche he taketh for the chiefe God, thynketh it to be the very same nature, to whose onlye deuyne myght and maiestie the som and soueraintie of al thinges, by the consent of all people, is attributed and geuen. Howe be it, they al begynne by litle and litle to forsake and fall from thys varietie of superstitions, and to agree togethers in that religion whiche semethe by reason to passe and excell the resydewe. And it is not to be dowted but all the other would longe agoo haue bene abolyshed; but that, whatsoeuer vnprosperous thynge happened to any of them as he was mynded to chaunge his religion, the fearefulnes of people dyd take it not as a thynge cummynge by chaunce, but as sente frome God owt of heauen; as thoughe the God, whose honoure he was forsakynge, woulde reuenge that wicked purpose against him.

But after they harde vs speake of the name of Christe, of his doctryne, lawes, myracles, and of the no lesse wonderful constancie of so manye martyrs, whose bloude wyllynglye shedde brought a great numbre of nations throughe out all partes of the worlde into theire secte; yowe wyll not beleue with howe gladde myndes they agreed vnto the same; whether it were by the secrete inspiration of God, or els for that they thought it next vnto that opinion which amonge them is counted the chiefest. Howe be it, I thynke this was no smal healpe and further-aunce in the matter, that they harde vs saye that Christ instytuted amonge hys all thynges commen; and that the same communitie dothe yet remayne amongest the rightest Christian companies. Verely, howe soeuer it came to passe, manye of them consented togethers in oure religion, and were wasshed in the hollye water of baptisme.

But because amonge vs foure (for no moo of vs was left alyue; two of oure companye beynge deade) there was no prieste, whiche I am ryghte sorye for, they, beinge entered and instructed in all other poyntes of oure relygion, lacke onelye those Sacramentes, whyche here none but priestes do minister. Howe be it, they vnderstande and perceyue them, and be verye desierous

OF UTOPIA

of the same. Yea, they reason and dispute the matter earnestly amonge themselfes, whether, without the sendyng of a christian bysshoppe, one chosen out of theire owne people may receaue the ordre of priesthode. And truly they were mynded to chuse one: but at my departure from them they hadde chosen none. They also, whiche do not agree to Christes religion, feare no man frome it, nor speake agaynste anye man that hath receyued it. Sauing that one of oure companye in my presence was sharpely punyshed. He, as sone as he was baptised, began against our willes, with more earnest affection then wisdome, to reason of Christes religion; and began to waxe so hotte in his matter, that he dyd not only preferre oure relygion before all other, but also dyd vtterlye despise an condempne al other, callynge them prophane, and the followers of them wicked and deuelishe, and the chyldren of euerlasting dampnation. When he had thus longe reasoned the matter, they layde holde on hym, accused hym, and condempned hym into exyle; not as a despyser of religion, but as a sedicious persone, and a rayser vp of dissention amonge the people. For this is one of the auncientest lawes amonge them: that no man shalbe blamed for reasonynge in the mayntenaunce of his owne religion.

For kyng Vtopus, euen at the first begynning, hearing that the inhabitauntes of the lande were before his commyng thether at contynuall dissention and stryfe among themselfes for their religions; perceyuing also that this common dissention, whyles euerye seuerall secte tooke seuerall partes in fyghting for theire countrey, was the only occasion of hys conquest ouer them all; assone as he had gotten the victory, first of all he made a decrie, that it shoulde be lawfull for euery man to fauoure and followe what religion he would, and that he myght do the beste he cold to bryng other to his opinion; so that he dyd it peaceably, gentelye, quyetly, and soberlye, without hastye and contentious rebuking and inuehyng against other. If he coulde not by fayre and gentle speche induce them vnto his opinion, yet he should vse no kinde of violence, and refrayne from displeasaunt and seditious woordes. To him that would vehemently and feruentlye in this cause striue and contend, was decreid bannishment or bondage.

This lawe did kynge Vtopus make, not only for the maintenaunce of peace, which he sawe through continuall contention and mortal hatred vtterly extinguished, but also because he thought this decrye shuld make for the furtheraunce of religion. Wherof he durst define and determine nothing vnaduisedly; as dowting whether god, desieryng manifolde and diuers sortes of honoure, would inspire sondrie men with sondrie kyndes of religion. And this suerly he thought a very vnmete and folishe thing, and a pointe of arrogant presumption, to compell all other by violence and threatenynges to agre to the same that thou beleuest to bee trewe. Furthermore though there be one religion whiche alone is trewe, and all other vayne and superstitious, yet did he well forsee (so that the matter were handeled with reason and sober modestie), that the trewthe of the owne powre woulde at the laste issue owte and come to lyght. But if contention and debate in that behalfe shoulde continuallye be vsed, as the woorste men be moste obstynate and stubburne, and in theire euell opynion moste constante; he perceaued that then the beste and holyest religion woulde be troden vnder foote and destroyed by moste vayne superstitions; euen as good corne is by thornes and weydes ouergrowen and choked. Therfore al this matter he lefte vndiscussed, and gaue to euery man free libertie and choyse to beleue what he woulde; sauinge that he earnestly and straytelye chardged them, that no man shoulde conceaue so vile and base an opinion of the dignitie of mans nature, as to thinke that the sowles do dye

and perishe with the bodye; or that the worlde
runneth at al auentures, gouerned by no diuine
prouidence. And therfore thei beleue that after this
lyfe vices be extreamely punyshed, and vertues
bountyfully rewarded. Hym that is of a contrary
opinion they counte not in the numbre of men, as
one that hath aualed the hyghe nature of his sowle
to the vielnes of brute beastes bodies; muche lesse
in the numbre of their citiziens, whoes lawes and
ordenaunces, if it were not for feare, he wold nothing
at al esteme. For yow may be suer that he wil study
other with crafte preuely to mock, or els violently to
breake, the commen lawes of his countrey, in whom
remayneth no further feare then of the lawes, nor no
further hope then of the bodye. Wherefore he that
is thus mynded is depryued of all honours, excluded
from all offices, and reiecte from all common adminis-
trations in the weale publyque. And thus he is of
all sorte despysed as of an vnprofitable and of a base
and vile nature. Howe be it they put hym to no
punyshemente, because they be perswaded that it is
in no mans powre to beleue what he lyst. No,
nor they constrayne hym not with threatninges to
dissemble his minde, and shewe countenaunce contrary to his thoughte. For deceite, and falshed, and
all maner of lyes, as next vnto fraude, they do
meruelouslye deteste and abhorre. But they suffre
him not to dispute in his opinion, and that onlye
emong the commen people. For elles a parte, emong
the pryestes and men of grauity, they doo not only
suffre but also exhorte him to dispute and argue;
hoopinge that at the laste that madnes will giue place
to reason.

There be also other, and of them no small numbre,
whych be not forbidden to speake their mindes, as
grounding their opinion vpon some reason; being in
their liuinge nother euell nor vitious. Their heresye
is much contrary to the other   For they beleue that

the soules of brute beastes be immortall and euerlasting; but nothinge to be compared with owers in dignitie, nother ordeyned and predestinate to like felicitie. For all they beleue certeinly and sewerly, that mans blesse shall be so greate, that they doo morne and lamente euerye mans sicknes, but no mans death; oneles it be one whom they see depart from his liffe carfully, and agaynst his will. For this they take for a very euell token, as though the sowle, beinge in dyspayre and vexed in conscience, through some preuy and secret forefeilyng of the punnishment now at hande, were aferde to depart. And they thinke he shall not be welcome to God, whyche, when he ys called, runneth not to hym gladly, but ys drawen by force and sore agaynste hys wyll. They therfore that see thys kynde of deathe doo abhorre it, and them that so die they burye wyth sorrow and silence. And when they haue prayed God to be mercifull to the sowle, and mercifully to pardon the infirmities therof, they couer the dead coorse with earthe.

Contrarye wise, all that depart merely and ful of good hoope, for them no man mournethe, but followethe the heerse with ioyfull synging, commending the soules to god with great affection. And at the last not with mourning sorrow, but with a great reuerence, they bourne the bodies; and in the same place they set vp a piller of stone, with the deade mans titles therin graued. When they be comme home they reherse his vertuouse maners and his good dedes. But no parte of his liffe is soo oft or gladly talked of as his mery deathe. They thinke that this remembraunce of their vertue and goodnes doth vehementely prouoke and enforce the quicke to vertue; and that nothing can be more pleasaunt and acceptable to the dead; whom they suppose to be present emong them when they talke of them, though to the dull and feoble eye sight of mortall men they be inuisible.

OF UTOPIA

For it were an vnconuenient thinge, that the blessed shoulde not be at libertye to goo whether they wold. And it were a poynte of greate vnkyndnes in them, to haue vtterly caste awaye the desyer of vysytynge and seynge their frindes, to whome they were in theyr lyfe tyme ioyned by mutuall loue and charytye; whych in good men after theyre deathe they cownte to be rather encreasede then dymynyshede. They beleue therefore that the deade be presentlye conuersaunte emong the quicke, as beholders and witnesses of all their woordes and deedes. Therefore they go more corragiously to their busines, as hauing a trust and affiaunce in such ouerseers. And this same belefe of the present conuersacion of their forefathers and auncetours emonge them fearethe them from all secrete dishonesty.

They vtterly despise and mocke sothe sayinges and diuinacions of thinges to come by the flighte or voyces of birdes, and all other diuinations of vayne superstition, which in other countreys be in great obseruation. But they highly esteame and worshippe miracles, that come by no helpe of nature, as workes and witnesses of the presente powre of God. And such they saye doo chaunce there very often. And sumtimes in great and dowtefull matters, by commen intercession and prayers, they procure and obteyne them with a suer hoope and confidence and a stedfast beleffe.

They thinke that the contemplacion of nature, and the prayse thereof cumminge, is to God a very acceptable honour. Yet there be many so earnestly bent and affectioned to religion, that they passe no thinge for learning, nor giue their mindes to no knowledge of thinges. But ydelnes they vtterly forsake and eschue, thinkinge felicitie after this liffe to be gotten and obteined by busy labors and good exercises. Some therfore of them attende vpon the sicke, some amend highe waies, clense ditches, repaire bridges, digge turfes, grauell, and stones, fell and cleaue woode, bring wood, corne, and other thinges into the cities in cartes, and serue not onlye in commen woorkes, but also in pryuate laboures, as seruauntes, yea, more then bondmen. For what so euer vnpleasaunte, harde, and vile worke is any where, from the which labour, lothsumnes, and desperation doth fraye other, all that they take vpon them willingly and gladly; procuring quyete and rest to other; remayning in continuall woorke and labour themselfes; not embrayding others there wyth. They nother reproue other mens liues, nor glorye in theire owne. Thies men, the more seruiseable they behaue them selfes, the moore they be honoured of all men.

Yet they be diuided into ii. sectes. The one is of them that liue single and chast, absteining not only from the company of women, but al so from the eating of flesh, and some of them from al maner of beastes. Which, vtterly reiectynge the pleasures of this present lyffe as hurtefull, be all hollye set vpon the dessire of the lyffe to come; by watchynge and sweatynge hoping shortely to obtaine it, beyng in the meane season meerye and lustye. The other sect is no lesse desyerous of labour, but they embrace matrimony; not despising the solace therof; thinking that they can not be discharged of theire bounden duetyes towardes nature withoute labour and toyle nor towardes their natiue countreye, wythowte procreacion of chyldren. They abstayne from no pleasure that dothe nothynge hynder them from laboure. They loue the fleshe of fourefoted beastes, bycause they beleue that by that meate they be made hardier and stronger to woorke. The Vtopians count this secte the wiser, but the other the hollier. Which, in that they preferre single liffe before matrimony, and that sharpe liffe before an easier liffe, if herin they grounded vpon reason, they wold mock them; but now, forasmuch as they say they be ledde to it by

OF UTOPIA

religion, they honour and worship them. And thies be they whome in their language by a peculyare name they call Buthrescas, the whyche woorde by interpretation signifieth to vs men of religion, or religious men.

They haue pryestes of exceding hollines, and therefore very few. For there be but xiii. in euery city, according to the number of theire churches, sauynge when they go furth to battell. For than vii. of them goo furthe wyth the armye: in whose steades so manye newe be made at home. But the other, at theyre retourne home, agayn reentre euery one into his own place. They that be aboue the numbre, vntyll suche tyme as they succede into the places of the other at theyre dyinge, be in the meane season continuallye in companye wyth the bishoppe. For he ys the chyeffe heade of them all. They be chosen of the people as the other magistrates be, by secrete voices for the auoyding of strife. After their election they be consecrate of their owne company. They be ouerseers of all deuyne matters, orderers of religions, and as it were jugers and maisters of maners. And it is a great dishonestye and shame to be rebuked or spoken to by anny of them for dissolute and incontinent liuing.

But as it is their offyce to gyue good exhortations and cownsell, so it is the deuty of the prince and the other magistrates to correct and punnyshe offenders; sauynge that the priestes, whome they find exceding vicious liuers, them they excommunicate from hauing any interest in diuine matters. And there is almoost no punnishment emonge them more feared. For they runne in verye great infamy, and be inwardly tormented with a secrete feare of religion, and shall not long scape free with their bodies. For onles they, by quycke repentaunce, approue the amendement of their lyffes to the priestes, they be taken and punnished of the cownsell as wycked and irreligious.

Both childhode and youth is instructed, and tought

of them. Nor they be not more deligente to instructe them in learning then in vertue and good maners. For they vse with very greate endeuour and deligence to put into the heades of their children, whiles they be yet tender and pliaunt, good opinions and profitable for the conseruation of their weale publique. Which, when they be ones rooted in children, do remayne wyth them all their lyfe after, and be wonders profitable for the defence and maintenaunce of the state of the commen wealthe; which neuer decaieth, but through vicis risinge of euell opinyons.

The pryestes, onles they be women (for that kynd is not excluded from pryesthode; howebeit fewe be chosen, and none but widdowes and old women): the men priestes, I saye, take to their wifes the chiefest women in all their countreye. For to no office emong the vtopians is more honour and preeminence geuen. In so much that if they committ any offence, they be vnder no commen iudgement, but be left only to god and themselfes. For they thinke it not lawfull to touch him with mannes hande, be he neuer so vityous, whiche after so singuler a sort was dedicate and consecrate to god as a holly offering. This maner may they easely obserue, bicause they haue so few priestes, and do chuse them with such circumspection. For it scasely euer chaunceth that the most vertuous emong vertuous, which in respect only of his vertue is auaunced to so high a dignity, can fal to vice and wickednes. And if it should chaunce in dede (as mans nature is mutable and fraile), yet by reason they be so few and promoted to no might nor powre, but only honour, it were not to be feared that anye great dammage by them should happen and ensue to the commen wealth. They haue so rare and few priestes, least, if the honour were communicate to many, the dignity of the ordre, which emong them now is so highly estemed, should runne in contempt; speciallye bicause they thinke it harde to find many so good, as to be meet for that dignity, to the execution and discharge wherof it is not sufficiente to be endued with mean vertues.

Furthermore, thies priestes be not more estemed of their owne countrey men, then they be of forrein and straung countreis. Which thing maye hereby plainly appere. And I think al so that this is the cause of it. For whiles the arm⟨i⟩es be fighting together in open feld, they a litle beside, not farre of, knele vpon their knees in their hallowed vestimentes, holding vp theyr handes to heauen ; praying first of all for peace, nexte for vyctory of theyr owne parte, but to neyther part a bluddy vyctory. If their host gette the vpper hand, they runne in to the mayne battayle, and restrayne theyre owne men from sleying and cruellye pursuynge theyre vanquyshed ennemies. Whyche ennemyes, yf they do but see them and speake to them, yt ys ynoughe for the sauegarde of theyr lyues ; and the towchynge of theire clothes defendeth and saueth al their gooddes from rauyne and spoyle. Thys thing hath auaunced them to so greate wourshyp and trew maiesty emong al nations, that many times they haue aswel preserued theire own citizens from the cruel force of their ennemies, as they haue their enemies from the furyous rage of theyre owne men. For yt ys well knowen that when their owne army hathe reculed, and in dyspayre turned backe, and runne away, theyr ennemies fyerslye pursuing with slaughter and spoyle, then the priestes cumming betwene haue stayed the murder, and parted bothe the hostes ; so that peace hath bene made and concluded betwine bothe partes vpon equall and indyfferent condytions. For there was neuer anny natyon so fiers, so cruell and rude, but they hadde them in suche reuerence, that they cownted theyr bodyes hallowed and sanctyfyed, and therefore not to be violentlye and vnreuerentlye towched.

They kepe hollye daye the fyrste and the laste day of euerye moneth and yeare, deuydynge the yeare into monethes; whyche they measure by the course of the moone, as they doo the yeare by the course of the sonne. The fyrste dayes they call in theyr language Cynemernes, and the laste Trapemernes; the whyche woordes maye be interpreted primifeste and finifest; or els, in our speache, first feast and last feast.

Their churches be very gorgyous, and not onelye of fyne and curious workemanship, but also (which in the fewenes of them was necessary) very wyde and large, and able to receaue a great company of people. But they be all sumwhat darke. Howbeit, that was not donne through ignoraunce in buylding, but as they say by the cownsell of the priestes. Bicause they thought that ouer much light doth disperse mens cogitations; where as in dimme and doutefull lighte they be gathered together, and more earnestly fixed vpon religion and deuocion. Which bicause it is not there of one sort emong all men; and yet all the kindes and fassions of it, thoughe they be sondry and manifold, agree together in the honoure of the deuine nature, as going diuers wayes to one ende; therfore nothing is sene nor hard in the churches, which semeth not to agre indifferently with them all. If there be a distinct kind of sacrifice, peculiare to any seuerall secte, that they execute at home in their owne houses. The common sacrifices be so ordered, that they be no derogatyon nor preiudyce to annye of the pryuate sacryfyces and religions.

Therefore no ymage of annye god is seene in the churche; to the intente it maye be free for euery man to conceyue god by their religion after what likenes and similitude they will. They call vpon no peculiar name of god, but only Mithra. In the which word they all agree together in one nature of the deuine maiestye, whatsoeuer it be. No prayers be vsed, but such as euerye man maye boldelye pronownce wythowt the offending of anny secte.

They come therefore to the churche the laste day of

OF UTOPIA

euery moneth and yeare, in the euenynge, yet fastyng, there to gyue thanckes to GOD for that they haue prosperouslye passed ouer the yeare or monethe, wherof that hollye daye ys the laste daye. The next daye they come to the churche earlye in the mornyng, to praye to GOD that they maye haue good fortune and successe all the newe yeare or monethe, whyche they doo begynne of that same hollye daye. But in the holly dayes that be the laste dayes of the monethes and yeares, before they come to the churche, the wiffes fall downe prostrat before their husbandes feete at home; and the children before the feete of their parentes; confessing and acknowleginge that they haue offended other by some actuall dede, or by omission of their dewty, and desire pardon for their offence. Thus yf anye cloude of preuy displeasure was risen at home, by this satisfaction it is ouer blowen; that they may be present at the sacrifices with pure and charitable mindes. For they be aferd to come there with troubled consciences. Therefore, if they knowe themselfes to beare anye hatred or grudge towardes anye man, they presume not to come to the sacrifices before they haue reconcyled themselfes and purged theyre conscyences, for feare of greate vengeaunce and punyshemente for their offence.

When they come thyther, the men goo into the ryghte syde of the churche, and the women into the left syde. There they place themselfes in suche ordre that all they which be of the male kind in euery houshold sitte before the goodman of the house; and they of the female kynde before the goodwyfe. Thus it is forsene that all their gestures and behauiours be marked and obserued abrode of them, by whose aucthoritye and discipline they be goucrned at home. This also they diligentlye see vnto, that the yonger euermore be coupled with his elder; lest, if children be ioyned together, they shold passe ouer that time in childish wantonnes, wherin they ought principallye to conceaue a religious and deuout feere towardes god ; which is the chieffe and almost the only incitation to vertue.

They kill no liuing beast in sacrifice, nor they thinke not that the mercifull clemency of god hath delite in bloud and slaughter ; which hath geuen liffe to beastes, to the intent they should liue. They burne franckensense and other sweet sauours, and light also a great numbre of waxe candelles and tapers ; nott supposinge this geere to be any thing auaylable to the diuine nature, as nother the prayers of men ; but this vnhurtfull and harmeles kind of worship pleaseth them. And by thies sweet sauoures, and lightes, and other such ceremonies, men feele themselfes secretly lifted vp, and encouraged to deuotion, with more willynge and feruent hartes. The people weareth in the churche white apparell: the priest is clothed in chaungeable coloures, whiche in workemanshyp be excellent, but in stuffe not verye pretious. For theire vestementes be nother embrodered with golde, nor set with precious stones ; but they be wrought so fynely and connyngly with diuers fethers of fowles, that the estimacion of no costelye stuffe is able to counteruaile the price of the worke. Furthermore, in thies birdes fethers, and in the dewe ordre of them, whiche is obserued in theire settyng, they saye is conteyned certayn deuyne misteries ; the interpretation wherof knowen, whiche is diligentlye tawght by the priestes, they be put in remembraunce of the bountyfull benefites of God towarde them, and of the loue and honoure whiche of theire behalfe is dewe to God, and also of theire dewties one towarde an other.

When the priest first commeth out of the vestrie, thus apparelled, they fall downe incontinent euery one reuerently to the grounde, with so styll silence on euery part, that the very fassion of the thinge striketh into them a certayne feare of God, as though he were there personally presente. When they haue lien

OF UTOPIA

a little space on the grounde, the priest giueth them a signe for to ryse. Then they sing prayses vnto God, whiche they intermixe with instrumentes of musick, for the moste parte of other fassions then thies that we vse in this parte of the worlde. And like as some of owrs bee muche sweter then theirs, so some of theirs doo farre passe owrs. But in one thynge dowteles they goo excedinge farre beyond vs. For all theire musicke, both that they playe vpon instrumentes, and that they singe with mans voyce, doth so resemble and expresse naturall affections; the sownd and tune is so applied and made agreable to the thynge; that whether it bee a prayer, or els a dytty of gladnes, of patience, of trouble, of mournynge, or of anger, the fassion of the melodye dothe so represente the meaning of the thing, that it doth wonderfullye moue, stire, pearce, and enflame the hearers myndes.

At the laste the people and the priest together rehearse solempne prayers in woordes, expresslye pronounced; so made that euerye man may priuatelye applye to hymselfe that which is commonlye spoken of all. In thies prayers euerye man recogniseth and knowledgeth God to be hys maker, hys gouernoure, and the principal cause of all other goodnes; thankyng him for so many benefites receaued at hys hande: but namelye, that through the fauoure of God he hath chaunced into that publyque weale, whiche is moste happye and welthye, and hath chosen that religion whyche he hopeth to be moste true. In the whyche thynge yf he doo annye thynge erre, or yf there bee annye other better then eyther of them is, beynge moore acceptable to GOD, he desiereth hym that he wyll of hys goodnes let hym haue knowledge thereof, as one that is readye too followe what waye soeuer he wyll leade hym. But yf thys forme and fassion of a commen wealthe be beste, and his owne religion moste true and perfecte, then he desyreth God to gyue

him a constaunte stedfastnes in the same, and to brynge
all other people to the same ordre of lyuyng, and to
the same opinion of God ; onles there be any thynge
that in this dyuersitie of religions doth delyte his
vnsercheable pleasure. To be shorte, he prayeth hym 5
that after his deathe he may come to hym ; but how
soone or late, that he dare not assygne or determine.
Howebeit, if it myght stande with his maiesties pleasure,
he would be muche gladder to dye a paynfull dethe
and so to go to God, then by long lyuing in worldlye 10
prosperytie to bee awaye from hym. Whan this
prayer is sayde, they fall downe to the ground agayne,
and a lytle after they ryse vp and go to dynner. And
the resydewe of the daye they passe ouer in playes,
and exercise of cheualrye. 15

Nowe I haue declared and descrybyd vnto yowe,
as truely as I coulde, the fourme and ordre of that
commen wealth, which verely in my iudgement is not
onlye the beste, but also that whiche alone of good
ryght may clayme and take vpon it the name of a 20
common wealthe or publyque weale. For in other
places they speake stil of the commen wealth ; but
euerye man procureth hys owne pryuate wealthe. Here
where nothynge is pryuate, the commen affayres be
earnestly loked vpon. And truely on both partes they 25
haue good cause so to do as they do. For in other
countreys who knoweth not that he shall sterue for
honger, onles he make some seuerall prouision for
hymself, though the commen wealthe floryshe neuer
so muche in ryches ? And therefore he is compelled, 30
euen of verye necessitie, to haue regarde to hym selfe
rather then to the people, that is to saye, to other.
Contrarywyse, there where all thynges be commen to
euerye man, it is not to be dowted that anye man shal
lacke anye thynge necessarye for hys pryuate vses, so 35
that the commen store houses and barnes be suffi-
cientlye stored. For there nothynge is distrybuted
after a nyggyshe sorte, nother there is any poore man

or begger. And though no man haue any thynge, yet
euerye man is ryche. For what can be more ryche
then to lyue ioyfullye and merylye without all griefe
and pensifenes; not caryng for hys owne lyuing, nor
vexed or trowbled with hys wyfes importunate com- 5
playntes, not drydynge pouertie to his sonne, nor
sorrowyng for his dowghters dowrey? Yea, they take
no care at all for the lyuyng and wealthe of themsefes
and all theirs; of theire wyfes, theire chyldren, theire
nephewes, theire childrens chyldren, and all the suc- 10
cession that euer shall followe in theire posteritie.
And yet, besydes thys, there is no lesse prouision for
them that were ones labourers, and be nowe weake
and impotent, then for them that do nowe laboure
and take payne. 15

Heere nowe woulde I see yf anye man dare be so
bolde, as to compare with thys equytie the iustice of
other nations. Among whom, I forsake God, if I can
fynde any signe or token of equitie and iustice. For
what iustice is this, that a ryche goldsmythe or an 20
vsurer, or, to be shorte, any of them, whyche other
doo nothyng at all; or els that whiche they do is
suche, that it is not very necessary to the commen
wealthe; should haue a pleasaunt and a welthy
lyuynge, other by Idilnes, or by vnnecessary busynes? 25
when in the meane tyme poore labourers, carters,
yronsmythes, carpenters, and plowmen, by so great
and continual toyle, as drawyng and bearyng beastes
be skant able to susteine; and agayn so necessary
toyle that with out it no commen wealth were able to 30
continewe and endure one yere; do yet get so harde
and poore a lyuing, and lyue so wretched and miserable
a lyfe, that the state and condition of the labouring
beastes maye seme muche better and welthier. For
they be not put to so contynuall laboure, nor theire 35
lyuynge is not mucho worse; yea, to them much
pleasaunter; takynge no thowghte in the meane season
for the tyme to come. But thies soilie poore wretches

be presently tormented with barreyne and vnfrutefull labour. And the remembraunce of theire poore indigent and begerlye olde age kylleth them vp. For theire dayly wages is so lytle that it will not suffice for the same daye; muche lesse it yeldeth any ouerplus, that may dayly be layde vp for the relyefe of olde age.

Is not thys an vniust and an vnkynd publyque weale, whyche gyueth great fees and rewardes to gentelmen, as they call them, and to goldsmythes, and to suche other, whiche be other ydell persones or els onlye flatterers, and deuysers of vayne pleasures; and, of the contrary parte, maketh no gentle prouision for poore plowmen, coliars, laborers, carters, yronsmythes, and carpenters; without whome no commen wealth can continewe? But when it hath abused the laboures of theire lusty and flowringe age, at the laste, when they be oppressed with olde age and syckenes, being nedye, poore, and indigent of all thynges; then, forgettynge theire so many paynfull watchynges, not remembrynge theire so many and so great benefytes; recompenseth and acquyteth them moste vnkyndly with myserable death. And yet besides this the riche men not only by priuate fraud, but also by commen lawes, do euery day plucke and snatche away from the poore some parte of their daily liuing. So, where as it semed before uniuste to recompense with vnkindnes their paynes that haue bene beneficiall to the publique weale, nowe they haue to this their wrong and vniuste dealinge (whiche is yet a muche worse pointe), geuen the name of iustice, yea, and that by force of a law.

Therfore when I consider and way in my mind all thies commen wealthes which now a dayes any where do florish, so god helpe me, I can perceaue nothing but a certein conspiracy of riche men, procuringe theire owne commodities vnder the name and title of the commen wealth. They inuent and deuise all meanes and craftes, first how to kipe safely without feare of

lesing that they haue vniustly gathered together; and
next how to hire and abuse the woorke and labour of
the poore for as litle money as may be. Thies deuyses
when the riche men haue decreed to be kept and
obserued for the commen wealthes sake, that is to
saye, for the wealth also of the poore people, then they
be made lawes. But thies most wicked and vicious
men, when they haue by their vnsatiable couetousnes
deuided emong themselfes all those thinges which wold
haue suffised all men, yet howe farre be they from the
wealth and felicity of the vtopian commen wealth?
owt of the which in that all the desire of moneye with
the vse therof is vtterly secluded and bannisshed,
howe great a heape of cares is cut away? How great
an occasion of wickednes and mischiefe is plucked vp
by the rotes? For who knoweth not that fraud, theft,
rauine, brauling, quarelling, brabling, striffe, chiding,
contention, murder, treason, poisoning; which by
dayly punishmentes are rather reuenged then refrained;
do dye when money dieth? And also that feare, griefe,
care, laboures, and watchinges, do perishe, euen the
very same moment that money perissheth? Yea,
pouerty it selfe, which only semed to lacke money,
if money were gone, it also wold decrease and vanishe
away.

And that you may perceaue this more plainly, consider with your selfes some barrein and vnfrutefull
yeare, wherin many thousandes of people haue starued
for honger. I dare be bolde to say, that in the end
of that penury so much corne or grain might haue
bene found in the riche mens barnes, if they had
bene searched, as being deuided emong them, whome
famine and pestilence hath killed, no man at all
should haue felt that plage and penury. So easely
might men gett their liuinge, if that same worthye
princesse, lady money, did not alon stoppe vp the way
betwene vs and our liuing; whiche a goddes name
was very excellently douised and inuented, that by

her the way therto should be opened. I am sewer the
ryche men perceaue thys, nor they be not ignoraunte
how much better yt werre to lacke noo necessarye
thynge then to abunde with ouermuch superfluyte;
to be rydde owte of innumerable cares and trowbles,
then to be beseiged wyth greate ryches. And I dowte
not that other the respecte of euery mans priuate
commoditie, or els the aucthority of oure sauioure
Christe (which for his great wisdom could not but
know what were best, and for his inestimable goodnes
cold not but counsell to that which he knew to be
best) wold haue brought all the wordle long agoo into
the lawes of this weale publique, if it were not that one
only beast, the princesse and mother of all mischiefe,
pride, doth withstonde and let it. She measureth not
wealth and prosperity by here own commodities, but
by the miseriies and incommodities of other. She
wold not by her good will be made a goddes, if there
were no wretches left, whom she might be lady ouer
to mocke and scorne; ouer whose miseries her felicity
might shine, whose pouerty she might vexe, torment,
and encrease by gorgiously setting furthe her riches.
This hell hound crepeth in to mens hartes, and
plucketh them backe from entering the right pathe
of liffe; and is so depely roted in mens brestes, that
she can not be plucked out.

This forme and fassion of a weale publique, which
I wold gladly wisshe vnto all nations, I am glad yet
that it hath chaunced to the Vtopians; which haue
followed those institutions of liffe, wherby they haue
laid such fondations of their common wealth, as shall
continew and last, not only wealthely, but also, as
farre as mans wit maye iudge and coniecture, shall
endure for euer. For seinge the chiefe causes of
ambition and sedition with other vices be plucked vp
by the rootes and abandoned at home, there can be
no ieopardye of domesticall dissention; which alone
hathe caste vnder fote and broughte to noughte the

OF UTOPIA

well fortefied and strongly defenced wealth and riches
of many cities. But for asmuch as perfect concord
remaineth, and holsome lawes be executed at home,
the enuy of all forrein princes be not able to shake or
moue the empire, though they haue many tymes long
ago gone about to do it, beinge euermore dreuen
backe.

Thus when Raphaell hadde made an ende of his
tale, thoughe manye thinges came to my mind which
in the manners and lawes of that people semed to be
instituted and founded of no good reason, not only in
the fassion of their cheualry and in their sacrifices and
religions, and in other of their lawes, but also, yea
and chieffely, in that which is the principall fondacion
of al their ordinaunces, that is to saye, in the communitie of theire liffe and liuinge, without anny
occupieng of money; by the whyche thynge onelye
all nobilitie, magnificence, wourship, honour, and
maiestie, the true ornamentes and honoures, as the
common opinion is, of a common wealth, vtterly be
ouerthrowen and destroyed; yet, bicause I knew that
he was wery of talkinge, and was not sure whether
he coulde abide that any thing shoulde be said againste
hys minde; speciallye bicause I remembred that he
had reprehended this fault in other, which be aferd
least they shoulde seme not to be wise enough, onles
they could find some fault in other mens inuentions:
therfore I, praising both their institutions and his
communication, toke him by the hand, and led him
into supper; saying that we wold chuse an other
time to way and examine the same matters, and to
talke wyth him more at lardge therin. Whiche wold
to God it might ones come to passe. In the mean
time as I can not agree and consent to all thinges that
he said; being els without dowte a man singulerly
well learned, and also in all wordely matters exactely
and profoundely experienced; so must I nedes confesse

and graunt, that many thinges be in the vtopian weal publique, which in our cities I may rather wisshe for then hoope after.

<blockquote>
Thus endeth the afternones talke of Raphaell Hythlodaye concerning the lawes and institutions of the Iland of Vtopia.
</blockquote>

¶ Imprinted at London

by Abraham Vele, dwelling in Pauls churcheyarde at the sygne of the Lambe. Anno. 1551.

NOTES

BOOK I

Utopia. There can be no doubt that More compounded the name from οὐ and τόπος, for in his letter to Erasmus dated London, 1517, he speaks of his book Utopia by the name of 'Nusquama,' and in a second letter to him dated September 3, 1517, he says '*Nusquamam* nostram nusquam bene scriptam ad te mitto' (Erasmi *Opera*, ed. Leyden, 1703; tom. iii. part ii. pp. 1629 and 1664); nor can there be the smallest doubt that 'Nusquama' was coined from 'Nusquam'; as is borne out by Budé's letter to Lupset prefixed to the *Utopia*—'Utopia vero insula quam etiam Udepotiam appellari audio.' 'Udepotiam' being obviously a play on οὐδέποτε. But, the play on οὐ and εὐ being so obvious, it is not surprising that that play on the words became common; so the Poet Laureate of the Island is made to say

> 'Utopia priscis dicta ob infrequentiam,
> Nunc civitatis aemula Platonicae...
> *Eutopia* merito sum vocanda nomine.'

See 'Hexastichon Anemolii Poetae Laureati,' in the preliminary matter to the *Utopia*. But this must not mislead us, as it has misled Dibdin, Bailey, the Italian translator, and others.

The word, as Scaliger observed, is not legitimately formed. [See for an interesting discussion on the subject *Notes and Queries*, seventh series, vol. v. pp. 101-2, 229-31.] Rabelais nowhere mentions More, but he has borrowed the name Utopia (*Pantagruel*, bk. ii. ch. xxviii; bk. iii. ch. i), just as he has borrowed his Amaurots and his kingdom of Achory from him (Id. bk. ii. ch. xxiv). Cf. too his island of Medamothy (Nowhere) (Μηδαμόθι), Id. bk. iv. ch. ii. It has been conjectured, but quite groundlessly, that the Englishman Thaumast (*Pantagruel*, bk. ii. ch. xviii-xx) was intended for More.

P. 1, l. 9. **king of Castell.** Charles V, afterwards (1519) Emperor was at this time (1515) a youth of fifteen, he had been proclaimed King of Castile on the death of his grandfather Ferdinand in January, 1516 (see Introduction).

l. 13. **cuthebert Tunstall.** Born in 1474 at Hackforth in the North Riding of Yorkshire. He studied both at Oxford and Cambridge, and was appointed to several ecclesiastical preferments, including the Prebend of Stowe Longa, Lincoln, and the Archdeaconry of Chester. In May, 1515, he was appointed Ambassador to Brussels, as is here recorded, and in the following May he became Master of the Rolls. In 1522 he was made Bishop of London, and in the following year Keeper of the Privy Seal. In 1530 he was translated to the See of Durham. On the accession of Queen Elizabeth he refused to take the oath of allegiance, and was accordingly deprived of his preferment in 1559, and died the same year at Lambeth where he was residing with Archbishop Parker. The high character given by More to Tunstall is not exaggerated; he was honourably distinguished not only by his scholarship but by his humanity. 'Dispeream si quid habet haec aetas cum eo viro conferendum' is Erasmus's expression about him (*Ep.* 241, c. 1658). For more about Tunstall's character see Jortin's *Life of Erasmus*, vol. I. i.

l. 25. **as the Prouerbe sayth.** The earliest forms of this proverb appear to be those given by Erasmus (*Adag.* 1629, p. 12) 'Lucernam adhibere in meridie,' and (p. 18) 'solem adiuvare facibus,' 'to bring up a lamp at noonday,' 'to assist the sun with torches.'

l. 26. **Bruges,** the chief mercantile town of Belgium for many centuries. As early as the seventh century it held the rank of a city. But in 1488, on account of a rising by its citizens against the Archduke Maximilian, it was deprived of its privileges, and thenceforth lost its commercial importance, which was for the most part transferred to Antwerp.

l. 29. **Marcgraue.** This title (= count of the marches), originally a territorial title possessed by the Princes of the Empire, came to be applied to the chief magistrate of Bruges.

l. 31. **George Temsice.** Georgius a Tempseca (de Theimsecke) was a native of Bruges, and wrote a history of Artois (Lupton); beyond these facts nothing seems to be known about him.

P. 2, l. 1. **Casselles.** Now Cassel, a town in the department du Nord of France, between Hazebrouck and Dunkirk.

l. 9. **Bruxelle,** Brussels, a French form of the word, now spelt Bruxelles.

NOTES: BOOK I

l. 15. **Peter Gyles.** Petrus Gillius, or Aegidius, to whom More dedicated the *Utopia*, was the son of Nicholas, 'quaestor urbis,' and was born at Antwerp in or about 1486. He was a pupil of Erasmus, who not only directed his studies, but remained through life his cordial friend. See the many affectionate letters addressed to him in Erasmus's correspondence. The *Epithalamium* in Erasmus's *Colloquia* (*Opera Omnia*, ed. 1703, vol. i. pp. 746-9) was composed in honour of his marriage. He had been made town clerk (Stadtschreiber) of Antwerp in 1510. Erasmus speaks of him in the highest terms in the *Epithalamium* as 'candidissimus ille iuuenis et omnibus politioris literaturae deliciis expolitissimus.' It would appear that Erasmus recommended More and Tunstall to Giles. (See Erasmus, *Letter* clv.) Giles was an accomplished Latin poet. He died Nov. 11, 1533. The character which More gives of him is amply borne out by what Erasmus says of him. See particularly *Epistolae*, cc, cciii, and *Appendix, Epist.* cxv.

l. 19. **the yong man.** Giles would be at this time about twenty-nine.

l. 28. **vsithe ... dyssymulatyon.** This is a very diffuse rendering of the original, which is 'nemini longius abest fucus' (from no man is paint—artifice—farther off). The distinction between simulation and dissimulation which Robynson was thinking of is given in the well-known line 'Quod non es simulas, dissimulasque quod es,' 'You pretend to be what you are not, and you pretend not to be what you are.'

P. 3, l. 1. **when I hadde herde.** Ed. 1, 'as I was herynge.'

l. 2. **our ladies churche.** The Cathedral of Notre Dame at Antwerp, which had been completed only a few years before, though begun early in the fifteenth century. It is still one of the finest specimens of Gothic architecture on the Continent, with a spire 366 feet high.

l. 5. **the seruice beynge done.** Ed. 1 reads 'when the deuyne was done.' The adjective seems occasionally to have stood alone in this sense. The N. E. D. quotes (*Will of Vavesour*) 'to sing devyne for my sowle.' Burnet paraphrases the original 'peracto sacro,' 'as I was returning home from Mass.'

l. 9. **homely,** plainly, carelessly. Cf. Chaucer, *Prol.* 325 'He rood but hoomly in a medlee cote,' and Latimer (*Second Sermon before Edward VI*), 'Homilyes, they may well be called, for they are homely handeled.' Dr. Lupton thinks there may be some allusion to the careless way in which More, according to Ascham, wore his gown (see *Scholemaster*, ed. Mayor, p. 180).

l. 10. fauour, appearance, aspect, or face, a common use of the word in sixteenth-century English. Cf. Skelton, *Poems against Garnishe*, 'The favyr of your face is voyd of all grace'; and Shakespeare, *Macbeth*, i. 5. 73 'to alter favour ever is to fear.'

This sense survives in the term 'ill-favoured,' 'well-favoured.'

l. 11. But when thys. Ed. 2 reads 'But the sayde Peter seyng me, came vnto me & saluted me.'

l. 23. Than I coniectured, i. e. 'then.' 'Then' is frequently spelt 'than' in older English. The two words 'than' and 'then' like *tum* and *tam*, *quum* and *quam* in Latin are closely connected, and are indeed simple variants of the same word. (See Abbott's *Shakespearian Grammar*, Ed. 1883, p. 52.)

l. 27. Palynure. Palinurus was the pilot of Aeneas. Virg. *Aen.* iii. 202, and v. 832 seqq.

l. 28. Ulisses. Ulysses the son of Laertes, the Greek chief, and Lord of Ithaca, whose adventures after the fall of Troy are related in Homer's *Odyssey*.

l. 29. Plato. Plato is said to have visited Egypt, Sicily, and other foreign places for the purpose of acquiring knowledge. To his travels there are many references in ancient writers. Cf. Cicero, *De Finibus*, v. 29, Valerius Maximus, viii. 7, § 3, and Diogenes Laertius, iii. 6.

l. 30. Raphaell Hythlodaye. Dr. Lupton derives this name from ὕθλος, babble or idle talk, and δαίειν, to distribute. But is it not more natural to suppose that the derivation is from δάϊος in its secondary sense of 'skilled in,' 'knowing in,' from δάω, or rather δαῆναι ? Stephens's *Thesaurus* under δάϊος paraphrases ἔμπειρος (skilled in) and translates 'peritus,' quoting *Anth. Plan.* iv. 119 to support this sense of the word, which is also preserved in δαίφρων. Dr. Lupton somewhat fancifully suggests that the Christian name Raphael is borrowed from Raphael Volaterranus, the voluminous author of the *Commentarii Urbani* printed in 1511. This is at any rate more plausible than the theory of the French translator (1559), who supposes that it is borrowed from the Archangel Raphael, and is meant to indicate the spiritual energy at work in the composition of the romance.

NOTES: BOOK I

l. 37. **Senecaes.** Lucius Annaeus Seneca, the Roman philosopher, and tutor of the Emperor Nero, by whom he was subsequently ordered to put himself to death. He flourished during the first half of the first century, dying A.D. 65. His philosophical writings are certainly more original than is common with Romans when treating of such subjects.

Ciceroes. Marcus Tullius Cicero, the great Roman orator and man of letters; born B.C. 106, assassinated B.C. 43. The reference is to his voluminous philosophical writings.

doinges. Now a rare use of the word as a synonym for 'works,' and always in plural in this sense.

P. 4, l. 1. **Portugalle.** The form commonly used in Elizabethan English for Portuguese. So Hakluyt speaks of 'the Spaniards and Portugales in Barberie,' *Voyages*, ii Ded., and Peele, *Battle of Alcazar*, iv. 2 'Now have I set these Portugals a work.'

l. 4. **Amerike vespuce.** Amerigo Vespucci was born at Florence, March 9, 1451, the son of a Notary. After passing some time as a clerk in the service of the Medici he entered the service of Juonoto Bernardi, a Florentine merchant who had fitted out the second expedition of Columbus in 1493. This brought Amerigo into contact with the spirit of exploration and travel so energetic at that time, and in 1497 he embarked on his first voyage. Between that date and 1504 he made, according to his own account, no less than four voyages, of which an account is given, drawn partly from his own narrative in the *Quatuor Americi Vesputii Navigationes*—the work referred to by More—appended to *Cosmographiae Introductio*, printed at St. Dié in the Vosges in 1507. For the portion of the narrative on which the *Utopia* was founded, see Introduction. After his return to Lisbon from his fourth voyage Amerigo went back to Spain and settled at Seville, where he died February 22, 1512. For an excellent account of him and a discussion of the attempt made to attribute to him the honour of having anticipated Cabot and Columbus in the discovery of the American Continent, see Major's *Life of Prince Henry of Portugal*, p. 366 seqq.

l. 13. **Gulike.** A very singular misinterpretation of More's Latin by Robynson. As he found Castellum printed with a capital C he supposed it to be the name of a place, and finding, as Dr. Lupton conjectures, in the old dictionaries that Castell'im was the Latin name for Jülich (the French Juliers, or as it was sometimes spelt, Gulike, a town twenty-three miles west of Cologne) he assumed that it was this place. More is no doubt referring to the passage in the *Quatuor Navigationes* (see Introduction), where it is described how a garrison or factory of twenty-four men with arms and provisions was left in Cape Frio by Vespucci in June, 1504: the words being 'Relictis igitur in castello praefato Christicolis xxiiii,' &c.

l. 14. **for hys mindes sake.** Lat. 'ut obtemperaretur animo eius,' to comply with his inclination.

l. 17. **He that hathe no graue,** &c. Lucan, vii. 819 'Caelo tegitur qui non habet urnam,' cf. too the line of Maecenas cited by Seneca, *Epp.* xiv. 4 'Nec tumulum curo: sepelit natura relictos.'

The second saying is, as Dr. Lupton notes, plainly an adaptation of the saying of Anaxagoras (preserved by Cicero, *Tusc.* i. § 104), who, on his friends asking him, when he was dying at Lampsacus, whether in the event of his death he would wish to be carried to his country Clazomenae, replied 'There is no necessity; for on all sides the way to the shades below is equally long,' 'Nihil necesse est, inquit, undique enim ad inferos tantundem viae est.' Cf. Roper's *Life of More*, p. 79 (Ed. Singer), where More is represented as saying of his prison the Tower, 'Is not this house as nighe heaven as myne owne?'

l. 24. **Gulykyans,** a mistranslation of Castellanorum, i.e. those in the fort (see note on *Gulike*, above).

l. 25. **Taprobane.** The Greek corruption of the native name for Ceylon, Ταπροβάνη, situated on the S.E. of the peninsula of Hindostan. Utopia would thus lie somewhere between India and S. America.

l. 26. **Calyquit.** Now *Calicut*; a seaport town in the province of Malabar, India. It was the first Indian port visited by Vasco de Gama in May, 1498. The name of the place is properly *Colicodu*.

l. 28. **nothynge lesse then lokyd for.** Anything rather than expected, quite unexpected by any one. The original has 'praeter spem'; N. E. D. quotes Greneway's *Tacitus*, xxx 'The Barbarous people know nothing less than engines and subtill devises.' French 'rien moins que.'

l. 35. **haylsede.** Hailed, greeted; from Old Norse *heilsa*, 'to greet,' say, hail. N. E. D. quotes from Palsgrave, 'I haylse, or greete, je salue.'

NOTES: BOOK I

P. 5, l. 1. torues. Middle-English plur. of *torf*, a form of *turf*. Cf. original 'in scamno cespitibus herbeis constrato.' The same sort of seat is mentioned in Chaucer's *Marchantes Tale* (990–1), 'Adoun him sette, Upon a bench of turves, fresh and grene.'

l. 9. **harmelese.** Free from harm: uninjured. Chaucer, *Leg. of Good Women*, 2664 'To passen *harmlesse* of that place.'

occupyed. In the earlier English sense of dealing or trading with; N. E. D. quotes Marbeck, *Boke of Notes*, p. 653 'He gained much by occupieing with the Jewes and Christians.' Cf. Tyndale's translation of St. Luke xix. 13 'Occupy till I come,'—that is, 'go on trading.'

l. 13. **mere.** Exactly the Latin *merus*, pure; cf. our modern expression, 'pure generosity.'

l. 17. **was in botys**, i.e. in boats, one of the many variants of 'boat,' and of the plural.

l. 21. **holsom.** Wholesome, but a more correct form, for the word comes directly from the Middle-English *holsum*, holsom, *halsum* being suggested by the Icelandic *heilsamr* (Skeat).

l. 22. **lyne equynoctyall**, i.e. the equator.

l. 28. **owte of fasshyon.** A curious translation of the original 'horrida,' which simply means 'rough.' 'Fashion' here = form or shape, so the phrase means 'out of shape,' or 'ill made,' so, 'rough, uncouth.'

P. 6, l. 1. borderers. The Lat. has 'finitimos,' neighbouring people.

l. 3. **occasion**, i.e. an opportunity afforded. Almost = the Latin *occasio*. Cp. Milton, *Par. Lost*, ix. 480 'Let me not let pass *Occasion* which now smiles.'

l. 11. **rydged kyeles.** Keels running like a ridge at the bottom of the ships. The original is 'acuminatas carinas,' sharpened or pointed.

l. 17. **feate**; here answers closely to 'use,' merely emphasizing that word—the original being simply 'usus.'

lode stone. Though the polarity of the magnetic needle had been known long before More's time, it was not, as Dr. Lupton remarks, till the fifteenth century that it seems to have been applied to purposes of navigation.

l. 22. **in so doynge, ferther frome care then ieopardye**; i.e. 'freer from anxiety than from danger,' a literal rendering of the Latin 'securi magis quam tuti.'

l. 25. **tourne them.** As the Latin shows, 'them' is here the dative, 'shall turn to evil and harm for them.'

l. 31. **in an other place.** That is, in the Second Book of the *Utopia*.

l. 36. **cyuyle pollycye.** Such a course of conduct as becomes citizens living as citizens should live—in the original 'civiliter conviventes.' Cf. Starkey's *Dialogue between Pole and Lupset*: 'I cal the cyuyle lyfe lyuyng togyder in gud and polytyke ordur, one euer redy to dow gud to a nother, and as hyt were conspyryng togydur in al vertue and honesty' (Ed. J. M. Cowper, Early English Text Soc., p. 11).

P. 7, l. 4. **Scyllaes.** Scylla, the monster represented by Homer, *Odyssey*, xii. 85 seqq., and Virgil, *Aen.* iii. 426 seqq., as residing on one of the two rocks between Italy and Sicily—the 'barking' is Homer's δεινὸν λελακυῖα, and Virgil's 'caeruleis canibus resonantia saxa.' For a full description of the monster see Ovid, *Met.* xiv. 51 seqq.

Celenes. Celaeno was chief of the Harpies; see Virgil, *Aen.* iii. 211.

Lestrygones. A savage tribe who destroyed eleven of Ulysses' ships with their crews. See *Odyssey*, x. 82 seqq.

l. 12. **ensample** = example, the reading of the second edition.

l. 15. **intreate.** Archaic form of 'entreat,' to deal with or treat of in a specified matter, so 'describe' or 'relate.' Frequently used without the preposition 'of.' Cf. Latimer, 2nd Serm. Convoc. i. 43 'It should be too long to *intreate* how the children of light are ingendered.'

l. 26. **connynge**—'knowing,' as we might say. 'Perfecte' is the reading of Ed. 2.

l. 29. **geaste wyse,** like or after the manner of a guest. The suffix 'wise' from old Saxon 'wisa,' Anglo-Saxon '*wīse*,' way, manner, was used more frequently in early English than it is now, though it is stereotyped in the adverbs and adjectives, 'anywise,' 'nowise,' otherwise,' 'sidewise,' 'crosswise,' &c.

l. 31. **I wondere greatlye, &c.** For the connexion of this passage with More's life see Introduction.

l. 37. **are meat.** Ed. 2 omits 'are.'

P. 8, l. 5. **I passe not greatly for them.** A common use of the word in earlier English, meaning 'care' or have regard to. It is almost universally found with the negative, like ἀλέγειν in Greek. 'As for these silken-coated

NOTES: BOOK I 153

slaves. I *pass* not' (Shakespeare, 2 *Hen. VI*, iv. 2. 156);
and Drayton, 'I pass not what it may be' (*Question of Cynthia*).

l. 17. Naye god forbedde, &c. Robynson's version
is here most inadequate and defective. The original Latin
is ' Bona verba, inquit Petrus; mihi visum est non ut servias
regibus, sed ut inservias. Hoc est, inquit ille, una syllaba
plus quam servias'; that is, 'soft and fair,' said Peter, 'I do
not mean that you should be a slave to kings, but an
assistant to them.' 'This latter,' said Hythlodaye, 'is only
a syllable longer than the former': that is, the one is
'servias,' the other 'inservias.' Dr. Lupton paraphrases
this as 'service at a Court is only short for servitude.'
Robynson omits the passage in Hythlodaye's reply containing
the play on the word.

l. 29. greate states...realmes. Robynson's paraphrase
of the single word 'Purpurati' of the original. For this
sense of 'States' cf. Middleton, *Game of Chess*, Prol. 'First
you shall see the men in order set, States and their Pawns.'
So Hexam (quoted in *Babees Book*) speaks of 'The twelve
Peeres or *States* of the Kingdome of France.'

l. 31. sike. Ed. 2 'sue.'

l. 32. thynke it. Note the imperative mood, 'Do not
you think it.'

P. 9, l. 11. For from the prynce. Cf. Starkey's *Dialogue*, J. M. Cowper (E. E. T. S.), p. 48: 'For lyke as
al wyt, reson and sens, felyng, lyfe and al other natural
powar spryngeth out of the hart, so from the prynces
and rularys of the State commyth al lawys, ordur and
pollycy, al justice, vertue and honesty to the rest of thys
polytyke body.'

l. 20. nother. See Glossarial Index.

l. 23. moste parte of all princes. This picture of the
Princes and Kings of More's time is amply illustrated by
Erasmus. Hallam in his Introduction to the *Literature of
Europe*, vol. i. pp. 286, 289, has collected and translated the
chief passages in the *Adagia* bearing on this question. The
most remarkable are in the commentary on the adage
'Scarabaeus aquilam quaerit,' chil. iii, cent. vii, prov. 1,
and 'Frons occipitio.' With these compare Philip de
Commines, *Mémoires*, bk. i. ch. x; bk. ii. vi; bk. v. xviii.
Both especially dwell on their ignorance, selfishness,
rapacity, cruelty, tyranny, and indifference to everything
except what concerns their ambitions or contributes to their

pleasure. The *Dialogue between Pole and Lupset* dwells with equal emphasis on the injuries inflicted on subjects by these vices and the necessity for reform by curtailing their power. Compare Swift's *Gulliver's Travels*, part iii. ch. viii: 'Three kings protested to me that in their whole reigns they never did once prefer any person of merit, unless by mistake or treachery of some minister in whom they confided, neither would they do it if they were to live again, and they showed with great strength of reason that their royal throne could not be supported without corruption, because that positive, confident, and restive temper, which virtue infused into a man, was a clog to public business.'

l. 34. **sauing that they do shamefully**, &c. More may have been thinking of Juvenal's description of the parasite, *Sat.* iii. 101 seqq.

P. 10, l. 2. **So both the rauen and the ape.** An adaptation or another form of proverbs quoted by Erasmus (*Adagia*, chil. iv. cent. x) as illustrating 'asinus asino, et sus sui pulcher.'

l. 5. **haue despite at.** Hold in contempt. Cf. Chaucer, *Melib.* 452 'Peradventure Christ hath thee in despit'; Caxton, *Golden Legend*, 'He hadde in despite fader and moder.'

l. 9. **fare**, behave. A rare use of the word. Nares quotes Heywood, *Troia Britannica*, 'His bottles gone, still stands he strangely faring.'

l. 12. **diserdes**, a variant of dizzards = clowns, jesters, blockheads. The word is found in many forms, 'disarde,' 'dysarde,' 'dyzerde,' and is probably derived from 'diseur' (Lat. *dicere*). N.E.D. quotes Skelton, *Image Ipocr.*: 'To go gaye With wonderful array As *dysardes* in a play.' See Glossarial Index.

l. 14. **fawt.** M.E. *faut*, from O.F. *faute*; *l* inserted in F. in the 16th century, and adopted by English writers.

l. 20. **As who should saye**, &c. This was the favourite cry of the Obscurantists; see *Epistolae obscurorum Virorum, passim*.

l. 28. **lewde, ouerthwarte.** *Lewd* is here used in the primary sense of unlearned, ignorant (see Glossary). *Overthwarte* = perversely. So in Nares's *Terence*, 'obstinate operam dat' is translated 'he deals overthwartly with me'; cf. *Euphues*, ed. Arber, p. 378 'Necessary it is that among friends there should be some overthwarting.'

l. 33. **insurreccion**, i.e. the Cornish insurrection of 1497. The men of Cornwall, led by Lord Audley and

NOTES: BOOK I   155

Flammock an attorney, and one Michael Joseph, marched on London, but were defeated at Blackheath, on June 22 of that year, the leaders being captured and executed. 'There were,' says Hall, 'slaine of the rebels whiche fought and resisted two thousand men and moo.' For a vivid account of this see Hall's *Chronicle*, Henry VII, *sub ann. XII Yere*; cf. Holinshed's *Chronicles*, ed. 1808, vol. iii. p. 515 seq., and Bacon's *Henry VII, sub ann.* 1497.

l. 38. **Jhon Morton.** Born either at Bere Regis or Milborne St. Andrew in Dorsetshire about 1420. He received his early education at the Abbey of Cerne, and then went to Balliol College, Oxford. While practising as an advocate in the Court of Arches, he attracted the notice of Cardinal Bourchier, who bestowed on him several preferments besides introducing him to King Henry VI. His fidelity to that unhappy monarch throughout his misfortunes attracted Edward IV, who on his accession took Morton into his councils, appointed him Master of the Rolls in 1473, and Bishop of Ely six years later, and made him one of the executors of his will. Richard III had no love for him, but put him into prison, nominally as a ward of the Duke of Buckingham; he escaped to the Isle of Ely, and shortly after fled in disguise to the Continent, where he joined the Earl of Richmond (subsequently Henry VII), and is said to have been the first to propose the union of the two Houses of York and Lancaster by marriage with Elizabeth, the eldest daughter of Edward IV. In 1486 he was made Archbishop of Canterbury, in 1487 Lord Chancellor, and in 1493 created a Cardinal by Pope Alexander VI. He died in September 1500, and was buried in Canterbury Cathedral. More's character of Morton is not corroborated by Bacon, who describes Morton as 'a wise man and an eloquent, but in his nature harsh and haughty, much accepted by the King, but envied by the nobility and hated of the people.' The unpopularity of the deviser of 'Morton's fork' is not difficult to understand.

P. 11, l. 25. **in the chiefe of hys youth,** 'ab prima fere iuventa'; 'almost from boyhood' would be a simpler rendering.

l. 28. **tumbled and tossed in the waues of.** The first edition reads 'troubled and tossed with'; which is not so near to the Latin, 'variis fortunae aestibus assiduo iactatus.'

l. 33. **a certayne laye man.** In More's time and previously it was not common for *laici*—that is, non clerios—to be acquainted with the law ; and therefore More emphasizes the fact that the speaker was a layman.

l. 37. **fellones.** The derivation of this word is very uncertain ; its general meaning is a vile or wicked person, a villain or wretch, and in that sense it is used here. The punishment against which More represents Hythlodaye as protesting continued to be the law in England till 1827 (7 and 8 George IV, c. 28, § 7) ; see Stephen, *Hist. of the Criminal Law in England*, vol. i. p. 472. Philanthropists had continually protested against the severity of the penalty, and with More's words may be compared what Starkey says in his *Dialogue between Pole and Lupset* (ed. Cowper, p. 119) : 'Wyth us for every lytyl theft, a man ys by and by hengyd wythout mercy or pitie, wych, me semyth, ys agayne nature and humanyte. Specyally when they steyle for necessyte wythout murdur or manslaughter commytted therein.' The remarks with which Coke, scarcely a century after More's death, concluded his Third Institute may also be compared. —'What a lamentable case it is to see so many Christian men and women strangled on that cursed tree of the gallows, insomuch as if in a large field a man might see together all the Christians that but in one year throughout England came to that untimely and ignominious death, if there were any sparke of grace or charity in him, it would make his heart to bleed for pity and commiseration.' *Coke upon Littleton*, Epilogue to Third Inst. (Ed. Hargrave and Butler, vol. vi. p. 244).

l. 38. **were for the moste part.** Robynson is not quite accurate in his rendering of the Latin original, 'quos passim narrabat nonnunquam suspendi viginti in una cruce,' who, he said, were being hanged in all quarters, sometimes twenty at a time on one gallows.

P. 12, l. 8. **the limites ⟨of⟩ Justyce.** Ed. 1 reads ' of the lymytes Justyce.'

l. 11. **refrayne men.** The proper sense of the word *refrenare*, 'hold in with a bit.' So Proverbs i. 15 ' my son, refrain thy feet from their path.' Ed. 2 reads ' refrayne and withhold.'

l. 32. **blacke heath filde.** See note on p. 10, l. 33.

l. 33. **warres in Fraunce.** On the death of Francis Duke of Brittany at the end of 1488, Henry VII, who had promised to protect his interests and was under great obligations to him, sent aid to his daughter Anne, whose territory was being overrun by the French king, Charles

NOTES: BOOK I

VIII. In October, 1492, he laid siege to Boulogne, but being secretly in treaty with King Charles, he soon terminated the expedition at the peace of Etaples on Nov. 14, 1492, being contented to receive an indemnity.

l. 37. **because warre lyke the tyde ebbeth and floweth.** This was altered in the second edition to 'forasmuch as warres have their ordinarie recourses,' which is also the reading of the subsequent editions.

P. 13, l. 5. **dorres** = drones. The word is said to be derived phonetically from the noise made by the insect. O.E. 'dora.' The word is vaguely used, being applied to a humble bee, a hornet, or a drone, as here.

l. 6. **polle.** Properly to remove the top or head (poll), so to cut the hair, and then generally to rob or pillage. It is frequently found in combination with 'pil'; so Spenser, *F. Q.* v. 2. 6 'Which pols and pils the poore in piteous wise.'

l. 7. **reysing their rentes.** This account of the poverty and misery prevalent in England and Europe, as well as of the causes of them, finds abundant illustration in contemporary testimony. The details are well summed up by Brewer. 'The arbitrary rule of its monarchs bent on their own aggrandizement, and careless of the improvement of their people,—the disputes among their Councillors, agreed in one point only, to flatter and mislead their sovereigns— the wide separation between the luxury of the rich and the hopeless misery of the poor—the prevalence of crime—the severe execution of justice, earnest for punishment but regardless of prevention—the frequency of capital punishment —the depopulation of villages,—the engrossing by a few hands of corn and wool—the scarcity of meat—the numbers of idle gentlemen without employment—of idle servingmen and retainers turned adrift on a life of vagabondism.' *Letters and Papers of the Reign of Henry VIII*, vol. ii. part i. Preface, p. ccxxii. For the grievance involved in raising the rents, see the Preambles to the Acts of 7 and 25 Henry VIII, and the 'Prayer for Landlords' in one of Edward's Liturgies, quoted in Cowper's Introduction to the *Select Works of Robert Crowley* (E. E. T. S.), p. xxii: 'We heartily pray Thee that they who possess the grounds, pastures and dwelling-places of the earth may not rack and stretch out the rents of their houses and lands nor yet take unreasonable fines and incomes . . . but so let them out to others that the inhabitants thereof may both be able to pay their rents

158   UTOPIA

and also honestly to live.' See also Crowley's sermon, *The Way to wealth*, where, speaking of landlords, he says: 'some have purchased and some taken by leases whole alleyes, whole rentes, whole rows, yea whole streats and lanes, so that the rents be reysed, some double, some triple and some four fould'; and his epigram on 'Rente Razers.' Emphatic expression is given to the same grievance in Brinklow's *Complaynt of Roderyck Mors*, in Starkey's *Dialogue*. The common term for landlords in Latimer's Sermons is 'rent raisers.'

l. 12. **a greate flocke or trayne of ydell**, &c. Cf. Starkey's *Dialogue between Pole and Lupset* (ed. Cowper, p. 77): 'Fyrst loke what an idul route our nobul men kepe and nurysch in theyr housys, wych do no thyng els but cary dyschys to the tabul and ete them when they have downe, and aftur gyuyng themselfe to huntyng, hawkyng, dysyng, cardyng and al other idul pastymes and vayne.' And these men, as ample testimony shows, when dismissed by their masters, or on the death of their masters, were turned loose on the country to swell the number of beggars.

l. 16. **incontinent** = immediately, forthwith; a common word in the English of the 15th–17th centuries, and in the adverbial form 'incontinently' not quite obsolete.

l. 25. **appayred their health.** Injure or damage, impair; cf. Prynne, *Power of Parliament*, ii. 71 'The ancient laws be greatly appaired.' Originally from the Lat. *adpeiorare* through the Old-French *empeire*. The word has a curious history. The prefix of the early *ampayre*, or *anpayre*, was subsequently treated like the native *an-* before a consonant and reduced to *a-* which in the fifteenth century was frequently though erroneously spelt *ap*. Caxton restored the Fr. form *empeyr*, *empayr*, which soon afterwards passed into the now current form *impair*. The word, common enough before, is rarely used after the sixteenth century.

l. 34. **iette.** Strut and swagger, boast or 'talk big.' See Glossarial Index.

l. 37. **Naye by saynt Marie, ser.** An interpolation of Robynson's.

P. 14, l. 1. **stomackes**—'temper,' 'inclination,' 'courage.' Cf. Shakespeare: 'He which hath no *stomach* to this fight, Let him depart' (*Henry V*, iv. 3. 35). The transition to this meaning comes from its use for 'appetite,' e.g. 'a good stomach for roast beef.'

ll. 7–9. **theues.** As the Latin context makes a distinc-

NOTES: BOOK I

tion, using 'fures' in ll. 7 and 8, and 'latrones' in l. 9, this should be preserved in the English; and Burnet very properly, in l. 9, translates 'robbers.'

l. 14. **Fraunce... plage.** Fortescue, in the third chapter of his *Governance of England*, comments on this custom and its inconveniences in France, adding: ' Lo, this is the fruit of his *Ius regale*.' With More's remarks on mercenaries may be compared the similar remarks of Macchiavelli, *Il Principe*, cap. xii.

l. 20. **wisefooles and very archedoltes.** In the original this is all comprised in the one word ' Morosophi,' which is the plural of a latinized Greek word Μωρόσοφοι, 'foolishly wise,' from Lucian (*Alexander*, 40). Pope has imitated the Oxymoron; 'the wisest fool much time has ever made.' *Moral Essays*, Epist. II. 124.

l. 21. **archedoltes.** 'As a prefix the usual sense of 'arch-' (Gk. ἀρχός) is 'chief,' 'principal,' 'high,' occasionally 'first in time,' 'original,' 'initial,' but in modern use it is prefixed intensively to words of bad or odious sense, as 'arch-traitor,' 'arch-enemy'' (N. E. D.).

l. 25. **fayne.** Ed. 2 reads 'forced.'

l. 28. **Saluste.** The quotation is from Sallust, *Cat.* **xvi** 'Ne per otium torpescerent manus aut animus.'

l. 34. **the Romaynes,** &c. Macchiavelli notices the ruinous effects on Rome and Carthage of employing mercenaries. With regard to the eastern nations, More may, as Dr. Lupton says, have had in his mind the Janizaries and Mamelukes. Dr. Lupton quotes Gibbon on the Mamelukes: 'The rage of these ferocious animals who had been let loose on the strangers was provoked to devour their benefactor' (*Decline and Fall*, ch. lix).

P. 15, l. 3. **inured.** Ed. 1 reads vrede = ' ured.'

l. 10. **vplandishe.** Belonging to the uplands or country-parts; so 'rude' or 'boorish.' Lumby quotes Puttenham, *Art of Poetry* (ed. Arber, p. 157): 'any *uplandish* village or corner of a realme where there is no resort but of poor rustical people.'

l. 16. **yf they.** Edd. 1 and 2 read 'they yf.'

l. 20. **spill.** To injure or destroy. A. S. *spillan*, an assimilated form of *spildan*, 'to destroy'; in this sense it became obsolete in the seventeenth century.

l. 25. **avayleable.** 'Serviceable,' ' that may avail.'

warre sacke = ' war's sake.' We frequently find 'sake' joined with an uninflected noun in Elizabethan

English; so Shakespeare, 1 *Henry IV*, i. 2. 174 'for recreation sake,' and *As You Like It*, iii. 2. 271 'for fashion sake.' It is found even now in nouns ending in *e*, 'for experience sake,' to avoid the clash of s's.

l. 29. noyous = 'troublesome,' 'grievous,' and Middle-English 'noyous'='noyes.' Cf. Chaucer, 'Thou art *noyous* for to carye' (*House of Fame*, i. 574); and Spenser, 'noyous' injuries (*F. Q.* ii. 9. 16).

l. 31. not onlye the = 'not the only.'

l. 35. your shepe, that were wont. More now enters specifically on the chief grievances of the time, namely (*a*) turning the arable land into pasture for the purpose of breeding sheep for their wool, and (*b*) the wrong done by the enclosures. The best comprehensive commentaries on More's view are the Preambles and First Sections of the Statutes 7 and 25 Henry VIII, and Starkey's *Dialogue between Pole and Lupset*, edited by J. M. Cowper for the Early English Text Society. To these may be added the 'Petition to Henry VIII' (cited in Furnivall's *Ballads from Manuscripts*, vol. i. 101-2); the ballad 'Now-a-dayes' and that of 'Vox populi, Vox Dei' in the same collection; Robert Crowley's *Sermons and Epigrams* (E. E. T. S.); Henry Brinklow's *Complaynt of Roderyck Mors*, printed by the same society; William Roy's *Rede me and be Nott Wrothe*; and *Certayne causes gathered together wherein is shewed the decaye of England only by the great multitude of Shepe, to the utter decay of household kepying, mayntenance of men, dearth of corne and other notable dyscommodityes approved by syxe olde Proverbes*, which was a supplication to Edward VI's Council 1550-3, also printed by the E. E. T. S. The sermons of Lever edited by Arber, and the sermons of Latimer edited for the Parker Society, throw much light on these subjects. These publications, ranging between about 1515 and 1553, very exactly illustrate every detail of More's terrible picture. Dr. Furnivall's Preface to the *Ballads from Manuscripts* and Mr. Cowper's Preface to Starkey's *Dialogue* may be consulted with advantage.

P. 16, l. 1. They consume, &c. Cf. Petition to Henry VIII (1514): 'The ploughes be decayed and the fferme houses and also other dwelling houses in many townes, so that where was in a towne XX or XXX dwelling houses they be now decayed ploughes and all, and all the people clene goon and decayed and no more parisshons in many parisshes, but a nettard and a sheppard, or a warner and a sheppard in the stede of 60 or 80 persones.' Cf., too, ballad of 'Now-a-dayes':—

> 'The townes go down, the land decayes;
> Off cornefeydes, playne layes;
> Great men makithe now-a-days,
> A sheepecott in the Churche.'
> (Furnivall's *Ballads from MSS.* i. 97.)

l. 5. certeyn Abbottes. Many and bitter are the complaints made in the ballads, and many and emphatic the supplications and protests against this action on the part of the Church. See particularly *A supplicacyon for the Beggers*, attributed to Simon Fish, which was answered by More himself, and Roy's *Rede me and be Nott Wrothe:*—

> 'The abbeys then full of covetyse,
> Whom possessions could not suffyse,
> Ever more and more encroachynge,'

but see the whole passage (ed. Arber), pp. 99-100, and *A proper Dyalogue*, ed. Arber, a full and elaborate review of those grievances, emphasizing and amply illustrating, what is condensed in the couplet:—

> 'Our patrimonie given away is
> Unto these Wolffes of the Clergye.'

See the complaint made to the Commons (Hall's *Chronicle*, Nov. 1529) that 'Priests beying surveiers stuardes and officers to Bishoppes, Abbotes and other spiritual heddes had and occupied Fermes, Graunges and grazing, in every country so that the poore husband men coulde have nothyng but of them; and yet for that they should pay derely.'

holy men. Of course satirical, the abbots being considered the chief offenders in this respect. The Civil Wars no doubt were a source of much loss to them, as the Black Death in the fourteenth century had been before. As they were not able to look after their lands, the property lost its value as productive soil, and they were only too glad to be able to derive any profit from their neglected estates; but it does not appear that they were more rapacious than lay landlords. See Gasquet's *Henry VIII and the English Monasteries*, vol. i. pp. 30-5.

l. 23. coueyne = fraud. The word is French *covin, covine*, from Low-Latin *convenium*, and properly means a coming together for agreement, so a compact or agreement.

From this it passed into meaning a *fraudulent* agreement, and since the fifteenth century is generally used in a bad sense.

l. 27. **pore, sylie, wretched soules.** For all this see the Ballads *passim* and Starkey's *Dialogue*. Ascham did not exaggerate when he wrote: 'Vita quae nunc vivitur a plurimis, non vita sed miseria est'; the life nowadays which most live is not life, but misery. 'Sylie' is of course used in the earlier sense of 'simple,' 'innocent,' being derived from A. S. *sælig*, happy, prosperous; the word then, following the analogy of εὐήθης in Greek, came to be used in a derogatory sense.

l. 35. **abyde the sale.** This obscure phrase can best be explained by reference to the Latin, 'haud magno uendibilem, etiam si manere possit emptorem,' i.e. their household stuff would not be worth much, even though it could await a buyer (an advantageous time for selling).

P. 17, l. 1. **God wote.** Literally 'God knows,' 'wote' being the third person singular present indicative of wit (A.S. *witan*, to know). It passed into a mere formula of emphasis. Ed. 2 changes the 'God wote' of the first edition into 'forsothe.'

l. 2. **a beggyng.** The common form of the verbal substantive still commonly used dialectally. This prefix, a form of 'on,' appears also in *a*board, *a*float, &c. So in A. V., John xxi. 3 'I goe a fishing.'

l. 6. **For one shepherde ...** Cf. Latimer. 'For where as have been a great many house-holders and inhabitants there is now but a shepherd and his dog.' (*First Sermon before Edward VI.*)

l. 7. Robynson has omitted a sentence in the Latin preceding this paragraph : 'Nam rusticae rei, cui assueuerunt, nihil est quod agatur, ubi nihil seritur,' which Burnet thus translates:—'For there is no more occasion for country labour, to which they have been bred, when there is no arable ground left.'

l. 11. **the pryce of wolle.** Cf. the tract *Certayne Causes* (Furnivall's *Ballads from MSS*. vol. i. p. 23): 'The more shepe the dearer is the wool'; and Becon's *Jewel of Joy* quoted by Dr. Lupton: 'Those beastes which were created of God for the nouryshment of man do nowe deceive man.... Since they ["gredy gentlemen"] began to be shepe maysters and feders of cattell we neyther had vyttayle nor cloth of any resonable pryce.'

l. 20. **morreyn** = murrain, cattle plague; from O. F.

NOTES: BOOK I 163

morine, M. E. *murrin*, *moreyne*, ultimately from Latin *mori*. It is not easy to identify the epidemic to which More refers. Dr. Lupton observes that the extreme wet of the year 1506 must have been injurious to cattle; and it would seem from Hecker's *Epidemics of the Middle Ages*, translated by Babington (p. 204), that there was a severe visitation of it in Germany and France. But in a state paper in the Record Office cited by Furnivall (*Ballads from MSS.* vol. i. p. 18), we find :—'the same selff yere thatt the warre ended there ffelle as greatt a generall Rott and Morregn amongst Cattelle as ever was seen eny time forty yeres beffore.' Brewer supposes that this refers to the termination of the French wars of 1523-5, but it may refer to the war concluded by the Treaty of Étaples in 1492: if so, this would fix the year.

l. 22. **And though the numbre of shepe, &c.** Robynson's version is inadequate. The Latin is ' Quod si maxime increscat ouium numerus, precio nihil decrescit tamen; *quod earum, si monopolium appellari non potest, quod non unus uendit, certe oligopolium est*.' The latter clause is thus rendered by Burnet, 'Though they cannot be called a Monopoly, because they are not engrossed by one Person, yet they are in so few Hands, and these are so rich,' &c. More's antithesis between *monopolium* and *oligopolium*—a word coined by himself—cannot be rendered in English. For the remark that though the number of sheep increase the price does not fall, see *Certayne Causes* (Furnivall, *Ballads*, i. 23), 'The more shepe, the dearer is the wool.'

l. 37. **incommoditie.** Inconvenience. French *incommodité*. Cf. Higden viii. 241: 'In the ende of harveste were so moche wete and reyne—whereby many incommodities followed.' The word is not quite obsolete in this sense.

l. 38. **make dearth,** i. e. raise the price. The Latin has 'reddunt cara.' M. E. *derthe*=dearness.

P. 18, l. 8. **in the whiche thyng.** That is, hospitalitie, as we gather from what follows.

l. 9. **this great dearth, &c.** Cf. *Certayne Causes*, cited by Furnivall (*Ballads*, i. 23): 'And where that the said persons were wont to have meate, drynche, rayment and wages, payinge Scot and lot to God and to our Kyng, now there is nothing kept there but onely Shepe . . . (they) go forthe from shyre to shyre to be scattered thus abroad . . . and for lacke of maysters by compulsyon dryuen, some of them to begge, and some to steale.'

l. 16. **this wretched beggerye.** On this *The Dialogue*

between Pole and Lupset furnishes a commentary (ed. Cowper, p. 95).

l. 19. **gentle.** Ed. 1 reads 'gently.'

l. 20. **handycraft men.** First Edit., 'hand y craft men.'

l. 24. **qweynes.** Loose women. The word is from the A.S. *cwene*, another form of *cwèn*, a woman, but from an early time having a bad sense attached to it. In M.E. the word was distinguished from its kindred word Queen by its open *e*, the one having the form *queyne*, the other *queene*. So in *Piers Plowman* (C) ix. 46 :—

> 'Other a knyght fro a knave,
> Other a queyne fro a queene.'

In Elizabethan English it is commonly spelt *quean*; so Shakespeare, 2 *Henry IV*, ii. 1. 51 'throw the *quean* in the Channel.'

l. 28. **tables,** i.e. backgammon. So Chaucer, *Boke of the Duchess*, 51 'Play either at Chesse or tables,' and Harington, *Epig.* i. 79 'Then with thy husband dost play false at tables.' The Latin word is *fritillus*, a dice-box. Dr. Lupton observes that More once spoke less harshly of such amusements, as 'to cast a coyte, a cokstele and a ball,' was one of the child's accomplishments in his pageant.

l. 31. **Caste out,** &c. Such is the advice given in *Dialogue*, p. 175.

l. 33. **towne** is here used in the old sense of an 'enclosed place,' and so a farmstead with its land.

l. 37. **ingrosse.** Buy up wholesale or monopolize the trade in any commodity: cf. Cranmer, *Catech*. 77 'Forestalling, regratyng, ingrossing of marchaundise.'

forstalle. To buy up beforehand in order to sell at a higher price to those who come later.

P. 19, l. 2. **let clothe workynge.** Cf. *Dialogue*: 'If thys stapul were broken or otherwyse redressyd & clothyng set up again in England ... the commodyte of our wolle & cloth schold bryng in all other thyngys that we haue need of.'

l. 9. **auuance your selfes of**=boast or pride yourselves on. Cf. Caxton, *Golden Legend*, 267 'He had no more wyll to advaunce him'; and Bishop Hall, *Hard Texts*, 477 'Thou advancest thyself to be as that glorious Cherub.'

l. 10. **For this iustice,** &c. The Latin is 'iusticiam nempe speciosam magis quam aut iustam aut utilem.' In his second edition Robynson turns it, 'is more beautiful in appearance and more florishyng to the shewe then either

NOTES: BOOK I

just.' . . . His first version is too cramped, his second too diffuse. Burnet has, 'which tho' it may have the Appearance of Justice, yet in itself is neither just nor convenient.'

l. 15. **they be commen.** Ed. 2, 'being come.'

l. 37. **Hold your peace.** There is a marginal note in the Latin calling attention to Morton's habit of cutting loquacious people short: 'Expressit morem ei Cardinali familiarem, interpellandi si quis loquacius ageret.'

l. 38. **by lyke** (= later, 'belike'), 'probably,' 'in all likelihood': now obsolete. Cf. Udall, *Aphor.* 'Harpalus who by like had a good insight in suche matters.' Ed. 2 substitutes 'it appeareth that.'

P. 20, l. 6. **earnest lette.** Serious hindrance. The original has 'nisi quid impediat aut te aut Raphaelem hunc.'

l. 8. **not worthy to be punished with death.** Compare the similar discussion between Pole and Lupset in the *Dialogue*, where Pole takes the same view as Hythlodaye, and Lupset the view of the Lawyer.

l. 22. **counteruayle** = make up for, be an equivalent for, Latin *contravalere*, to be of the same value as; commonly used in the English of the 16th and 17th centuries.

l. 25. **is recompensed** = is repaid, finds retribution. 'Recompense' was frequently used in earlier English for good or evil, but has now lost the latter meaning.

l. 28. **so streyte rules.** This is Robynson's translation for 'tam Manliana imperia,' which is to be found in Livy iv. 29, and implies 'stringent decrees.' Cf. 'Draconian laws.' Lucius Manlius, surnamed from the imperious harshness of his character Imperiosus, was dictator B.C. 363. Both he and his son Titus M. C. Torquatus were noted for their sternness and severity.

l. 30. **by and by.** At once, immediately; so generally in 16th and 17th century English.

l. 31. **stoycall.** The later Stoics considered that all crimes were equal, 'omnia peccata esse paria'—an absurd paradox very pleasantly ridiculed by Cicero, *Pro Murena*, xix, and Horace, *Sat.* i. 3. 94 seqq.

l. 34. **bothe a matter**, i.e. both one matter, equally guilty. *án* is the A. S. form of 'one,' and in M. E. the *n* is sometimes dropped. N. E. D. quotes Hampole, *Prose Tr.* 32 'Some ere of a tree and some er of another.'

P. 21, l. 16. **daunger** = jurisdiction, or power—a sense illustrating the history of the word, which is derived from *dominium* through O. F. *dangier*: so it comes to mean from 'power,' 'power to hurt or harm,' and so liability to come within that power.

l. 23. **Moyses.** The Greek form of Moses (Μωϋσῆς). The reference is to Exodus xxii. 1-9. Dr. Lupton appositely refers to Colet's *Letters to Radulphus*, where he observes that Moses adapted his language to 'the uncultivated nature of those poor people, but lately occupied among the bricks and clay': 'Sed crassiter et pingue docenda fuit stulta illa et macra multitudo.'

l. 28. **the newe lawe**, i. e. the teaching of the Gospel.

P. 22, l. 6. **care.** Ed. 2 reads 'feare.'

l. 7. **bewrayed**, i. e. betrayed. From A. S. *wrégan*, to accuse, through M. E. *bewraien*. Cf. A.V. of Isaiah xvi. 3 'Bewray not him that wandereth,' and Shakespeare, *Lear*, ii. 1 'He did bewray his practice.'

l. 8. **rydde**, removed.

l. 9. **vttered**, put forth, made public. Cf. Elyot, *Governour*: 'Marchauntes do utter ... wares and commodoties'; now used chiefly in the sense of circulating coins, genuine or counterfeit.

l. 10. **discriued** = descried, detected. See Glossarial Index.

l. 12. **single fellonye** = mere theft.

l. 30. **abowt the wordle.** So often spelt in M. E. Skeat quotes *Ayenbite of Inwyt*, p. 7, l. 10. Robynson repeatedly spells it so.

l. 32. **the polylerytes.** Like the Utopians, an imaginary people. Their name is derived from πολὺς λῆρος, 'much nonsense.'

l. 33. **wyttelye** = wisely, the common meaning in the English of the early sixteenth century and later.

P. 23, l. 8. **to their chiefe lord and kinge.** The first edition, misreading the original, which is 'rerum potienti' as 'potenti,' translated 'the myghtye Kynge.'

l. 10. **gallawnte** = comfortable, rather than gay or showy. Gallant is from French *galer* 'to rejoice.'

l. 16. **that they stoole.** Ed. 2 has 'that which' for 'that.'

l. 21. **paide of**, i. e. paid out of.

l. 29. **be not only tied**, &c. The Latin has 'non tam vinculis cohercent quam excitant uerberibus,' 'they not so much imprison as flog them,' i. e. they more often resort to flogging than imprisonment. The English version is therefore misleading.

l. 35. **indyfferent good** = fairly or moderately good.

NOTES: BOOK I

Cf. Shakespeare, *Hamlet*, iii. 1. 122 'I am myself *indifferent* honest.'

P. 24, l. 1. that = that which, the reading of the second edition.

l. 4. In some places ... mainteined. The Latin has simply, 'alibi reditus quidam publici ad id destinantur'; 'landis' is interpolated by Robynson. The first edition reads 'fownde' for 'mainteined,' both meaning the same thing.

l. 9. for so be thies, &c. This is not in the Latin here, but comes afterwards with reference to 'seruynge men' in l. 29. It may have been an omission which Robynson inserted later in the wrong place; or possibly he thought it desirable to introduce this phrase earlier. Damned, condemned, in the Latin *damnati*.

l. 19. sum thynge, i.e. their earnings, which they were not allowed to keep.

P. 25, l. 1. openeth, i. e. discloses. Cf. A. V. Acts xvii. 2, 3 'Paul ... reasoned with them ... *opening* and alleging, that Christ must needs have suffered.'

l. 5. of that they were of councell in that pretence, i. e. for being of counsel = Latin *conscientiae*.

l. 22. to theyre guydes, i. e. *for* their guides.

l. 23. sheyre. This is a good example of Robynson's or his printer's fondness for varying the spelling of words. He has already spelt this 'sheire' and 'shyere,' and further on we have 'shere.'

l. 28. wyth the maner, i. e. red-handed. The word is derived from *manus*, hand, and *opus*, work, act; whence *manuopere* = 'in the very act.' 'Mainour' in Cowell's *Law Dictionary* (quoted by Nares) is thus explained: 'Mainour, alias manour, alias meinour from the French manier, i. e. "manu tractare," in a legal sense, denotes the thing that a thief taketh away or stealeth; as to be taken with the mainour is to be taken with the thing stolen about him.' Cf. Latimer: 'even as a thief is taken with the maner that he stealeth' (*Sermons*, ed. Parker Society, p. 110). 'The manner of it is, I was taken *with the manner*;' *Henry IV*, ii. 4. 437, and *Love's Labour's Lost*, i. 1. 205 'O villain ... thou wert taken *with the manner*.'

l. 35. But. In the Latin 'At' (raising an objection) = 'But, some one will say.'

l. 36. dowted. To fear or be afraid, common in old English and not obsolete now. Cf. Holinshed, *Chron.* ii. 19

'The French king began to doubt of the puissance of King William,' and Shakespeare, *passim*.

P. 26, l. 8. **of their cownsell.** Depending on 'make'; i. e. they would not confide in, or take into their confidence.

l. 11. **openner** = discloser, detector, cf. *supra* 25. 1.

l. 17. **For euery yeare.** As Dr. Lupton remarks, an anticipation of our 'ticket-of-leave' system, instituted by the Penal Servitude Act of 1853.

l. 27. **made a wrie mouth.** Lat. 'distorsit labrum,' twisted his lip, i. e. pouted. *Cent. Dict.* quotes Scott, *Quentin Durward*, 'Die like a man without making wry mouths.'

l. 31. **withowte a proffe,** i. e. without putting it to the proof: Lat. 'nullo facto periculo.'

l. 34. **differryd** = deferred. Both words come from Lat. *differre*. But 'defer' in the sense of submit, or lay before, is from *deferre*.

l. 35. **saintuaries.** Originally every church or churchyard was a sanctuary for criminals. Some had special reputation, e. g. Westminster Abbey and Beverley Minster. The right of sanctuary in relation to common law was extended to any person accused of felony, who might thus preserve his life. There is ample testimony that this right was grossly abused. The *Dialogue* (p. 140) again illustrates More on this point, as well as the abuse of the privilege. 'And what think you by privylegys graunted to Churchys and al Sanctuarys? Can you judge them to be convenient? Thinke you that hyt ys wel a man when he hath commytted murder, or outragyouse robbery, decycevued hys credytorys, to run to the sanctuary with al hys godys? . . . Who wil be aferd to kyl hys enemy, yf he may be sauyd by the pryuylege of sayntuary?' On the gross abuses of the rights of Sanctuary, More comments at length in his *History of King Edward V*, in the speech he puts into Buckingham's mouth, when he is urging the Council to take the Duke of York out of the sanctuary to which his mother had fled with him (ed. 1641, pp. 68–76).

P. 27, l. 14. **sad** = serious. From O.E. *sæd*, full; so sated, heavy, with other meanings naturally deduced. Cf. in sense of text, 'Sadde resoun,' *Piers Plowman*, B. xv. 541; 'A few sad words,' Beaumont and Fletcher, *King and no King*, ii. 1.

l. 17. **parasite.** From Greek παρά, 'beside,' and σῖτος, 'food,' one who eats beside another at another's table; so a hanger-on or sycophant.

l. 18. **which wold seme** = who wished to simulate.

NOTES: BOOK I

ll. 25-6. **indifferent and reasonable.** Lat. 'non absurda,' not absurd; 'indifferent' practically qualifies 'reasonable,' and here means 'neither very reasonable nor very unreasonable.'

l. 27. **he that shoteth oft,** &c.: in the Lat. 'crebro iactu iaci aliquando Venerem.' Erasmus gives the Lat. proverb in his *Adagia*, chil. i. cent. iii. prov. 13 'Si saepe iactaveris, aliquando Venerem iacies,' i.e. 'If you throw [the dice] often, you will at some time or other throw a *Venus*.' The highest throw was called a *Venus*, and the lowest a *Canis*; so Propertius iv. 8. 45-6 'Me quoque per talos Venerem quaerente secundos, Semper damnosi subsiluere canes.'

l. 34. **vnweldye,** unwieldy. Used in an active sense; here practically synonymous with 'impotent,' 'that cannot wield.' Cf. Chaucer, *Rom. of the Rose*, 359 'Al woxen was hir body unwelde.'

l. 37. **For I had rather then anye good** = For I had rather than anything.

P. 28, l. 2. **with their lamentable teares,** &c. The Lat. is stronger: 'cum querulis illis opplorationibus flagitarent pecuniam,' 'when with that pitiful weeping they kept imploring me for money.'

l. 9. **leese** = lose. Cf. Shakespeare, Sonnet v. 14 'But flowers distill'd ... leese but their show'; it is very common in Elizabethan English.

l. 14. **into houses of religion.** Lat. has 'in Benedictinorum coenobia,' into the monasteries of the Benedictines. The Benedictines are an order of monks and nuns following the precepts of St. Benedict (*c.* 480–*c.* 543). Fifty Benedictines have already occupied the Papal throne. As they were by far the most numerous and most important of the Monastic Orders, their establishments are to some extent synonymous with 'houses of religion.'

l. 15. **laye bretherne,** i.e. those who take the habits and vows of religion, but are employed mostly in manual labour, and are not admitted into even minor orders.

l. 33. **towchyd one the quicke**—touched on the quick. 'Quick' from A. S. *cwic*, alive; so 'the quick' means what is sensitively alive, as in the phrases 'stung to the quick,' &c.

hit on the gawl. This and the above phrase combined are Robynson's equivalent for the Latin 'tali perfusus aceto' (an expression borrowed from Horace, *Sat.* i. 7. 32 'At Graecus, postquam est Italo perfusus aceto,' &c.), meaning literally 'deluged with such vinegar.' 'Gall' here means a 'blister,' and is especially applied to the sore on a horse produced by rubbing. It is possible that the word is connected with 'gall,' in the sense of bile, gall-bladder; the notion of venom being transferred to 'envenom'd spot.'

l. 34. fret = fretted. This word originally meant 'to eat' (A. S. *fretan*, German *fressen*); in 1835 it was used in an absolute sense 'to champ the bit.' Not to be confounded with fret-work, fretted ceilings, and the like, where the word is from *frætwan, frætwian*, to adorn or ornament.

l. 37. iauell. A low worthless fellow, a rascal. The derivation is uncertain. Cf. More's *English Works*, p. 1272 'a lewde, vnthriftye javell'; and Spenser, *Mother Hub. Tale*, 309 'These two javells' (N. E. D.).

P. 29, l. 4. Patient iourself. Compose yourself. A not uncommon use of the word in earlier English. Cf. Shakespeare, *Titus Andron.* i. 2. 58 'Patient yourself, Madam, and pardon me.'

l. 8. gallous = gallows, i.e. the name adjectivally used for one deserving of it, 'a gallows bird.' Cf. Shakespeare, *L. L. L.* v. 2. 12 'He hath beene five thousand yeeres a Boy. I, and a shrewd unhappy *gallowes* too.'

l. 10. be you angry. The reference is to Ps. iv. 4, where the A. V. reads, 'Stand in awe, and sin not'; but More follows the Septuagint and the Vulgate, corroborated by St. Paul's citation in Eph. iv. 26, as Dr. Lupton points out.

l. 14. the zeale of thy house. Ps. lxix. 9.

l. 16. The skorners of Helizeus, &c. The original lines are, as Dr. Lupton points out, from the *De Resurrectione Domini* of Adam of St. Victor: 'Irrisores Helisaei, Dum conscendit domum Dei, Zelum calvi sentiunt.' *Helizeus* = the Greek and Latin form of 'Elisha.' The 'scorners' of course refer to the children who mocked him for his baldness; see 2 Kings ii. 23. To indicate the Friar's want of scholarship More makes him use *zelus* for *zelum* as if (see marginal note) it were a neuter noun like *scelus*.

l. 22. set your wit to a fooles witte. Lat. 'Si te ita compares, ne cum homine stulto et ridiculo ridiculum tibi certamen instituas.'

l. 26. Answer a foole, &c. Prov. xxvi. 5.

l. 29. bald man. The monks and friars of course shaved the crown of their heads.

l. 33. excommunicate, suspended, and acursed. A periphrastic rendering of the original, which has simply *excommunicati*.

NOTES: BOOK I

l. 35. preuy beck. A secret signal. Lat. has *nutu*.

turned. The Latin has an adverb, *commodum*, meaning 'opportunely.' Neither Robynson nor Burnet translates it.

l. 37. heare his sueters. Up to 1858 all probate matters were under ecclesiastical jurisdiction; and the fact of his being also Lord Chancellor of England would make the Cardinal's legal duties particularly heavy.

P. 30, l. 5. hit. So frequently spelt till the middle of the sixteenth century.

parcell. In its original meaning of 'portion' or 'part,' still preserved in the phrase 'part and parcel.'

l. 9. improued. This is from the Latin *improbare=probare*, 'to approve of,' with the negative prefix in-, so that the word means 'to disapprove of.' The N. E. D. quotes Bale, *Eng. Votaries*, 8 'They have improved that doctrine and taught the contrarye.'

l. 10. incontinent = immediately; that is, hearing the Cardinal allow them, or let them pass, they immediately gave their approval to what was said. The Lat. original is *euestigio*.

l. 18. ensure = assure.

l. 24. of a child, i.e. as a child. Lat. has simply *puer*. For the reference see Introduction. Cf. Mark ix. 21.

l. 36. youre Plato. The passage referred to is in the *Republic*, bk. v. 473: 'Until philosophers are kings, or the kings and princes of this world have the spirit and power of philosophy, and political greatness and wisdom meet in one, and those commoner natures who follow either to the exclusion of the other are compelled to stand aside, cities will never cease from ill.' More, quoting probably from memory, gives only the general sense. By '*youre* Plato' he seems to mean the Plato whom you have plainly so carefully studied, and whose philosophy has had so much influence on you, a well-known Latin usage.

P. 31, l. 4. wyll ⟨not⟩ vouchesaufe. Original omits 'not,' which Lupton supplies. Latin *nec dignentur*.

l. 16. Dionise. Dionysius the Younger succeeded his father as tyrant of Syracuse in 367 B.C. He was indolent and dissolute, and Dion, his father's son-in-law, sought to improve him by inviting Plato to Sicily to instruct him in philosophy. He improved for a while; but a faction led by Philistus, the historian, succeeded in poisoning his mind against both Dion and Plato. Dion was accordingly banished, and Plato, not succeeding in obtaining his recall, left Syracuse. Thereupon Dionysius resumed his old life, and gave himself up to unrestrained debauchery. He was afterwards in turn driven out of Syracuse by Dion (who was later murdered), and several tyrants succeeded each other, until he at last retook the city in 346 B.C. After his return his conduct and mode of living were worse than ever, and two years later he was driven out by Timoleon, and spent the remainder of his life in Corinth (v. Plutarch, *Dion*).

l. 19. **noughtenes.** Much stronger than our use of it, and with the force of its derivation, A. S. *nawiht*, nothing, worth nothing. Cf. 1 Sam. xvii. 28 'I know thy pride, and the naughtiness of thy heart.'

l. 20. **laughynge stocke.** 'Stock' meant originally a 'stump,' 'stake,' 'post,' and came to mean an object especially stupid or dull, such a thing as would provoke scornful laughter; but 'laughing-stock' seems to mean a fixed object for laughing at; cf. the phrases 'laughing matter,' 'laughing thing,' and the like.

l. 22. **Frenche kynge.** Louis XII (1498–1515). On his accession he asserted his claims to the duchy of Milan, derived from his grandmother Valentina Visconti, and forthwith marched with an army into Italy and took possession in 1499. Encouraged by this he laid claim to Naples, derived from the Anjous, which had been unsuccessfully asserted by his predecessor, Charles VIII. Frederic, king of Naples, applied for assistance to Ferdinand, king of Spain, his relative, who thereupon sent him an army led by the celebrated Gonzalo of Cordova. Louis then secretly proposed to divide the kingdom of Naples with Ferdinand, who readily agreed; and they were joined in this infamous transaction by Pope Alexander VI. The unhappy Frederic, perceiving his hopeless condition, surrendered to Louis, who bestowed upon him the duchy of Anjou and a pension. Ferdinand and Louis, however, soon quarrelled over their respective shares; and after two battles the French were defeated and Naples was lost, 1503. A few years after Pope Julius II joined with Ferdinand, and after several campaigns Louis was finally driven out of Italy in 1513.

l. 29. **fugatyue.** Lat. *fugitivam*. So called because it was always slipping out of the grasp of the French.

l. 30. **Venetians.** At the treaty of Cambray (1508) Venice was divided between Louis XII, Ferdinand of Spain, Maximilian I of Austria, and Pope Julius II.

NOTES: BOOK I

l. 32. Flaunders. From the death of Count Louis III in 1384, as he left an only daughter married to Philip of Burgundy, Flanders had practically formed part of this duchy. But in 1477 Mary of Burgundy married Maximilian of Austria, so that at this time Flanders was included in the Austrian Netherlands.

Brabant. Formerly a most important province of the Netherlands. On the death (1477) of Charles the Bold, the last independent duke of Burgundy, Brabant, which was part of their dominion, passed with Flanders to the Empire.

Burgundie. This duchy should also have passed with Brabant and Flanders to Mary of Burgundy; but her right to it was disputed by Louis XI, who affirmed that, as it had been given to Philippe le Hardi as an appanage, it reverted to the Crown in default of male heirs. It was therefore annexed to France, while its possessions passed to the House of Austria. See Bryce, *Holy Roman Empire*, Appendix.

P. 32, l. 5. **Germaneynes.** The 'lance-knights' served as mercenaries with the French. They were particularly conspicuous at the battle of Ravenna in 1512 when opposed to the Spaniards.

l. 6. **Swychers.** Later, 'Switzers.' The Swiss were notorious as mercenary infantry. (See Book II. ch. viii, with the Notes.)

l. 7. **emperours maiestie.** This refers to Maximilian of Austria. Though he is said to have taken pay when serving with the English at Tournay, and generally to have been mean and grasping, his country's debt to him was incalculable. He consolidated both the power of his House and that of the Empire. He reformed German law and created German discipline, and was the first to establish an organized standing army. He also secured the reversion of Hungary and Bohemia to his descendants, by a diplomatic marriage of his grandchildren.

l. 10. **kynge of Arragone.** Ferdinand, husband of Isabella of Castile, and father of Catharine of Arragon, first wife of Henry VIII.

l. 11. **Nauarra.** Navarre, a province on the borders of France and Spain. This kingdom shared the fate of the other little states over which France and Spain were disputing in the sixteenth century; and in 1512 the portion south of the Pyrenees passed to Ferdinand of Spain. The

P

portion north of the Pyrenees was afterwards united to the crown of France by Henri IV. It is now known as the department of the Lower Pyrenees.

l. 13. wyth his .v. egges. A proverb indicating some paltry, worthless proposition, or a statement officiously intruded; the full phrase seems, as Ray gives it, to be 'five eggs a penny, and four of them addle.' N. E. D. quotes Udall, *Apoph.* 272 'Persones comying in with their five egges,' &c. In Swift's *Journal to Stella*, where the proverb frequently occurs, 'two' is substituted for 'five.' There is nothing to correspond to it in More's Latin.

l. 14. Castell. The reference here seems to be to the recent negotiations for a marriage between Charles, Prince of Castile, and Madame Renée, the youngest daughter of Louis XII, and to the anxiety of Charles and his German ministers for an alliance with France. See Brewer, *Reign of Henry VIII*, vol. i. pp. 79 and 148-52.

l. 17. staye = stick, stop.

l. 23. skottes. The French were ever ready for an alliance with the Scots, to aid them against England.

l. 24. in aunters = usually, *inaunter, enaunter*, 'in case that.' French, *aunter, aventure* = English 'adventure,' thus 'in adventure,' 'at adventure' = in case that. Cf. 'peradventure.'

l. 29. peere of Englande. The definite reference, if any, cannot be explained. Dr. Lupton thinks it refers to Perkin Warbeck; and Gilpin (*Utopia*, vol. i. p. 105) suggests Richard de la Pole, fifth son of John de la Pole, Duke of Suffolk; but neither conjecture is quite satisfactory.

l. 34. affiaunce = O.F. *afiance*, trust or confidence. So Coverdale, *Erasm. Paraphr.* 'puttyng his *affyaunce* in God.'

l. 38. turne ouer the leafe, and learne a newe lesson. Robynson has adopted an entirely different metaphor from the Latin 'uerti iubeam uela,' should order the sails to be shifted, i.e. 'to go on another tack,' as Dr. Lupton points out.

P. 33, l. 8. Achoriens. Derived from ἀ, priv., and χώρα, place = those without a place of habitation, who dwell in a non-existent place. Cf. 'Utopia.' In classical Greek the adjective ἄχωρος would mean literally 'homeless,' as in Aelian.

l. 13. aliaunce, i.e. an alliance by marriage. Lat. *affinitas*.

l. 23. pylled = plundered. Cf. French *piller*, Lat.

pilare (common in compound *compilare*), 'scrape together and carry off.' Cf. Engl. 'compile.' Cf. Shakespeare, *Richard the Second*, ii. 1. 246 'The Commons hath he *pill'd* with grievous taxes.'

l. 26. peace nothynge better then warre. Lat. 'pacem nihilo tutiorem.'

l. 32. set by. A synonym for 'regarded' or 'esteemed.' Cf. 'His name was much *set by*,' 1 Sam. xviii. 30.

P. 34, l. 3. mo = more. In M. E. 'mo' and 'more' were different words, 'mo' relating to number, and 'more' to size. Cf. Chaucer, *Prol.* 578 '*Mo* then thries ten.'

l. 5. take hym for his muletṭour. Another form of the proverb 'qui aliena servat sua negligit.' moyles = mules. Cf. 'And at the sayd Noualassa we toke *moyles* to stey us vp the mountayne.' Sir R. Guylforde, *Pylgrymage*, p. 80.

l. 12. hys sake. Referring to the French king.

l. 13. hurley-burley = commotion, tumult, turmoil. Cf. *Macb.* i. 1. 3 'When the Hurley-burley's done, When the Battaile's lost and wonne.' The phrase 'hurling and burling' preceded this. 'Hurling' itself means a 'disturbance,' and 'burling' is merely an initially varied repetition to intensify the meaning. Cf. 'topsy-turvy.'

l. 21. endeuoure himself. Used reflexively. Cf. Caxton, *Gold. Leg.* 422, 423 'He ... moche *endeuoyred hym* to make hym to lerne the deuyne Scripture'; and Elyott, *Gov.* Pref. 2 'I endeavoured myself while I had leisure ... to translate.'

l. 26. turne hym to, i.e. turn his attention to.

l. 29. suppose that some kyng. In the passage which follows More is glancing at abuses notorious in his time. Edward IV and Henry VII dealt with the coinage as More describes: Edward issuing, for the old coins, nobles and half-nobles worth respectively 6*s*. 8*d*. and 3*s*. 4*d*.; angels and angelots which, though considerably inferior in weight to the former coins, were ordered to pass as equivalent in value; and Henry VII securing great profit by calling in minished or impaired coins and receiving them at the Mint by weight. See Dr. Lupton's Note.

P. 35, l. 1. to fayne warre. The particular reference seems to be to the subsidy levied in 1490, of a tenth and fifteenth for the maintenance of the army which was being raised for the defence of Brittany against France, and the subsidy of two entire tenths and fifteenths granted by the Parliament of January, 1492. The King came to peace with

France at the treaty of Etaples, and appropriated the rest of the subsidy. See Stubbs, *Lectures on Mediaeval and Modern History*, ed. 3, 410 sq.

l. 10. **certeyn olde and moughte-eaten lawes.** This refers to the rapacious proceedings of Empson and Dudley under Henry VII, who put into force obsolete (moth-eaten) laws in order to exact a fine from those who were able to afford it and so increase the revenue. Lupton appositely quotes Hallam, *Const. Hist.* ch. i, who says that Statutes passed in previous reigns were 'raked out from oblivion,' and Henry, 'prosecuting such as could afford to endure the law's severity, filled his treasury with the dishonourable produce of amercements and forfeitures.' See Bacon's *Henry VII*; Kennett, i. 629.

l. 19. **dispence for money with.** This is a literal translation of the mediaeval Latin phrase *dispensare cum*, which More employs in the original. It means to arrange administratively with a person so as to grant him a relaxation or remission of a penalty incurred by breach of law, or special exemption or release from a law or obligation— N. E. D., which quotes Latimer, *2 Serm. before Edw. VI*, 'God had dispensed wyth theym to have many wives,' and Holland, *Suet.* 104 'He dispensed with a gentleman of Rome for his oath . . . never to divorce his wife'; the condition being expressed in English by 'for.'

not be vsed = not to be used.

l. 25. **preuyleges and licences,** i.e. monopolies; an abuse which reached its height in the reign of James I.

l. 31. **endaunger** = 'subject (the judges) to his absolute control,' which is the primary meaning of 'endanger.'

l. 35. **And they muste be called,** &c. The second edition reads 'yea, and further to call them into his palace, and to require them there to argue,' &c.

P. 36, l. 3. **pike a thanke** = pick a thank or favour; one who picks a thank, i.e. filches a favour. Hence a 'pickthank' came to mean a 'toady'; cf. Shakespeare, *Henry IV*, iii. 2. 25 'By smiling *pickthanks* and base newsmongers.' So Wither, *Britain's Remembrancer*, 'By slavish fawning or by *picking thanks*' (Nares).

l. 5. **take . . . in a trippe.** As we say, 'catch them tripping.'

l. 10. **fyt occasion.** Robynson has apparently, as Dr. Lupton notes, mistaken the adverb *commodum*. 'seasonably' or 'opportunely,' for an adjective agreeing with *ansam*.

NOTES: BOOK I

l. 16. **equitie of.** The second edition reads 'on.' But it is by no means uncommon to have 'of' for 'on' or 'for.' See Glossarial Index.

l. 17. **wrythen and wrested**=distorted and twisted. 'Wrythen' is the old past participle of 'writhe.'

l. 22. **Crassus.** Marcus Licinius Crassus, surnamed, from his ancestor Publius Licinius Crassus Dives, and celebrated for his enormous wealth. He was elected consul with Pompey in B.C. 70 and joined him and Caesar in forming the first triumvirate. While endeavouring to conquer the Parthians he was defeated and taken prisoner by Surenas, their general, who put him to death. Dr. Lupton observes that this passage looks like a reminiscence of Pliny, *Hist. Nat.* xxxiii. 10 'M. Crassus negabat locupletem esse, nisi qui reditu annuo legionem tueri posset.'

P. 37, l. 6. **if I shuld declare.** This doctrine, so daring in a subject of the Tudors, finds emphatic expression in one of More's Latin Poems to which he affixes as a title 'Populus consentiens regnum dat et aufert'—

> Quicunque multis vir viris vnus praeest,
>   Hoc debet his quibus praeest:—
> Praeesse debet neutiquam diutius
>   Hi quam volent quibus praeest.'

The same is maintained in Starkey's *Dialogue between Pole and Lupset*, ii. 1: 'After the deceise of the prynce, by electyon of the common voyce of the parlyamant assemblyd to chose one most apte to that hye offyce and dygnyte, wych schold not rule and govene al at hys owne plesure and lyberty but ever be subjecte to the ordur of hys lawys.' Monarchy on this principle and of this kind is one of the remedies proposed for the lamentable condition of the kingdom.

l. 9. **wealthily,** i. e. well. So also supra, 47. 5 'wealthely deuysed'; wealthe=well-being. See Glossarial Index.

l. 13. **to feade his shepe.** Lupton compares Ezek. xxxiv. 2 'Woe be to the shepherds of Israel that do feed themselves: should not the shepherds feed the flocks?' and Plato, *Repub.* i. 343 'You fancy that the shepherd or neatherd fattens or tends the sheep or oxen with a view to their own good, and not to the good of himself or his master.'

l. 26. **behated**=thoroughly hated. The prefix 'be' here, as usual, intensifies the word. Cf. belove.

l. 35. **hardie and couragius.** This is hardly a translation of the Latin 'vir erecti ac sublimis animi,' which Burnet more correctly translates 'A man of a noble and exalted Temper.'

l. 36. **Fabrice.** This is Caius Fabricius Luscinus who was elected consul in 282 B.C., and was renowned for his frugality and incorruptibility. After the defeat of the Romans by Pyrrhus king of Epirus, 281 B.C., Fabricius was sent to treat with that king, who tempted him with large bribes to enter his own service. Fabricius, though poor, refused. It is also said that Pyrrhus's own physician proposed to Fabricius to poison his master for a bribe; at which the consul indignantly put him in chains and sent him back to the king, who was greatly impressed by this example of Roman integrity. The saying attributed to him in the text is to be found in Valerius Maximus iv. 5 : but is there related of M'. Curius Dentatus who finally defeated Pyrrhus in 275 B.C.

P. 38, l. 6. **be taking from them.** 'Be' is an old form of 'by' still retained in compounds. Cf. supra, p. 26, and p. 55, 15.

l. 8. **feate.** Properly an action or deed (*factum*), then an art or trick. Cf. Chaucer. *Clerks Tale*, 429 'Griseldis—Coude all the feate of wifely homeliness.'

l. 9. **let hym,** &c. This could scarcely have been palatable advice to Henry VIII, to whom it plainly relates.

l. 11. **runne in** = incur, from Lat. *incurrere*, which, however, never means 'incur' in classical Latin.

l. 13. **Let him do coste not aboue his power** = let him adapt his expenditure to his income.

l. 18. **callynge agayne lawes** = reviving laws. The favourite device of the sharks under Henry VII.

l. 19. **lawes, whiche a custome.** Cf. supra, p. 35, l. 10, note on Empson's and Dudley's Extortions. *Hist. of Henry VII*, Kennett, p. 629.

l. 22. **take suche fynes,** &c. Cf. what Bacon says of Empson and Dudley, *Henry VII*, ed. Lumby, p. 190: 'Their manner was to cause divers subjects to be indicted of sundry crimes ... to suffer them to languish long in prison and by sundry devices and terrors to extort from them great fines and ransoms which they termed compositions and mitigations.' Dibdin sees a pointed allusion to Henry VII's treatment of More's father.

l. 26. **Macariens.** The happy people. From the Greek, μίκαρες, fortunate, blessed. It is not difficult to understand why this epithet is bestowed on them. Some, however,

NOTES: BOOK I

fancifully think that it refers to the *Fortunatae Insulae* or
'Islands of the Blessed.'

l. 30. golde or syluer. Dr. Lupton compares with this
the fortune which Henry VII is said to have left at his
decease, amounting to not less than £1,800,000, or in modern
equivalent, certainly not less than eighteen millions. The
Lat. says 'a thousand pounds of gold in weight, or silver of
equivalent value.'

l. 35. The translation is here somewhat obscure. The
Latin of this passage is, ' Nempe eum thesaurum videbat
suffecturum, sive regi aduersus rebelleis, sive regno adversus
hostium incursiones esset confligendum ; caeterum minorem
esse quam ut animos faciat invadendi aliena.' ' He thought
that sum sufficient should the King require it against rebels,
or the country against invasion, yet insufficient to encourage
the prince to invade the rights or possessions of others.' As
Dr. Lupton remarks, 'invadendi aliena' may mean foreign
wars.

P. 39, l. 3. able = enable, which is the reading of the second
edition.

l. 10. prescript some = prescribed sum.

l. 13. of euell, of good = by ... by.

l. 14. informatyons. Lat. 'haec ... si ingererem.'

l. 25. cleane contrarye. Though ' clean ' in this sense
is now colloquial, it was commonly used in dignified composition in the sixteenth century.

l. 26. schole philosophie. Lat. *scholastica*.

l. 27. in the counselles of kynges ... phylosophye
hadde no place among *Kinges*. Cf. Philip de Commines,
Memoirs (English trans., bk. ii. ch. x), 'They are brought
up to nothing but to make themselves ridiculous. They
have no knowledge of letters; no wise man is suffered to
come near them to improve their understandings.'

l. 35. cyuyle. The Lat. *civilis* = pertaining or adapted
to citizens: *civil* in this sense is not yet obsolete.

P. 40, l. 3. Plautus. T. Maccius Plautus (or M. Accius
Plautus as he is also, but incorrectly, called) was the most
prolific and original of Roman comic dramatists; twenty
of his plays are extant. Born about 250 B.C., he died
184 B.C.

l. 4. vyle bondemen, i.e. the slaves who were impersonated in the comedy.

l. 8. Seneca. Lucius Annaeus Seneca, the philosopher,
born about 4 B.C.; he was a very versatile author. The

tragedies which he wrote, among which *Octavia* which he certainly did not write is included, are imitations of Greek Alexandrian models and distinguished rather for rhetorical than dramatic power. He was accused of taking part in the Pisonian conspiracy against Nero, and condemned. He elected to open his veins, and so perished, 65 A.D.

l. 8. **dysputeth with Nero.** This occurs in the second act of *Octavia*, and forms a very animated dialogue.

l. 9. **domme persone.** The *muta persona*, or, in Greek, the κωφὸν πρόσωπον; the character who plays a 'thinking' part and says nothing.

l. 12. **gallymalfreye** (or 'gallimaufry' as it is more commonly spelt), was originally a 'dish made up of odds and ends of food,' a 'hodge-podge'; then used for any confused jumble or mixture. Here it means 'a ridiculous medley.' This is probably the earliest use of the word in English; from fourteenth-century Fr. *galimafrée*.

l. 37. **wyttelye**, i.e. wisely; **handsomely** = 'handily,' 'in a suitable manner.'

P. 41, l. 9. **as for to speake** = as for speaking.

l. 19. **as much.** First edition 'a smuch.'

l. 20. **seuerall**, separate. Cf. Milton, *Hist. Eng.* ii *fin.* 'So different a state of things requires a *several* relation.' Cf. the modern phrase 'they went their *several* ways.'

l. 26. **hedlonges**, adverbial genitive in -s. The word was originally 'headling,' but altered by erroneous assimilation to '-long.' '-ling' is an old suffix for forming adverbs from nouns.

l. 32. **wyncke at,** 'shut our eyes to.' Cf. Shakespeare, *Macbeth*, i. 4. 52 'Let not night see my black and deep desires; The eye *wink at* the hand!'

l. 36. **in open howses.** The expression is not clear in the English. The original is 'palam in tectis,' openly on the housetops. See Luke xii. 3.

l. 37. **dissident from**, at variance with.

P. 42, l. 3. **euel willing,** evil or ill willing, and so 'unwilling.'

l. 4. **wrested,** twisted. 'Wrest once the law to your authority: To do a great right do a little wrong,' Shakespeare, *M. of V.* iv. 1. 215. **wriede,** turned or twisted, and so 'perverted.' The verb 'wry' meant to turn or twist: the verb is now almost obsolete in all forms, but the phrase 'awry' still remains, as well as the adjective 'wry.'

NOTES: BOOK I   181

l. 5. **a rule of leade** (Greek μολίβδινος κανών, *plumbea regula* in More's Latin) was used in ancient Greece in 'Lesbian building'—probably because, being *flexible*, it could be adapted to curved 'Lesbian' mouldings: it is mentioned for its adaptability by Aristotle, *Ethics*, V. 10. 7, whence More drew the metaphor. (For other examples in English literature, see N. E. D. s.v. Lesbian, and see *in loc.* Stewart's *Notes.*)

l. 6. **at the leaste waye**, at least.

l. 9. **sickerlye**, securely, surely. M. E. *sikerly*, in its turn derived from the Lat. *securus*.

l. 10. **asmuche.** The second edition reads 'as little.'

l. 13. **Mitio saieth in Terence.** *Adelphi*, i. 2. 66 'Verum si augeam Aut etiam adiutor sim eius iracundiae, Insaniam profecto cum illo.'

Terence. P. Terentius Afer is the only Roman comic dramatic poet, with the exception of Plautus, whose works have come down to us. He died 159 B.C.

l. 15. **traine.** That which draws or lures on, so an artifice. Now obsolete in this sense, but common in earlier English. Cf. Spenser, *F. Q.* i. 3. 24 'Subtil Archimag that Una sought By traynes into new troubles to have toste,' and Shakespeare, *Macbeth*, iii. 4. 118 'By many of these traines hath sought to win me.'

l. 20. **there.** The emphasis is on this word, as it renders *ibi* in the original.

l. 27. **occasyon.** This is the meaning of the Latin word *occasio*, opportunity.

l. 33. **layde in hys necke**, i.e. laid to his charge: cf. infra 114, l. 26, 'and them they sette in theyre neckes.' The metaphor appears applicable to a yoke rather than to setting on dogs to the neck of a hunted animal. Compare Cicero, *Ad Fam.* xii. 23 'Cogitabat legiones ad urbem adducere *et in cervicibus nostris* collocare,' and many similar instances in Lewis and Short's Latin Dictionary.

l. 36. **Plato.** From *Repub.* vi. 496: 'And he [the wise man] reflects upon all this and holds his peace and does his own business. He is like one who retires under the shelter of a wall in the storm of dust and sleet which the driving wind hurries along; and when he sees the rest of mankind full of wickedness, he is content if he only can live his own life and be pure from evil or unrighteousness, and depart in peace and goodwill with bright hopes.'

P. 43, l. 10. **as my mynde geueth me**, as my feelings

incline or move me. The verb is still retained in 'my mind *misgives* me.'

l. 11. **beareth all the stroke,** i. e. has the chief influence. 'He has a great *stroke* with the reader when he condemns any of my poems, to make the world have a better opinion of them ' (Dryden).

l. 25. **had in pryce.** The Latin is ' ut et virtuti precium sit, et tamen aequatis rebus omnia abundent omnibus '; which seems to mean 'that, while worth receives its proper wage, nobody shall lack.'

l. 26. **common.** On this, the basis of the Utopian Commonwealth, see Introduction.

l. 38. **holde well with Plato,** agree with Plato. This anecdote is related by Diogenes Laertius in his Life of Plato (*De Vitis Clar. Phil.* iii. 17); translated, it runs thus : ' Pamphila says in the twenty-fifth book of her *Commentarii* that the Arcadians and Thebans, after building a great city, asked him [Plato] to be its legislator; but that, on learning that they would not consent to an equality of rights, he declined to go thither.' Aelian (*Var. Hist.* ii. 42) tells the same story at greater length.

P. 44, l. 12. **all the riches that there is.** Ed. 2 reads 'all the whole riches.' Robynson here seems to regard the word as sing., no doubt correctly (= M. E. *richesse*); but it also occurs as plur. from the *Ayenbite* onwards (see Skeat's *Etymological Dictionary*).

l. 25. **propriety,** ownership ; right of possession. The Lat. *proprietas.*

l. 32. **a certein measure of ground.** In the draft of a Bill of 1548 by Hales preserved in the Record Office, which in its preamble sums up the distresses and miseries caused by the wrongs and grievances here indicated, the limitation suggested by More was proposed. See transcript in Appendix to Introduction to *A discourse of the Common Weale of England*, edited by Miss Lamond, pp. 47, 48.

l. 37. **offices shold not be obteined.** The all but universal corruption which More here exposes is the theme of almost all who illustrate the social history of the time. See the ballad of *Now a dayes*, and others in Furnivall's *Ballads from Manuscripts*, the *Dialogue between Pole and Lupset*, and the *Sermons* of Latimer and Lever. 'The saying is now,' says Latimer, ' that money is heard everywhere : if he be rich he shall soon have an end of his matter.'

Everything was for sale—employments, offices, justice. In his own rigid incorruptibility More stood alone.

suyte, suit, solicitation.

P. 45, l. 4. **gather vp their money again,** recoup themselves.

l. 9. **kept vp.** Ed. 2 reads 'kept and betched vp for a time.'

l. 17. **taken from an other.** Cf. Publilius Syrus (*Sent.* ed. Nisard, p. 785), 'Lucrum sine damno alterius fieri non potest': and Bacon's 'Whatsoever is somewhere gotten is somewhere lost' (*Of Seditions and Troubles*). Spenser, *F. Q.* v. 2. 39, furnishes a picturesque illustration; and the proverb, 'Serpens nisi serpentem comederit non fit draco,' a fancifully practical one.

l. 32. **what place it maye haue,** i. e. how it can have a place.

l. 38. **presently** = personally (Lat. *praesens*).

P. 46, l. 33. **impery.** A form of the word directly from the Latin *imperium*. The commoner form in early English is 'empery,' from the old French 'emperie.'

l. 36. **So great proffyte ... from hence.** This is a little obscure, through being so literal; the original is 'tanto bono fuit illis aliquos hinc semel illuc esse delatos.' Burnet turns it 'so happily did they improve that accident of having some of our people cast upon their shore.'

P. 47, ll. 16, 17. This is an interesting illustration of the purely capricious spelling common with Robynson, his predecessors and contemporaries, and printers. 'Their' is spelt in the course of two lines in no less than four different ways.

l. 25. '**Content ... be it.**' Original has *fiat*, 'let it be done.'

BOOK II

CHAPTER I

P. 48. In the title, for 'Godly' gouernement, Ed. **2** reads 'politike.'

Topography and general description of Utopia; its havens, defences and cities; its capital and the connexion of the capital with the cities and country districts; rural life and its organization; its agricultural system, transference of produce to the cities, and relation of the cities to the rural districts.

The general description of Utopia is plainly modelled on Plato's picture of Atlantis in the *Critias*, pp. 112-20 (see Jowett's translation). It bears also some resemblance, as Mr. Cannan has pointed out to me, to Tacitus's account of Britain. *Agricola*, cap. x 'Formam .... eloquentissimi auctores oblongae scutulae vel bipenni assimilavere. . . . Immensum et enorme spatium procurrentium extremo iam littore terrarum velut in cuneum tenuatur.' In More's Latin this becomes 'fines versus paulatim utrimque tenuatur'; ... while the ends 'insulam totam in lunae speciem renascentis effigiant.' There can be little doubt that the contrast presented by such towns as Bruges and Antwerp to London must have greatly contributed to draw More's attention to the deficiencies in English social life and its surroundings. The same contrast was noticed some years later by Starkey. 'Methought, when I came fyrst into Flaunders and Fraunce, that I was translatyd as hyt had byn in a nother world, the cytes and townes apperyd so gudly, so wel bylded and so clene kept: of the wych ther ys in every place so grete cure and regard that every towne semyd to me to stryue wyth an other, as hyt had byn for victory, which schold be more beautiful and strong, bettur byld and clennur kept' (*Dialogue*, ed. Cowper, pp. 92, 93).

l. 16. **Whiche.** Referring to 'endes.'

fetchynge about a circuite or compasse, i. e. forming a circle, making a circular course. N. E. D. quotes Coverdale, *Eccles*. i. 6 'The wynde goeth toward ye South & fetcheth his compase about unto the North'; and Gilpin, *Demonol*. 56 'He falls not directly upon what he intended, but fetcheth a compass.'

.v.c. = 500.

l. 18. **Betwene thys two corners**, &c. The island would be roughly horse-shoe shaped, the two extremities being only eleven miles apart in a bee line, whilst the sea, enclosed like a harbour, would be of a circular shape and 160 miles across, the whole island being 360 miles in diameter. The general description of the haven recalls what may possibly have suggested it, Virgil, *Aen*. i. 159-64:

'Est in secessu longo locus: insula portum
Efficit obiectu laterum, quibus omnis ab alto
Frangitur inque sinus scindit sese unda reductos.
Hinc atque hinc vastae rupes geminique minantur
In caelum scopuli, quorum sub vertice late
Aequora tuta silent.'

NOTES: BOOK II

l. 20. **surmounteth**, mounts over the two corners, that is, the *fons Anydri* and the *ostium Anydri* (as marked in the woodcut opposite the title-page of the original edition), and forms a bay.

l. 23. **nor mountith not.** This is like the Greek double negatives, not making, of course, an affirmative but intensifying one other; it is common in Elizabethan English. Cf. 'This England never did (nor never shall), Lie at the proud foot of a conqueror.' Shakespeare, *K. John*, v. 7. 113.

P. 49, l. 1. **fordys.** A ford is properly a shallow place which may be crossed by wading. Here it means 'shallow tracts of water.' **shelues**, shoals, sand-banks.

l. 5. **bicause it is in sight.** There is nothing to correspond to this in the Latin.

l. 15. **translatynge** = transferring. *translatus* is used as p.p. of *transferre*, but *-latus* is from a different root, *tal*, 'to bear,' or 'carry across,' whence Lat. *tollere*. For Robynson's now obsolete use of it cf. A. V. Heb. x. 15 'By faith Enoch was translated that he should not see death.'

l. 18. **The out side.** Ed. 2 adds 'or vtter circuite of.'

l. 19. **suerly** = securely. **what by . . . what by.** Like 'what with . . . what with,' supra l. 1; the two 'whats' meaning 'partly, partly,' or 'both, and'; *aut, aut* in the original.

l. 26. **Abraxa.** Dr. Lupton suggests that this name may be derived from or connected with the Greek ἄβρεκτος, 'unwetted' or 'wanting rain'—a city on which no rain fell,—and he compares 'Anyder,' though the derivation there has certainly more point. But there can be little doubt that what suggested the word to More was what suggested to him the letters of the Utopian alphabet, namely the symbols or gems of the Gnostics. See the plates in King's *Gnostics and their Remains*. More says in the ninth chapter that the Utopians worshipped Mithras. Now, by the Gnostics, Abraxas was frequently associated with Mithras in the gems. Abraxas is a mystic name said to mean either in actual Coptic 'Holy Name,' or, as seems equally probable, merely the Hebrew 'Ha-B'rachah,' i. e. 'The Blessing.' The symbolic figure embodying the idea of the Abraxas god has a reference to the sun in all its components. See King's *Gnostics*, pp. 117 seqq. and pp 251-9. 'Abraxas,' there can be little doubt, suggested this name to More.

l. 28. humanitie = civilization, 'culture' exactly, the Lat. *humanitas*. N. E. D. quotes Wyclif, 2 Macc. iv. 11 'Because of humanytee or curtasie.'

l. 32. vplandyshe, i.e. up country, = right inland, or possibly in the sense used supra, 15. 10.

l. 35. because = that, in order that. Cf. Matt. xx. 31 'And the multitude rebuked them because they should hold their peace.'

l. 38. into = among. A rare use of the word.

P. 50, l. 6. .liiii. Dr. Lupton thinks that More had England in his mind. Harrison (*Description of England*, ed. Furnivall, pp. 96-7) gives the number of English counties as fifty-three, and More may have reckoned the City as a county in itself, and so made up his number.

l. 7. agreyng all together. So Tacitus on the Germans. *Germ.* ch. ii.

l. 10. as farfurth as. The difference between 'farfurth' and 'far' is not easy to grasp.

l. 14. Amaurote. The 'dark,' 'dim,' 'obscure' city, Gk. ἀμαυρός, a fitting name for the capital of Utopia. It is applied in the *Odyssey* (iv. 824) to a spectre or vision which Athene sends to Penelope—εἴδωλον ἀμαυρόν.

l. 15. entreate = treat. Cf. 'Richarde, the third sonne, of whom we now entreate.' More's *Rich. III*, xxxvii. 1.

l. 17. in the myddes. In the midst. The Lat. has *in umbilico*, 'in the navel.'

l. 28. husbandes, i. e. husbandmen. Cf. Fabyan, *Chron.* vii. 421 'In this yere ... fell so excedynge rayne that husbondys myght not bring in their store of corne'; and Dryden, 'When Husbands have survey'd the last Degree, ... and order'd ev'ry Tree' (Virg. *Georg*. ii. 578).

l. 32. of the cytezens, by the citizens, common use of 'of.' N. E. D. quotes Gower, *C. A.* iii. 1332 (Macaulay), 'The Cite ... Of worthi folk ... was enhabited here and there.'

l. 33. by course, i. e. in turn, alternately. Cf. Sidney, *Arcadia*, i. 5 'They took their journey. ... Claius and Strephon by course carrying his chest for him.' Tacitus notes that the same custom prevailed among the Germans: 'Agri pro numero cultorum ab universis in vices occupantur' (*German*. xxvi). *Vices* has been corrected to *vicis* in modern editions; see Stubbs, *Const. Hist.* i. p. 19, n. 3.

l. 35. bonden men. Men who have transgressed the law and are made slaves. They are attached to the

NOTES: BOOK II

soil, and pass transferred accordingly to its successive owners.

ll. 36, 37. **good man, good wyfe.** Still used commonly for the master and mistress of a house.

P. 51, l. 1. **Phylarche.** Strictly 'chief of a tribe or clan' from the Greek φύλαρχος, φυλή, clan, and ἀρχός, chief. Robynson is more accurate than the original, which misprints it 'philarchus,' the reading at the end of this chapter being correct—'phylarchi.' Cf. Macaulay on Croker's *Boswell* (Essays, ed. 1861, p. 161).

l. 2. **baylyffe.** After 1531 applied to a landlord's agent: here he is acting for the State. O. F. and M. E. *baillif*, from the late Latin *baiulivus*, properly meaning one charged with public administrative employment in a certain district.

l. 15. **occupiers**, i. e. 'those occupied in.'

l. 16. **solempne** = customary. Lat. *sollemnis*, literally 'annual,' applied to religious rites which occurred annually; hence solemn = serious. For the sense in which it is here employed cf. Milton, *Par. Lost*, iv. 646-7 'silent night with this her *solemn* bird.'

l. 22. **bryde vp** = breed or bring up: a variant not noticed by the N. E. D.

l. 25. **pulleyne**, i. e. poultry. Low Lat. *pulla*, a hen. **policie**, i. e. contrivance. The Lat. has *artificium*. For the account in the text Dr. Lupton quotes Bacon, *Nat. Hist.*, cent. ix. 856, and Pliny, *Hist. Nat.* x. 54, and refers to a curious passage in the pseudo-Maundeville's *Travels* (ed. 1883, p. 49). The whole subject is discussed and amply illustrated by J. A. St. John in his *Egypt and Mohamed Ali*, vol. ii. p. 327.

l. 31. **nor non.** Another instance of a double negative emphasizing the negation.

very fearce ones. The idea of horses being employed for this purpose may have been suggested, as Dr. Lupton thinks, by Plato, *Repub.* v. 467 'We must mount them on horses in their earliest youth, and when they have learnt to ride take them on horse-back to see war: the horses must not be spirited and war-like, but the most tractable and yet the swiftest that can be had.' Cf. too Xenophon, *Cyropaedia*, iv. 3.

l. 36. **at a sodeyne brunt ... dead lifte.** Ed. 1 reads 'as' for 'at a.' According to the N. E. D. the primary meaning of 'brunt' is 'a sharp blow.' The derivation is doubtful; it is probably an onomatopoeic word. 'At a brunt,' means 'at one blow,' 'at once.' *tout à coup.* Here it means 'spurt'; and a dead lifte=lifting a dead weight, being still used dialectally for the pull of a horse exerting his utmost strength at a dead weight beyond his power to move. The original is 'boves ... equis impetu cedere.'

l. 37. they = oxen, which is the reading of the second edition.

P. 52, l. 2. so manye dysseases. The many infirmities to which horses are subject became proverbial. So Shakespeare, 'He's mad that trusts in the tameness of a wolf, a horse's health,' &c. (*K. Lear*, iii. 6. 18).

l. 7. other wyne, i.e. either, a common M.E. variant. N.E.D. quotes Wyclif, 'ether to kyng, other to deukes,' cf. 'nother' for 'neither.' See Glossarial Index.

l. 8. methe = mead. A.S. *medu*. A drink made from honey and water.

l. 9. liqueresse. 'Liquorice' is derived from Lat. *glycyrrhiza*, Gk. γλυκύς = sweet + ῥίζα = root.

sodde, i.e. sodden, boiled. Cf. 'Can *sodden* water, ... their barley broth, Decoct their cold blood to such valiant heat?' Shakespeare, *Hen. V*, iii. 5. 18.

l. 13. spende. Consume or dispose of. Whitney quotes Hakluyt's *Voyages*, i. 276 'a little bread which they spent by Thursday at night.'

l. 22. Philarches. This mode of spelling the word makes the derivation from Gk. φίλαρχοι, fond of rule. But in the Latin it is here *phylarchi*, 'clan-chiefs,' as at p. 51, l. 1, *philarchi* thus affording another instance of Robynson's fondness for variety in spelling.

CHAPTER II

OF THE CYTIES AND NAMELY OF AMAUROTE.

The cities are modelled on the Capital; particular description of the Capital: the river Anyder and its bridge: the water supply, defences of the city, its streets, houses and gardens described in detail.

This description of Amaurote was drawn from London, and its reference to London is marked in the marginal notes of the Latin text; in some of its features it recalls London as it was, in others London as it ought to be, the satire

NOTES: BOOK II

being implied in the touches of description. Stow, in his *Survey of London and Westminster*, vol. ii. pp. 573–4, after observing that More's description of Amaurote 'doth in every particular thing so exactly square and correspond with our City of London that I make little doubt that writer did thereby mean the same place,' transcribes More's account of it as a picture of London in Henry VIII's time. In its excellent sanitary arrangements Amaurote certainly did not square with London. See the General Introduction, and compare particularly the letter of Erasmus to Francis, Wolsey's physician, cited and translated by Brewer, *Letters and Papers of Henry VIII*, pref. ccix: 'Englishmen never consider the aspect of their doors or windows; next, their chambers are built in such a way as to admit of no ventilation. Then a great part of the house is occupied with glass casements which admit light but exclude the air, and yet they let in the draught through holes and corners, which is often pestilential and stagnates there. The floors are in general laid with white clay and are covered with rushes occasionally removed, but so imperfectly that the bottom layer is left undisturbed, sometimes for twenty years, harbouring expectoration, ale-droppings, scraps of fish, and other abominations not fit to be mentioned.' And to these unhealthy and noisome conditions he is inclined to attribute the epidemics which so often visited London.

P. 53, l. 2 (title). **namely** = in particular, especially.

l. 7. **skylleth not** = it does not matter. Cf. 'It *skills not* whether I be kind to any man living.'—Shirley, *Gamester*, O. Pl. ix. 36.

l. 17. **Anyder.** A fitting name for the river of No-Peace-Land, from the Greek ἄνυδρος, waterless—a river which is no river. Its general description recalls, as was intended, the Thames. See Stow, *Survey*, ii. 458.

l. 25. **.lx.** The Latin has *sexaginta*. Ed. 2 has 'fortie.' London is 40 miles in a bee-line to the sea, and about 60 miles following the course of the river, London Bridge to the Nore.

l. 26. **By al that space**, i. e. throughout the whole of this area. The Lat has 'Hoc toto spacio.' The marginal note in the Latin directs attention to the same thing occurring in the Thames: 'Idem fit apud Anglos in flumine Thamysi.'

l. 27. **a good sorte** = colloquial 'lot,' a good many miles. Ed. 2 reads 'certen.'

P. 54, l. 1. chaungethe. Lat. has *corrumpit.* So 'chaungethe' is used in the sense of 'taints'; cf. the dialectal or colloquial use, 'the milk is changed' (by thunder, &c.).

ll. 3, 11. **forby,** for-by, past. Cf. German *vorbei.*

l. 7. **a brydge.** London Bridge is intended.

l. 8. **stonewarke.** Many bridges were erected on piles in More's time; London Bridge was of stone.

l. 12. **lette** = hindrance. A reference to the drawbridge at the fourteenth arch of London Bridge, which was raised to allow the larger ships to pass through.

an other ryuere. 'This,' says Stow, 'must be the river of the Wells that ran down by Walbrook,' probably not the Flete river.

l. 23. **deryued,** i.e. diverted, turned aside. Lat. *dirivatur.*

l. 24. **cannellis,** i.e. channels or canals. The reference is to the Conduits: the Conduit in Cheapside, erected in 1289; the Tonne in Cornhill (1401); the Bosses of Water at Paul's Wharf and Cripplegate (1423); the Little Conduit in Fleet Street and Aldermanbury (1471), and others (Stow).

dyuers wayes: and so distributed in all directions.

l. 30. **full of turrettes,** i.e. with a long array of turrets. The Lat. has *turribus frequens.* This is a reminiscence of the Wall of London and the moat or ditch round it; and More, in speaking of the 'drye dyche' of Amaurote, is contrasting it with the filthy city ditch of London, one of the most noisome and disgusting features of the London of his time. References to this horror are frequent in the writers of those times.

l. 35. **appoynted,** i.e. laid out. Here the satire on London comes in. For a description of the streets of London see Introduction.

l. 36. **carriage,** i.e. transport. The Lat. has *rectura.*

P. 55, l. 2. twenty fote brode. The streets of London were as a rule about ten or twelve feet broad. See Brewer, *Henry VIII,* vol. i. p. 204. In this part of the description More was no doubt drawing on his experience of Bruges, which he could not fail to contrast with London. (See Dr. Lupton's Introduction, p. xxx.)

l. 8. **with two leaues,** i.e. they were folding doors. The original has *bifores.*

l. 11. **Euerye man that wyll.** In the marginal note of the Latin it is pointed out how this savours of Plato, 'Haec sapiunt communitatem Platonis.' The reference is

NOTES: BOOK II

to the conclusion of the third book of the *Republic*. 'None of them (the citizens) should have any property beyond what is absolutely necessary, neither should they have a private house with bars and bolts closed against any one who has a mind to enter' (Jowett's Trans.).

l. 15. **They sett great stoore be**, &c. In his account of the gardens, More recalls the pleasantest features of the London of his time. It is represented by Fitz Stephen, writing as early as about 1170, as 'a city of gardens.' 'Undique extra domos suburbanorum Horti civium arboribus consiti, spatiosi, et speciosi, contigui habentur' (*Descriptio nobilissima Civitatis Londonicæ*, printed in Appendix to Stow's *Survey*, ed. 1603). See too the verses by Sir Thomas Chaloner, describing the gardens of London in Elizabeth's reign, quoted by Stow, *Survey*, vol. ii. p. 459:—

'An quod amoena tibi facies hinc, inde viretis
Clauditur? Arboribusque frequens, quod villa sub ipsis
Moenibus erigitur patulis umbrosior hortis.'

l. 16. **vyneyardes**. In More's time London was not without its vineyards, as is still indicated by the name Vine Street, Saffron Hill, which marks the site of the great vineyard of Ely Palace. Dr. Lupton says there was another at Westminster, near St. John's Church, and that even as late as towards the end of the eighteenth century there was one on the site of what is now Addison Road Station.

l. 18. **thynge** = anything.

l. 31. **platte fourme**, French *plateforme*, Italian *piatta forma*, the ground plan.

l. 38. **M.viic.lx.**, i. e. one thousand seven hundred and sixty.

P. 56, l. 2. **verye lowe**. This is a reference to the 'mean hovels, mud walls, thatched roofs struggling with overhanging gables and shutting out both air and light' (Brewer, *Henry VIII*, vol. i. p. 294), which in More's time and long afterwards disgraced London.

l. 4. **at all aduentures**. The Lat. has *temere*, at random, hap-hazard, anyhow. This is the primary meaning of the phrase. Hence it came to mean 'at all hazards,' 'at any risk,' and then 'at all events,' 'at any rate.' Cf. Smeaton, *Edystone Lighthouse*, p. 275 '*At all adventures* they were to fit the outside shell of the building.'

l. 8. **storries**. From the O. F. *estorée*, a building, pp.

of *estorer*, late Latin *staurare*, Latin *instaurare*, to erect, build.

l. 9. **Flynte.** This word has no connexion with the Welsh county of that name; but is possibly cognate with the Gk. πλίνθος, a brick.

l. 14. **peryshe.** Used actively, 'destroy,' 'kill.' Cf. 'You are an innocent, A soul as white as Heaven: let not my sins *Perish* your noble youth,' Beaumont and Fletcher, *Maid's Tragedy*, iv. 1. Cf. also our colloquialism, ' You look *perished* with cold.'

l. 17. **glasse.** In the houses of the richer classes glass was coming into use in the reign of Henry VIII (see Erasmus to Francis, Brewer, *Letters and Papers*, vol. ii. pt. 1, p. ccix), but in ordinary houses it was not common till the reign of James I. As late as 1567 it was such a rarity that special precautions were used to protect it. See Eden's *State of the Poor*, vol. i. p. 77. As it was commonly used for windows in the great towns of the Low Countries, More was no doubt pressing its use in England.

l. 18. **sumwhere,** i.e. in some places; the Lat. is *interim*, which, used in the sense of *interdum*, means here ' sometimes,' a rare use of the word which may have puzzled Robynson.

l. 19. **oyle or ambre,** Lat. *succinum*, amber in its resinous state ; or probably spirit of amber, succinic acid. When heat was applied to amber it was resolved into a sticky substance like resin or pitch. Cf. Tacitus, *Germ.* xlv 'si naturam succini admoto igni tentes. . . . mox ut in picem resinamve lentescit'; and of this More may have been thinking.

CHAPTER III

OF THE MAGYSTRATES.

The Syphogranti and Tranibori and their functions: method of electing Princes of the cities: the Tranibori and other officers: duration of their time of office: mode of conducting consultations. With the functions of the Syphograuntes and Tranibores may be compared Tacitus's account of the German *principes* and *comites*, *Germ.* xi, xii.

NOTES: BOOK II

P. 57, l. 3. fermes, i. e. farms.

l. 6. **Syphoagrauntes.** The Lat. is *Syphogranti.* Whether any derivation can be traced for this word is as yet an unsolved problem. Dr. Lupton half humorously but most ingeniously suggests that the only Greek word to which it bears a resemblance, συφεός, 'a sty,' may throw light on its origin, and that More was thinking of the Benchers and Steward (Sty-ward) of his old Inn. Certainly the title *Tranibori*, which is associated with it, savours at least of Greek, θρανιβόροι, 'bench-eaters,' and so points in this direction. It is just possible that More may, fancifully and erroneously coining, have written the word *Syphogronti*, the printer changing the 'o' into 'a,' and that the third syllable of the word may be traced to γέροντες, so that it would mean 'seniors of the sty,' i. e. συφεοῦ γέροντες. But all this is very unsatisfactory.

l. 7. **300.** The second edition corrects 'thirtie'; which of course comes to the same thing, meaning '*each* with their thirty families.'

l. 12. **secrete electyon.** An election held privately. The 'prince' elected is of course the chief magistrate of each city only, not of the whole island.

l. 16. **put vp.** Lat. *unus commendatur senatui.*

l. 20. **lightlye.** For a slight or trivial reason.

l. 26. **by and by.** Latin has *mature*, speedily, quickly.

l. 32. **It is deathe,** i. e. it is considered a capital crime. The Lat. is *capitale habetur.*

P. 58, l. 6. Therfore matters of greate weyghte. With this passage cf. Tacitus, *Germ.* xi 'De minoribus rebus principes consultant, de maioribus omnes, ita tamen ut ea quoque, quorum penes plebem arbitrium est, apud principes praetractentur.'

l. 16. **Bycause that.** In order that. Cf. supra 49, 35. Lat. has *ne quis.*

l. 17. **that** = what, that which. Cf. P. B., 'to do always *that* is righteous in thy sight.'

l. 18. **fyrste to hys tonges ende.** 'Fyrste' is omitted in the second edition.

l. 19. **defendo and confyrme,** i. e. strengthen. The second edition has 'defende and mainteine.' The Lat. has *tueatur.*

l. 24. **existymatyon.** Estimation, esteem, reputation. His worth in the opinion of himself and of others. Cf. *Moral*

State Eng., Pref.: 'He who striveth to wound his Brother's Existimation, at the same time stabbeth his own.'

wolde not for shame ... be cowntede annye thynge ouerseen in the matter at the fyrste. The second edition reads 'wolde be ashamed ... to be at the firste ouersene in the matter,' i. e. be ashamed to appear to have been lacking in foresight at the beginning. The Lat. has 'ne initio parum prospexisse videatur.' ouerseen = deceived, deluded. The verb 'oversee,' as well as its past participle in this sense, is now obsolete except in literary use. Cf. Fuller : 'The most expert gamester may sometimes oversee,' i. e. see wrongly, go astray. So Middleton, *Chaste Maid*, iv 'They're mightily o'erseen in it methinks.'

CHAPTER IV

OF SCYENCES

Craftes and Occupatyons.

Importance attached to husbandry: other trades and occupations of the Utopians: regulations of labour; of their recreations; no idlers and fribbles—the pest of other communities—allowed to exist: employments of those who are too old or otherwise unfit for manual labour. Why there is less need for incessant work, such as house-building and clothesmaking, and more leisure for mental cultivation, than in other states.

This chapter is full of satirical strokes at the customs and condition of things in England, tacitly satirizing them by depicting, in contrast, the Utopian treatment of artisans and labourers.

P. 59, l. 8. **brought vp.** Robynson, as Dr. Lupton points out, has confused the Lat. *educti* for *educati*. It should be 'taken out,' i. e. into the fields outside the city.

l. 13. **seuerall.** Separate, distinct.

l. 14. **clothe-workinge.** For the point of this, see Introduction and notes on bk. i.

l. 18. **For their garmentes**, cf. Tacitus, *Germ.* xvii.

l. 24. **weldynge.** Wielding, exercising.

l. 26. **maketh theire owne.** In the *Dialogue*, Starkey (ed. Cowper, pp. 94-5) represents Lupset as saying that much of the poverty so rife arose from people preferring foreign-made garments to home-made: 'Now you se ther ys almost no man content to were cloth here made at home in our owne countrey, nother lynyn nor wolen, but every man wyl were such as ys made beyond the sea.'

P. 60, l. 2. stonde, i. e. tend.

l. 4. fantasy = to fancy, as often in Elizabethan English.

l. 10. occupyethe whether, i. e. he 'takes up' which of the two he wishes.

l. 15. applye, i. e. ply. The Latin has *incumbere*, to devote oneself to. *Apply*, from O. F. *aplier*, Lat. *applicare*, means first to put a thing into practical contact with another, then to devote one's energy to something. N. E. D. quotes Elyot, *Gov.* iii: 'Quintius ... repaired again to his plough and applied it diligently.' The form now in use is 'ply.'

l. 20. the myserable and wretced condytyon, &c. More is here glancing at the hard lives of labourers and artisans in England, their severe work, and their long hours. Dr. Lupton quotes an Act passed in 1496, and, though repealed, revived with but little modification in 1514 (2 Henry VIII, cap. 22), which enacted that every artificer and labourer was to be at his work, between the middle of March and the middle of September, before five in the morning; that he was to have only half an hour for his breakfast, an hour and a half for his dinner : 'and at such time as is here appointed hee shall not sleep ; then hee to have but one houre for his dinner, and halfe an houre for his noone-meate ; and that hee depart not from his worke between the midst of the said moneths of March and September, till between seven and eight of the clock in the evening . . . and that from the midst of September to the midst of March every artificer and labourer be at their work in the springing of the day and depart not till night of the same day.'

l. 24. iust, i. e. equal.

l. 25. iii. before none. 'iii.' is omitted in Ed. 2.

l. 31. voide time, i. e. unoccupied time.

l. 36. lycensed, i. e. freed.

P. 61, l. 1. solempne, l. 3. namelye ; see Glossary.

l. 10. ryse not in = are not elevated ; the Lat. is 'consurgit in nullius contemplatione disciplinae.'

l. 11. scyence lyberal. The Lat. has simply *disciplinae*, branches of education, departments of knowledge.

l. 14. After supper, &c. This reminds us of Cresacre

More's account of More's own household at Chelsea : 'Every one was busied about somewhat or other : no cards, no dice . . . their recreation was either music of voices or viols' (*Life of More*, ed. Hunter, p. 107).

l. 21. **the battell of nombers**, in original Latin *numerorum pugna*, was known later (see Burton's *Anatomy of Melancholy*, fol. 172, col. 2) as 'philosopher's game,' and is thus described by Strutt (*Sports and Pastimes*, 4th ed., p. 277) : 'It is called a " number fight " because in it men fight and strive together by the art of counting or numbering how one may take his adversary's king and create a triumph upon the deficiency of his calculations.' The second game 'the fyghte with vertues' is a moralization of the game of chess probably suggested by Jacobus De Cassulis, *Liber Moralis de Ludo Scaccorum*, the French version of which, *Le Jeu des Echecs moralisé* or *Le Traité des Nobles et des Gens du Peuple selon le Jeu des Echecs*, was translated by Caxton, and enjoyed extraordinary popularity. Possibly the Moralities may have suggested the idea to More. For a very curious moralization of the game for satirical purposes see Middleton's *A Game of Chess*. In any case, these games are More's proposed substitutes for the 'folish and pernycious' games to which he has referred. Plato proposes (*Laws*, bk. i. p. 643) that children's games should be subservient to the useful purpose of fitting them for the several serious occupations of life. Rabelais, who was a diligent reader of the *Utopia*, represents Gargantua as receiving useful instruction from the games prescribed for him (see *Hist. of Gargantua and Pantagruel*, bk. i. ch. xxiii).

l. 24. **set fyld.** A 'set field' is little more than a synonym for 'battle array.' Cf. Latin original, *collata acie*.

l. 31. **puissaunce**, power.

l. 32. **frustate.** The omission of the 'r' is probably a misprint.

l. 33. **sieight**=cunning, dexterity, trick. The word is now only used in the phrase 'sleight of hand.' It is akin to 'sly.'

l. 35. **lease**=lest. One of the many variants of the word. See N.E.D. ; it gives no example of this precise form.

l. 36. **looke more narrowly vpon.** We now say 'into.'

P. 62, l. 10. **be ydle.** The Latin is more vigorous, *stertunt*, 'are snoring.'

l. 12. **relygyous men.** One of the commonest complaints in the literature of More's time. For ample illustrations see Starkey's *Dialogue*, Latimer's *Sermons*, and Furnivall's *Ballads from Manuscripts*. Dr. Lupton pertinently quotes Erasmus, *De sarcienda Ecclesiae concordia*, the passage beginning 'Dolendum est tam multos esse monachos.'

l. 13. Put there to, i. e. add.

l. 16. flocke of stout, bragging, russhe bucklers. Lat. has 'cetratorum nebulonum colluvies,' meaning 'a rabble of shield-bearing ruffians.' 'Russhe-bucklers' here simply means what we should call 'swashbucklers'; it is very improbable that it has anything to do with the idea of 'bucklers as flimsy or as worthless as if they were made of rushes.'

l. 18. valiaunt, i. e. lusty, strong. From the Latin *valere*, through O. F. *vaillant*, or *valant*.

leffe = life. One of the many variants of 'life,' but not given by N. E. D.

l. 21. that men vse. In Ed. 2 Robynson turned this more diffusely: 'that in men's affaires are daylye vsed and frequented.'

l. 24. where money beareth all the swing. Where money is everything. Lat. has 'ubi omnia pecuniis metimur,'—'where we measure all things by money.' Swing means 'sway' or 'control'; cf. Sackville, *Induct. Mir.* 'That whilome here bare swinge among the best.'

l. 29. so few = only so many as.

l. 33. bisiede, i. e. busied.

P. 63, l. 9. scaselye, i. e. scarcely. So spelt by Robynson, 49, 13; 108, 12; 132, 26. It may have been adopted for the sake of euphony; cf. the Spanish *escaso*. Or it may be dialectal: cf. e. g. the local pronunciation of Carisbrooke and Carshalton, where the *r* disappears.

l. 12. licensed. Freed (after French *licencier*). Ed. 2 adds 'and discharged from.' N. E. D. quotes from Sir H. Wotton, 'When he listed he could license his thoughts,' i. e. dismiss them (*Parallel in Relig.* 17).

l. 22. expectation and hoope of him conceaued, i. e. expectation conceived of him.

l. 27. handy occupation, i. e. manual labour.

l. 31. Barzanes. The name was probably suggested to More either by that of the king of Armenia who, according to Diodorus Siculus (ii. 1), was one of the tributaries of the Assyrian Ninus; or that of the Satrap of the Parthyaei mentioned by Arrian, *Anabasis*, iv. 7. There is of course no

Persian or oriental word which can connect it etymologically with ἄδημος.

l. 32. **Ademus.** This name Robynson mis-spells 'Adanus' in his first edition, and misprints 'Adamus' in his second. More spells it with the 'e,' intending it of course to mean a king without a people, from the Greek *a* privative and δῆμος; cf. Anydrus. The word is More's invention. There is no such word as ἄδημος in Greek, except as the poetical form of ἀπόδημος, 'away from one's people.'

P. 64, l. 2. **asketh**, i. e. demands, requires. Lat. *requirit*. Cf. Dryden, *Virg. Georg.* iii. 478 'Goats of equal profit ask an equal care.'

l. 9. **stoode one man in**=cost one man. This idiom is still in common use.

l. 28. **Now, Syre.** The Latin has *Iam*, introducing a new subject.

l. 30. **homely,** i. e. in a plain style.

l. 36. **spende,** i. e. use, cf. 52, 13. The *Cent. Dict.* quotes Campion (Arber's *English Garner*, i. 56): 'The oils which we do spend in England for our cloth are brought out of Spain.'

P. 65, l. 5. **that ys no thynge passed for,** i. e. that is not cared for at all. See note supra, on 8, 5.

l. 12. **hapt.** Wrapped. The derivation of this word is unknown. It occurs as early as the fourteenth century, and is probably of Norse origin, meaning to cover up, to wrap or tuck up. N. E. D. quotes *York Mysteries*, xviii. 195 'I pray þe Marie *happe* hym warm,' and *Paston Letters*, 1465 'Worsted for dobletts to *happe me* thys cold wynter.'

l. 27. **pretended.** This is almost in the literal sense of the Latin word from which it is derived, *praetendere*, 'stretch forth,' 'put forward,' and so 'set before' (their eyes).

l. 32. **garnisshing.** Culture. The Lat. has *cultus*.

CHAPTER V

OF THEIR LYUING AND MUTUAL CONUERSATION TOGETHER.

Constitution of social life; regulations and distribution of the population, the surplus employed to colonize and cultivate the waste lands of the continent which are claimed as a right. Family life; regulations about markets and slaughter-houses. Thirty families under a Syphograntus occupy one of the large Halls which are set at equal distances in every street. Arrangements made for the sick. How the meals are arranged in the Halls, and in what order and position the men, women, and children are disposed; moral instruction and recreation provided for them.

In this interesting chapter satire is subordinate to suggestions for increasing the comforts of social life.

P. 66, l. 4. **occupieng and enterteynement.** Lat. *commercia* = intercourse.

l. 7. **tamilies.** It must be remembered that More uses the word *familia* in the Latin sense of the term, i.e. a household including all who belong to it either in kinship or in association.

l. 8. **kinredes.** The early and more correct spelling, as the word is derived from *cyn* = kin, and *reden* = condition. The *d* is excrescent; cf. 'thun*d*er.'

l. 19. **fewer chyldren,** &c. This is very diffuse and misleading. More's word is simply *puberes*, by which he means adults as distinguished from children (*impuberes*).

l. 22. **appointed.** In Ed. 2 Robynson prefixed 'prescribed, or' to 'appointed.'

l. 31. **in the nexte lande,** i.e. on the mainland nearest the island. Lat. 'in continente proximo.'

l. 32. **waste and vnoccupied grounde.** The right here claimed by the Utopians is defended by Grotius, *De Belli Iure ac Pacis*, bk. ii. chap. ii. sect. 17: 'And if there be any waste or barren land within our dominions, that also is to be given to strangers at their request or may be lawfully possessed by them, because whatever remains uncultivated is not to be esteemed a property, only so far as concerns jurisdiction, which always continues the right of the ancient people.' But Puffendorf, *Law of Nations* (Kenneth's translation), bk. iii. ch. iii. sect. 10, denied the right, basing it merely on the consent of the original occupiers: 'they are not to fix themselves as it were by some right in any spot of waste land they find, but ought to rest satisfied with the station and privileges we assign them'; and Barbeyrac (see note on Grotius *ad loc.*) agrees with Puffendorf against Grotius.

P. 67, l. 1. **the inhabitauntes to them,** i.e. 'the same countrcy people to them' (the reading of the second edition). Lat. 'ascitis una terrae indigenis.'

l. 12. **limited** Defined. The Latin is *describunt* = 'which they now mark out for themselves.'

200   UTOPIA

l. 14. iust cause of warre. According to Grotius, but not according to Puffendorf. See note supra on 66, 32.

l. 24. pestilente plage. The population of London and England greatly suffered from 'sweating sickness,' of which there were several severe visitations between 1485 and 1517. See Hecker's *Epidemics of the Middle Ages*, 181 seqq.

l. 26. forreyne townes, i. e. on the mainland inhabited by their own countrymen; Latin *colonia*.

l. 30. conuersation, society, intercourse. Cf. Parsons's *Conference concerning the next Succession*, I. i. 6 'the natural instinct which man hath to live in *conversation*.'

l. 35. foure equall partes, i. e. the four wards, quarters; supra, 57, 14.

P. 68, l. 1. seuerall. Used adverbially, = separately. Cf. 'We'll dress us all so *several*, They shall not us perceive.'— 'Robin Hood and the Golden Arrow,' in Child's *Ballads*, v. 385.

l. 5. without annye gage or pledge, i. e. without any security. The second edition reads 'gage, pawne or pledge,' Lat. *hostimentum*, a rare word found in Ennius and Plautus, but obsolete in classical Latin.

l. 19. meate markettes. 'Meat' here means any kind of food, not necessarily flesh. The word comes probably from a root connected with Lat. *mandere*, to chew. Cf. Matt. iii. 4 'his *meat* was locusts and wild honey.' In the R. V. of the Bible, the 'meat-offering' of the A. V. has been replaced by 'meal-offering.' In this passage More is again glancing at the London of his time. As far back as Edward III's reign, we find a royal order, forbidding the slaughter of beasts in the city, the preamble of which ran: 'Whereas by reason of the slaughters of great beasts in the city, from the putrefied blood of which running in the streets, and the extracts therefrom thrown into the water of the Thames, the air in the same city has been greatly corrupted and infected, and whereby the worst of abominations and stenches have been generated,' &c. See Riley's *Memorials of London and London Life*, p. 356. And the nuisance was not abated.

l. 38. seuerall name, i. e. 'special name,' Lat. *nomine suo*, 'by its own name.'

P. 69, l. 5. numbre of their halles, i. e. 'the number (of persons) in their halls.'

l. 8. hospitalles. Hospitals grew out of the 'infirmaria' attached to every monastery. In More's time there was only one hospital in our sense of the term, St. Bartholomew's,

NOTES: BOOK II

founded by Rahere, Henry I's jester and minstrel. More here makes several suggestions not carried out till our own time. **cured**, i. e. looked after, taken care of. Lat. *curantur*.

l. 14. **thronge**, i. e. thronged, crowded. See *Dialect Dictionary*, s. v.

strayte, i.e. confined in space, close. Der. from Lat. *strictus* = drawn tight, through O.F. *estrait* (*étroit*). It is a doublet of 'strict.'

P. 70, l. 7. **of small honestie**, i. e. rather dishonourable behaviour, in the Latin sense of *honestas* = 'honour.'

l. 8. **dresse**, make ready, prepare. O. F. *dresser*, to arrange. Cf. 'make oneself ready' = to dress, of the Elizabethan dramatists.

l. 13. **by course** = in turns, Lat. *per vices*. Cf. A. V., 1 Cor. xiv. 27.

l. 14. **sethinge**, i. e. boiling. 'Thou shalt not *seethe* a kid in his mother's milk,' A. V., Exod. xxiii. 19.

l. 30. **Euery mother**, &c. Such is the provision in Plato. See *Republic*, v. p. 460, and Plutarch, *De Liberis Educandis*, ch. v: 'The next thing is the nursing of children, which in my judgment the mothers should do themselves, giving their owne breasts to what they have borne.' So Tacitus notes of the German women, 'sua quemque mater uberibus alit, nec ancillis aut nutricibus delegantur' (*Germania*, cap. xx).

P. 71, l. 5. **meruelous silence**. For the behaviour of children at table, see ample information in *The Babees Book*. For the particular qualities noted by More, cf. 'Latte curtesye and sylence with you dwell' (p. 6); 'Tylle thou have thy fulle servuyse Touche noo misse in noo wyse' (p. 18). Cf. too the 'Stans puer ad mensam,' pp. 28–33 in the same collection. Plutarch also lays great stress on insisting on silence (*De Liberis Educandis*, cap. 14).

l. 12. **ouer wharte** = overthwart, across. **ouer** = upper.

l. 14. **meesse**. The word 'mess,' O.F. *mes*, is from the Latin *missus*, p.p. of *mittere*, to send, in Low Latin to set or place. It originally meant a portion set or placed, viz. on a table, and afterwards came to mean those sitting at the table. All these arrangements resemble what More must have been familiar with at the Messes of the Inns of Court; but were undoubtedly suggested by those of Lycurgus described by Plutarch in his Life. See his description of the ἀνδρεία or φειδίτια.

l. 23. **yongers.** We do not use this plural now, but say 'young people' or 'young ones.' The grouping of the young with the old at these messes was no doubt suggested by Plutarch's account of the regulations of Lycurgus referred to above.

l. 31. **dainties.** After this in the Latin there follows a clause in parentheses, omitted by Robynson, 'quarum non tanta erat copia ut posset totam per domum affatim distribui' = of which there was not enough to go round.

l. 32. **of both sides them.** Ed. 2 reads 'on eche side of them.'

l. 36. **of reading** = by reading. This was the usual custom in the monasteries, but a marginal note in the Latin version points to its decline: 'Id hodie vix monachi obseruant. Sermones in conviuiis.' In More's own household it was the custom. 'He used to have one read daily at his table, which being ended he would ask of some of them how they understood such and such a passage,' Cresacre More, *Life of More*, p. 103.

P. 72, l. 7. **towardnes** = tendency, inclination.

l. 12. **more strengthe.** First ed. erroneously inserts 'no' before 'more.'

l. 14. **musicke.** More's own fondness for music and belief in its composing effects were very great. Cresacre More says that the recreation of his family 'was either music of voices or viols, for which cause he procured his wife to play thereon to draw her mind from the world, to which by her nature she was too much addicted' (*Life*, p. 107). Dr. Lupton points out that, in Holbein's picture of More's household, a viol is seen hanging up.

nor . . . no. Another instance of the double negative, though special emphasis seems unnecessary.

l. 15. **bankettes** = banquets. See Glossary. Lat. *mensa secunda.* **conceytes nor ionckettes.** The Latin has *bellaria* = what we should call 'dessert,' i.e. fruits, nuts, &c. Conceit orig. a 'conception,' and so a 'fancy' or 'fancy trifle,' as here. Cf. 'He wolde gladlye se *conseytes* and fantesies at his table' (Ld. Berners' *Froissart*, ii. 26. 72). A junket was originally a basket made of rushes (Lat. *iuncus*). It then got the meaning of a cream cheese or any preparation of cream served on a rush mat. Now it is almost exclusively confined to the popular Devonshire dish consisting of sweetened and flavoured curds with a layer of scalded cream on the top. Here of course the word is used loosely,

NOTES: BOOK II

and means simply 'a dainty delicacy.' Cf. 'Bread pasties, tartes, custardes and other delicate *ionckettes* dipped in honie,' Adlington, trans. of Apuleius's *Golden Ass*, x. xlv.

l. 16. **for perfumes.** Ed. 2 reads *or* perfumes.

l. 19. **maketh for,** i.e. contributes to, favours. Cf. 'Not that I neglect those things that *make for* the dignity of the commonwealth.' Cf. infra, 103, 31.

l. 26. **as from whome,** seeing that from them.

CHAPTER VI

OF THEIR IOURNEYENGE OR TRAUAYLYNGE A BRODE, &C.

Regulations as to the Utopians leaving their country on visits; as to their recreations; their industrial and mercantile employments; their contempt for gems, the precious metals, and gorgeous apparel; their education and studies in leisure hours; their ethical philosophy based on the tenets of Epicureanism, tempered with Platonism; their ideal of the *Summum Bonum* — that is, 'pleasure' rationally defined and interpreted; their intelligence, and sympathy with Greek literature and philosophy; their eager welcome of strangers from other countries who can tell them about these countries or teach them anything.

P. 73, l. 9. **som profitable let** = a very good reason to prevent them from going.

l. 13. **retourne.** Dr. Lupton thinks that this curtailment by law of their visits to foreign countries may have been suggested by the provision of Lycurgus for the Spartans: 'He would not permit all that desired it to go abroad and see other countries, lest they should contract foreign manners, or gain traces of a life of little discipline and of a different form of government' (Plutarch, *Lives* (Langhorne), ed. 1805, p. 155).

l. 23. **gentilly enterteined.** Lat. *humanissime tractantur*.

l. 24. **of his owne head,** on his own authority.

l. 28. **sharpely.** Ed. 1 reads 'shapely.'

P. 74, l. 12. **There be nether,** &c. A contrast with the state of things in London, where one of the worst of these iniquities was licensed.

l. 15. **in the present sight,** 'in full view' (Burnet).

l. 28. **the lacke of the one is performed** — i.e. the

want is at once supplied. Cf. Chaucer, *Astrolabe*, ii. 10: 'Yif thow abate the quantitee of the houre in-equal by daye out of 30, than shal the remenant that leveth *performe* the hour inequal by night.'

P. 75, l. 3. **proffe**, proof. The meaning is the uncertainty of what next year's crop may prove or turn out. Lat. *euentus*.

l. 6. **madder**. A plant of the genus *Rubia*: it yields a valuable red dye. The Lat. word here is *coccum*, cochineal.

purple die felles. Ed. 2 has 'died.' See Glossary. A 'fell' is the skin or hide of an animal.

l. 10. **meane** = moderate.

l. 19. **at a daye** = on an appointed day.

l. 20. **in so doyng**. This is a mistranslation of the original, arising apparently from Robynson's ignorance of the meaning of the Latin phrase *nomina facere* = to lend (Lupton).

followe the credence of pryuat men: i.e. rely on the credit of individuals. For this meaning of 'credence' cf. Hall, *Chron.* 212. b 'The Merchaunt should stande in adventure, both of losse of stocke and *credence*.'

l. 22. **instrumentes** = legal documents, formal agreements. Cf. 'We shall show that *Instrument*, that was made under the Hand and Seal of the Prisoner at the Bar, as well as others, for Execution of the King; that Bloody Warrant' (*Trials of the Regicides*, 45).

l. 31. **they thinke it no righte nor conscience**. Lat. 'haud aequum credunt,' 'they do not think it fair.' 'To think a thing not conscience' is to think it such a thing as the conscience or innate sense of right cannot approve.

P. 76, l. 1. **straunge** = foreign. Lat. *externi*.

l. 6. **sette togethers by the eares**. Said of animals fighting; Lat. 'inter se committi.'

l. 10. **beleued**. The contempt shown for the precious metals and for gold, of which More proceeds to speak so much and so humorously by way of illustration, appears to have been suggested by Vespucci's account of the tribes visited in his fourth voyage. (See Introduction.) Plato also forbids the use of the precious metals in his Commonwealth, *Laws*, v. p. 742; cf. his remarks in the *Republic*, iii. p. 417. Tacitus's *Germania*, v, notes that the Germans had the same contempt for the precious metals. Cf. too Bacon, *New Atlantis* (Ed. Bohn, p. 287).

l. 16. **guyse and trade**, i.e. manners and ways; Lat.

simply *moribus*. 'Guise' is now obsolete in this sense. Cf. 'A military roughness, resembling most of the Lacedaemonian *guise*' (Milton, *Areop.*, ed. Arber, 37). 'Trade' is akin to 'tread' (O.E. *tredan*, v), and so primarily meant a 'footstep,' hence 'path,' 'way,' and so 'way of living,' a 'practice.' Cf. 'Thy sin's not accidental, but a *trade*' (Shakespeare, *M. for M.* iii. 1. 149). The transition to 'occupation' and 'business' is easy.

l. 18. indyfferente estymer, i.e. impartial judge. 'I leave to all worthy and *indifferent* men to judge,' Raleigh, *Apol.* 21. *estymer* = one who esteems or estimates.

l. 22. applyed = adapted. Lat. *accommodetur*.

l. 23. occupye. See Glossary.

l. 31. vnder, i.e. lower in value, inferior to.

l. 34. lacke, i.e. miss, endure the absence of; so, 'I shall be lov'd when I am *lack'd*,' Shakespeare, *Cor.* iv. 1. 15.

P. 77, l. 3. thynges. For the sentiment, cf. Horace, *Odes*, iii. 3. 49 seqq.:—

'Aurum irrepertum et sic melius situm,
    Cum terra celat, spernere fortior
        Quam cogere humanos in usus
            Omne sacrum rapiente dextra,'

and Milton, *Paradise Lost*, i. 687-8.

l. 10. plat, i.e. plate. Lat. 'phyalas . . . aliaque id genus opera fabre excusa.' ('Vessels,' Burnet.)

l. 19. from ours: depending on *discrepant* and *repugnaunt*—i.e. 'very different from ours.'

l. 24. properlie = finely, handsomely; 'proper' is very commonly used in this sense; the Latin is *elegantissimis*.

l. 31. infamed, i.e. disgraced.

P. 78, l. 1. forgo, i.e. give up, go without.

l. 2. at ones. Lat. *semel*, 'on one single occasion,' 'once.' Robynson seems to mistake it for *simul* (Lupton).

l. 15. shamefastenes. This is the correct orthography of the modern form, 'shamefacedness,' and has been adopted by the Revisers of the A.V.

l. 17. nuttes, brouches, and puppettes. Dr. Lupton illustrates 'nuttes' (*nuces*), 'brouches'(*bullae*), and 'puppettes' (*pupae*), from Persius, *Sat.* i. 10, v. 31, and ii. 70 respectively. All three expressions, as he points out, refer to 'putting away childish things.'

l. 22. Anemolians. From Gk. $\dot{a}\nu\epsilon\mu\omega\lambda\iota\sigma s$, 'windy'; $\dot{a}\nu\epsilon\mu\omega\lambda\iota a\ \beta\dot{a}\zeta\epsilon\iota\nu$, 'to talk words of wind,' is a common phrase in Homer. Dr. Lupton compares Cicero's description of Lepidus, 'homo ventosissimus.' 'Anemolius' was the Poet Laureate of Utopia, the alleged author of the Utopian Hexastichon included in the preliminary matter prefixed to the text (Lupton, p. xciii).

l. 25. those .iii. citizeins, i.e. the old wise men sent yearly from the country to confer about the common matters of the land. See supra, 50, 14.

l. 31. enfamed. Infamed, despised.

P. 79, l. 3. dasell = dazzle. A diminutive and frequentative form of 'daze.'

l. 4. silie = plain, simple. This satire by implication on the ostentatious pomp in dress common in More's time is illustrated by Hall's account of Henry VIII's appearance on the occasion of his procession to the Tower before his marriage with Catharine: ' His grace wered in his upperst apparrell a robe of crimsyn velvet furred with armyns [ermines]: his jacket or cote of raised gold; the placard embroidered with diamonds, rubies, emeraudes, greate pearles and other riche stones: a greate bauderiche [baldric] about his neck of large balasses [rubies]' (*Chronicle*, p. 508, ed. 1809).

l. 5. in chaungeable colours. This may mean either a parti-coloured material or else what is called 'shot' silk. The Lat. is *versicolori*, which may seem to favour the former meaning.

l. 11. aglettes here means 'small pendants.' The word is the French *aiguillette*, a small needle; hence it was used for the point or tag of a lace. 'Aiguillette' at the present day, both in French and English, has passed from the tag to the braid itself, and is the technical name for the cord hanging from the shoulder to the breast on certain military and naval uniforms.

l. 15. infamed. Lat. *infamare*, and French *infamer*, to render infamous, to disgrace. N. E. D. quotes Holinshed, *Chron.* i. 66, 2 'Because ... he somewhat persecuted the Christians, he was infamed by writers.'

l. 17. howe proudelye... them selfes. A good instance of how Robynson expands; the Lat. has simply ' quo pacto cristas erexerint.'

P. 80, l. 2. lubbor = a dull, clumsy fellow; a dolt. The word is now chiefly used by sailors with 'land' prefixed. The derivation is obscure.

l. 23. For they marueyle, i.e. the Utopians.

NOTES: BOOK II

l. 30. **a shepe weare.** Cf. Pope, *Essay on Man*, iii. 44 'The fur that warms a monarch warm'd a bear.'

l. 32. **of the owne nature** = of its own nature, in itself. Lat. has *suapte natura*.

l. 37. **lumpyshe blockehedded churle.** The Lat. has *plumbeus quispiam*, transl. by Burnet as 'a Man of Lead.'

P. 81, l. 1. **noughtenes** = wickedness. See 31, 19 supra.

l. 6. **wyle.** The second edition reads 'wyle and cautele,' the latter word being practically a synonym for the former and derived from the Lat. *cautela*, a caution, precaution.

l. 9. **dreuell**, earlier form of 'drivel' = driveller. As it is here a synonym for 'slave,' it perhaps does not so much mean 'imbecile' as 'drudge.' Cf. Erasm. *Par.* 1 Cor. xi. 11 'To use his wife as a vile *dreuell*, because she is commaunded to obeye.' The Lat. has *nebulonem*.

then shortely after. The sense is that *money* is the important thing and the first consideration; the *man* is, as it were, 'thrown in.'

l. 14. **daunger**, i. e. power. See, for an exhaustive account of this interesting word, N. E. D.

l. 16. **nigeshe penny fathers.** 'Nigeshe' = niggardly (see Skeat, s. v.). 'Penny father' = a miserly person, a skin-flint; the idea being possibly that the attempt to draw one penny from him is attended with the greatest difficulty. Cf. Drayton, *Mirrour*, p. 1262 'To nothing fitter can I thee compare, Than to the son of some rich *penny father*.'

l. 35. **They be taughte learninge.** We now come to a very important part of More's work—his account of the educational system of the Utopians—which is of course satire by implication on the pre-Renaissance theory and practice of it.

P. 82, l. 1. **syde of the wordle.** For this form of the word see Glossary.

l. 8. **comen.** The strong past participle. Cf. 'knowen.'

l. 13. **clerkes.** Originally a 'cleric' or 'ecclesiastic' in holy orders. As learning was in the Middle Ages practically confined to the clergy, the word came to mean as here a 'scholar.' It is also used of the old pre-mediaeval philosophers, Aristotle, &c.

l. 15. **For they haue not douysed,** &c. The marginal note in the Latin, 'Apparet hoc loco subesse nasum,' prepares us for sarcasm. More is here ridiculing the logical studies so extensively, and to so little purpose, cultivated in the Schools and Universities of the Middle Ages and of his own time. Cf. Bacon's remarks, *Advancement of Learning*, bk. i, on barren logical subtilties. Butler also ridicules them—*Hudibras*, part i. canto i. 65 :—

> 'He was in Logic a great critic,
> Profoundly skill'd in Analytic
> He could distinguish and divide;
> A hair twixt south and south-west side.'

And see too Mephistopheles' sensible sneers at the same thing in Goethe's *Faust* :—

> 'Mein theurer Freund, ich rath' euch drum,
> Zuerst Collegium logicum,
> Da wird der Geist euch wohl dressirt,
> In spanische Stiefeln eingeschnürt &c.'
> Ed. Tetot, ii. p. 167.

l. 16. **restryctyons, amplyfycatyons, and supposytyons in the small Logycalles.** Logical terms found in the book referred to by More, viz. the *Parva Logicalia*, the name given to the last part of the *Summulae Logicales* of Petrus Hispanus, afterwards, it is said, Pope John XXI, who died in 1277, only eight months after his election. There seems to be some doubt, however, as to the identification of the author with the pope.

l. 19. **seconde intentyons.** *Rabelais*, II. vii 'Questio subtilissima, utrum chimera in vacuo bombinans possit comedere secundas intentiones' [in ridicule of subtle discussions of Schoolmen]. As it would be impossible to give a clearer definition and account of what is meant by 'second intentions' than is given by Mansel in his edition of Aldrich's *Logic*, I shall content myself with transcribing his note.

'A *first intention* or *notion* is a conception under which the mind regards *things*, whether facts of external or of internal perception. Thus, the individual Socrates is regarded by the mind as *man, animal, body, substance*. All these are first intentions. And a mental state may be successively regarded as a *smell*, a *sensation*, a fact *of consciousness*. These again are first intentions.

'A *second intention* or *notion* is a conception under which the mind regards its first intentions as related to each other. Thus the relation of *animal* to *man* and of *man* to *animal* is expressed in the second intention *genus* or *species*. First intentions as conceptions of things are predicable in the individuals conceived under them. Thus we may say " Socrates is man, animal," &c. Second intentions are not so predicable: we cannot say, " Socrates is species, genus," ' &c.—Mansel's *Aldrich* (ed. 1842), pp. 20, 21. For a very lucid and interesting dissertation on First and Second Intentions see Mr. Shadworth Hodgson's *Time and Space*, 33-45. Marcus Aurelius l. xvii, agreeing with More, enumerates among the things which he was thankful for, the fact that he had not wasted time on the subtilties of Logic.

l. 21. **man hymselfe in commen**, i.e. man in the abstract, man regarded not as an individual, but καθόλου (in general).

l. 24. **the course of the starres, &c.** Observe how the good sense of the Utopians separates Astronomy, which they study, from Astrology which they despise. Rabelais (*Pantagruel*, bk. ii. ch. viii), in the admirable letter which Gargantua writes to Pantagruel, recalling in many respects More's scheme of education and dated from Utopia, speaks in the same way of Astrology and Astronomy.

P. 83, l. 9. **manners and vertue.** We now come to the moral philosophy of the Utopians. It is founded partly on the doctrines of Epicurus, partly on those of Stoicism, and partly on those of Christianity: from the first is derived the tenet that the *summum bonum* of life is pleasure in the *proper sense of the term*; from the second the precept that life should be regulated 'according to nature'; from the third, the association of Theology, and Theological belief, with Ethical Philosophy. For the two former More has drawn almost perhaps entirely on Cicero's *De Finibus*.

l. 16. **felycytye of man.** Cf. *De Finibus, passim*.

l. 20. **chiefyste parte of mans felycytye, &c.** This was the teaching of Epicurus. Vespucci had said of some of his newly discovered tribes, from which More (see Introduction) seems partly to have derived the fable of the *Utopia*, that they were followers rather of the Epicureans than of the Stoics; ' vivunt secundum naturam, et Epycuri potius dici possunt quam Stoici ' (*Mundus Novus*, fol. 3 verso).

l. 23. **sharpe, bytter, and rygorous.** The epithets are unsuitable and hardly the meaning conveyed by the Latin, ' grauis et seuera est ferequo tristis et rigida.' Burnet's is an improvement : ' notwithstanding its severity and roughness.'

P. 84, l. 3. **the lesse pleasure should not be a let, &c.** *De Finibus*, i. cap. 14.

l. 14. **onlye in that pleasure that is good.** Cf. *De*

Finibus, ii. 15 'Idem (Epicurus) dicit ... non posse iucunde vivere nisi etiam honeste.'

l. 18. **life ordered according to nature.** To this phrase the Stoics attached different meanings, but the meaning attached to it by More is no doubt that attached to it in *De Finibus,* iv. 10. 27 'secundum naturam vivere; quod est ... habere ea quae secundum naturam sunt, vel omnia, vel plurima et maxima.' To live 'according to nature' was to live in accordance with the entire course of the world, as opposed to individual and special ideas and impulses, and according to a man's whole nature, not to a part of it only. See Grant's *Ethics of Aristotle,* vol. i. p. 255, and Long's *Marcus Aurelius* (ed. Bohn), p. 56.

l. 24. **of whoes goodnes it is that we be,** i. e. have our being, exist.

l. 25. **in possibilitie.** Misprinted 'impossibilitie' in Ed. 1.

l. 26. **leade our lyfe out of care.** Cf. *De Finibus,* i. 12. 41.

l. 31. **inioyne** = enjoin. From Lat. *iniungere* = to impose (a penalty or duty).

laboures, watchinges, and fastinges. There is an allusion here evidently to 2 Cor. vi. 5, though, as Dr. Lupton points out, it is only in the English rendering.

P. 85, l. 5. **For a ioyful lyfe.** Robynson's punctuation is here rather perplexing; dashes after 'euell' and 'hurtefull' instead of commas would make the sense clearer.

l. 12. **natur biddeth the.** Cf. *De Finibus,* i. 9. 30.

l. 18. **accordyng to the prescrypt of nature,** i.e. according to the law or ordinance of nature. Lat. 'ex cuius praescripto.'

l. 21. **not without.** Lat. 'quod certe merito facit.'

l. 23. **carke.** A synonym of 'care.' From the late Latin *carcare,* 'to load'; cf. charge. Hence 'to load oneself with care.' See N. E. D. So in Kingsley, *Alton Locke's Song* 9 'Why for sluggards *cark* and moil?'

l. 30. **Wherfore their opinion is.** St. John quotes Hobbes, *De Cive,* i. 3. 36 'Cum omni homine vel servanda est fides vel non paciscendum: hoc est, vel declaratum bellum vel certa et fida habenda est pax.'

l. 36. **constitute** = constituted. This form of the p. p. is still retained in technical phraseology in Scotland (N. E. D.).

P. 86, l. 1. **Thies lawes not offendid.** Nominative

NOTES: BOOK II

absolute, not often used in English. It is an attempt to translate the essentially Latin ablative absolute; the original has 'Hiis inoffensis legibus,' 'so long as these laws are not violated.'

l. 8. **they selfe** = thy self.

l. 9. **humanitie** = politeness.

l. 27. **Appetite they ioyne to nature.** That is to say, in their definition of pleasure they not only include every motion and state of the body, &c., but healthy or right desires or inclinations. The Lat. is 'Appetitionem naturae non temere addunt,' *naturae* being, as Dr. Lupton suggests, not dative but genitive.

P. 87, l. 1. **taken place**, i. e. become deeply seated. Lat. *insederunt*.

l. 11. **counterfeat kinde of pleasure.** From his reference to false notions of pleasure, More goes on to satirize directly some leading foibles of his time—vanity in dress and in ancestry.

l. 19. **thought.** Both editions misprint 'thoughe.'

l. 21. **and not by their mistakyng**, i.e. and not through a mistake on their own part.

l. 30. **vayne and vnprofitable honoures.** With this passage compare Erasmus's comments on 'Sileni Alcibiadis,' *Adagia*, chil. iii. cent. iii. prov. 1, the passage beginning: 'Videas in nullis minus esse verae nobilitatis quam in Thrasonibus istis qui vetustis stemmatibus, qui torquibus aureis, qui splendidis cognominibus summam iactant nobilitatem,' &c.

l. 35. **for the opinion of nobilitie**, i. e. in considering themselves of noble birth.

P. 88, l. 5. **of one heare**: i.e. even by a single hair, not a whit, the less noble, a Latin idiom; cf. Cicero, *Q. Fr.* ii. 16 'ego ne pilo quidem minus me amabo.'

l. 6. **take pleasure . . . in gemmes.** The rage of Henry VIII and his courtiers for the ostentatious display of jewelry is notorious, and is frequently commented on by the writers of the time. More's own simplicity, and contempt for such distinction as he has here described, is well illustrated by an anecdote told of him by Cresacre More: 'He exercised acts of humility that he made most worldie men to wonder at him. On the Sunnedaies euen when he was Lord Chancellor he wore a surplice and sang with the singers at high mass and matins in his parish church at Chelsea, which the Duke of Norfolk on a time finding sayde, "*God bodie, God bodie*—My Lord Chancellor, a Parish Clarke! you disgrace the king and his office." "Nay," sayde Sir Thomas, smiling, "your grace may not thinke I dishonour my prince in my dutifulness to his Lord and Yours"' (*Life of More*, p. 19).

l. 12. styll = constantly, continually.

l. 27. Or of them, i.e. or what shall I say of them?

l. 35. hoppest = dancest; N. E. D. quotes Coverdale 1 Kings xviii. 26 'They hopped aboute the altare as their vse was to do.' Psalms lxviii. 16 'Why hoppe ye so, ye greate hilles?' The Lat. has *gestis*, to throw oneself about, to be transported.

P. 89, l. 9. thu = thou, the reading of Ed. 2.

l. 24. reiected, i.e. given over.

l. 26. they counte huntyng. This tenderness to animals and objection to unnecessary slaughter—one of the great notes of the *Utopia*—More shared in common with Pythagoras and the Pythagoreans. With his remarks here compare what Plutarch says in his *De Solertia Animalium*, i and ii, about hunting, to which pursuit he traces the cruelty and inhumanity of men: 'Men became insensible and inhuman, having once tasted of murder and being accustomed by hunting and following the chase not only to behold without pity the wounds and blood of wild beasts, but to rejoice at their being killed and slaughtered': and see also his *De Esu Carnium, Orat.* ii; cf. Ovid, *Met.* xv. 75 seq.; Gay, Fable xxxvi; Pope, *Essay on Man*, Ep. iii. 160-8, and Thomson's eloquent invective, *Autumn*, 384-457; Shelley, *Queen Mab*, viii. 77-82 and 111-18.

P. 90, l. 20. of the good lyfe past. In the Latin this sentence is followed by 'et spes non dubia futuri boni,' omitted by Robynson. Burnet: 'and the assured Hope of a future Happiness.'

l. 28. voided = evacuated.

l. 32. scratchynge. First ed. stratchinge.

P. 91, l. 2. vpright. The Latin is *aequabili* = here 'well balanced,' with all the 'humours' in harmonious concert.

l. 5. yf yt be not letted nor assaulted with no greiffe, i.e. if it be not checked or attacked by pain.

l. 20. whyche sayde that stedfaste and quyete healthe. The substance of this passage seems to have been partly suggested by the arguments of Cicero and Torquatus on the *summum bonum* in bk. i of the *De Finibus*, and partly by the argument between Socrates and Callicles in Plato's

NOTES: BOOK II

Gorgias, pp. 494-5, but mainly by the discussion in bk. ix of the *Republic,* pp. 583-7.

ll. 24-5. **by some owtwarde motion.** Robynson is translating the *extrario* of the first three Latin editions, printed by Dr. Lupton *contrario.* The allusion is to the 'externall or outwarde pleasure' of l. 7, supra. Robynson has omitted *nisi* (which is in the Latin editions) before *motu*; 'nisi motu quopiam extrario sentiri.'

P. 92, l. 3. **procedyng,** i. e. progress. A synonym to 'onwardnes' following.

ll. 8-9. **thee pristynate strengthe,** i. e. its former strength. Lat. *pristinatus.*

l. 11. **imbrace the owne wealthe,** i. e. cling to and take to itself *its* own good. Lat. 'bona sua amplexabitur.'

l. 12. **For that,** i. e. for where, as in the second edition.

l. 13. **For what man wakynge,** &c. Robynson is here a little obscure. Burnet's version is better : 'for what man is in health, that does not perceive it [is not conscious of it] when he is awake ? '

l. 16. **stonyshe** = stony.

sleping sicknes. Robynson changed this in the next version to 'lethargie.' Sleeping sickness is, as is well known, the name now popularly given to the disease called 'nelavan,' which attacks the negroes on the west coast of Africa and in Uganda, and generally ends fatally.

l. 21. **they imbrace.** This in the Latin is properly followed by *ergo,* therefore, omitted by Robynson.

l. 32. **preuelye stealynge one,** i. e. secretly stealing on.

l. 35. **carefull greyffes,** i. e. pains which give care and trouble.

l. 37. **sealynge.** Robynson's translation is obscure ; it has been suggested that *sealynge* may be a misprint for *fealynge* or *healynge.* The Latin is: 'ita hoc quoque voluptatis genere non egere quam deliniri praestiterit.' Ed. 2 reads, 'then thereby to be eased of the contrarie grief.'

l. 38. **The whyche kynde** of pleasure. Cf. Plato, *Republic,* ix. p. 583 : 'There are many other cases of suffering in which mere rest and cessation of pain ... is extolled as the highest pleasure ? ' 'Yes.' . . . 'When pleasure ceases, that sort of rest will not be pleasant but painful ? ' 'Doubtless.' 'Then the intermediate state of rest will be pleasure and will also be pain ? ' 'That is assumed.' 'But can that which is neither become both ? ' 'I should say not.' 'And both pleasure and pain are motions in the soul, are they not?' 'Yes.' 'But that which is neither was just now shown to be rest and not motion and in a mean between them?' 'Yes.' 'How then can we be right in saying that the absence of pain is pleasure or that the absence of pleasure is pain?' 'Impossible.'

P. 93, l. 11. egal = equal. O. F. *egal*; this form of the word, preserved also in the substantive *egality* and the verb *egall*, was common till about the middle of the seventeenth century.

l. 20. which of necessitye, &c. The second edition is clearer: 'to the necessarie vse whereof they must from time to time continually be forced and driuen.'

l. 29. no other kind. Cf. the well-known lines in Ovid, *Met.* i. 85-6 'Os homini sublime dedit, caelumque tueri Iussit, et erectos ad sidera tollere vultus,' with the comments of Cicero, *De Nat. Deorum*, ii. 10. 56; *De Senectute*, 21; *De Legibus*, i. 9, where the same idea is put very strikingly: 'Nam cum ceteros animantes abiecisset ad pastum, solum hominem erexit, ad caelique quasi cognationis, domiciliique pristini, conspectum excitavit.'

l. 35. allowe = commend, approve of. The English word identifies, after O. F., the two Latin words, *allaudare*, to praise, and *allocare*, to assign. Hence its various meanings. reioysinges. Robynson, as Dr. Lupton points out, has not given the force of the Latin *condimenta* in the above word. Burnet is better: 'as the pleasant Relishes and Seasonings of Life,' but it may possibly be a misprint for *releysinges*, relishes.

l. 36. cautell = precaution.

P. 94, l. 2. yet to dyspyse, &c. In this most interesting passage (to which a marginal note in the Latin original directs special attention), More seems to question the wisdom of that severe ascetic discipline which, in the milder form, he himself practised. But he is guarded, and merely condemns it in its harsher form where it is not conducive to the common good. It is a condemnation of such fanatics as St. Simeon Stylites.

l. 4. sloughishnes = sluggishness.

l. 9. forborne, i.e. denied, refrained from. Cf. 'Fruits—Whose taste, too long *forborn*, at first assay Gave elocution to the mute' (Milton, *P. L.* ix. 747).

l. 10. at Goddes hand. Ed. 1 reads 'of GOD.'

l. 18. in her daunger, i.e. in her power, under an obligation to her; v. supra, 81, 14.

NOTES: BOOK II

l. 26. **lores and ordenaunces.** Lat. *instituta*. Burnet better: 'constitution and principles.' See Glossary.

l. 36. **defende them.** Note how More prudently guards himself.

l. 37. **husbande theyr grounde:** cultivate.

P. 95, l. 4. **exploited and furnished,** i. e. performed, achieved, administered. Lat. has simply *administrata*. Cf. 'They departed without *exploytinge* their message' (Elyot, *Gov.* I. xxvi). 'Exploit' has lost this meaning, and now means either technically to work (a mine, &c.), or else in a derogatory sense 'to utilize for one's own ends.'

l. 20. **Greke.** For the point of this, and the association of Utopian ideals with classical, see General Introduction.

l. 38. **free.** Both editions misprint *faee*.

P. 96, l. 2. **lesse then iii. yeres.** Milton, in his *Tractate on Education*, allows one year for mastering the rudiments and making much progress in Greek.

ll. 4-5. **wythout anny staye,** i. e. without any stopping or hesitating; Lat. *inoffense*.

l. 5. **if the booke were not false,** i. e. if the text were not at fault.

l. 7. **allyaunte,** i. e. allied, akin. The word is very rare.

l. 15. **pretye** = moderately large. The word was used to express moderately great in size, quantity, duration, &c. It is now used almost exactly in the same way, but adverbially, necessitating an adjective or adverb after it. For the former use, cf. 'A *pretty* while these pretty creatures stand, Like ivory conduits coral cisterns filling' (Shakespeare, *Lucrece*, i. 1233).

fardell, i. e. bundle. The word is possibly akin to the Arabic *fardah*, a package. It is common in English of this period, though now obsolete. Cf. 'There lyes such Secrets in this *Farthell* and Box, which none must know but the King' (Shakespeare, *W. T.* iv. 4. 783).

l. 16. **rather neuer than shortelye,** i. e. never to return rather than quickly (to return).

l. 18. **Theophrastus.** A Greek naturalist and philosopher, born at Eresos in Lesbos about 370 B.C. He afterwards went to Athens and heard Plato and Aristotle, to the latter of whom he was particularly attached and from whom he inherited the whole Aristotelian library, the largest then known. He succeeded Aristotle as head of the Peripatetic school, over which he presided for thirty five years till his death in 288 B.C. He was the reputed author of 227 works, most of which however are lost. The *History of Plants*, *Causes of Plants*, and the well-known *Characters* are perhaps his most important extant works.

l. 20. mormosett. A 'marmoset' is a small kind of American monkey (*Hapale jacchus*). For the history of the word, see Skeat's Dictionary. The Lat. has *cercopithecus*, a long-tailed ape.

l. 24. Lascaris. The *Erotemata* or *Grammatica Graeca* of Constantine Lascaris was published at Milan in 1476, and has the distinction of being the first Greek book ever printed.

Theodorus. Theodorus Gaza was born at Thessalonica in 1398. The Greek Grammar, his chief work, was first published by Aldus at Venice in 1495. This work was held in very high estimation by subsequent scholars, and was generally recognized as the best of its kind. Theodorus died in 1478.

l. 25. Hesichius. Hesychius, a Greek grammarian of Alexandria, was the author of a Greek lexicon. Although the text is very corrupt, the book has been of considerable use in interpreting obscure and rare words and phrases of the great Greek classical writers. It was not known till the sixteenth century, when it was published by Aldus in 1514. Little is known about the author, but he flourished probably towards the end of the fourth century A.D.

l. 26. Dioscorides. Pedanius Dioscorides was a native of Anazarbus in Cilicia, and flourished in the reign of Nero. In early life he probably accompanied the Roman armies through many countries as physician. He has left us his celebrated *Materia Medica* in five books, which treats of all the then known medicinal substances and their properties. This work enjoyed a universal celebrity and popularity for over sixteen centuries. The first edition of the Greek text was published by Aldus in 1499 at Venice.

l. 27. Lucianes. Lucian, the Greek Voltaire, was born at Samosata in Syria about 125 A.D., and is one of the most interesting and amusing of Greek writers. He was evidently a great favourite with More as he was with Erasmus, and More translated four of his dialogues into Latin (see Introduction).

ll. 28-9. **Aristophanes.** The greatest of the Greek comic poets, born about 448 B.C. He is said to have written fifty-four plays, but only eleven are extant in their entirety.

NOTES: BOOK II

He died about 388 B.C. The first printed edition, containing nine plays, was published by Aldus at Venice in 1498.

l. 29. **Euripides.** The third and last of the great Greek tragedians. Born at Salamis in 480 B.C., died 406 B.C. The first edition of his plays, consisting however only of four, was published by J. Lascaris at Florence at the end of the fifteenth century. But Aldus in 1503 brought out an edition containing seventeen.

Sophocles. The second of the trio of Greek tragedians, born 496 B.C. He entered into competition with his great predecessor Aeschylus in 468 B.C. Only seven of his plays are now extant, which in their probable order are *Ajax, Antigone, Electra, Oedipus Tyrannus, Trachiniae, Oedipus Coloneus, Philoctetes.* He died in 405 B.C. The first edition of his plays was printed at Venice in 1502.

Aldus. From the preceding notes it may be perhaps correctly inferred that Aldus was the most celebrated of the early printers. Aldus Pius Manutius was the founder of the firm which was carried on after him by his two sons. The works that issued from this establishment were renowned for the correctness of the typography, and so great was the demand for them that the printers of Lyons and Florence began the system of issuing counterfeit Aldines as early as 1502. The press continued in active operation for upwards of 100 years, from 1490 to 1597, and printed 908 different works. The distinguishing mark is an anchor, entwined by a dolphin, inscribed either with *Festina lente* or *Sudavit et alsit.*

l. 30. **Thucidides.** The greatest Greek historian. He was born probably in 471 B.C. and wrote a history of the Peloponnesian War in eight books, though it is doubtful if the whole of the eight is from his hand. After living in exile for twenty years he returned to Athens in 404 B.C. But the date and manner of his death are unknown. The Greek text of his work was first published by Aldus in 1502.

l. 31. **Herodotus.** The 'father of history.' Born about 484 B.C. at Halicarnassus. His *History*, written in nine books, is a general history of the Greeks and Barbarians (i.e. non-Greeks) between the fall of Croesus 546 B.C. and the capture of Sestos 478 B.C. He is said to have died at Thurium, but the date is unknown. The first Greek edition of his work was printed by Aldus in 1502.

Herodian. A Greek historian. Wrote a history in eight books of the Roman Emperors of his own lifetime, beginning with the death of Marcus Aurelius A.D. 180 and ending with the accession of the younger Gordianus in 238 A.D.

ll. 31-2. **Tricius Apinatus.** A name coined by More to signify a 'trifler' or 'fribble.' Apina and Trica were two towns in Apulia said to have been sacked by Diomede, but so vile and insignificant before their destruction that they had become proverbs for vileness and insignificance. See Forcellini's *Lexicon*, sub verb. Apina. Martial in two epigrams, i. 112. 2 and xiv. 1. 7, uses them to signify trifles: 'Sunt apinae tricaeque et si quid vilius istis.'

l. 33. **Hippocrates.** The 'father of medicine.' Born at Cos 460 B.C. Before his time the science of medicine was confined to the priests or else taken up in a subordinate way by the philosophers of the age. He wrote many medical books, and died in 357 B.C. The first Greek edition of his works was published by Aldus in 1526.

Galenes Microtechne. Claudius Galenus, the famous Greek physician, was born at Pergamus 131 A.D. He attended M. Aurelius, the Roman Emperor, and also his two sons, and was afterwards physician to the Emperor Severus. He died about 201 A.D. His most important works are *De Anatomicis Administrationibus*, and *De Usu Partium Corporis Humani*. The *Microtechne* mentioned, i. e. 'Little Art,' was in contradistinction to the larger book known as *Megalotechne* or *Methodus Medendi*, a fuller and more elaborate work.

l. 36. **Phisick,** i. e. medicine. Lat. *res medica*.

P. 97, l. 8. **maruelous and gorgious frame.** With this cf. the fine passage in Plato's *Republic*, vii. p. 529, which probably suggested it. St. John compares Cicero, *De Natura Deorum*, ii. 37-8.

l. 14. **maruelour,** i. e. admirer. Lat. *admirator*.

l. 20. **feates,** i. e. devices, arts.

l. 33. **rides,** i. e. reeds. Lat. *papyrus*, whence our word 'paper.' The papyrus reed from which paper was originally made is now very scarce in lower Egypt, but it still exists about the lake Menzaleh, near Damietta, as well as in Sicily.

l. 36. **assayinge,** i. e. essaying, attempting. The word is now archaic, except as applied to the testing of metals. Cf. Spenser, *Sonn.* lib. 8 'Never ought was excellent *assayde* Which was not hard t'atchieve and bring to end.'

feate, i. e. method of doing, knack.

P. 98, l. 7. **sene,** i. e. versed, skilled; an imitation of the

Lat. *spectatus* not uncommon in Elizabethan English. Cf. Hakluyt's *Voyages*, ii. 2 'She was *seene* in the Hebrew, Greeke and Latin tongues'; and Spenser, *F. Q.* vi. 6. 3 'For he right well in Leache's craft was *seene*.'

l. 10. **wonders**, i. e. wondrously. The old genitive case of 'wonder' used adverbially. Cf. *needs*, &c.; 'Me mette swiche a swevenyng, That lykede me *wonders* wel.'—*Rom. of the Rose*, Chaucer, ed. Skeat, i. 27.

l. 17. **geer.** For the derivation of this word see Glossarial Index, and for the order of senses N. E. D. Its earliest meanings were 'apparel,' 'dress'; 'arms,' 'accoutrements'; 'harness'; 'apparatus,' 'machinery'; 'movable property'; 'material substance,' &c. Hence it came to mean 'affairs,' 'business generally,' as here. Cf

'But I will remedy this *gear* ere long,
Or sell my title for a glorious grave.'
(Shakespeare, 2 *Henry VI*, iii. 1. 91.)

l. 20. **owte landes**, i. e. foreign countries.
vre : not from same root as *use*, being adapted from O. F. *eure*, Lat. *opera*, 'work.' It was common in M. E., but became obsolete about the middle of the seventeenth century.

CHAPTER VII

Of Bondemen, Sicke Persons, etc.

Slave labour, performed either by criminals convicted of some heinous offence, or criminals condemned to death in some other state, or by voluntary slaves. Their treatment of the sick and encouragement of suicide in particular cases. Their marriage regulations: when divorce is allowed, their treatment of adulterers. How criminal offences are punished by them. Their delight in social buffoons; their abhorrence of jesting at deformed people, and contempt for such vanity as the application of cosmetics to the face. Their encouragement of noble and virtuous actions by the institution of rewards. The fewness of their laws and their dislike to lawyers and pettifoggers. Their regard for justice, and their incorruption, the admiration of neighbouring states. Why they make no leagues—reflections on the characters and practices of contemporary princes.

P. 99, l. 6. nor bondemens, i.e. nor of bondemens, which is the reading of ed. 2. So also 'annye man'='of any man' in l. 7.

l. 15. for gramercye, i. e. *gratis*, which is the word in the Latin. A contraction for 'grand merci,' great thanks. 'Gramercy' was an interjection meaning originally 'thanks'; hence 'for gramercy' means 'for a thank you,' 'for nothing.' Cp. 'He made Corn to be distributed to the People at a very mean price to some, and *for gramercy* to the poor' (North, *Plutarch*, 966).

l. 17. bandes. Bonds.

l. 21. godlye. In a godly way. Latin 'ad virtutem egregie instructi.'

l. 25. drudge. One employed in mean or servile work a 'hack.' The derivation of the word is obscure; it is probably allied to the Lowland Scotch verb 'dree,' which means to 'endure,' 'undergo.' Cf. 'Many they held as *drudges* and captyues' (Fabyan, *Chron.* vii. 497).

l. 27. handle and order. Edition 2 reads 'intreate and order,' possibly so as not to repeat the word from the second sentence preceding. The Lat. has *tractant*.

l. 30. as thereto accustomede. Being accustomed to it.

P. 100, l. 3. as I sayde. Supra, ch. v. pp. 69 sqq.

l. 4. lette nothynge at all passe, i.e. omit nothing at all, which is the literal translation of the Latin, viz. 'nihil prorsus omittunt.'

l. 9. But yf the dysease, &c. In so devout a Christian as More this defence of suicide is truly remarkable, even when we consider the conditions under which it is alone represented as justifiable. Orthodox Christian ethics have always been unanimous against it. More's favourite divine St. Augustine absolutely forbids it under any circumstances (see *De Civit. Dei*, lib. i. ch. xv–xxiv), though some 'heretics' allowed it: see Fulke's Defence, *Works*, vol. i. p. 23, and Whitgift, *Works* (Parker Society), vol. iii. p. 57. But suicide *under the condition specified by More* was unanimously allowed and even encouraged by the Ancients, Stoics and all other sects alike, even by Plato: see *Laws*, bk. ix. p. 873; for it is doubtful whether the apparently unqualified condemnation of it by Pythagoras (see Cicero, *De Senectute*, ch. xx), by Plato in the *Phaedo* and *Apology*, and by certain

NOTES: BOOK II

philosophers, was meant to include such cases as More describes. At Marseilles, according to Valerius Maximus, II. vi, 'Poison, a compound of hemlock, was kept in the city and given to those who could assign to the Council of Six Hundred a sufficient reason for wishing to rid themselves of life: for, though the Council took care that no one should have it without being able to assign such sufficient reasons, they were quite willing to provide the means of easy death to such as could assign such reasons.' For the whole question see Lipsius, *Manuductio ad Stoicam Philosophiam*, and lib. iii. *Diss.* 22 and 23; Donne's *Biathanatos, passim*; Hume's *Essay on Suicide*; More, *Essay on Suicide*; and Lecky's *Hist. of European Morals*, vol. i. In 1872 what More here inculcates was seriously proposed in a powerful and eloquent little work by Mr. S. D. Williams entitled *Euthanasia*. See for an account of it, and for an interesting discussion on the subject, Tollemache's *Stones of Stumbling*, pp. 1–32. But above all see the admirable disquisition in Sidney's *Arcadia*, lib. iv, Ed. 1628, pp. 419–23; a short passage from which may be quoted:—'To prejudicate his (i. e. God's) determination is but a doubt of goodnesse in him who is nothing but goodnesse. But when indeed he doth either by sicknesse or outward force lay death upon us, then are wee to acknowledge that such is his pleasure, and to know that all is well that hee doth. That we should be masters of ourselves we can show at all no title nor claime; since neither we made ourselves, nor bought ourselves, we can stand upon no other right but his gift, which hee must limit as it pleaseth him.'

l. 13. **overlyuing hys owne deathe.** 'Overlive' is of course the literal translation of the Latin *supervivat*; we should now say 'outlive' or 'survive.' More means that a man is to all practical purposes dead when he ceases to be of any further use in the world, after which he is outliving his death. For 'overlive' in this sense, see Sidney, *Arcadia*, iii 'Basilius will not long *overlive* this loss.'

l. 18. **take a good hope to hym,** i.e. rely on good hope; Lat. 'bona spe fretus.'

l. 22. **by other,** i.e. by others.

l. 24. **lyse,** i. e. 'lose,' a variant not recognized by the *Cont. Dict.*

l. 30. **dye in theyre sleape.** The phrase is sufficiently expressive for a death by anaesthetics. The Lat. has *sopiti soluuntur*, 'having been put to sleep, they are released.'

l. 31. **wythowte annye fealinge.** Both editions misprint 'fealnige.'

ll. 32-3. **nor they vse no lesse dilygence.** They do not relax their care and attention over him, even though he does not terminate his life.

l. 34. **beleuynge thys to be an honorable deathe.** Robynson has here mistranslated through mistaking *persuasos* for *persuasi*, and connecting it with the former clause. Burnet turns it correctly, though loosely: 'They believe that a voluntary death, when it is chosen upon such an authority, is honourable.'

Elles, 'on the other hand'; Lat. *alioqui*. With this cf. Plato, *Laws*, ix. p. 873: 'The suicide who deprives himself by violence of his appointed share of life, not because the law of the State compels him, nor yet under the compulsion of some painful and inevitable fortune which has come upon him, nor because he has had to suffer from irremediable and intolerable shame,'... should be 'cast naked out of the city, and all the magistrates on behalf of the whole city shall carry stones, and each of them shall cast a stone upon the head of the dead man,... and after that they shall bear him to the borders of the land and throw him out unburied.'

l. 37. **of fyer,** i.e. of being cremated.

P. 101, l. 1. **XVIII. yeres.** This is the age prescribed by Aristotle, *Politics*, vii. 16; but he thinks the proper age for a man to be thirty-seven or thereabouts.

l. 3. **bodely.** Ed. 2 'actually.'

l. 5. **whether** = whichever, which one (of two). Cf. '*Whether* of them twaine did the will of his father?' (Matt. xxi. 31, A.V.).

l. 21. **sheweth the woman.** No doubt suggested by the custom sanctioned by Lycurgus. See Plutarch's *Life of Lycurgus*, ch. xiv. Cf. Bacon who refers to this passage, *New Atlantis* (ed. Bohn, p. 291).

l. 22. **wower** = wooer.

l. 24. **disalowed it** = disapproved of it. Cf. 'Though they... do take liberty to... use... sports and exercises upon the Lord's Day, yet most of their ministers *disallow* it' (Ray, *Journ.* 436).

l. 28. **in hassarde,** 'at stake.' Cf. 'My reputation, and my worship had beene *in hazard*' (Fleming, *Panopl. Epist.* 260).

l. 36. **esteme, i.e. value,** estimate her worth. Lat. *aestiment*.

NOTES: BOOK II

P. 102, l. 2. myslyke, i. e. disgust, offend. Cf. 'Bellaria .. oftentimes comming herselfe ... to see that nothing should be amis to *mislike* him,' Greene, *Pandosto* (1581). For a commentary on what More says here see Milton, *Doctrine and Discipline of Divorce*, ch. iii.

l. 13. **well a worthe,** 'alas!' See Glossarial Index; and cf. 'wellaway,' which occurs in Chaucer and in *Piers Plowman* in this sense.

l. 29. **a greate poynte of crueltie.** Swift, with characteristic cynicism, reverses this, and makes old age a ground *ipso facto* for divorce (*Gulliver's Travels*, part III. ch. x). The thought, as Dr. Lupton points out, is from Terence, *Phormio*, iv. 1 'CH. Pol me detinuit morbus. DE. Unde? aut qui? CH. Rogas? Senectus ipsast morbus.'

l. 33. **withall.** This is another form of 'with,' not infrequently used when 'with' ended a sentence. Cf. 'These banished men that I have kept *withal*' (Shakespeare, *T. G. of Verona*, v. 4. 152).

l. 34. **man and the woman cannot well agree.** Here More is again as paradoxical from the orthodox point of view as he was in his defence of suicide, but Milton agrees with him, seriously contending 'that indisposition, unfitness and contrariety of mind arising from a cause in nature unchangeable, hindering, and ever likely to hinder, the main benefits of conjugal society, which are solace and peace, is sufficient cause for divorce provided there be "mutual consent"' (*Doctrine and Discipline of Divorce*, ch. i).

P. 103, l. 11. auoutrers, i. e. adulterers. O. Fr. *avouttre*. Cf. 'God wyll condempne *advouterers* and whorekepers' (Bale, *Yet a Curse at the Romyshe Foxe*, fol. 70 c).

l. 12. **luste,** 'like,' 'wish.'

l. 22. **eftsones :** 'eft' = a second time, again, + soon. Thus it means lit. 'soon afterwards,' or simply 'soon.' Cf. 'If he do not accomplishe the order ... to be *eftsones* taken and whipped' (*Act 22 Hen. VIII*, c. 12).

l. 28. **husbandes chastice,** &c. The old Common Law of England allowed the husband to give his wife 'moderate correction,' says Dibdin. The Civil Law gave him the right to castigate her severely with whips and cudgels ('flagellis et fustibus acriter verberare uxorem '). See Dibdin's Note, and Blackstone's *Commentaries* (vol. 1. p. 44, edit. 1787).

l. 30. **open punyshemente,** i.e. public punishment. Cf. 'If Demetrius ... have a matter against any man, the law is *open*' (Acts xix. 38).

l. 31. **maketh for**, i. e. is for the advantage of, favours, tends to. Cf. Ben Jonson, *Epicoene*, v. 1 'Not that I neglect those things that *make for* the dignity of the commonwealth.'

l. 32. **But moste commenlye**. Perhaps suggested by the policy of Anysis in Herodotus (ii. 137), who, when an Egyptian committed any crime, would not have him put to death, but employed such criminals on public works, apportioning their labour and the time of it to the magnitude of their offences.

P. 104, l. 1. **feare other**, i. e. frighten others. Lat. has *deterrent*, which is stronger than the English word derived from it. For the active use of 'fear,' cf. 'Shall it not *feare* us from so foule a custome?' (Babington, *Commandm.* 135). Also, 'Warwicke was a Bugge that *fear'd* us all' (Shakespeare, 3 *Hen. VI*, v. 2. 2).

l. 4. **desperate**. First ed. reads *desperace*.

l. 14. **moueth to** = attempts.

l. 17. **pretensed** = pretended, i. e. intended or designed. Lat. *praetensus*, p. p. of *praetendo*. Cf. Matt. v. 28; and Juvenal, xiii. 208-9 'Nam sceluṣ intra se tacitum qui cogitat ullum Facti crimen habet.'

l. 19. **too haue no lette**, i. e. to have no hindrance, to be successful.

l. 21. **sette greate store by fooles**. Plutarch tells us that Lycurgus dedicated a little statue to the god of laughter in each hall, as 'he considered facetiousness a seasoning of their hard exercises and diet, and therefore ordered it to take place on all proper occasions' (*Life of Lycurgus*, Langhorne's version, ed. 1846, p. 61). Gregorius Lamprechter, Chancellor of Wirtemberg, and afterwards of Charles V's council, used to say that every prince should have two fools, one whom he might tease, and the other who might tease him, 'einen den er vexirt, den andern der ihn vexirt' (Flogel, *Geschichte der Hofnarren*, p. 7). Rabelais set the same store by them; see *Pantagruel*, bk. iii. ch. xxxvii. More's fool, Henry Pattinson, is introduced into Holbein's well-known sketch of More's family.

l. 27. **tuition**. Here simply 'care,' the original meaning of the word. Cf. *Paston Letters*, i. 103 'The ... *tuycyon* of your seid realme of Fraunche.'

l. 34. **dishonestie**, i. e. dishonour or dishonourable conduct. Also cf. 'Shame, that eschueth alle *deshonestee*' (Chaucer, *Persones Tale*, 759).

NOTES: BOOK II

l. 36. **imbrayde, or embrayde** = upbraid. M. E. *up-breiden*, A. S. *up-bregdan*, to attack, accuse, &c., cognate with *braid*, to weave. Elyot, *Gov.* 16, has ' He was of his enimies *embrayded*, and called a schoole master.'

P. 105, l. 2. **payntinges**, i.e. painting the complexion with rouge. In all ages men have objected to this practice, as in all ages it has been practised by women. See Strutt's *Manners and Customs*, vol. iii. p. 103, and for much curious information Dibdin's Note, *More*, pp. 318-19, ed. Boston, 1878.

l. 6. **honest conditions**, honourable behaviour, respectful deference. Lat. 'morum probitas et reuerentia.'

l. 7. **loue is oftentimes wonne.** So Crabbe of his Phoebe Dawson, ' Admirers soon of every age she gained, Her beauty won them and her worth retained.' *Par. Reg.* ii.

l. 17. **may sturre and prouoke.** Lat. has 'calcar et incitamentum sit,' i. e. may be a spur and an incitement. This was also suggested by a regulation of Lycurgus; see Plutarch, *Instituta Laconica*, xviii.

l. 22. **hawte or ferefull** = haughty or terrifying.

l. 23. **vse themselfes**, i.e. show, behave themselves. Lat. has *exhibent*, where there is an ellipse of *se*.

l. 27. **cappe of maintenaunce.** The 'cap of maintenance,' also called 'cap of dignity,' is a cap of crimson velvet lined with ermine with two points turned to the back. Originally worn by dukes only, it is carried in the hand before the sovereigns of Great Britain on the occasion of their coronation, whence in all probability its name. In the Latin text, *diadema* serves for all three head-dresses.

l. 31. **Thei haue but few lawes.** Tacitus remarks that it is in the corruptest states that there are most laws: 'Corruptissima republica plurimae leges' (*Annals*, iii. 27); while he observes of Germany 'plus ibi boni mores valent quam alibi bonae leges' (*Germania*, xix).

ll. 31-2. **instructe and institute**, i.e. instructed and trained. The original has *institutis* only.

l. 38. **blinder and darker.** Lat. has *obscuriores*, more obscure.

P. 106, l. 2. **proctours and sergeauntes at the lawe.** With the contempt which More here shows for lawyers and the technicalities of their profession compare the equally contemptuous expressions of Cicero, *Pro Murena*, xi and xii, and Rabelais, *Pantagruel*, bk. iii, ch xxxix-xliv, and bk. v. xiv-xvi. See, too, Swift, whose contempt for lawyers equalled his contempt for soldiers, *Gulliver's Travels*, pt. ii. ch. vi (Scott's ed. vol. xii. p. 168). A proctor (Lat. *procurator*, one who acts for another) was a person who performed the duties of an attorney or solicitor in the Ecclesiastical and Admiralty Courts in England. Proctors were formerly a distinct body from solicitors, but the office is now merged in the latter class, any solicitor being allowed to practise in these Courts since 1877, at which time jurisdiction had already been taken from the clergy, and the Admiralty Court included in the Probate, Divorce, and Admiralty Division of the High Court of Justice. The serjeant-at-law was formerly the highest degree of barrister, ranking next to the judge, and could only be appointed after sixteen years' standing. Moreover, he had exclusive audience in the Court of Common Pleas. He was appointed by a writ or patent of the crown. This distinction was entirely honorary, merely giving precedence over ordinary barristers. The order is now practically extinct, for, since 1868, no person except a Judge-Designate has taken the degree, though it has never been formally abolished. The Lat. has simply *causidici*, advocates, for both these titles.

l. 8. lesse circumstaunce of wordes, i. e. circumlocution, Lat. *minus ambagum*.

l. 13. circumuertions, perversions. Lat. *calumnias*.

chyldren, i. e. people. As often in the Bible. Cf. Ps. cxliv. 7 'And deliver me . . . from the hand of strange *children*.' Also 1 Pet. i. 14 'As obedient *children*, not fashioning yourselves according to the former lusts in your ignorance.' So *passim*, 'the children of Israel.'

l. 25. grosse, i. e. the obvious, general. The original has *crassa*.

l. 30. blynde an interpretacion. For an excellent commentary on this see Cicero, *pro Murena*, xi, xii.

P. 107, l. 18. affection, i. e. bias, feeling, prejudice. Cf. Harrison, *Exhort. to Scottes*, 227 'Weigh the querell indifferently and without *affeccion*.'

auryce = avarice.

take place, i. e. have a place.

l. 19. breake, i. e. break down.

l. 27. neuer . . . none. Another instance of a double negative for emphasis.

l. 35. here in Europa. For what follows see the General Introduction. The bitter irony of this passage will be obvious. The direct references seem to be to the shameful treachery of the French and of Ferdinand against Frederick of Naples when Ferdinand joined with Louis XII in the Treaty of Grenada to portion out Naples between them in 1500; to the treachery of Julius II when in 1510 he deserted his allies the French, and formed a league with the Swiss, the Venetians, the Emperor and the Kings of Spain and England to expel the French from Italy; and to the circumstances which in 1514 broke up the Holy League. See Erasmus's commentaries on the *Adagia* 'Simulatio et Dissimulatio ' and ' Imperitia.'

P. 108, l. 1. through the reuerence, &c. The second edition reads 'at the reuerence and motion of the head byshoppes.' The Latin reads 'summorum reverentia metuque pontificum.' Robynson afterwards apparently read *motuque*.

l. 7. thynke well, i. e. rightly think.

l. 10. faythfull, holding the faith, i. e. Christianity.

l. 12. lyne equinoctiall, the equator.

l. 16. some cauillation founde in the woordes, i. e. some legal quibble as to the meaning of the words. To cavil, Lat. *cavillari*, is properly to 'mock' or 'jest,' hence to raise frivolous objections. For the substantive N. E. D. quotes Lydgate, *Pylgr. Sowle*, iv. xxix ' Yf lawes be keped stably withoute ony *cauyllacions.*'

l. 27. a shamefull death. Lat. has *furca*, the cross, i. e. crucifixion, this being the most ignominious death amongst the Romans.

euen verye they, i. e. even these very men. Lat. *hi ipsi*.

l. 31. aualeth it self, i. e. lowers itself. The word is directly from O.F. *avaler*, to descend, from the Lat. *ad vallem*, to the valley (speaking of rivers flowing down). Cf. ' Phœbus gan availl His weary waine.'—Spenser, *Sheph. Cal.*, Jan. 73. The root is also found in ' avalanche.'

l. 34. by lowe = below. This was altered in the second edition to ' lowe by the ' = near. The Lat. has *humirepa* for the whole phrase.

l. 36. because it shall not run at rouers, i. e. that it may not run wild. The Lat. has ' neve usquam septa transilire queant'—that it may nowhere be able to leap over the bounds. ' To shoot at rovers' is a term of archery meaning to shoot an arrow at random and not at any particular object or target. Cf. Drayton, *Polyolbion*, xxvi ' With broad arrow or prick, or roving shaft, At marks full fortie score they used to prick or sore,' and South's *Sermons*, 'Providence never shoots *at rovers*.'

P. 109, l. 4. **so euyll kepers of**, i.e. who so loosely observe.

l. 9. **was verye euel begonne**, i.e. it was a bad thing ever to have commenced them.

ll. 9-10. **this causeth men.** A reference to the ill-feeling between England and Scotland, particularly from the time when James IV allied himself with France to the results of the Battle of Flodden Field.

CHAPTER VIII

OF WARFARE.

Dislike of the Utopians to war, and their method of conducting it. Their chief aim to minimize bloodshed. Preference of stratagem to force. Immoral intrigues and practices to which they resort. Employment of mercenaries and the character of those mercenaries. How their battles are conducted and their camps fortified. Cost of the war imposed on the conquered.

With this chapter should be compared Erasmus's *Pacis Querela* and his commentary on 'Dulce bellum inexpertis,' *Adagia*, chil. iv. cent. iv. prov. 1. More's opinions on this subject were identical with those of his friends Erasmus and Colet, but they were shared also by the Anabaptists and afterwards by the Quakers.

P. 110, l. 1. **beastelye**, i.e. fit for beasts. Lat. 'rem plane beluinam.'

l. 6. **glory gotten in warre.** With More's abhorrence and contempt for war should be compared Swift's *Gulliver's Travels*, the remarks of the King of Brobdingnag, part ii. ch. vii. The Anabaptists and Quakers have always held the same view. In modern poetry it is a distinct note. Cf. Browning's *Love among the Ruins*; Tennyson's *Locksley Hall*; Whittier's Poems *passim*; and Longfellow, *In the Arsenal at Springfield*:—

'The warrior's name should be a name abhorrèd,
And every nation that should lift again
Its hand against a brother, on its forehead
Should bear for ever more the curse of Cain.'

NOTES: BOOK II

l. 11. **to seke in the feat of armes**, i.e. unaccustomed to the use of arms. 'To be to seke' = to be wanting in. Cf. 'Does he not also leave us wholly *to seek* in the art of political wagering?'—Swift, *Tale of a Tub*, v.

l. 12. **goo to battayle.** So Ed. 2; Ed. 1 inserts 'to' before 'goo.'

l. 19. **not euer**, i.e. not always.

l. 24. **probable**, i.e. able to be substantiated, a just one, exactly in the Latin sense. Cf. Milton, *Civil Power in Eccles. Causes*, 'He who maintains tradition not *probable* by Scripture'; and Jeremy Taylor, *Holy Living*, iv. 5 'a probable necessity.'

the contrarye parte, i.e. the other side.

ll. 29, 30. **much more mortally**, i.e. with much more rancour. Lat. *multo infestius*.

l. 30. **frindes marchauntes**, i.e. the merchants with whom their friends do business.

P. 111, l. 4. **Nephelogetes.** A very appropriate Utopian name, 'the people of Cloudland.' Νεφελόγεται, a word coined by More and no doubt suggested by the Homeric νεφεληγερέτα, which has of course quite a different meaning. From Gk. νεφέλη.

Alaopolitanes. The inhabitants of the 'City of Blind men.' From Gk. ἀλαός, blind, and πόλις, a city.

l. 13. **shrewedely** = severely. Cf. 'The air bites *shrewdly*; it is very cold,'—Shakespeare, *Hamlet*, i. 4. 1. Also, 'I knew one *shrewdly* gor'd by a Bull,'—Dampier, *Voyages*, II. ii. 99.

l. 25. **wiped**, i.e. defrauded, cheated. Cf. 'We are but quit; you fool us of our moneys, In every cause, in every quiddit *wipe* us.'—Fletcher, *Spanish Curate*, iv. 5. The expression is more common in Greek and Latin than in English. Cf. Greek ἀπομύσσειν and Lat. *emungere*. **beside** = out of. Cf. 'That no God was able to put him *besides* his Kingdom.'—Ussher, *Ann.* v. 88. N. E.D. quotes Fox, *Acts and Mon.* ii. 384 'He put the new Pope Alexander *beside* the cushion, and was made pope himself.'

l. 27. **occupieng.** See Glossary.

l. 32. **frindes marchaunte men.** Those who are trading with their friends. The Lat. is *amicorum negotiatores*.

l. 33. **leise** = lose. There are four variants of the spelling of this word by Robynson.

P. 112, ll. 3, 4. **nother in his liffe, nother in his liuingo,**

230   UTOPIA

i. e. there is no loss of life nor livelihood.   Lat. *aut vita aut victu*.

l. 19. **sett vp a pyller.** With this cf. Plutarch, *Instituta Laconica*, xxv: 'Whenever a victory was gained through a well-contrived stratagem, and thereby with little loss of men and blood, they always sacrificed an ox to Mars: but when the success was purely owing to their valour and prowess, they only offered up a cock to him; it being in their estimation more honourable for their generals and commanders to overcome their enemies by policy and subtlety than by mere strength and courage' (Goodwin's paraphrase of Plutarch's *Morals*, vol. i. pp. 94-5.

l. 22. **cracke**, i. e. brag. 'Crack' is primarily to make a sharp noise; hence, to utter or tell in a loud voice. We still use the word in 'crack a joke.' Then, as here, 'to talk big,' 'boast.' Cf. 'Thou art always *cracking* and boasting.'— Addison, *Drummer*, I. i. **when.** Lat. *quoties*, how often.

l. 26. **puisance.** Ed. 1 reads 'pusyaunce.'

l. 34. **moued battayle**, i. e. made war.

l. 37. **aferde**, i. e. afeard, afraid. Cf. 'Fye, my Lord, fie! A Souldier and *affear'd*.'—Shakespeare, *Macbeth*, v. 1. 41.

P. 113, l. 1. **sette forewarde**, i. e. further the interest of, help on. Cf. *Prayer Book*, 'In the Ember Weeks,' 'that ... they may set forth thy glory, and set forward the salvation of all men.'

l. 5. **denounced**, i. e. proclaimed. Lat. *indicto bello*.

ll. 5, 6. **manye proclamations.** The whole of this passage with all that follows is an exact account of the intrigues of Henry VIII and his minister Lord Dacre against Scotland. See Brewer, *Letters and State Papers*, vol. ii. pt. i. Introduction, p. cclxix. It may be added that this would be brought home to More, as the correspondence passed through Tunstal's hands when minister in the Netherlands.

l. 19. **takinge their partes**, i. e. if they will join them.

ll. 22-3. **they haue**, i. e. their enemies, the reading of the second edition.

l. 29. **So that, &c.** There is no 'consequence' here. The original is 'Tam facile quodvis in facinus impellunt munera,' 'so easily do gifts drive men to any kind of deed.'

l. 30. **enforce**, i. e. force, impel. Cf. 'My serving you ... *Enforced* this to come to pas' (Tusser, *Husbandry* (1878), 5).

l. 31. **they kepe no measure**, i. e. they fix no limits.

l. 33. **endeuoure themselfes**, reflexive. See Glossary.

NOTES: BOOK II

P. 114, l. 4. amonge other people ys dysallowed, i. e. is not permitted by other people. Lat. 'apud alios improbatum.'

ll. 6-7, 36. **as who** = as those who.

l. 14. **basse** = lower.

ll. 20-1. **occasyons of debate and dyssentyon.** The best commentary on this will be an extract from Lord Dacre's dispatch to the Lords of the Council dated August 1, 1515 : 'Received their letter ... directing him as of himself to practise with the Lord Chamberlain and other lords of Scotland to induce the sending of an embassy for peace, to foment quarrels between Albany and Angus, and between Albany and the Chamberlain, so as to drive the Duke out of Scotland' (Brewer, *Letters & State Papers*, vol. i. pt. ii. p. 205).

l. 33. **intyerlye** = entirely, i. e. singularly. The Lat. original is *unice*.

P. 115, l. 5. **of** = from. Lat. *ex*.

Zapoletes. The people intended are the Swiss, and the word, as Dr. Lupton has pointed out, is plainly coined by More from the Greek, and means 'ready sellers' (of themselves), or 'readily sold.' Ζαπωλῆται or Ζαπωλῆτοι from Ζα-, the intensive, and πωλεῖν, to sell. More's character of the Swiss is amply corroborated by their conduct in the Italian wars. They first fought against their own countrymen on the side of Ludovico Sforza, when they simply sold themselves to the highest bidders. In 1500 they deserted Sforza and went over to the French. In 1513, entering the service of Leo X, they defeated the French at the battle of Novara. More gives them this prominence because, at the very time he was writing, Henry, through Pace, was bargaining for their assistance in the war against France, they 'being willing to assist him with 20.000 men at 40,000 florins a month' (Brewer, *Letters and State Papers*, vol. ii. pt. i. p. 264).

l. 7. **hydeous.** The Lat. is *horridus*, and probably simply means 'rough.'

l. 10. **abide**, i. e. endure. Cf. 'He could not *abide* an ass' (De Foe, 'Hist. Apparitions,' *Works*, xv. 370). The word in this sense is extremely rare in an affirmative sentence as we have it in the text, being almost invariably used with a negative or quasi-negative, e. g. 'I cannot abide,' 'He could scarcely abide,' &c.

ll. 10, 11. **abhorrynge from**, i. e. shrinking from, Lat. *abhorrere*. Cf. Fynes Moryson, l. 3. 1. 208 'Must part of the Mariners are Greekes, the Italians *abhorring from* being sea men.'

l. 15. **breede** = breeding.

l. 25. **whomewyth they be in wayges**, i.e. from whom they receive pay.

l. 31. **lytle more moneye.** For the greed of the Swiss, cf. Pace's letter to Burbank (Brewer, *Letters and Papers of Henry VIII*, Preface, lviii): 'The Swiss be unreasonable in asking money, and remedy there is none, "quia talis est illorum barbaries ut pecuniam petitam neganti mortem minentur."'

l. 32. **there awaye**, i.e. in those parts, an interpolation of Robynson's.

l. 34. **nye** = nigh, i.e. near in relationship.

l. 37. **separate** = separated, Lat. *distracti*.

P. 116, l. 7. **taken a smacke in**, i.e. acquired a taste for.

l. 16. **abuse**, use ill.

l. 20. **on liue** = 'alive,' the reading of Ed. 2.

l. 31. **ioyne to** = join-to, i.e. add. Lat. 'suos ciues adiungunt.'

l. 33. **conductyon**, i.e. leadership, command. Cf. Holinshed, *Chron.* ii. 221 'English horsemen under the *conduction* of the lord William Evers.'

ll. 37-8. **by inherytaunce.** The Lacedaemonian custom. Thucyd. iv. 38 (Lupton).

l. 38. **miscarry** = fail, or be incapacitated. The original is 'ex euentu.' Cf. 'Two ill-looking Ones, that I thought did plot how to make me *miscarry* in my journey' (Bunyan, *Pilg. Prog.* i. 256).

P. 117, l. 10. **be.** Ed. 1 misprints 'by.'

l. 13. **so that** = provided only that.

l. 14. **dyspose them**, i.e. set them out.

l. 15. **maye not flye.** The original is 'non sit refugiendi locus,' there may be no occasion for flight.

ll. 16, 17. **what for ... what for**, see supra, 49, 19.

ll. 22-3. **women ... accompanye their husbandes.** Suggested no doubt either by Plato, *Republic*, v. p. 457: 'Then let the wives of our guardians strip, having virtue for their robe, and share in the spoils of war and the defence of their country' (Jowett's translation), or by Tacitus, *German.* xviii 'ne se mulier extra virtutum cogitationes *extraque bellorum* casus putet, ipsis incipientis matrimonii auspiciis admonetur venire se laborum periculorumque sociam, idem in pace, *idem in praelio passuram ausuram*que.'

NOTES: BOOK II

l. 26. **sett fylde**, i. e. line of battle, battle array; Lat. *in acie.*

l. 29. **alliaunce**, i. e. kindred, Lat. *cognati.* Cf. 'Therefore let our *Alliance* be combin'd' (Shakespeare, *Jul. Caes.* iv. 1. 43).

P. 118, l. 7. **bronte** = shock, onslaught. See Glossary.

l. 10. **gyue backe**, i. e. retreat. Cf. 'So they (Fiends) gave back and came no further' (Bunyan, *Pilg. Prog.* i. p. 108).

l. 14. **pensifenes** = M. E. *pensifnesse*, gloomy thought.

l. 17. **knowledge in cheualrye**, i. e. practical knowledge of military discipline. Lat. *militaris disciplinae peritia.*

l. 18. **putteth them in a good hope**, i. e. gives them confidence.

l. 28. **honestie** = honour, exactly the Latin *honestas.*

l. 31. **bende** = band, modification of 'band.' *bende* is rare in this sense, from F. *bande*, Low Lat. *banda*, 'a gang,' after 1600 (N. E. D.).

l. 34. **inuade** = attack.

P. 119, l. 10. **rerewarde**, i. e. the rear guard. 'Rere' is short for M. E. *arere*, behind. 'Warde' is an O. F. form of *garde.* Cf. 'The God of Israel will be your rereward' (Isa. lii. 12).

l. 24. **spyte of there tethes** = in spite of their teeth, their direct opposition; i. e. despite all resistance. The phrase 'in the teeth' means 'in direct opposition to.' The Cent. Dict. quotes Urquhart's Rabelais, i. 49 'They met Picrochole in the teeth'; and Shakespeare, *C. of E.* ii. 2. 22 'Dost thou geer and flout me in the teeth?'

l. 37. **pollicie**, i. e. stratagem. Lat. *stratagemate.*

l. 38. **softely** = quietly. Lat. *sensim.*

P. 120, l. 8. **in harneis**, i. e. under arms. The Lat. is 'in armis,' and cf. the same phrase in l. 18, 'armati.' M. E. *harness*, O. F. *harneis.* Cf. Ital. *arnese*; it properly means 'tackle, gear.' It was afterwards applied to armour and particularly to a coat of mail, and in Elizabethan English is commonly so used. So Shakespeare, *Macbeth*, v. 5. 52 'At least we'll die with harness on our back.'

l. 9. **auentures**, i. e. events, surprises.

l. 19. **afarre of**, i. e. for long-distance fighting.

l. 22. **mortall**, i. e. death-dealing, deadly. Lat. *letales.*

l. 23. **foynes**, i. e. thrusts made with the point of the weapon thrust forward, as distinct from the strokes made with the edge of the weapon. Usually derived from O. F. *foine*, a three-pronged fish-spear. Lat. *fuscina*.

l. 30. **handsome** = handy, easy to manipulate. Cf. 'Neither were the barbarous huge targets, and long spikes so *handsome* among trees and low shrubs as darts and swords.' Grenewey, *Tacitus's Ann.* ii. 4. 37.

P. 121, l. 3. **espiall**, i. e. a spy. This is an obsolete meaning of the word, which now means 'the action of espying.' For the former meaning cf. Holinshed, *Chron.* i. 174 'His (Harold's) vnskilfull *espials* took the Normans for priests.'

ll. 18, 19. **laye it vpon theire neckes that be conquered**, i. e. 'put it down to the conquered.' The Lat. has simply *victis imputant*.

ll. 26–7. **vii. hundreth thousand ducates.** This is probably the gold ducat, which was worth 9s. 4d., and was current in Holland, Sweden, Austria, and Russia, and not the Italian or silver coin worth about 3s. 6d. The total amount would therefore be about £326,500.

CHAPTER IX

OF THE RELIGYONS IN VTOPIA.

Of the various forms of religion in Utopia. Readiness with which many of the Utopians embraced Christianity. Their remarkable tolerance, and dislike of intolerance, inculcated by King Utopus; his reasons for such indulgence; his two restrictions on liberty of thought, and why they were imposed. Utopian belief in the immortality of the souls of brutes. Burial of the dead, and how it is conducted. Belief in the presence among the living of the souls of the dead; contempt for soothsaying and divination. Importance attached to the study of natural history, to manual labour, and to good exercises as a preparation for an after-life. Devout citizens divided into two sects; tenets and practices of these sects. The Utopian priests; their characteristic functions. Festivals of Churches and religious services in Utopia. Concluding reflections of Hythlodaye and More on the application of Utopian theories and practices to contemporary life.

P. 123, l. 5. **Some worshyp.** In this account of the forms of religion current in Utopia, More simply specifies the forms which religion has actually assumed among mankind, possibly drawing on the first book of Cicero's *De Natura*

NOTES: BOOK II

Deorum and the first book of Lactantius, *De Falsa Religione*, where those forms are enumerated. Cf. also Tacitus, *Germania*, ix.

ll. 5, 6. **the sunne ... the mone.** Cf. Cicero, *De Nat. Deorum*, I. ii. 27 'Crotoniates Alcmaeon, qui soli et lunae reliquisque sideribus ... divinitatem dedit.' It was the religion of the primitive Germans (see Caesar, *De Bello Gall.* vi. 10) and of many other barbarous peoples.

l. 7. **to a man.** As Gaudama the Buddha, Confucius, Zoroaster (Lupton).

l. 10. **the moste.** This pantheistic conception of Deity reminds us of the accounts given of the Pythagorean creed (Lactantius, *De Falsa Religione* (ed. 1685), i. p. 11) and of that of Zeno (Diogenes Laertius, *Vita Zenonis*, lx. 2); it is also the conception of Deity formulated by Cicero and constituting apparently his own creed. See *Tusculanae Quaestiones*, lib. i. 26. 66.

l. 18. **Nother they,** i.e. nor do they.

l. 25. **Mythra.** Mithras was the Persian Sun-God. See Strabo, xv. p. 732 (Casaub.) 'The Persians ... worship the sun, whom they call Mithras.' As the Utopian language was 'not unlike the Persian tongue,' it is not unnatural that they should worship the same God. The worship of Mithra was attended with elaborate ritual observances and ceremonial mysteries, and spread far and wide, being also practised in Rome under the early Empire, especially in the army, for upwards of 300 years. There is proof of the presence of Mithraism in Britain, tablets being found in the Roman wall at York relating to it.

P. 124, l. 8. **as he was mynded,** i.e. while he was making up his mind. Lat. *inter mutandae religionis consilia*, thinking of a change of creed. The reminiscence here of St. Augustine's *De Civitate Dei* is unmistakable. That work was written to refute the popular opinion that the fall of Rome had been the result of the wrath of the Pagan deities at the neglect of their worship through the substitution of Christianity for Paganism.

l. 12. **reuenge,** i.e. exact retribution for. Lat. *vindicante*.

l. 22. **next vnto,** i.e. nearest to; the second edition reads 'nieghest.' 'That opinion' is explained by what follows, namely, that Christ approved of communism.

l. 26. **Christ instytuted.** The original merely says 'Christo placuisse,'=that Christ approved.

l. 28. **rightest Christian companion.** The marginal

note in the Latin, *coenobia*, seems to show that More meant monasteries.

l. 32. **amonge vs foure.** Originally Hythlodaye had five companions. Cf. Book I, and General Introduction. Note the touch of realism.

l. 35. **entered,** i.e. initiated, Lat. *initiati*. Cf. Ellwood, *Autobiography*, 202 'He asked me if I would *enter* his Children in the Rudiments of the Latin Tongue'; and Shakespeare, *Cor.* i. 2. 2 'They of Rome are *entred* in our Counsailes.'

l. 37. **minister,** i.e. administer, confer. Cf. 'Christ hath commanded prayers to be made, sacraments to be *ministered*, his Church to be carefully taught and guided' (Hooker, *Eccles. Pol.* III. ii).

P. 125, l. 5. **mynded to chuse one.** It was this passage which suggested and gave point to what More relates in his letter to Peter Giles, namely, that a certain godly man was anxious to go out as a missionary to Utopia, hoping to be made bishop. (See Appendix.)

ll. 9, 10. **one of oure companye,** i.e. of those who had been converted.

l. 12. **with more earnest affection then wisdome,** i.e. with greater zeal than prudence.

l. 21. **not as a despyser,** &c. This conception of religion purely in its political aspect is very remarkable in a man tempered like More. (See Introduction.) For the sentiment cf. Dryden, *Religio Laici*, 447-50:—

'... Private reason 'tis more just to curb
Than by disputes the public peace disturb;
For points obscure are of small use to learn,
But common quiet is mankind's concern.'

l. 31. **seuerall partes,** i.e. different sides. As the country was thus split up by these religious factions Utopus found little difficulty in conquering it.

P. 126, l. 20. **trewe.** For the discrepancy of what is here inculcated with More's measures against the Protestants, see Introduction.

l. 24. **trewthe of the owne powre.** The original has 'ipsa per se ueri uis,' the mere force of truth by itself.

P. 127, l. 7. **aualed,** i.e. lowered, degraded, see Glossary. With the sentiment cf. Bacon's *Essay on Atheism*: 'They that deny a God destroy man's nobility ... as Atheism is in all respects hateful, so in this, that it depriveth human nature of the means to exalt itself above human frailty.'

NOTES: BOOK II

ll. 8, 9. **muche lesse in the numbre of their citiziens,** i. e. he is not even counted in the number of *men*, much less as one of their *citizens*.

l. 13. **breake, the commen lawes.** For this idea that a man who is an atheist will have no regard for the law or for morality, cf. the freethinker Collins's reply, when he was asked why he was careful to make his servants go to Church: 'I do it that they may neither rob nor murder me'; and Tillotson's sermon on the Advantages of Religion to Societies (*Works*, vol. iii. 43 *seqq.*), both quoted in Pattison's *Tendencies of Religious Thought in England*, 1688-1750, reprinted from *Essays and Reviews* in Pattison's *Essays*, Oxford, 1899, vol. ii.

l. 17. **reiecte,** i. e. rejected.

ll. 18, 19. **of all sorte,** i. e. by all classes; 'sort' is commonly used in old English for a number of persons, and for a particular class.

l. 21. **punyshemente.** This of course refers to physical punishment. The original has *supplicium*.

l. 22. **beleue.** The original has *sentiat*, i. e. be of such opinion.

l. 28. **dispute in his opinion,** i.e. discuss his opinion.

and that onlye. The omission of these three words and the comma makes the meaning clear.

l. 29. **elles a parte,** i. e. otherwise. Lat. *alioquin*.

l. 37. **liuinge.** Ed. 1 misprints 'gliuine.'

P. 128, l. 4. **all they,** i. e. they all.

l. 5. **blesse,** i. e. bliss. This spelling is very rare, though 'blisse' is common. It occurs, however, in Walkington, *Opt. Glass*, 65 'The soul is ... wrapt up into an Elysium and paradise of *blesse*.'

l. 8. **carfully,** i. e. full of care, anxiously and reluctantly.

l. 11. **forefeilyng**=fore-feeling, presentiment.

l. 22. **merely**=merrily, cheerfully.

l. 24. **ioyfull synging.** Suggested perhaps by what Herodotus says (*Hist.* v. 4) of the Trausi: τὸν δ' ἀπογινόμενον παίζοντές τε καὶ ἡδόμενοι γῇ κρύπτουσι, ἐπιλέγοντες ὅσων κακῶν ἐξαπαλλαχθείς ἐστι ἐν πάσῃ εὐδαιμονίῃ ('one that dies they bury in the earth, making merry and rejoicing, recounting the many evils from which being released he is now in perfect bliss'); or possibly Euripides (Fragments of the *Cresphontes*), where he says that, considering the evils of life, we ought rather to mourn those who enter life, τὸν δ' αὖ θανόντα καὶ πόνων πεπαυμένον, χαίροντας, εὐφημοῦντας, ἐκπέμπειν δόμων ('but him who is dead and hath ceased from his labours we ought with rejoicings and congratulations to escort from his home to the grave'). Cf. too Sir Thomas Browne, *Religio Medici*, part i. sect. xliv: 'The first day of our jubilee is death; the devil hath therefore failed of his desires: we are happier with death than we should have been without it.'

l. 33. **their vertue**, i. e. of the dead.

l. 38. **feoble**. This form is recognized in N. E. D.

inuisible. Ed. 1, 'invisibly.'

P. 129, l. 6. **charytye**. Ed. 2 reads 'amitie.' Lat. *charitas*.

ll. 9, 10. **be presentlye conuersaunte**, i. e. are personally present among the living. The original is *versari*, 'to turn oneself about.' Hence 'to turn oneself about much in a place,' and so 'frequent.' There is no word corresponding to 'presentlye' in the Latin, but here it probably means 'in presence,' 'actually.' See also 'present conuersacion' in l. 14; Lat. 'credita maiorum praesentia.' The beautiful superstition of which More here speaks was no doubt suggested by the Roman Lares and Manes. Cf. ll. 13-16, with the sentiment of Tennyson, *In Memoriam*, i.

l. 17. **despise and mocke sothe sayinges**, &c. The favourite butts of Euripides' scorn and contempt.

ll. 21-2. **esteame and worshippe miracles**. Cf. More's confutation of Tyndale, quoted in Tyndale's *Works*, 'Answer to More's *Dialogue*' (Parker Soc. ed., p. 100): 'I say that the Catholic Church bringeth miracles for their doctrine, as the Apostles did for theirs, in that God ceaseth no year to work miracles in his Catholic Church, many and wonderful, both for his holy men quick and dead.' And see chaps. iv-xvii of the First Book of the *Dialogue*.

l. 30. **the prayse thereof cumminge**, i. e. the praise given to God which is inspired by the contemplation of nature.

l. 33. **nor ... no**. Double negative for emphasis. 'No' is changed to 'any' in ed. 2.

l. 34. **of thinges**, i. e. except religion.

l. 36. **exercises**, i. e. duties. Lat. *officia*. It is on the salutary effect of such 'exercises' as these that Ruskin lays so much stress; see *Sesame and Lilies* and *Fors Clavigera*, passim.

P. 130, l. 7. **lothsumnes** = loathsomeness.

fraye, i. e. frighten. Cf. 'Instead of *fraying* they themselves did feare' (Spenser, *F. Q.* ii. 12. 40).

NOTES: BOOK II

l. 13. seruiseable. Not in our sense of the word 'useful,' but ' as servants,' 'proffering their services.' The Latin has ' sese servos exhibent,' behave themselves as slaves. Cf. Milton, *Ode on the Nativity*, 244 ' And all about the courtly stable, Bright-harness'd Angels sit, in order *serviceable.*'

ll. 18, 19. flesh . . . beastes. Whilst the former (Lat. *caro*) would mean 'meat,' the latter (Lat. *animal*) would also include birds and fish.

l. 22. sweatynge, i. e. toiling, labouring. Cf. Cowley, *Tree of Knowledge*. st. 4 ' Henceforth, said God, the wretched Sons of Earth shall *sweat* for Food in vain.'

l. 27. labour and toyle. Ed. 1 misprints 'tiole.'

P. 131, **l. 1. worship them.** After these words comes a sentence in the Latin which Robynson omits to translate : 'Nihil enim sollicitius observant, quam ne temere quicquam ulla de religione pronuncient' (translated by Burnet, 'There is nothing in which they are more cautious, than in giving their Opinion positively concerning any Sort of Religion ').

l. 3. Buthrescas. From Gk. βου- (βοῦς, an ox), used in compounds for something ' very big,' 'huge,' as βούπαις, 'a big boy,' βουλιμία, ' ravenous hunger ' (cf. our ' horse ' in ' horse-chestnut,' &c.); and θρῆσκος, ' religious,' ' devout.' So that it means ' extraordinarily religious.'

ll. 5, 6. therefore very few. More's dislike of priests finds strange illustration in this remark.

l. 18. a⟨uoyding of strife. The first edition omits everything between ' a ' in ' auoyding ' and ' consecrate.'

l. 20. religions, i.e. religious ceremonies and services. Cf. Milton, *Par. Lost*, i. 372 ' The invisible Glory of him that made them to transform Oft to the image of a brute adorn'd With gay *religions* full of pomp and gold.'

l. 23. dissolute. Both editions misprint ' dissolate.'

l. 28. sauynge that the priestes, &c. This is a Latin construction, and perhaps not quite clear in the English. We should say, ' except that the priests excommunicate those whom they find exceeding vicious livers from having any interest in divine matters.'

l. 32. runne in verye great infamy, i. e. incur very great disgrace ; a not uncommon use of the word even now, as ' run in debt,' or ' run in danger.'

l. 35. approue, i. e. prove, demonstrate. Cf. Shakespeare, *Cymbeline*, v. 5. 245 ' One thing . . . which must *approve* thee honest.'

P. 132, **l. 11. risinge of,** i. e. arising from.

l. 12. **women.** It is remarkable that in his controversy with Tyndale there were no points more emphatically and intemperately denounced by More than Tyndale's vindication of women as ministers of religion and the contention that priests should be allowed to marry. See More's *Confutation*, bk. v, and Tyndale's *Answer* (*Works*, Parker Soc. ed., pp. 18, 29, 30, 98, 176). What More says about women in the text was perhaps suggested by Plutarch, *Laconica*, xxxv. The Lacedaemonians did not 'exclude either sex from their temples and religious services, but as they were always bred up to the same civil exercises so they were to the same common performances of their holy mysteries' (Plutarch, *Morals*, Goodwin's translation, vol. i. p. 97). Possibly More may have been thinking of Phoebe, who is described as a διάκονος in Epistle to the Romans, xvi. 1. Among the Collyridian heretics women were admitted to the priesthood. See Lecky, *Hist. of European Morals*, ii. 365.

l. 19. **commen.** As before, 'public.'

l. 22. **after so singuler a sort,** i.e. in so special a manner.

l. 37. **runne in,** &c. 'Incur,' as above.

P. 133, l. 3. **mean,** i.e. average, mediocre.

l. 4. **thies priestes.** In this picture of the conduct of the priests in Utopia we have another oblique satire on the part too often played by Christian priests both in mediaeval times and in More's own day. Instead of composing, they had too often inflamed war, as Henry the Fifth's bishops had done and such a Pope as Julius II. Wolsey had encouraged Henry VIII in his invasion of France, and More had just seen the Archbishop of St. Andrews and the bishops of Caithness and of the Isles abetting James IV in his ambitious designs, and falling at his side at the battle of Flodden Field.

l. 14. **in to the mayne battayle,** i.e. into the thick of the fight. Lat. *acies* = fighting-line.

l. 26. **reculed,** i.e. recoiled. Fr. *reculer*.

P. 134, l. 4. **Cynemernes.** 'Lynemernes' is the reading of the first English editions; probably a misprint. Dr. Lupton expresses his surprise that Robynson should have altered 'Cynemernos' into 'Lynemernos'; but he does not, at least in the editions I have consulted. Dr. Lupton's explanation (and I have no better one to give) is that the word is meant 'to suggest κυνημερινός [κυνός and ἡμέρα], "the dog's day of the month," strictly the night between the old and the new,

NOTES: BOOK II

when food was placed out at the crossways, and the barking of the dogs was taken as a sign of the approach of Hecate (see Theocritus, *Idyll.* ii. 35-6).'

Trapemernes. This Dr. Lupton explains as τραπημερινός, 'the turning or closing day of the month': from τρέπειν and ἡμέρα, through the adjective ἡμερινός.

l. 8. **curious.** In the Latin sense of 'careful' or 'elaborate.'

l. 14. **ouer much light.** From the earliest times it was usual for churches to be brilliantly lighted. More's suggestion that in an ideal church the light should be dim and subdued, because such subdued light was conducive to devotion, appears to be original. Possibly the idea may have been suggested to him by Euripides' *Bacchae*, 485-6, where it is said that in religious rites darkness adds solemnity:—

Pentheus. τὰ δ' ἱρὰ νύκτωρ ἢ μεθ' ἡμέραν τελεῖς;

Dionysus. νύκτωρ τὰ πολλά· σεμνότητ' ἔχει σκότος.

All readers will recall Milton's 'Storied windows richly dight, Casting a dim religious light' (*Il Penseroso*, 159-60).

l. 23. **indifferently,** i. e. equally, alike, impartially. So till the eighteenth century. Cf. Steele, *Tatler*, No. 57 'All Mankind are *indifferently* liable to adverse strokes of Fortune.'

l. 24. **sacrifice.** As the Utopians had no sacrifices (see p. 136, l. 4), the Latin (*sacrum*) would be more correctly translated 'rite.'

P. 135, l. 1. **yet,** i. e. still.

l. 20. **knowe themselfes to beare,** &c. The parallel between this passage and the Rubric before the Communion Service in the Liturgy will be obvious: 'The same order shall the Curate use with those betwixt whom he perceiveth malice and hatred to reign; not suffering them to be partakers of the Lord's Table, until he know them to be reconciled.'

l. 26. **the men goo,** &c. The separation of the sexes in the Christian churches, Dr. Lupton observes, is as old as the *Apostolical Constitutions*.

l. 27. **the women** in both editions.

l. 30. **goodman.** The original has *paterfamilias*. **Good wyfe,** Lat. *materfamilias*. Words not yet wholly obsolete. Cf. Macaulay's *Horatius*, st. lxx :—

'When the *goodman* mends his armour,
  And trims his helmet's plume;
And the *goodwife's* shuttle merrily
  Goes flashing through the loom.'

l. 32. **forsene.** Not 'seen beforehand,' but 'seen *to* beforehand,' 'provided for.' Cf. Act 8 Elizabeth, cap. 13 'The Master, Wardens and Assistants of Trinity House . . . are bound to *foresee* the good Increase and Maintenance of Ships' (*Statutes of the Realm*, iv. p. 496).

l. 33. **abrode,** i. e. away from home, out. Lat. *foris.* Cf. 'I am glad to see your Lordship *abroad*: I heard say your Lordship was sicke' (Shakespeare, 2 *Henry IV*, i. 2. 107).

P. 136, ll. 4–7. **They kill...franckensence.** So Diogenes Laertius relates of Pythagoras: 'He used to practise divination . . . but not by means of burnt offerings except only the burning of frankincence. And all the sacrifices which he offered consisted of inanimate beings' (*Life of Pythagoras*, xviii).

l. 10. **geere,** see Glossary. The Latin has simply *haec* = 'these things.'

l. 22. **diuers fethers of fowles.** This may have been suggested by the passage in Plato's *Timaeus* (Jowett's translation, p. 91): 'The race of birds was created out of innocent light-minded men, who, although their minds were directed toward heaven, imagined, in their simplicity, that the clearest demonstration of the things above was to be obtained by sight; these were remodelled and transformed into birds, and they grew feathers instead of hair.' For the association of birds with divination and prophecy, which was no doubt in More's mind, cf. Plutarch, *De Solertia Animalium*, xxii, where, speaking of the prophetic nature with which terrestrial creatures are endowed, he says of birds: 'The quickness and intelligible faculty of birds, together with their capability to receive all impressions of fancy, afford the Deity a convenience to make use of those faculties as instruments.'

l. 23. **counteruaile.** Literally 'to be of worth against,' from Lat. *contra* and *valere*, and so 'to be equivalent in value to,' 'to equal.' Cf. supra, p. 20, l. 22 'All the goodes in the world are not able to *countervayle* man's life.'

l. 33. **vestrie.** Lat. has *adytum*, the innermost part of the temple.

P. 137, ll. 8, 9. **For all theire musicke.** The whole of this passage so closely resembles Aristotle's remarks on Music and its effects (see *Politics*, viii. 5) that it is difficult to suppose that More had it not in mind. Cf. 'Different harmonies differ from each other so much by nature that those who hear them are differently affected. . . . The one for instance

NOTES: BOOK II

occasions grief and contracts the soul, as the mixed-Lydian; others soften the mind and as it were dissolve the heart; others fix it in a firm and settled state.... It is evident then what an influence music has over the disposition of the mind and how variously it can fascinate it.' See too, for a similar view, Plato, *Republic*, iii. pp. 399-401; and cf. Elyot's remarks in his *Governour* on music and dancing, bk. i. ch. xix-xxi.

l. 20. **expresslye.** i.e. definitely, in set terms. Cf. Hawes, *Pastime of Pleasure*, XIV. ix 'The Pamflete shewith it *expressely*.'

P. 138, l. 5. **vnsercheable**, i.e. inscrutable. Cf. Milton, *Paradise Lost*, viii. 8 'Thou hast vouchsafed This friendly condescension, to relate Things else by me unsearchable.'

ll. 6, 7. **how soone or late.** Cf. *Paradise Lost*, xi. 550-1 'Nor love thy life, nor hate; but what thou liv'st, Live well, how long or short permit to Heav'n.'

l. 8. **stande with**, i.e. be in accordance with. Cf. Burton, *Anat. of Mel.* 634 (*fol. edit.*) 'It cannot *stand with* God's mercy that so many should be damned.'

l. 15. **cheualrye** = military training.

ll. 35, 36. **so that,** provided that.

P. 139, l. 10. **nephewes.** Here 'grandsons.' The Latin has *nepotes*. The word 'nephews' was commonly used in M.E. for 'grandchildren.' Cf. Jeremy Taylor, *Works*, i. 776 '*Nephews* are very often liker to their grandfathers than to their fathers.'

l. 18. **I forsake God.** A strong asseveration. The Latin has *dispeream*, 'may I utterly perish.'

l. 20. **ryche goldsmythe.** See Introduction. In and before More's day till after the Restoration the goldsmiths were also bankers. See Macaulay's *History* (crown 8vo ed.), ii. 479.

l. 28. **drawyng and bearyng beastes,** i.e. draught-cattle and beasts of burden. Latin has *iumenta*.

l. 29. **skant,** i.e. scarcely, hardly. Cf. '*Scant* one is to be found worthie amongst us for translating into our Countrie speach' (Ascham, *Scholemaster*, p. 7).

ll. 32, 33. **so wretched and miserable a life.** See Introduction, and cf. Ascham's remark on the condition of the poor: 'Nam vita quae nunc vivitur a plurimis non vita sed miseria est.' See also 'A Supplication of the Poor Commons,' Furnivall's 'Forewords' to *Ballads from Manuscripts*, p. 6.

P. 140, l. 1. **presently**, i.e. at the present time. Lat. *in praesenti*.

l. 3. **kylleth them vp**. 'up'=off. Cf. Shakespeare, *As You Like It*, ii. 1. 62 'To fright the animals and *to kill* them *up*, In their assign'd and native dwelling-place.'

l. 22. **acquyteth**, i.e. requiteth. Cf. Gower, *Confess. Amant.* (ed. Macaulay), bk. viii, ll. 2298-9 'This wold I for my laste word beseche, That thou mi love *aquite* as I deserve.'

l. 24. **commen lawes**. A reference to the Statute of Labourers passed in 1495-6, and again in 1514.

l. 31. **by force of a law**. The Statute of 1514.

P. 141, l. 17. **rauine**. From O.F. *ravine, rabine* (Lat. *rapina*), robbery, rapine, and so plunder. The original sense of the word is lost in French, where it now means 'a violent rush of water' (N. E. D.).

brabling, i.e. cavilling or wrangling. The derivation of the word is obscure. Cf. Raleigh, *History of the World*, i. 172 'The *brabblings* of the Aristotelians.'

l. 36. **lady money**. The Latin is simply *beata illa pecunia*, translated by Burnet 'that blessed thing called money.' Robynson was no doubt thinking of the phrase 'lady Pecunia' which became so common afterwards among the Elizabethans. See Barnfield's *Encomium of Lady Pecunia*; and the 'Queen' or 'Lady' Pecunia in Ben Jonson's *Staple of News*.

l. 37. **a goddes name** = in God's name. Latin has *scilicet*. Cf. Chaucer, Prol. 854 'What, welcome be the cut, *a Goddes name!*'

P. 142, ll. 8, 9. **oure sauioure Christe**. This association of Christ with communism was one of the heresies of the Anabaptists, which makes More's insistence on it the more remarkable. See Bullinger's *Letters* (Parker Society ed.), vol. ii. 18, 21, iv. 18; and Hooper's *Works* (Id.), vol. ii. p. 42. It is a heresy condemned in one of the articles, *Liturgy*, Edw. VI. 536. But see More's repudiation, supra, p. 45 foll.

l. 13. **not that one**. Ed. 1, 'No that one.'

l. 14. **princesse**. The first edition reads 'prince.' What More here says of 'pride' he says with equal emphasis in his 'De Quatuor novissimis' (*English Works*, 1577, pp. 82, 1270, referred to by Dr. Lupton). It is condemned not less strongly, and for the same reasons, by his contemporaries, by Warner, as Satan's chief instrument for leading men astray, see Farr's *Select Poetry*, p. 379; 'as the headspring of all

NOTES: BOOK II

evil' by Becon, *Works*, i. 198; 'as the source of heresies' by Tyndale, *Works*, ii. 140.

l. 18. **by her good will**, i. e. of her own will.

l. 23. **hell hound**. The original has *auerni serpens*, 'serpent of Avernus.'

l. 28. **yet**, i. e. at least. Lat. reads *saltem*.

l. 29. **chaunced to**, i. e. fallen to. Lat. *contigisse*.

l. 32. **wealthely**, happily, successfully. Lat. *feliciter*.

l. 37. **ieopardye of domesticall dissention**. Lat. 'nihil impendet periculi ne domestico dissidio laboretur,' i. e. no risk of party strife.

P. 143, l. 1. **well fortefied and strongly defenced wealth and riches of many cities**. Robynson has once more paraphrased the Latin: 'quae una multarum urbium egregie munitas opes pessundedit.' For *defenced*, cf. A.V., Jer. i. 18 'I have made thee this day a *defenced* city.'

l. 25. **other** = others. Lat. *quosdam*. Cf. P.B. version (Coverdale's) of the Psalms, vii. 16 'He is fallen himself into the destruction that he made for *other*.'

l. 29. **communication**, i. e. conversation. See Glossary.

l. 33. **ones** = at some *future* time.

l. 35. **els**, Lat. *alioquin*; i. e. but for Raphaell's love of fault-finding.

APPENDIX

I.

⁋ To the right honourable Hierome Buslyde, prouost of Arien͂, and counselloure to the catholike kinge Charles, Peter Gyles Citizien of Antwerpe, wisheth health and felicitie.

Thomas More the singular ornamente of this our age, as you your self (right honourable Buslide) can witnesse, to whome he is perfectly wel knowen, sent vnto me this other day the ylande of Vtopia, to very few as yet knowen, but most worthy which, as farre excelling Platoes commen wealthe, all people shoulde be willinge to know: specially of a man most eloquent so finely set furth, so conningly painted out, and so euidently subiect to the eye, that as oft as I reade it, me thinketh that I see somwhat more, then when I heard Raphael Hythloday himselfe (for I was present at that talke aswell as master More) vtteryng and pronouncing his owne woordes: yea, though the same man, accordinge to his pure eloquence, did so open and declare the matter, that he might plainely enough appeare to reporte not thinges, which he had learned of others onelye by hearesay, but which he had with his own eyes presently sene, and throughly vewed, and wherein he had no smal time bene conuersant and abiding: a man trulie, in mine opinion, as touching the knowledge of regions, peoples, and worldly experience, muche passinge, yea euen the very famous and renowmed tranailer Vlysses: and in dede suche a one, as for the space of these viij. c. yeres past I think nature into the worlde brought not furth his like: in comparison of whome Vespuce maye be thought to haue sene nothing.

Moreouer, wheras we be wont more effectually and pitthely to declare and expresse thinges that we haue sene, then whiche we haue but onelye hearde, there was besides that in this man a certen peculiar grace, and singular dexteritie to discriue and set furth a matter withall. Yet the selfe same thinges as ofte as I beholde and consider them drawen and painted oute with master Mores pensille, I am therwith so moued, so delited, so inflamed, and so rapt, that sometime me think I am presently conuersaunt, euen in the ylande of Vtopia. And I promise you, Ican skante beleue that Raphael himselfe by al that fiue yeres space that he was in Vtopia abiding, saw there somuch, as here in master Mores description is to be sene and perceaued. Whiche description with so manye wonders and miraculous thinges is replenished, that I stande in great doubt wherat first and chieflie to muse or marueile: whether at the excellencie of his perfect and suer memorie, which could welniegh worde by woorde rehearse so manye thinges once onely heard : or elles at his singular prudence, who so well and wittyly marked and bare away al the originall causes and fountaynes (to the vulgare people commenly most vnknowen) whereof both yssueth and springeth the mortall confusion and vtter decaye of a commen wealth, and also the auauncement and wealthy state of the same may riese and growe: or elles at the efficacie and pitthe of his woordes, which in so fine a latin stile, with suche force of eloquence hath couched together and comprised so many and diuers matters, speciallie beinge a man continuallie encombred with so manye busye and troublesome cares, both publique and priuate, as he is. Howbeit all these thinges cause you litle to maruell (righte honourable Buslid) for that you are familiarly and throughly acquainted with the notable, yea almost diuine witte of the man.

But nowe to procede to other matters, I suerly know nothing nedeful or requisite to be adioyned vnto his writinges. Onely a meter of .iiij. verses written in the Vtopian tongue, whiche after master Mores departure Hythloday by chaunce shewed me, that haue I caused to be added thereto, with the Alphabete of the same nation, and haue also garnished the margent of the boke with certen notes. For, as touchinge the situation of the ylande, that is to saye, in what parte of the worlde Vtopia standeth, the ignoraunce and lacke whereof not a litle troubleth and greueth master More, in dede Raphael left not that vnspoken

of. Howbeit with verie fewe wordes he lightly touched it,
incidentlye by the way passing it ouer, as meanyng of
likelihod to kepe and reserue that to an other place. And
the same, I wot not how, by a certen euell and vnluckie
chaunce escaped vs bothe. For when Raphael was speaking
therof, one of master Mores seruauntes came to him, and
whispered in his eare. Wherefore I beyng then of purpose
more earnestly addict to heare, one of the company, by
reason of cold taken, I thinke, a shippeborde, coughed out
so loude, that he toke from my hearinge certen of his
wordes. But I wil neuer stynte, nor rest, vntil I haue gotte
the full and exacte knowledge hereof: insomuche that
I will be hable perfectly to instructe you, not onely in the
longitude or true meridian of the ylande, but also in the
iust latitude therof, that is to say, in the subleuation
or height of the pole in that region, if our frende Hythloday
be in safetie, and aliue. For we heare very vncerten newes
of him. Some reporte, that he died in his iorney home-
warde. Some agayne affirme, that he retorned into his
countrey; but partly, for that he coulde not away with the
fashions of his countrey folk, and partly for that his minde
and affection was altogether set and fixed vpon Vtopia, they
say that he hathe taken his voyage thetherwarde agayne.

Now as touching this, that the name of this yland is
nowhere founde amonge the olde and auncient cosmographers,
this doubte Hythloday himselfe verie well dissolued. For
why, it is possible enoughe (quod he) that the name, whiche
it had in olde time, was afterwarde chaunged, or elles that
they neuer had knowledge of this iland: forasmuch as now
in our time diuers landes be found, which to the olde
Geographers were vnknowen. Howbeit, what nedeth it in
this behalfe to fortifie the matter with argumentes, seynge
master More is author hereof sufficient? But whereas he
doubteth of the edition or imprinting of the booke, in deede
herein I both commende, and also knowledge the mannes
modestie. Howbeit vnto me it semeth a worke most vn-
worthie to be long suppressed, and most worthy to go abrod
into the handes of men, yea, and vnder the title of youre
name to be publyshed to the worlde: either because the
singular endowmentes and qualities of master More be to no
man better knowen then to you, or els bicause no man is
more fitte and meete then you, with good counselles to
further and auaunce the commen wealth, wherin you haue
many yeares already continued and trauailed with great

glory and commendation, bothe of wisedome and knowledge, and also of integritie and vprightnes. Thus o liberall supporter of good learninge, and floure of this oure time,
  I byd you moste hartely well to fare. At
        Antwerpe .1516. the first daye of
              Nouember.

II.

¶ Thomas More to Peter Giles
sendeth gretynge.

I **am** almoste ashamed, right welbeloued Peter Giles, to sende vnto you this boke of the vtopian commen wealth, welnigh after a yeares space, which I am suer you loked for within a moneth and a half. And no marueil. For you knewe welenough, that I was already disbourdened of all the labour and study belonging to the inuention in this work, and that I had no nede at all to trouble my braynes about the disposition or conueyaunce of the matter; and therefore had herin nothing els to do, but only to rehearse those thinges, which you and I togethers hard maister Raphaell tel and declare. Wherefore there was no cause whie I shold study to set forth the matter with eloquence; for asmuch as his talke cold not be fine and eloquent, being firste not studied for, but sodein and vnpremeditate, and then, as you know, of a man better sene in the greke language then in the latine tong. And my writing, the nigher it shold approche to his homely, playne, and simple speche, somuch the nigher shold it go to the trueth; whiche is the only marke, wherunto I do and ought to direct all my trauail and study herin.

I graunt and confesse, frende Peter, meself discharged of somuch labour, hauing all thies thinges redy done to my hand, that almoost there was nothing lefte for me to do. Elles other the inuention, or the disposition of this matter, might haue requyred of a witte, nother base nother at all vnlearned, bothe some time and leasure, and also some studye. But yf yt were requysyte and necessary, that the matter shoulde also haue bene wryten eloquentelye, and not alone truelye: of a suerty that thynge coulde I haue perfourmed by no tyme nor studye. But nowe, seynge all

APPENDIX II

thyes cares, stayes, and lettes were taken awaye, wherin elles somuche laboure and studye shoulde haue bene employed; and that there remayned no other thynge for me to doo, but onelye to write playnlye the matter as I hard it spoken; that in dede was a thynge lyghte and easye to be done. Howe beit, to the dyspatchynge of thys so lytell busynes my other cares and troubles did leaue almooste lesse then no leasure. Whyles I doo daylye bestowe my tyme abowte lawe matters; some to pleade, some to heare, some as an arbytratour wyth myne awarde to determyne, some as an vmpier or a judge with my sentence finallye to discusse; whiles I go one way to see and visite my frend, an other way about mine owne privat affaires; whiles I spend almost al the day abrode emonges other, and the residue at home among mine own; I leaue to meselfe, I meane to my boke, no time.

For when I am come home, I muste commen with my wife, chatte with my chyldren, and talke wyth my seruauntes. All the whyche thynges I reken and accompte emonge busynes, forasmuche as they muste of necessytye be done: and done muste they nedes be, oneles a man wyll be a straunger in hys owne howse. And in any wyse a man muste so fassyon and order hys condytyons, and so appoynte and dyspose hym selfe, that he be merye, iocunde, and pleasaunte amonge them, whome eyther nature hath prouyded, or chaunce hathe made, or he hymselfe hathe chosen, to be the fellowes and companyons of hys lyfe: so that wyth to muche gentle behauyoure and famylyaryte he doo not marre them, and, by tomuche sufferaunce, of hys seruauntes make them hys maysters. Emonge thyes thinges nowe rehearsed stealethe awaye the daye, the moneth, the yeare. When doo I wryte, then? And all thys whyle haue I spoken no woorde of slepe, nother yet of meate, whyche emonge a greate number doth waste no lesse tyme then dothe slepe, wherin almooste halfe the lyfe tyme of man crepethe awaye. I therefore doo wynne and gette onelye that tyme, whyche I steale from slepe and meate. Whyche tyme bycause yt ys verye littell, and yet somwhat it is, therfore haue I ones at the last, thoughe it be longe first, finished Vtopia, and haue sent it to you, frende Peter, to reade and peruse; to the intent that if anye thynge haue escaped me, you might putte me in remembraunce of it. For though in this behalf I do not greatly mistruste meself (whiche woulde God I were somewhat in witte and learnyng, as I am not all

of the worste and dullest memory), yet haue I not so great
truste and confidence in it, that I thinke nothing could fall
out of my mynde.

For John Clement my boye, who as yow knowe was there
present with vs, whome I suffer to be awaye from no talke,
wherin may be anye profit or goodnes (for out of this yong
bladed and newe shotte vp corne, whiche hath alredy begonne to sprynge vp bothe in Latine and Greke learnynge,
I looke for plentiful increase at length of goodly rype
grayne), he, I saye, hath brought me into a greate doubte.
For wheras Hythlodaye (oneles my memory fayle me) sayde
that the bridge of Amaurote, which goeth ouer the riuer
of Anyder, is fyue hundreth paseis, that is to saye, half
a myle, in lengthe; my Jhon sayeth that ii. hundred of those
paseis must be plucked awaye; for that the ryuer conteyneth
there not aboue thre hundreth paseis in bredthe. I praye
yow hartely call the matter to youre remembraunce. For
if you agree with hym, I also wyll saye as you saye, and
confesse me selfe deceaued. But if you cannot remember
the thynge, then suerly I wyl write as I haue done, and
as myne owne remembraunce serueth me. For as I will take
good hede that there be in my booke nothyng false, so, if
there be anythynge in doubte, I wyll rather tell a lye then
make a lye; bicause I had be good then wise rather.

Howbeit this matter maye easely be remedied, if yow wyll
take the paynes to aske the question of Raphaell himselfe,
by worde of mouthe, if he be nowe with yow, or els by youre
letters. Which you must nedes do for an other doubte also,
whiche hath chaunced, throughe whoes faulte I cannot tell,
whether throughe myne or youres or Raphaels. For neither
we remembred to enquire of hym, nor he to tell vs, in what
parte of that newe worlde Vtopia is situate. The whiche
thinge I had rather haue spent no small somme of money
then that it should thus haue escaped vs; aswell for that
I am ashamed to be ignoraunt in what sea that Ilande
standeth, wherof I write so longe a treatyse, as also because
there be with vs certayne men, and especially one deuoute
and godly man, and a professour of diuinitie, who is excedynge desierous to go vnto Vtopia; not for a vayne and
curious desiere to see newes, but to the intent he maye
further and increase our religion, whiche is there already
luckely begoune. And that he may the better accomplyshe
and perfourme this his good intent, he is mynded to procure
that he maye be sent thether of the byshoppe, yea and

APPENDIX II

that he hymselfe may be made bishop of Vtopia; beynge nothynge scrupulous herein, that he must obteyne this byshopricke with suete. For he counteth that a godley suete, whiche procedeth not of the desiere of honour or lucre, but only of a godly zeale.

Wherfore I moste earnestly desyere you, frende Peter, to talke with Hythlodaye, if you can, face to face, or els to wryte youre letters to hym; and so to worke in this matter, that in this my booke there maye neyther any thynge be founde whiche is vntrue, neither any thinge be lacking whiche is true. And I thinke verely it shalbe well done that you shewe vnto hym the booke it selfe. For if I haue myssed or fayled in any poynte, or if any faulte haue escaped me, no man can so well correcte and amende it, as he can: and yet that can he not do, oneles he peruse and reade ouer my booke written. Moreouer by this meanes shal you perceaue, whether he be well wyllynge and contente that I should vndertake to put thys worke in wryting. For if he be mynded to publyshe and put forth his owne labours and trauayles hymselfe, perchaunce he woulde be lothe, and so would I also, that in publyshynge the Vtopiane weale publyque, I should preuente and take from hym the flower and grace of the noueltie of this his historie.

Howbeit, to saye the verie truthe, I am not yet fully determined with me selfe, whether I wyll put forth my booke or no. For the natures of men be so diuers, the phantasies of some so wayewarde, theire myndes so vnkynde, theire iudgementes so corrupte, that they which leade a merie and a iocunde lyfe, followinge theire owne sensuall pleasures and carnal lustes, maye seme to be in a muche better state or case, then they that vexe and vnquiete themselfes with cares and studie for the puttynge forth and publyshynge of some thynge, that maye be either profett or pleasure to other; whiche neuertheles wyl disdaynfully, scornefully, and vnkyndly accepte the same. The moste parte of al be vnlearned: and a great numbre hath learnynge in contempte. The rude and barbarous alloweth nothynge but that which is verie barbarous in dede. If it be one that hath a lytell smacke of learnynge, he reiecteth as homely and commen ware whatsoener is not stuffed full of olde moughteaten wordes, and that be worne out of vse. Some there be that haue pleasure onely in olde rustie antiquities; and some onely in theire owne doinges. One is so sowre, so crabbed, and so vnpleasaunt, that he can awaye with no myrthe nor sporte. An other is so narrow in the sholders, that he can beare no iestes nor tawntes. Some selie poore soules be so aferd that at euery snappishe worde theire nose shalbe bitten of, that they stande in no lesse drede of euerye quicke and sharpe worde, then he that is bytten of a madde dogge feareth water. Some be so mutable and waueryng, that euery houre they be in a newe mynde, sainge one thynge syttynge, and another thynge standynge. An other sorte sytteth upon theire allebencheis, and there amonge theire cuppes they geue iudgement of the wittes of wryters, and with greate aucthoritie they condemne euen as pleaseth them euery wryter accordyng to his writinge; in moste spiteful maner mockynge, lowtynge, and flowtynge them: beynge themselfes in the meane season sauffe, and, as sayth the proverbe, out of all daunger of gonneshotte. For whye, they be so smugge and smoethe, that they haue not so much as one heare of an honest man, whereby one may take holde of them. There be moreouer some so vnkynde and vngentell, that thoughe they take great pleasure and delectation in the worke, yet for al that they can not fynde in theire hartes to loue the author therof, nor to aforde hym a good worde; beynge muche lyke vncourteis, vnthankefull, and chourlishe guestes, whiche, when they haue with good and deyntie meates well filled theire bellyes, departe home, geuynge no thankes to the feaste maker. Go youre wayes, nowe, and make a costly feaste at youre owne chargeis for guestes so deyntie mouthed, so dyuers in taste, and bisydes that of so vnkynde and vnthankefull natures.

But neuertheles, frende Peter, do I praye you with Hythlodaye as I willed you before. And as for this matter, I shalbe at my lybertie afterwardes to take newe aduisement. Howebeit, seynge I haue taken great paynes and laboure in wrytynge the matter, if it may stande with hys mynde and pleasure, I wyll, as touchinge the edition or publishing of the booke, followe the counsell and aduise of my frendes, and specially yours. Thus fare you well, ryght
    hartely beloued frende Peter, with
        youre gentell wyfe; and loue
        me as you haue euer done;
          for I loue you better
           then euer I dyd.
            (∴)

GLOSSARIAL INDEX

PRINCIPAL CONTRACTIONS.

a. = adjective. acc. = accusative. *adv.* = adverb. **adv.** Gen. = adverbial Genitive. AF. = Anglo-Norman French. cf. = *confer*, compare. *conj.* = conjunction. dat. = dative. dim. = diminutive. F. = French. G. = German. Gk. = Greek. Icel. = Icelandic. *int.* = interjection. Ital. = Italian. L. = Latin. MDu. = Middle Dutch. ME. = Middle English. MHG. = Middle High German. MLG. = Middle Low German. Mod. Eng. = Modern English. OE. = Old English (Anglo-Saxon). OF. = Old French. OHG. = Old High German. OLG. = Old Low German. ON. = Old Norse. part. = participle. pl. = plural. *ppl. a.* = participial adjective. *prep.* = preposition. *pron.* = pronoun. q. v. = *quod vide*, which see. *sb.* = substantive. *v.* = verb. *vbl. sb.* = verbal substantive.

Proper names invented by More (or Robynson) are distinguished by *.

A

A, a. one, 20. 34. OE. *ān*, numeral and article; ME. *ān, ōn*, a.

A, *prep.* in, on. A Goddes name, in God's name, 19. 14, 141. 37. A beggynge, on begging, 18. 13. OE. *on*, prep.; ME. *on, o, a.*

Abhor from, *v.* dislike, shrink from, 115. 10. L. *ab*, from; *horrēre*, to dread.

Able, *v.* enable, empower, 39. 3. From *Able*, **a.** OF. *hable*; L. *habilis*.

* *Abraxa*, 49. 26.

Abrode, *adv.* abroad, 17. 34. OE. *on*, prep. + *brād*, a. broad.

Abunde, *v.* abound, 142. 4. ME. *abunden, abounden*; L. *abundāre*, to overflow, *ab*, from, away + *unda*, wave.

Accorded, *ppl. a.* come to an agreement, 109. 16. OF. *accorder*, to agree; late L. *accordāre*, from *cor, cordis*, heart.

* *Achoriens, the*, 33. 8, 9.

Acquyte, *v.* requite, 140. 22. Late L. *acquitāre*, to appease, satisfy.

* *Ademus*, 63. 32.

Aduance, auaunce, *v.* exalt, 79. 20, 105. 5, 132. 27. OF. *avancer*; late L. *abanteare* (*ab*, away, *ante*, before), to go forward; *d* inserted from mistaken derivation from L. prefix *ad.*

Aduauncemente, *sb.* furtherance, advancement, 103. 31.

Aduentures, auentures, *sb.*; at

al a., 56. 3, 127. 2, haphazard, at random. OF. *aventure*, a chance occurrence. Also with *a* changed to *ad* after L. *adventura*.

Aduisement, *sb.* consideration, deliberation, 109. 19. OF. *avisement*, from *aviser*, v.; late L. *advīsāre*.

Aduoutrye, *sb.* adultery, 104. 14. OF. *avoutrie*, with *ad-* for *a-* after L. *adultĕrium*.

Aduoyded, *v.* avoided, shunned, 102. 15. For *Avoid*, OF. *esvuidier*, from *es*, (L. *ex*, out) and *vuidier*, to empty; *ad-* for *a-*, as in prec.

Aferd, *aferde*, *ppl. a.* afraid, frightened, 22. 13, 128. 12, 135. 19, 143. 25. OE. *a*, intensitive prefix, + past part. of *fĕran*, to frighten. Cf. dialectal *afeared*.

Affectioned, *ppl. a.* disposed, inclined, 129. 32. From *Affection*, v. F. *affectionner*, from L. *affectio* (-ōnem), disposition.

Affiaunce, *sb.* confidence, reliance, 129. 13. OF. *afiance*, cf. *afier*, to trust; L. *ad + fīdere*.

Aglette, *sb.* hanging ornament, pendant, *properly* a tag, 79. 11. OF. *aiguillette*, dim. of *aiguille*, needle, late L. *acūcula*, for *acicula*, dim. of *acus*, needle.

A goo, *adv.* ago, 31. 33. Past part. of OE. *āgān*, to go away; ME. *āgō(n)*.

Agreable (to), *a.* in keeping with, consonant with, 77. 18. OF. *agréable*, from *à gré*, favourably; L. *ad grātum*, neut. of *grātus*, pleasant.

Alaopolitanes, 111. 4, 7, 15, 19.

Aldus Manutius, 96. 29, 97. 25.

Allow, a lowe, *v.* praise, approve, sanction, 22. 38, 31. 12, 39. 20, 95. 22. OF. *alouer*; L. *allaudāre*, to praise. Cf. *allow* from L. *allōcare*, to assign, allow.

All togethers, *adv.* altogether, 123. 21. OE. *tógædre*, together, with intensitive prefix *all*, and adv. suffix *-s*, as if an adv. Gen.

Allyaunte, *ppl. a.* allied, akin, 96. 7. Pres. part. of *ally*; L. *ad + ligāre*, to bind.

Amaurote, city of, 50. 14, 53. 8, 13, 74. 24.

Amaurotians, 54. 18.

Ambre, *sb.* amber, 56. 19. Oyle or ambre, probably for 'oil of amber' obtained by distillation of the resin. F. *ambre*; Arab. *anbar*, ambergris, extended by confusion to the yellow amber.

Amerike, see *Vespucci*.

Amityes, *sb.* friendships, i. e. favourable conjunctions, 82. 31 (with reference to the relative positions of the planets). F. *amitié*; late L. *amicitas*, friendship.

Amonge, **amonges**, *prep.* among, amongst, 5. 8, 44. 12. OE. *on gemonge*, in the throng, shortened to *on-monge, amonge*, and used as a prep. Also with adv. Gen. *-s*, corrupted later to *-st*, cf. *against*.

An, *conj.* and, 33. 14, 125. 16. Weakened form of *And*.

Anemolians, 78. 22, 33.

Angerlye, *adv.* angrily, 87. 27. ME. *angerlich*, a. or adv.; ON. *angrligr* from *angr*, grief, anger. Mod. Eng. remodelled on *Angry*.

Antwerp, 2. 12, 16.

GLOSSARIAL INDEX

Anyder, river, 53. 17, 20, 54. 16.

Appayre, *v.* to injure, weaken, impair, 13. 25, 91. 38. OF. *em-, am-peirer*; L. *pejorāre*, to make worse; ME. *am-, an-, ap-payren.*

Applye, *v.* ply, practise, 60. 15. OF. *aplier*; L. *applicāre*, to apply to.

Appoynt. *v.* plan, arrange, 54. 35. OF. *apointer*; late L. *appunctāre*, to prick, mark with a point.

Aragon, King of, 32. 10.

Archedolte, *sb.* arch-dullard, chief of fools, 14. 21. ME. *dolte,* related to OE. *dol,* dull.

Aristophanes, 96. 28.

Aristotle, 96. 17.

Artyfycers, *sb.* handycraftsmen, 60. 22.

Asmuche as, *conj.* so much as, 26. 5. OE. *eallswā . . . eallswā*; ME. *alse . . . alse, as . . . as,* often combined with OE. *swā,* ME. *so.*

Assay, *v.* try, practise, 97. 36. OF. *essai, assai,* a trial; L. *exagium,* trial of weight.

Assentacion, *sb.* assenting, agreeing, 9. 37. L. *assentātio* (*-ōnem*), from *assentāri,* to assent.

Aswell, *adv.* as much, in a like degree, 46. 9.

Attayntede, *ppl. a.* convicted, found guilty, 23. 15, sixteenth-cent. form for older *Attaint.* OF. *ateint,* from *atteindre,* to accuse, convict; L. *attingere,* to hit.

Auale, *v.* lower, debase, 108. 31, 127. 7. OF. *avaler,* to let descend, from *aval,* down; L. *ad + vallem,* to the valley.

Auaunce, *v.* 105. 5, 132. 27. See Aduance.

Auaunce, auuance, *v.* boast, vaunt oneself, 19. 9, 108. 28. A contamination of *avaunt,* OF. *avanter* (late L. *vānitāre,* to boast) with *avaunce,* OF. *avancer.* See Aduance.

Auaunte, *v.* boast, vaunt, 112. 16. See Auaunce.

Auentures, *sb.* chances, hazards, 120. 9, 127. 2. See Aduentures.

Auncetours, *sb.* ancestors, progenitors, 10. 17, 87. 37, 88. 2, 105. 17. OF. *ancestre*; L. *antecessor,* a foregoer, predecessor; ME. *ancetre, aunceter,* dialectal *anceter, anster*; remodelled in sixteenth cent. on F. *auncestre* + L. suffix *-or.*

Auncyetnes, *sb.* Error for *Auncyentnes,* ancientness, antiquity, 46. 15. From *Ancient,* OF. *ancien*; L. *antiānus.*

Aunswere to, *v.* answer meet, rebut, 19. 34. OE. *andswarian* with Dat.; hence in ME. with *to*; Cf. F. *répondre à.*

Aunters. See In aunters.

Auoutrers, *sb.* adulterers, 103. 11. See Aduoutrye.

Avaleth, *v.* 108. 31. See Auale.

Avayleable, *a.* available, serviceable, 15. 25. From *Avail, v.* new formation for *vail,* F. *valoir,* to be worth; L. *valēre.*

A-worke, 17. 5. On work, i. e. to work. *A* weakened form of *On.*

Ayer, *sb.* variant of *Air,* 94. 35, 36. OF. *air*; L. *āer.*

Bandes, *sb.* bonds, fetters, 99. 17. Same word as *Bond*; both from Icel. *band.*

258 GLOSSARIAL INDEX

Bankettes, *sb.* banquets, 72. 15. OF. *banquet*, feast, dim. of *banc*, from G. *bank*, bench.

* *Barzanes*, 63. 31.

Be, *prep* by, 38. 6, 16, 84. 1. Weak form of *By*. OE. *bī*.

Be it, *v. imper.* let it be so, 47. 25.

Be to seke. Be to be sought i. e. be wanting, 110. 10.

Beareth all the stroke, 43. 10, all the swing, 62. 24; has the chief power, is reckoned as the most important thing. Cf. *To have the blow* or *swing*, to have the power.

Beastelye, *a.* bestial, pertaining to beasts, 110. 2. OF. *beste*; L. *bestia*; ME. suffix *-lich*, *-ly*.

Beck, *sb.* gesture, sign, 29. 35. From *Beck*, v. shortened form of *Becken*, from OE. *béacn*, sb. sign.

Beggerlye, *adv.* in beggarly fashion, 43. 20. From *Beggar*, OF. *begard*; late L. *begardus*, one of the order of lay mendicants.

Behalfe, in thys. On, in behalf of this, 25. 9. A confusion of two constructions; *on his halve*, and *bi halve him*, on, by his side.

Behate, *v.* hate, dislike, 37. 26. OE. *hātian*, to hate, made transitive by prefix *be-*.

Bende, *sb.* band, troop, 118. 31. From confusion of *Band*, OF. *bande*, a company, with *Band*, Icel. *band*, bond, fetter; and further with *Bend*, OE. *bende*, bond.

Bente, *ppl. a.* inclined, prone, 60. 1. Past part. of *Bend*; OE. *bendan*.

Bethinkynge hymselfe, *v. refl.* reflecting, calling to mind, 47. 34. OE. *beðencan*, call to mind, used reflexively.

Bewray, *v.* betray, expose, 22. 7. OE. *bi* + *wrēgan*, to accuse, denounce.

Bicause, bycause that, *conj.* because, by reason that, 40. 19, 58. 16, 64. 3. ME. *bi (be, by)*, prep., *cause*, sb., L. *causa*.

Blackheath, *defeat of Cornish rebels at*, (1547), 10. 33, 12. 32.

Blesse, *sb.* bliss, joy, 128. 5. Confusion of *Bliss*, v. to make glad, OE. *blīþsian*, with *Bless*, OE. *bletsian*.

Bloodis, *sb.* persons of gentle blood, 18. 13. OE., ME. *blōd*, with Northern pl. *-is*.

Bonden men, *sb.* bondsmen, serfs, 50. 35. For *Bonde-men*, representing OE. *bŏnda*, bondsman. *Bonde* wrongly regarded as a strong past part. in *-en*.

Borderours, *sb.* those dwelling on their borders, next neighbours, 23. 14.

Brabant, 31. 32.

Brabling, *sb.* contention, 141. 17. From *Brabble*, to quarrel; cf. Du. *brabbelen*, to stammer.

Breed, *sb.* breeding, 115. 15. From *Breed*, v. OE. *brēdan*, a derivative of the usual sb. *brōd* (Mod. Eng. *brood*).

Bretherne, *sb.* brethren, 28. 15. ME. *breþeren*; OE. *brēþer*, pl. of *brōþer*, with weak pl. ending *-en*.

Brode, *a.* broad, wide, 53. 24. **Brodest,** *superl.* 48. 12. OE. *brād*; ME. *brōd*.

Bronte, brunt, *sb.* brunt, first rush or attack, 118. 7. **Sodeyne brunte,** 51. 36, a sudden rush or exertion. (Origin unknown.)

GLOSSARIAL INDEX 259

Brouches, *sb.* brooch, trinket, *properly* a pin, 78. 17. OF. *broche,* spit; late L. *brocca,* pointed stick.
Bruges, 1. 26. *Marcgrave of,* 1. 29.
Brussels, 2. 9.
Bryde, bryed, *v.* breed, rear, 51. 22, 52. 14. Variants of *Breed*; OE. *brēdan.*
Burgundy, 31. 32.
* *Buthrescas,* 131. 3.
By and by, *adv.* straightway, 57. 26. OE. *bī*, prep. by, *hence* close at hand, at once; cf. similar change to future time in *presently.*
Bycause that, *conj.* 40. 19, 58. 16. See Bicause.
Bye, *v.* buy, purchase, 17. 34, 18. 36, 112. 15. OE. *bycgan,* to buy; ME. *bien, buyen.*
By lowe, *adv.* below, 108. 34. OE. *bī*, by; Icel. *lāgr*, low.
By lyke, *adv.* belike, probably, 19. 38. *By,* prep. + *like,* a. or sb.

C

Calicut, Calyquit, 4. 26.
Call agayne, *v.* recall, revive, 38. 18.
Cannellis, *sb.* channels, 54. 24. OF. *chanel, canel*; L. *canālis,* a channel. Northern pl. *-is.*
Cappe of maintenaunce, 105. 27. *See* Note.
Careful, *a.* full of care, anxious, 92. 35. OE. *caru,* anxiety, sorrow.
Carfully, *adv.* sorrowfully, 128. 8.
Carke, *v.* to be anxious, to trouble, 85. 23. North. F. *carkier*; late L. *carricāre,* to load.
Carpente, *sb.* carpenter, 59. 16. AF. suffix *-er* confused with Eng. agent suffixes *er, -e* (OE. *-ǣre, -a*).
Carthaginians, 14. 34.
Cast, *v.* to find guilty, convict, condemn, 27. 2. Figurative use of *Cast,* v. to throw, overthrow. ON. *kasta.*
Castile, King of, 1. 9, 32. 14.
Cauillation, *sb.* quibble, objection, 108. 16. OF. *cavillacion*; L. *cavillārī,* to wrangle, object.
Cautell, *sb.* precaution, device, 93. 36. OF. *cautele,* cunning; L. *cautēla.*
Celenes (Celaenos), 7. 4.
Chaffare, chaffayre, *sb.* trade, traffic, 5. 38, 39. 8. OE. *céap,* bargain, *faru,* dealing; ME. *chapfare, chaffare.*
Chardge, *sb.* expense, 64. 8, 14. OF. *charge,* burden; late L. *carricum,* load (of a car).
Charles, King of Castile, 1. 9.
Charye, *a.* careful, 101. 28. OE. *cearig,* full of care.
Chastyce, *v.* chastise, correct, 24. 15, for older *Chasty*; L. *castigāre.*
Chaunce, *v.* to come by chance, to happen (to come) into, 42. 28. From *Chaunce,* sb.; late L. *cadentia.*
Chaungeable coloures, 79. 5, 136. 17, changing or shot colours. Cf. Shakesp. *Twelfth Night,* ii. 4. 76 'Changeable taffeta.'
Cherissyng, *sb.* care, tending, 45. 8. From pres. part. of F. *chérir,* to cherish; from F. *cher,* L. *carus,* dear.
Chesse, *sb.* the game of chess, 61. 20. OF. *esches,* pl. of *eschec,* check; from Persian *shah,* king.
Cheualry, *sb.* military art, knightly exercises, 9. 25, 138. 15, 143. 12. OF. *chevalerie*;

from **L.** *caballārius*, horseman.

Cheuse, chewse, chuese, *v.* choose. Variant spellings of *Chuse*, OE. *cēōsan*, ME. *chēsen, chōsen, chusen.*

Christen, *a.* Christian, 41. 31. OE. *cristen.*

Chueseth, *v.* 37. 6. *See* Cheuse.

Church, our Lady's, at Antwerp, 3. 2.

Chyldren, *sb.* persons, people, 106. 13. OE. *cildru,* pl. + weak pl. *-en.* Used in ME. in a general sense. Cf. *Psalm* cxliv (A.V.), 7, 11 'strange children.'

Cicero, 3. 37.

Circumstaunce, *sb.* circumstantiality of detail, circumlocution, 106. 8. (Without indef. art., cf. 'To use great circumstance of woordes, to goe aboute the bushe.' Baret's *Alvearie,* 1580.) L. *circumstantia,* standing round, environment.

Circumuertion, *sb.* Error for *Circumuention,* overreaching, malicious device or stratagem, 106. 13. L. *circumvenire,* to encompass, 'get round.'

Cleane, *a.* pure, unadulterated, 52. 8. Cleane contrarye, 39. 25, 40. 34, the very opposite. OE. *clǣne,* clear, pure.

Cloke, *sb.* cloak, covering, 74. 11. Late L. *cloca,* a bell, *also* a bell-shaped cape.

Coliars, *sb.* colliers, 140. 14. OE. *col,* coal, with Romanic suffix *-ier.*

Come to their handes, fall to their lot, reach them, 117. 35.

Commen, *a.* public, general, 23. 36. Common boxe, 75. 26, public chest. L. *communis.*

Commen, see Man in, 82. 21. *See* Note.

Commeth in, *v.* contracts, draws together, 48. 15.

Commoditie, *sb.* comfort, convenience, 8. 22, 56. 19, 63. 37, 71. 34, 140. 36. L. *commoditas,* from *commodus,* fit, suitable.

Commodye, *sb.* comedy, 40. 3. L. *cōmœdia.*

Common boxe. *See* Commen.

Communicate, *ppl. a.* communicated, granted, 132. 35. L. *commūnicātus,* past part. of *commūnicāre.*

Communycatyon, *sb.* speech, converse, 2. 33; conversation, personal intercourse, 11. 8, 72. 1; discourse, 143. 29. L. *commūnicātio (-ōnem),* action of communicating.

Concelour, *sb.* concealer, hider, 26. 10. AF. *concelour,* from *conceler,* to conceal.

Conceytes, *sb.* skilfully or fantastically devised dishes, 72. 15. From *Conceive,* OF. *concevoir;* cf. *deceit* from *deceive.*

Condition, -dytyon, *sb.* conduct, behaviour, 25. 21, 105. 6. L. *condicio (-ōnem),* compact, *also* situation, nature, manner.

Conductyon, *sb.* conduct, management, 116. 23. From L. *conductus,* past part. of *condūcere,* to lead.

Conscience, *sb.* consciousness, 86. 12, 92. 24. According to conscience, i. e. just, 75, 31. L. *conscientia.*

Consecrate, *ppl. a.* consecrated, 131. 19, 132. 23. L. *consecrātus,* past part. of *consecrāre* (*con* + *sacrāre*).

Constitucions, *sb.* decree, ordinance, 21. 4, 14. L. *constitutio* (*-ōnem*), that which is constituted or established.

Constitute, *ppl. a.* constituted, established, 85. 36. L. *constitūtus*, past part. of *constituere*, to make to stand together.

Conuersation, *sb.* intercourse, 66. 2. Late L. *conversātiō-nem*; from *conversārī*, to live with.

Conuict, conuycte, *ppl. a.* convicted, proved guilty, 22. 2, 24. L. *convictus*, past part. of *convincere*.

Cormaraunte, *sb.* cormorant, an insatiably greedy person, 16. 19. OF. *cormoran*, *cormaran*, corruption of L. *corvus marīnus*, sea-raven; ME. corruption of *-an* to *-ant*.

Coueyne, couyne, *sb.* fraud, deceit, 16. 23, 111. 24, 114. 2. Late L. *convenium*, a coming together, *hence* with treacherous intent.

Counteruaile, counteruayle, *v.* to counterbalance, be equivalent to in value, 20. 22, 136. 23. AF. *countrevaloir*; L. *contra valēre*, to be of worth against.

Courage, currage, *sb.* disposition, temper, 14. 2, 36. 37; spirits, 80. 18. OF. *corage, curage*; L. **corāticum* (*cor*, heart).

Course, *a.* coarse, 87. 19, 24. Earlier form of *Coarse*, apparently from *course*, sb. denoting anything usual or ordinary, as in phrases *In*, *Of course*.

Cowardenes, *sb.* cowardice, 117. 10, 19. OF. *couard*, coward; OE. suffix *-ness*.

Cowardyshe, *a.* cowardly, 114. 5. OF. *couard*; OE suffix *-isc*.

Coytes, *sb.* quoits, 18. 28. ME. *coite, quoite*.

Cracke, *v.* brag, boast, 15. 4, 112. 22. OE. *cracian*, to make a cracking noise.

Crassus, 36. 22.

Credence, *sb.* belief, 75. 21. L. *crēdentia* (*crēdo*, I believe).

Cummeth of, *v.* proceeds from, is caused by, 55. 20.

Cunnyng, *a.* wise, knowing, 69. 22. Pres. part. of ME. *cunnen*, to know; OE. *cunnan*.

Cure, *v.* care for, tend, 69. 8. L. *cūrāre*, to care for, from *cūra*, care.

Currage, *sb.* 14. 2, 80. 18. See Courage.

Customablie, customablye, *adv.* customarily, usually, 4. 16, 36, 51. 16. From *Custom*, sb., OF. *coustume*, from shortened form of L. *consuētudo*, custom.

*Cynemernes, 134. 4.

Cyuyle philosophy, 39. 35. That which is adapted to the public life of the community, politic. L. *cīvīlis*, belonging to citizens.

D

Damned, *ppl. a.* condemned, sentenced, 24. 9. L. *damnāre*, to condemn.

Dasell, *v.* dazzle, 79. 3. Earlier form of *Dazzle*, a frequentative and dim. of *Daze*; ME. *dasen*, of Norse origin.

Daunger, *sb.* jurisdiction, power, 21. 16, 81. 14. In her daunger, 94. 18, in her power. OF. *dangier*; late L. **domināriun* from *dominium*, lordship.

Decrey, *v.* decree, appoint, 25. 2, from *Decree*, sb.: see next.

Decrye, *sb.* decree, 125. 34.

126. 11. ME. variant of *Decre, decrey*; L. *dēcrētum*, the thing decreed.

Dedicate, *ppl. a.* dedicated, 132. 22. L. *dēdicātus*, past part. of *dēdicāre*, to devote.

Defenced, *ppl. a.* defended, protected, fortified, 49. 19, 143. 1. From L. *defensus*, past part. of *defendĕre*, to defend.

Delectacion, -atyon, *sb.* delight, pleasure, 11. 15, 87. 4. L. *dēlectātio* (-*ōnem*), action of delighting.

Delete, *sb.* delight, pleasure, 51. 19. Variant of *Delite*.

Delite,-yte,*sb.*delight,pleasure, 9. 24, 11. 9, 136. 5. From the verb. See Delyte, *v.*

Delycte, *sb.* delight, 33. 29. The *c* was apparently after L. *delectāre* : see next.

Delyte, *v. refl.* to take pleasure, gratify oneself, 7. 35. ME. *deliten*, OF. *deliter*, L. *dēlectāre*, to delight. Misspelt *delight* in Mod. Eng.

Denounce, *v.* to declare, proclaim war, 113. 5. OF. *denoncer*; L. *dēnuntiāre*, to declare.

Deryue, *v.* obtain, 54. 23. L. *dērivāre*, to drain off water.

Descriue, *v.* discover, detect, 22. 10, 25. 35. Properly *Descry*. From ME. confusion of OF. *descrier*, to publish, with *descrivre* to describe.

Deuise, *v.* say, imagine, 45. 34, 46. 14. OF. *deviser*; late L. **dīvīsāre*, to divide.

Deuyse, *sb.* device, purpose, plan, 58. 11. Late L. *dīvīsum*, a division, also a device; from *dīvidere*, to divide.

Differryd, *v.* deferred, postponed, 26. 34. L. *differre*, (1) to delay, (2) to differ. Mod. Eng. *defér* on analogy of *delay*, but *differ*. Northern *-yd* for *-ed*.

Dionysius, 31. 16.

Dioscorides, 96. 26.

Disallow, *v.* refuse to praise, disapprove, refuse to accept, 27. 9, 30. 9. OF. *disalower, desalouer*. Cf. Allow.

Diserde, *sb.* fool, blockhead, 10. 12. Apparently from OF. *disour, -eur*, a professional jester, with change of suffix.

Dispatched from, *ppl. a.* quit, rid of, delivered from, 28. 23. Ital. *dispacciare*; Span. *despachar*; L. type **dispactiare*, from L. *pactus*, past part. of *pangere*, to fix.

Displeasaunt, *a.* unpleasant, disagreeable, 126. 4; OF. *desplaisant*, pres. part. of *desplaire*, to displease.

Disproue. *v.* disapprove, disallow, 28. 31. OF. *desprover*, to disprove.

Dissident, *a.* dissenting from, 41. 37. L. *dissidens* (-*entem*) pres. part. of *dissidēre*, to sit apart, disagree.

Distribute, *ppl. a.* distributed, 28. 13. L. *distribūtus*, past part. of *distribuere*.

Do coste, *v.* make outlay, incur expense, 38. 13. Cf. Tindale, *Acts* xxi. 24 'do cost on them.'

Domesticall, *a.* domestic, 142. 37. From L. *domesticus*, belonging to a household.

Domme, *a.* dumb, 40. 9. OE. *dumb*; ME. *dumb, domb*, with *b* silent, therefore not always written.

Dorre, *sb.* drone, idler, 13. 5. OE. *dora*, a humming insect.

GLOSSARIAL INDEX

Dowt, v. doubt, 22. 18 ; fear, 138. 34. OF. *douter.* Changed to *doubt* after L. *dubitāre.*

Dreuell, sb. menial, drudge, 81. 9. Cf. MDu. *drevel,* scullion, turnspit.

Drydynge, *pres. part.* dreading, 139. 6. ME. *drēden*; OE. *drǣdan,* to dread.

Dyffucultlye, adv. with difficulty, 76. 12. From a variant of *Difficult,* a.

Dysanulled, v. abolished, 83. 37. L. *annullāre,* to bring to nothing. Prefix *dis-* here intensifying the negatory force of the verb.

Dyscryue, v. 25. 35. See Discriue.

Dystyncte, *ppl. a.* distinguished, differentiated, 24. 30. L. *distinctus,* past part. of *distinguere.*

Dytty, sb. song, ditty, 137. 14. OF. *dité,* poem ; L. *dictātum,* from *dictāre,* to dictate.

E

Earnest, a. serious, 20. 5. OE. *eorneste,* from *eornust,* sb.

Effemynatede, *ppl. a.* rendered unmanly, enervated, 15. 16. Past part. of *Effeminate,* from L. *effemināttus.*

Eftsones, adv. afterwards, again, 103. 22. OE. *eft,* again, afterwards ; *sōne,* soon ; with adv. suffix *-s* from the adv. Gen.

Egal, a. equal, 93. 11. OF. *egal* ; L. *aequālem.*

Egerly, adv. zealously, keenly, 111. 22. OF. *egre*; L. *acer, acrem,* sharp, keen.

Egyptians, 46. 29.

Elder, a. older, 101. 2. OE. *ieldra, eldra,* mutated comparative of *eald,* old. Displaced by new form *older* from the positive.

Elles, adv. else, otherwise, 28. 20. OE. *elles,* adv. Gen.

Embrayd, imbrayde, v. upbraid, reproach, 104. 36, 130. 10. OF. *em-* (L. *im-,* in) ; OE. *bregdan,* denoting sudden movement, as to weave, brandish ; *hence* to attack.

Embrodered, *ppl. a.* embroidered. OF. *embroder,* to embroider.

Emong, *prep.* variant of Among. ME. *among, ymong,* also *emong.* See Amonge.

Emperor, 32. 7.

Enbrace, v. to embrace, welcome as a friend, 11. 17. OF. *embracer*; L. **imbracchiāre* from *in* and *bracchia,* arms.

Endaunger vnto, v. bring under the jurisdiction of, 35. 31. See Daunger.

Endeuoure, sb. effort, 46. 23. OF. *en,* in + *deveir,* duty, *properly* to owe ; L. *dēbēre.*

Endeuoure, v. *refl.* try, exert oneself. 34. 21, 40. 35, 42. 17, 113. 33. See prec.

Enfamed, infamed, *ppl. a.* defamed, branded with infamy, 77. 31, 78. 31. L. *infāmāre,* to render infamous.

Engines for warre, sb. implements, machines, 120. 23. L. *ingenium,* an invention.

England, 32. 18, 29.

Englishmen, 15. 33, 32. 19, 25; *the western,* 10. 34.

Enhaunce, v. increase, augment, 34. 34. AF. *enhauncer,* OF. *enhaucer,* to lift.

Entreat of, v. deal with, discuss, 78. 24. OF. *entraiter,* to treat of; L. *tractāre.*

GLOSSARIAL INDEX

Espiall, *sb.* spy, 121. 3. OF. *espiaille*, the action of spying.

Estymer, *sb.* estimator, judge, 76. 18. L. *aestimāre*, to value.

Euel willing, *ppl. a.* unwilling, averse, 42. 3. *Euel*, OE. *yfel*, in sense of *un-*, *not*.

Euen verye they, 108. 27; even those very persons. OF. *verai*, true.

Euennynge, *sb.* evening, 60. 18. OE. *ǣfnung*, from v. *ǣfnian*, to become evening.

Euer, *adv.* always, at all times, 49. 23, 110. 19. OE. *ǣfre*.

Euripides, 96. 29.

Europe, 107. 35.

Excommunicate, *ppl. a.* excommunicated, 29. 33. L. *excommūnicātus*, past part. of *excommūnicāre*.

Existimacion, -ymatyon, *sb.* estimation, valuation, 10. 10, 58. 24. L. *existimātio* (*-ōnem*), estimation.

Exploit, *v.* perform, achieve, 95. 4. From *Exploit*, *sb.* L. *explicitum*, that which is unfolded, ended.

Expresslye pronounced, 137. 20, uttered clearly or with emphasis; *or possibly*, exactly, according to a set formula. L. *expressus*, distinct.

F

Fabricius, 37. 36.

False, *a.* faulty, an erroneous or corrupt version, 96. 5. L. *falsus*, false, from *fallere*, to deceive.

Falshed, *sb.* falsehood, 127. 25. From OF. *fals*, with ME. suffix *-hed*, denoting quality.

Fantasy, *v.* to fancy, desire, 60. 4. From *Fantasy*, *sb.*; late L. *phantasia*.

Fardell, *sb.* burden, load, 96. 15. OF. *fardel*, **dim. of** *farde*, a burden.

Farfurth, ferfurth, *adv.* far, far on, 50. 10, 53. 5, 109. 19. OE. *feor*, far; *forþ* forward, with **u** from the compar. *furðor*.

Fasion, fassion, -yon, *sb.* method, manner, fashion, 19. 22, 66. 6, 67. 4, 78. 28. OF. *façon*; L. *factio* (*-ōnem*), from *facere*, to make.

Fauour, *sb.* countenance, looks, 3. 10. L. *favor* (*-em*).

Faute, fawt, *sb.* fault, 10. 14, 80. 6; defect, 64. 19. OF. *faute*. Mod. Eng. *fault*.

Fayne, *v.* feign, make pretence of, 35. 1; imagine, invent, 41. 15. OF. *feindre* (*feignant*), L. *fingere*, to form, feign.

Fearce, *a.* fierce, spirited, 51. 32. OF. *fers*, *fiers*; Mod. F. *fier*; L. *ferus*.

Feare from, *v.* frighten from, make afraid of, 104. 1, 105. 10, 125. 8, 129. 15. OE. *fǣran*, to frighten, terrify.

Feate, *sb.* act, deed, 9. 25, 26; crafts, industries, 97. 20; art, employment, 6. 17, 38. 8. OF. *fait*, *feit*; L. *factum*, a thing done.

Felles, *sb.* skins, 75. 7. OE. *fell*.

Fellones, *sb. pl.* felons, 11. 37. OF. *felon*, a. and *sb.*; low L. *fellōn-em*.

Ferefull, *a.* terrible, causing fear, 105. 22. OE. *fǣr*, sudden danger, fear.

Ferfurth, *adv.* 53. 5. *See* Farfurth.

Feruent, *a.* eager, hot, 118. 31. L. *fervens*, pres. part. of *fervēre*, to boil.

Fetch about a circuit **or com-**

GLOSSARIAL INDEX

passe, 48. 16, to describe a compass, make a circuit, go round in circular form.
Finifest, 134. 5. *See* Note.
Flanders, 1. 12, 31. 32.
Flickering, *a.* unstable, wandering, 87. 7. OE. *flicorian*, to flutter.
Fond, *a.* foolish, silly, 7. 9, 9. 35. Past part. of archaic *v. Fon*, to lose savour.
Forbie, forby, *prep.* beside, past, 54. 3, 11 ; *for*, adv. and prep. + *by*, prep.
Forefrontes, *sb.* front, foreshore, 48. 29. OE. *fore*, before, OF. *front*, forehead, L. *frons, -tem*.
For euer more, *adv.* perpetually, 59. 22.
Forrein, -eyn, *a.* foreign, 39. 1, 67. 26, 27, 133. 5, 143. 4. OF. *forain*, alien, strange; late L. *forāneus*, belonging to outside ; *g* inserted as in *sovereign* from false analogy with *reign*.
Forsake, *v.* I forsake God, 139. 18. A form of oath representing L. *dispeream*. Lit. I deny, renounce. OE. *forsacan*.
Forsene, *ppl. a.* provided, 135. 32. A literal translation of L. *prŏvidēre*.
Forstalle, *v.* to intercept goods before the market, to buy up in order to obtain a monopoly, 18. 37. From OE. *foresteall*, *sb.* intercepting, plot.
For whíe, why, wherefore, 65. 26. ME. *for whi*; cf. OE. *to hwȳ*; *huȳ*, instr. of *hwæt*, what.
Foynes, *sb.* thrusts, 120. 22. OF. *foine*, an eel-spear ; L. *fuscina*, trident.

France, 12. 33, 14. 14, 33. 3, 34. 18.
Franckely, *adv.* readily, liberally, 75. 9. From *Frank*, a. low L. *francus*, free, from OHG. *franko*, a Frank.
Fraye, *v.* make afraid, frighten, 130. 7. A shortened form of *Affray*; OF. *effraier*, to frighten.
Freare, *sb.* friar, 28. 18, 32, 29. 5, 7, 11, 30. ME. *frere*; OF. *frere*, brother.
French, 14. 32, 15. 2. French king, 31. 22.
Frie, *a.* Variant of free, 68. 28. OE. *frēo, frīo*.
Frindes marchauntes, *sb.* merchant-friends, friends who are merchants, 110. 30. The two nouns in apposition.
Frindes marchaunte men, 111. 32 ; the merchants of their friends. L. *amicorum negotiatores*.
From thens, *adv. phr.* from that place, 18. 2. OE. *þœnnes*, adv. Gen.
Frustate, *v.* 61. 32. Error for *Frustrate* ; from stem of L. *frustrāri*, to render vain.
Fugatyue, *a.* having run away, 31. 29. L. *fugitīvus*; *-ative* from analogy with *fug-ator, -acious*.

G

Galen's Microtechne, 96. 33.
Gallaunt, -awnte, *a.* showy, gorgeous, 23. 10 ; rich, goodly, 55. 33. OF. *galant*, pres. part. of *galer*, to make merry.
Gallous, *a.* fit for the gallows, villainous, wicked, 29. 8. From *Gallows*, sb. OE. *gealga*∙ ME. *galwe, galuw*, usually pl.

Gallymalfreye, *sb.* medley, hotchpotch, 40. 12. OF. *galimafrée.*

Garnishing, *sb.* adornment, furnishing, 55. 33, 65. 32. From *Garnish,* v. ; OF. *garnir (garniss-ant)*, to fortify, garnish ; OHG. *warnōn.*

Gather boldenes, gain heart, pluck up courage, 33. 30.

Gawl, *sb.* to hit on the gawl, to touch on a sore or tender point, 28. 34. OE. *gealla,* a gall or sore on a horse.

Geaste wyse, *adv.* guest-wise, in manner of a guest, 7. 29. OE. *giest,* guest ; *wīse,* manner.

Geer, *sb.* gear, tackle, stuff, 98. 17 ; trappings, appurtenances, 136. 10. Icel. *gervi,* gear, apparel, from *görr,* prepared, past. part. of *göra, gera,* to make, prepare.

Gentle, *a.* of gentle birth, 18. 19. OF. *gentil* ; L. *gentīlis,* from *gens,* race, family. Confused with adj. in *-ly.*

Germaneynes, *sb.* Germans, 32. 5. L. *Germānus* ; ME. *Germayne, Germanys.*

Geue, *v.* as my mynde geueth me, 43. 10, imparts (to), teaches, directs, moves.

Gieste, *v.* jest, 50. 3. From *Jest,* sb. ; OF. *geste,* tale, romance : L. *rēs gesta,* a thing done.

Giles, Peter, of Antwerp, 2. 15, 3. 7, 4. 30, 7. 30, 46. 6, 47. 30.

Gladlier, *adv.* more gladly, 47. 21. Compar. of *Gladly* ; OE. *glædlīc.*

Gode wote, *int.* God knows, 35. 7. OE. *wāt,* he knows ; from *witan,* to know.

Godlye, *adv.* in godly fashion, piously, 99. 20. OE. *God,* sb. + adv. suffix *-līce.*

Goo to, *int.* go to! come! 31. 22. Cf. L. *age.*

Gown, *sb.* garment, 87. 12. OF. *goune,* a loose robe ; mediaeval L. *gunna,* a garment of fur.

Gramercye, for. For nothing, *literally* for thanks, 99. 15. OF. *grand,* great ; *merci,* thanks.

Greeks, 96. 9.

Greued, *ppl. a.* troubled, bored, 71. 38. F. *grever* ; L. *gravāre,* to burden.

Greyffes, *sb.* griefs, 92. 35. OF. *grief, gref.*

Grislye, *a.* terrible, 28. 20. From *Grise,* v.; OE. *āgrīsan,* to shudder.

Grosser, *a.* plainer, simpler, 106. 17. Compar. of *Gross* ; L. *grossus,* fat, thick.

Ground upon, *v.* take as one's basis, take one's stand on, 130. 37. From OE. *grund,* sb. ground.

*Gulike, country of, 4. 13, 5. 5.

*Gulikians, 4. 24.

Guyse, *sb.* way, manner, 76. 16. OF. *guise,* from OHG. *wīsa,* way, manner.

Gyaunte, *sb.* giant, 82. 23. OF. *geant, geiant* ; ME. *geant* ; L. *gigantem.*

Gyell, *sb.* guile, 85. 36. ME. *gile, gyle* ; OF. *guile.*

Gyues, *sb.* fetters, shackles, 23. 26. ME. *give,* fetters, specially for the legs.

H

Habilitye, *sb.* ability, capacity, 9. 20. Be in habylyte, 8. 2, be able to. OF. *ableté, habilité* ; L. *habilitātem.* L.

GLOSSARIAL INDEX

initial *h* common in sixteenth cent., but probably silent.

Handsome, *a.* manageable, convenient, fit, adapted, 120. 14, 30. From *Hand*, v. to handle, manage.

Handy, *a.* belonging to the hands, mechanical, 63. 27. A new formation from *Hand* in place of OE. *hendig*.

Handycraft, *sb* handicraft, 18. 20. For *Handcraft*, remodelled on *hand-ywork*, OE. *hondgeweorc*.

Hapt, *ppl.a.* wrapped, covered, 65. 12. Past part. of *Hap*, v. to cover, perh. from Norse.

Hard, harde, *v. pret.* and *part.* heard, 21. 32, 34. 27, 46. 25, 95. 20, 124. 15, 134. 22. OE. *hieran*, past part. *gehiered*; ME. *hēren*, *herd*, *hard*. Cf. influence of *r* + consonant on pronunciation of *e* in *clerk*, *Derby*.

Hardenes, *sb.* hardship, 15. 23. OE. *heardness*, hardness. For sense cf. *hardship*.

Hardynes, *sb.* hardihood, boldness, daring, 6. 25. From OF. *hardi*, *a.* with OE. suffix *-ness*.

Harneis, *sb.* armour, 120. 8, 13. 18. OF. *harneis*.

Hastie to, *a.* eager, precipitate, 20. 38. OF. *hastif*, pl. *hastis*, whence a new sg. *hasti*.

Hawte, *a.* haughty, 105. 22. In fifteenth cent., *haute*, from F. *haut* o, high, L. *alt-us*: later *haught*; with *gh* from analogy with native words, cf. *delight* for *delite*.

Haylse, *v.* greet, salute, 4. 35. ON. *heilsa*, to greet, hail.

Heare, *sb.* hair. Of one heare, by one hair, 88. 5. OE. *hēr*, hair; ME. *heer*, *hear*, *haire*.

Hedlonges, *adv.* headlong, precipitately, 41. 26. ME. *heuedlinges*; OE. *heafod*, head, with *adv.* suffix *-linga*, *lunga*, corrupted from analogy with *long*, and addit. suffix *-s* from adv. Gen.

Helizeus (Elisha), 29. 16, 28.

Helpes, *sb.* remedies, aids, 100. 9. OE. *help*, sb.

Henry VIII, 1. 2.

Herodian, 96. 31.

Herodotus, 96. 31.

Hesychius, 96. 25.

Hippocrates, 96. 33.

Hole, *a.* whole, 120. 7. OE. *hāl*, whole; Mod. Eng. has a dialectal spelling with *wh*.

Holsom, *a.* wholesome, 5. 21. OE. *hāl*, whole, + suffix *-sum*; ME. *holsum*, *-som*. See prec.

Holy, *adv.* wholly, utterly, 44. 30. From prec. + *-ly*, OE. *-līce*.

Homely, *a.* and *adv.* plain, simple, 64. 33; in homely fashion, plainly, simply, 3. 9, 64. 30.

Homer, 96. 29.

Honest, *a.* honourable, 89. 29. L. *honestus*, honourable.

Houses, *sb.* households, 18. 10.

Howke, *v.* to hook or drag one in against his will, 32. 13. From *Hook*, sb.; OE. *hōc*.

Howke, *sb.* by howke or crook, 16. 26, by any device, by fair means or foul. A common phrase from the sixteenth cent. on, of doubtful origin.

Hundreth, *a.* hundred, 121. 26. OE. *hundred* corrupted by Icel. *hundrað*.

Hurley-burley, hurlie-burlie, *sb.* tumult, confusion, 34. 13, 37. 23. OF. *hurlee,* howling, from *hurler*; L. *ululāre,* to howl. *Burly,* a reduplication of *hurly.*

Husbande, *v.* till, cultivate, tend as a husbandman, 94. 37. From *Husband, sb.; see* next.

Husbandes, *sb.* tenders, husbandmen, 50. 28. OE, *hūsbŏnda,* one dwelling in a house, the master of the house.

*Hythloday, Raphael, 1. 3, 3. 30, 4. 34, 7. 21, 47. 31.

I, J

Iauell, *sb.* a rascal, a worthless fellow, 28. 37. ME. *iavelle.*

Ieopardye, Ioperdie, *sb.* hazard, danger, 6. 23, 10. 11, 22. 1, 11. OF. *jeu parti*; L. *jocus partītus,* a divided game, *hence* uncertainty, hazard.

Ieoperdous, *a.* dangerous, hazardous, 49. 2. From prec.

Iette, *v.* strut, swagger, 13. 34. OF. *jetter,* to throw; L. *jactāre.* Meaning influenced by L. *jactāri,* to boast, strut.

Ight, *a.* eighth, 1. 2. OE. *eahtōða*; ME. *eighthe, ighthe.*

Ilande, *sb.* island, 48. 11. OE. *īgland* (*īg,* island, + *land*); ME. *iland.* Mod. *isl-* from analogy with *isle.*

Imbrayde, *v.* 104. 36. *See* Embrayd.

Impery, *sb.* empire, 46. 33. L. *imperium,* empire.

Importunate, *a.* unseasonable, troublesome, 18. 8. L. *importūnus,* + suffix *-ate.*

Importune, *a.* importunate, 4. 10. L. *importūnus.*

Imprint letters, *v.* print in type, 97. 34. From OF. *empreinte,* sb. a stamp, print; past part. fem. of *empreindre,* L. *imprimere,* to impress. Hence the Mod. Eng. shortened form *print.*

Imprintyng, *sb.* printing, 97. 23. *See* Imprint, *v.*

Improue, *v.* disapprove, disallow, 29. 9. L. *improbāre,* to condemn, disapprove, from *improbus,* bad.

Impudency, *sb.* effrontery, insolence, 11. 14. L. *impudentia,* shamelessness.

In awnters, in case, *properly* in the adventure, 32. 24. F. *en aventure.*

Incommoditie, *sb.* inconvenience, discomfort, 17. 37, 85. 29, 103. 33, 112. 2. L. *incommoditas.* *See* Commoditie.

Incommodyous, *a.* uncomfortable, 23. 34. *In* + Med. L. *commodiōsus.*

Incontinent, incontynente, *adv.* immediately, forthwith, 13. 16, 19. 29, 30. 10, 32. 25, *et passim.* F. *incontinent*; L. *in continenti,* in continuous time, without break.

Indifferent, indyfferente, *a.* moderate, reasonable, just, 27. 25, 76. 18, 133. 31. L. *indifferens*(*-entem*), of medium quality.

Infamed, *ppl. a.* 77. 31. *See* Enfamed.

Ingrosse, *v.* to monopolize, buy up the whole market, 18. 37. From the phrase *In gross*; F. *en gros,* in the lump, wholesale.

Iniurie, *sb.* injury, hurt, 20. 27. L. *injūria,* wrong, hurt.

Inordinate, *a.* excessive, uncontrolled, 44. 33. L. *inor-*

dinātus, from *ordināre*, to order.

Insensibilitie, *sb.* absence of feeling, 92. 15. Late L. *insensibilitās*, the condition of being insensible.

Institute, *ppl. a.* established, constituted, 105. 32. L. *institūtus*, past part. of *instituere*, to establish.

Instructe, *ppl. a.* instructed, taught, 59. 5, 81. 30, 105. 31. L. *instructus*, past part. of *instruere*, to instruct (*struere*, to build).

Instrumentes, documents, 75. 22. L. *instrūmentum*, instrument, tool; from *instruere*.

Into, *prep.* among, 49. 38. OE. *intō*, in, into, among.

Intreataunce, *sb.* entreaty, intercession, 4. 9. From OF. *entraiter*; L. *in* + *tractāre*, to treat, handle.

Intreate, *v.* See Entreat.

Inuade, *v.* attack, make war on, 118. 34. L. *invādere*; *in*, in, + *vādere*, to go.

Inuehyng, *pres. part.* inveighing, sailing, 126. 1. L. *in* + *vehere*, to carry, bear.

Inuisibly, *a.* for *inuisible*, 128. 38. L. *invīsibilis*, that cannot be seen.

Inurede, *ppl. a.* accustomed, exercised, practised, 15. 3, 33. 27, 97. 18. L. *in*, in + *ure*, to exercise, use.

Ionckettes, *sb.* junkets, sweetmeats, delicacies, 72. 15. Ital. *giuncata*, a kind of cream-cheese, so-called because served on rushes. (L. *juncus*, rush.)

Italy, 31. 31, 33. 2.

Juger, *sb.* arbiter, judge, 131. 21. Agent from *v. Judge*; F. *juger*, L. *judicāre*.

K

Kendle, *v.* kindle, 84. 23. ME. *kindlen*; ON. *kynda*, to kindle.

King, the (*of England*), 11. 23.

Kinrede, *sb.* kindred, members of the same family or race, 66. 8. OE. *cyn*, kin, + suffix *-rǣden*, state, condition. Mod. Eng. has excrescent *d*.

Kipe, kype, *v.* keep, maintain, 14. 19, 140. 38. OE. *cēpan*; ME. *kepe*, also *kip*, possibly influenced by ME. *kip*, to seize. (ON. *kippa*.)

Knowledge, *v.* acknowledge, 53. 9, 93. 17, 137. 24. ME. *knowlechen*, *v.* from *know* + vbl. suffix *-lēchen*, OE. *lǣcan*. Hence Mod. Eng. *acknowledge*.

Kyele, *sb.* keel. Rydged Kyeles, 6. 11, keels projecting below the bottoms of the vessels. Icel. *kjölr*, keel.

Kyll, *v.* kylleth them vp, 140. 3, kills them off. Cf. Shakesp. *As You Like It*, ii. 1. 62 'Kill them up.'

L

Laborsome, laboursome, *a.* laborious, toilsome, 46. 23, 59. 30, 70. 11. OF. *labour*, L. *labor*, + OE. suffix *-sum*.

Laestrygones (*Lestrygones*), 7. 4.

Landed, *a.* having land, land-owning, 62. 14. Formed as if a past part. from *Land*, *sb.*

Lascaris, 96. 24.

Lauasse, *a.* lavish, profuse, 13. 9. OF. *lavasse*, *lavache*, *sb.* a deluge of rain; ME. *lavasse*, *lavesse*, *sb.* and *a.*, later corrupted to *lavish*.

Laundes, *sb.* glades, grassy plains, 16. 15. OF. *lande*;

Mod. Eng. (with loss of *d*), *lawn*.

Lay their heddes togither, take counsel together, 25. 36.

Layde in hys necke, laid to his charge, at his door, 42. 33.

Leade one's life, 43. 18.

Leage, *sb.* bond, alliance, league. 31. 35. Late L. *liga*, from *ligāre*, to bind.

Leaned vnto, *v.* depended upon, derived support from, 11. 24. OE. *hlænan*, to lean.

Lease, *conj.* lest, 61. 35. A form of *Less*; OE. *ðy lǣs ðe*, by that the less that, generally shortened to Mod. Eng. *lest*.

Leaste, *conj.* lest, 15. 16. See Lease.

Leaue, *v.* to forsake, give up, 20. 14. OE. *lǣfan*.

Leese, leise, *v.* lose, 37. 25, 88. 31, 111. 33; lose, waste, 28. 9. OE. *leōsan*, to lose; ME. *lēsen, lōsen*.

Leffe, *sb.* 62. 18. Variant of *Life*. OE. *līf*.

Lese, *a.* less, 113. 25. OE. *lǣssa* used as comparative of *lȳtel*.

Let, *v.* to prevent, hinder, 61. 11, 86. 31, 91. 5. OE. *lettan*, to hinder, make late; from *læt*, a. late.

Let, lette, *sb.* hindrance, impediment, 20. 6, 23. 9, 59. 23, 104. 19. From the prec.

Lewde, *a.* ignorant, worthless, 10. 28, 90. 8, 118. 26. OE. *lǣwed*, ignorant; *properly*, belonging to the laity; from L. *lāicus*, lay.

Licensed, lycensed from, *ppl. a.* exempt from, excused, 60. 36, 63. 12. From *Licence*, L. *licentia*, freedom to act.

Lieuetenauntes, *sb.* lieutenants, deputies, 121. 28. F. *lieu tenant*; L. *locum tenens* (*tenentem*), one who takes another's place.

Lightlye, *adv.* easily, for any slight cause, 57. 20 OE. *lēohtlīce*, from *lēoht*, easy, trifling.

Liqueresse, *sb.* liquorice, 52. 9. AF. *lycorys*; L. *liquirītia*, liquorice.

Logycalles, 82. 17. See Note.

Looke, *v.* see, 16. 2. OE. *lōcian*.

Lores, *sb.* doctrines, opinions, 94. 26. OE. *lār*, learning, doctrine.

Lubbor, *sb.* dolt, 80. 2. ME. *lobre*; cf. MDu. *lobbe*, clown, *Lucian*, 96. 27.

Lumpyshe, *a.* clumsy, stupid, 80. 37. From *Lump*, sb., cf. Norw. *lump*, block; Dutch *lomp*, clumsy.

Lust, *v.* please, desire, 17. 26, 103. 12. OE. *lystan*, impers. to please; ME. *listen, lusten*, pers. or impers.

Lustye, *a.* joyful, 130. 23. From OE. *lust*, sb. delight, joy.

Lycensed, 60. 36. See Licensed.

Lyghtly, *adv.* easily, 55. 25. See Lightlye.

Lyse, *v.* lose, 100. 24. See Leese.

Lyst, *v.* desire, please, 127. 22. See Lust.

M

* *Macariens, the*, 38. 26.

Madder, *sb.* a plant used in dyeing, 75. 6. OE. *mæddre*.

Made away, *ppl. a.* made away with, destroyed, 23. 21.

Make nothing to, make no difference to. 91. 31.

GLOSSARIAL INDEX 271

Make out of the waye, put out of the way, dispose of, 103. 37.

Maner, *sb.* Taken with the maner, 25. 28, caught in the act. AF. *manere*; Ital. *maniera*, manner, mode of handling (L. *manus*, hand).

Mansleers, *sb.* manslayers, killers, 14. 27. From OE. *manslēan*, to kill, murder, with agent suffix *-er*. Cf. OE. *manslaga*, man-slayer.

Marcgraue, *sb.* Margrave, count or earl of the Marches, 1. 29. Du. *markgraaf*; *mark*, boundary, *graaf*, a count.

Marchaunte-men, *sb.* traders, merchants, 111. 6. OF. *marchant*, merchant.

Marrish, *sb.* marsh, swamp, 100. 38. OF. *mareis*, late L. *mariscus* from *mare*, sea.

Marueil, *sb.* marvel, wonder, 28. 32. F. *merveille*; L. *mīrābilia*, wonderful things.

Master of the Rolls, 1. 16.

Me selfe, *pron.* myself, 43. 38, 44. 22. OE. *mē*, dative of pers. pron. + emphatic pron. *self*. In ME. often weakened to *miself*, and *mi* confused with the possessive, cf. Mod. Eng. *myself*.

Meanes, *sb.* by thys meanes, 24. 17, with the help of this. Pl. form of *adj.* used as *sb.* and treated as singular. AF. *meien*, medium, *hence* aid, help; L. *mediānus*, from *medius*, middle.

Meate, *sb.* food, provision, 68. 19. OE. *mete*, food.

Meerye, *a.* merry, 130. 23. OE. *myrge*, merry; ME. *merie*, *mirie*.

Meesse, *sb.* a dish, portion, course, 71. 14. OF. *mes*, dish, course; L. *missum*, that which is sent up.

Merely, *adv.* gaily, joyfully, merrily, 128. 22. ME. *meriliche*; OE. *myrig* + *līce*.

Methe, *sb.* mead, a sweet drink usually made of honey, 52. 8. OE. *medu*; cf. ME. *forth* for *ford*.

Middes, **myddes**, midst, 67. 35. OE. *midd*, a. + adv. Gen. *-es*; *tō middes*, in the midst. Cf. *againes*, Mod. Eng. *against*.

Milan, 31. 28.

Mind, *sb.* to mi mind, 28. 4, to my taste or liking.

* Mithra, Mythra, 123. 25, 134. 33.

Mitio, 42. 13

Mo, moo, *a.* more (in number), more numerous, 34. 3, 65. 11, 83. 16, 105. 37, 108. 15, 124. 32. OE. *mā*, more; in Bible of 1611 *moe* : Ps. xl. 12 'they are moe then the haires of mine head.'

Morderer, *sb.* murderer, 21. 37. From OE. *myrðrian*; ME. *murðren*, *morðren*, with agent suffix *-er* (OE. *ǣre*).

More, Sir Thomas, 9. 18, 11. 2, 30. 1, 43. 9.

Morton, Cardinal John, 10. 38, 12. 7, 15. 34, 26. 30, *et passim*.

Moses, law of, 21. 23.

Moughte-eaten, *ppl. a.* motheaten, 35. 10. OE. *mohða*, *moððe*, moth; ME. *moughte*, *mothe*.

Mouinge, mouynge, *sb.* movement, motion, 82. 25, 97. 16. 120. 15. From *Moue*, v.; L. *movēre*.

Moyles, *sb. pl.* mules, 34. 6. L. *mūlus*.

Mulettour, *sb.* muleteer, muledriver, 34. 6. F. *muletier*, from *mulet*, a mule. With

exchange of suffixes *-ier,
-or*.

Myddes. See Middes.

Myenes, *sb. pl.* mines, 22. 28.
From *Mine*, v., F. *miner*.

Myke, *a.* meek, quiet, 15. 36.
Variant of *Meek*. Icel.
mjukr; ME. *meke*.

*Mythra. See *Mithra*.

N

Namelye, *adv.* especially, particularly, 61. 3, 137. 27; literally 'by name'; OE. *nama*,
name, + adv. suffix *-līce*.

Naples, 31. 29.

Navarre, *kingdom of*, 32. 11.

Neades, nedes, *adv.* needs, of
necessity, 26. 25, 38. 7. OE.
niedes; ME. *nēdes*; adv.
Gen. from *nied*, sb. need,
necessity.

Nephelogetes, the, 111. 4, 17, 19.

Nephewes, *sb.* 139. 10, nephews,
or (possibly) grandsons, cf.
L. *nepos* which may mean
either. OF. *neveu*; L. *nepotem*,
acc.; with partial assimilation to L. spelling in sixteenth cent.

Nero, 40. 8.

Nether, . . . nor, *conj.* neither
. . . nor, 74. 12. OE. *ne* +
ægþer from *æghwæþer*, either
of two. Perhaps a misprint
for the usual form *Nother*.

Newe fanglenes, *sb.* love of
novelty, 18. 22. See Newfangled.

Newfangled, *a.* novel, newfashioned, 41. 14. ME. *newefangel*, a. fond of what is
new (OE. **fangol*, grasping
after) + suffix *-ed*, as if a
past part.

Nexte, *a.* nearest, 103. 6, 106.
37. OE. *nēhst*, superl. of *nēh*,
neah, nigh.

Nigeshe, *a.* niggardly, 81. 16.
From Icel. *hnöggr*; Swed.
njugg, niggardly, with suffix
-ish.

Nother, *adv.* or *conj.* neither,
88. 15, 136. 11. Nother . . .
nother = neither . . . nor, 63.
33, 85. 34, 94. 24, 29, 100. 1.
Nother . . . nor, 9. 20, 25,
47. 11, 63. 11, 72. 2, 99. 4, 6.
Alone after a negative = nor,
12. 14, 65. 13, 68. 31, 93. 33,
119. 7, 138. 38. ME. *nowðer*,
nawðer; OE. *nāwðer* from
nāhwæðer, pron. adj. neither
of the two, cf. L. *neuter*.
Further shortened in ME.
to *nor*; ME. adv. use
probably influenced by *oðer*,
either, or.

Noughte, nowght, *sb.* nothing,
a thing of no value, 41. 30,
42. 29. OE. *nāwiht*, *nāht*,
nothing.

Noughtenes, *sb.* worthlessness,
31. 19, 81. 1. From prec.

Noughty, *a.* worthless, evil,
40. 24. From *Nought*, see
Noughte.

Noyinge, *pres. part.* annoying,
harming, 16. 10. Pres. part.
of ME. *nuien* for *anuien*, to
annoy; from OF. *anoi*, *anui*,
vexation; L. *in odiō*, in
hatred.

Noyous, *a.* harmful, noxious,
15. 29. From OF. *anoi*, vexation + suffix *-ous*.

Noysome, *a.* troublesome,
harmful, 5. 31. ME. *noy*
for *anoy*, OF. *anoi*, vexation,
+ OE. suffix *-sum*.

Nyggyshe, *a.* niggardly, 138.
38. See Nigeshe.

Nyse, *a.* particular, fastidious,
65. 9. OF. *nice*, foolish,

simple ; L. *nescius*, ignorant, with change of meaning in ME.

O

Occupie, occupye, *v.* use, employ, trade with, 76. 23, 88. 29, make use of, practise, 60. 10, 115. 11. L. *occupāre*, to lay hold of.

Occupieng, occupyenge, *sb.* use, employment, 88. 26, 143. 17 ; trade, traffic, 39. 8, 111.27; intercourse, dealing, 66. 4. From Occupie, *v.*

Of, *prep.* (1) from, out of (denoting the source), 23. 21, 24. 1, 24. 5, 81. 26, 89. 34, 107. 11 ; (2) by (denoting the agent), 14. 28, 38, 34. 4, 82. 23, 84. 20, 89. 20, 21, 131. 36, 137. 23 ; (3) with, by, from (denoting the instrument), 29. 19, 38. 13, 70. 36, 110. 17 ; of his owne head, 73. 24, of his own will or motion. OE. *of*, prep. of, from, out of.

Of, *prep.* on. Of both sides, &c. ; on, 5. 22, 36. 13, 48. 21, 98. 20, 133. 12 ; of the contrarye part, on the other hand, 24. 38, 76. 36, 91. 25 ; of both sides them, 71. 32, on both sides of them ; of one heare, 88. 5, by one hair.

Of a child, 30. 24, from childhood. Cf. Mark ix. 21 'Of a child.'

Of that, 25. 4, for that, because.

Of, *adv.* off, 24. 22. OE. *of*, adv. off, away.

On liue, alive, 116. 20. OE. *on līfe*; *on* weakened to *o*, *a* in ME.

One, *prep.* on, 28. 33, 92. 32. OE. *on*.

Onely, onlye, *adv.* alone, 15. 31, 115. 23. OE. *ān-līc*, a. singular, only.

Ones, *adv.* once, formerly, 22. 6, 57. 8 ; once, sometime, 143. 33. Adv. use of Gen. of OE. numeral *ān*. Mod. Eng. has *ce* for final voiceless *s* ; cf. *mice*, *pence*.

Onles, *conj.* unless, 43. 14. OE. *on + lǣs*, less, hence *on lesse that*, on a less supposition than that.

Onwardnes, *sb.* advance, progress, 92. 4. From *Onward*, adv. ; OE. *onweard*, against, *tōweard*, approaching, going forward.

Openner, *sb.* revealer, discloser, 26. 11. From OE. *openian*, to open, reveal, with agent suffix *ēre*.

Order, *v.* control, dispose, 25. 16. From F. *ordre*, sb. order ; L. *ordo*, -*inem*.

Orelles, orels, or else, 9. 32, 15. 14, 20. *See* Elles.

Other, *adv.* or *conj.* either. Other ... or = either ... or, 13. 22, 33. 21, 46. 33, 51. 10, 55. 26. Other ... or els (else), 30. 28, 52. 7, 58. 6, 10. 33, ... or elles, 31. 20, 100. 21, 105. 36. ME. *oþer* ... *oþer*, *oþer* ... *or* ; OE. *oððe* ... *oððe*, with compar. suffix *-er*, and shortening to *or*. Also strengthened by adv. *Els*, *elles*, q. v.

Ouerlyuing, *v.* outliving, surviving, 100. 13.

Ouerrunned, *ppl. a.* overrun, 14. 37. ME. *runnen* ; OE. *urnen*, past part. of *irnan*, to run ; treated as a weak verb. Prefix *ofer*, over.

Ouerseen, *ppl. a.* having committed an oversight, imprudent, 58. 26. Active use of past part. of *Oversee*; OE. *oferséon*, overlook.

Ouerthwarte, *a.* perverse, cross, 10. 28. Icel. *þvert*, neut. of *þverr*, perverse.

Ouer wharte, *prep.* across, athwart, transversely across, 71. 12. Dialectal for *Overthwart*, used as adv. and prep.

Owte, *adv.* out, forth, 126. 25. The use of the adv. alone to supply the sense of the vb. of motion is common in OE. and ME.

P

Palinurus, 3. 27.

Parson, *sb.* person, 27. 1. ME. *persone*; L. *persōna*, a mask, character in a play. ME. also *parsone*, with change of *e* to *a* before *r* + cons. Mod. Eng. differentiates according to meaning.

Partein, *v.* pertain, belong, 27. 16. OF. *partenir*; L. *pertinēre*, to belong.

Partie, partye, *sb.* the person, 22. 8, 102. 3. OF. *partie*, a part, party; L. *partīta*, fem. of *partītus*, divided.

Passe, *v.* surpass, 87. 21. Late L. *passāre*, to pass, from *passus*, step.

Pass for, *v.* care for, trouble about, 8. 5, 17. 31, 65. 5, 107. 31, 116. 23, 129. 32. Cf. Shakesp. *2 Henry VI*, iv. 2. 156 'I pass not.'

Payntinges, *sb.* painting, artificial means, 105. 2. From ME. *peinten*, to paint; OF. *peint*, past part. of *peindre*; L. *pingere*.

Penny father, *sb.* miser, niggard, one who hoards his pence. 81. 16.

Pensifenes, *sb.* care, anxiety, 118. 14, 139. 4. From *Pensive*, OF. *pensif*; cf. *penser*, to think; L. *pensāre*, weigh, ponder.

Performe, *v.* complete, supply, 74. 28. AF. *parformer*, OF. *parfournir*, lit. to furnish thoroughly.

Persia, 22. 31; *King of*, 22. 36, 23. 8.

Peruocation, *sb.* for *Provocation*, 20. 18. From L. *prōvocātus*, called forth.

Peryshe, *v.* destroy, make to perish, 56. 14. Transitive use of *Perish*. From OF. *periss-*, lengthened stem of *perir*; L. *perīre*.

*Phylarch, 51. 1, 52. 22, 57. 6, 9, 27, 58. 8.

Pike a thanke, 54. 3, to curry favour, hence *pickthank*.

Plain, *a.* obvious, evident, 91. 9. L. *plānus*, flat.

Plat, *sb.* plate, 77. 11. OF. *plat*, flat; late L. *platta*, plate of metal.

Plato, 3. 28, 30. 36, 31. 15, 41 15, 42. 36, 96. 17.

Platte fourme, *sb.* ground plan 55. 31. F. *plate-forme*, platform, model.

Plautus, 40. 3.

Plesauntnes, *sb.* pleasingness, delight, 87. 5. From *Pleasant*, *a.*; OF. *plesant*, pleasing, pres. part. of *plesir*; L. *placēre*.

Plotte, *sb.* plot of ground, site, 50. 10, 64. 17. ME. *plot*.

Pluck, *v.* to snatch, take, 44. 11, to pull, 17. 30, 18. 32; plucked back, 63. 23, recalled, fetched back. OE. *pluccian*, to pluck, tear.

Plutarch, 96. 26.

Policie, *sb.* practice, mode of procedure, 51. 25. L. *politia*.

GLOSSARIAL INDEX

Gr. πολιτεία, polity, government.

Polle, *v.* to cut or crop the hair, 24. 20, 37. 28, fig. to shear, clip bare, 13. 6. ME. *pollen*, to cut the hair; LG. *polle*, head, pate.

*Polylerites, the, 22. 32.

Portugalle, *sb.* a native of Portugal, a Portuguese, 4. 1. The usual ME. name.

Possible, *adv.* possibly, 18. 11, F. *possible,* a.; L. *possibilis,* able to be done.

Posternne, *sb.* a small backdoor, 55. 7. OF. *posterne, posterle,* L. *posterula,* from *posterus,* behind.

Praye, *sb.* prey, booty, 32. 1, 110. 28, 121. 15. AF. *preie*; L. *praeda,* prey.

Precyncte, *sb.* boundary, limit, 24. 33. L. *praecinctus,* past part. of *praecingere,* to gird about.

Preparaunce, *sb.* preparation, making ready, 34. 11. From *Prepare,* v.; L. *praeparāre,* to make ready before.

Prescript, *ppl. a.* prescribed, 39. 10, 44. 33, 66. 15, 103. 24. L. *praescriptus,* past part. of *praescrībere,* to write beforehand.

Presently, *adv.* in one's very presence, being present, 45. 38, 76. 14, 91. 24, 129. 9. From *Present,* a.; L. *praesens* (*-sentem*), being in front.

Pretensed, *ppl. a.* intended, purposed, 104. 17. Late L. *praetensus* for *praetentus,* alleged, held before.

Preuy, *a.* privy, secret, 29. 35. ME. *privi, previ,* F. *privé*; L. *prīvātus,* private.

Primifest, 134. 5. *See* Note.

Pristynate, *a.* pristine, original, 92. 8. L. *pristinus,* ancient, + suffix *-ate.*

Proctour, *sb.* procurator in the law-courts, 106. 2. Short for *procurator;* late L. acc. *prōcūrātōrem,* manager, deputy.

Profe, proffe, *sb.* trial, proof, evidence, 26. 31, 83. 35. Nexte yeares proffe, 75. 3, what next year may prove to be. Older spellings of *Proof,* ME. *prove, preve*; F. *preuve,* sb. Double forms from the ME. verb.; cf. OF. *prover,* to prove; *preuve,* he proves; L. *proba're, pro'bat.*

Profitable let, *a.* reasonable hindrance, 73. 9.

Properlie, *adv.* singularly, peculiarly, 77. 24. From F. *propre,* a.; L. *proprius,* (*-um*), one's own, peculiar to oneself.

Psalmist, The, 29. 10.

Puisaunce, puysaunce, *sb.* power, might, 14. 4, 61. 31, 111. 12. F. *puissance,* power.

Pulleyne, *sb.* chickens, 51. 25. OF. *poulaine,* young of an animal; late L. *puleanus* from *pullus.*

Puppettes, *sb.* dolls, 78. 17, MF. *poupette,* dim. of *poupée,* doll; cf. L. *pūpa,* girl, doll.

Purple die fells, skins of purple dye, 75. 7.

Putt furthe, *ppl. a.* brought forward, 58. 15.

Putt to, apprenticed to, given into charge of, 60. 6.

Puyssaunte, *a.* powerful, mighty, 32. 7. F. *puissant,* powerful; L. *possens* (*-entem*) for *potens.*

Pyked, *ppl. a.* picked, chosen, 95. 36. ME. *pikken*; ON. *pikka.*

Pylled, *v.* plundered, 33. 23. F. *piller*; L. *pīlāre*, to pillage.

Q

Quicke, quycke, *sb.* living, 128. 34, 129. 10, the vital part, 13. 7. Towchyd one the quicke, 28. 33, wounded in the most vital part. OE. *cwic*, a. living.

Quod, *v.* quoth, said, 8. 17, 9. 18. OE. *cwœð*, pret. singular of *cweðan*, to say; ME. *quath, quoth*, weakened to *quod*.

Quyte, *a.* quit, free, 21. 15. OF. *quite*, released, free; late L. *quiētus*.

R

Ranke, *a.* abundant, plentiful, 12. 5. OE. *ranc*, strong, proud.

Rauin, rauyne, *sb.* rapine, plunder, 45. 3, 68. 13, 133. 20, 141. 17. OF. *ravine*, L. *rapīna*, plunder.

Recule, *v.* retreat, recoil, 133. 26. F. *reculer*, to recoil; from L. *cūlus*, hinder part.

Refrayne, refreyn, *v.* to check, restrain, 12. 11, 99. 22, to restrain oneself, refrain from, 42. 37. L. *refrēnāre*, to curb; from *frēnum*, a curb, bridle.

Reiecte, *ppl. a.* rejected, excluded, 127. 17. Past part. of *Reject*, v., OF. *rejecter*; L. *re*, back, *jactāre*, to throw.

Relygyous men, *sb.* members of the religious or monastic orders, 62. 12.

Render, *v.* give up, surrender, 112. 8. F. *rendre*; L. *reddere*, to give back.

Renowme, *sb.* renown, fame, 105. 16. F. *renom*; from L. *nōmen*, name.

Reparacions, *sb.* repairs, 64. 22. From L. *reparātus*, past part. of *reparāre*, to repair, make ready again.

Repriued, *ppl. a.* reprieved, 26. 38. Properly, having one's sentence re-proved or disallowed. ME. *reproven, repreven*; OF. *reprover*, to disallow—3rd sg. pres. *repreuve*.

Reprochefull, *a.* full of reproach, disgraceful, 78. 32, 79. 30. F. *reprocher*; late L. **reprobicāre*, from *prope*, near; hence to bring near to.

Retche, *sb.* reach, 123. 13. From OE. *rǣcan*, to reach; ME. *rechen*.

Reuenewes, reuennues, *sb.* revenues, incomes, 16. 6, 24. 5. From F. *revenu*, past part. of *revenir*, to come back; L. *revenīre*.

Reuerende, *sb.*, 45. 31. Probably an error for *Reverence*; L. *reverentia*, from *reverērī*, to revere.

Reyalme, *sb.* realm, kingdom, 35. 32. AF. *realms*; late L. **rēgālimĕn*, from *rēgālis*, royal.

Ribauld, ribbald, *sb.*, worthless fellow, scoundrel, 28. 37, 29. 19. Low L. *ribaldus*, ruffian; from OHG. *hrība*, prostitute, with masc. suffix *-wald* (power), cf. Reginald.

Ride, *sb.* Variant of *Reed*, 97. 33. OE. *hrēod*.

Romans, 14. 34, 46. 29.

Rome, Empire of, 46. 34.

Rotte, *sb.* a disease of sheep, 17. 18. Cf. OE. *rotian*, to rot.

Roundinge, *sb.* the rounding

GLOSSARIAL INDEX

of his head, the manner in which his hair is rounded off when cut, 25. 35. Cf. p. 24, l. 21.

Rubbers, *sb.* robbers, 20. 14. OF. *robeor*; derived from OHG. *rouba*, booty, spoil.

Run at rouers, run at random, rove about, 108. 36. Cf. Du. *roover*, robber, pirate.

Runne in, *v.* incur, 38. 11. A literal translation of L. *incurrere*.

Russhe bucklers, *sb.* a worthless boaster, a good-for-nothing fellow, 62. 17. *Properly,* one whose shield is made of rushes. OF. *bucler*, shield.

Rydde, *ppl. a.* got rid of, dispatched, 22. 8. OE. *hreddan*, to free from.

Ryffe, *a.* rife, abundant, 12. 5. OE. *rīf*; Icel. *rífr*, abundant, frequent.

Ryght, *a.* genuine, 88. 22. OE. *riht*, true, correct.

S

Sacke, *sb.* sake, 15. 26. ME. *sake*, sake, cause; OE. *sacu*, dispute, litigation.

Sad, sadde, *a.* sober, serious, 27. 14, 101. 20, 104. 25. OE. *sæd*, sated; hence quiet, serious.

Saintuarie, *sb.* sanctuary, 26. 35. OF. *saintuarie*, shrine; L. *sanctuarium*.

Sallust 14. 28.

Sauegarde, *sb.* safeguard, 25. 22, 36. 31, 133. 18. OF. *sauf-garde*; from L. *salmus*, safe, and OLG. *wardōn*, to watch, guard.

Sauffe, *prep.* save, except, 37. 9. OF. *sauf*, a., L. *salvus*, safe. Used in ME. as a prep. and conj. with meaning 'these things being safe,' i.e. 'excepted.'

Sauitie, *sb.* safety, 37. 3. OF. *sauveté*; L. *salvitas*.

Scasely, skaselie, *adv.* scarcely, hardly, 49. 13, 63. 9, 101. 36, 108. 12. ME. *scars-līche*, OF. *escars*, scarce; late L. *excarpsus* for L. *excerptus*, selected.

Schole philosophie, philosophy of the schoolmen, 39. 26.

Sclaunderer, *sb.* slanderer, 28. 37. From *Slander*; ME. *sclaundre*; OF. *esclandre*, popular form of L. *scandalum*.

Scoupe, *sb.* scope, 21. 30. Cf. Ital. *scopo*, a mark to shoot at; Gr. σκοπός, look-out man, mark aimed at.

Scyence liberal, *sb.* any accepted branch of knowledge, 61. 11.

Scyllas, 7. 4.

Sealynge, *pres. part.* 92. 37, putting an end to, curing. But possibly an error for *Healing*.

Seconde Intentyons, 82. 19. See Note.

Seely, seilie, sely, *a.* simple, 32. 37, 89. 20, 139. 28. OE. *sǣlig* from *sǣl*, time; = 'timely' then 'happy, innocent'; 'simple, foolish.'

Seneca, 3. 37, 40. 8.

Sergeauntes at the lawe, *sb.* Sergeants at law, 106. 2. OF. *sergant*, *serjant*; late L. *serviens* (*-ientem*), an officer.

Seruiseable, *adv.* usefully, 130. 13.

Set by, *ppl. a.* esteemed, 93, 16. Cf. next.

Sette greate store, make much of, esteem highly, 104. 21.

Sette in theyre neckes, set on them, 114. 26.

Set fyld, field arranged for battle, 61. 24, 117. 26.

Setting furth, *vbl. sb.* execution, carrying out, 55. 34.

Seuerall, *a.* separate, distinct, 24. 30, 68. 38, 71. 7, 125. 31, 138. 28; *adv.* separately, apart, 68. 1, 70. 23. OF. *several*; med. L. *sĕparālis*, separate, from *sĕparāre*, to separate.

Sewer, *a.* sure, 68. 11, 142. 1. OF. *seur*, for *segur*; L. *secūrus*.

Sewerly, *adv.* surely, 14. 8, 37. 30, 120. 3.

Sewter, 11. 10. Variant of *Sueter*, q. v.

Shamefastenes, *sb.* shamefacedness, 78. 15. From OE. *scamfæst*, a.; OE. *scamu*, shame, modesty; *fæst*, firm. Corrupted in Mod.Eng. to *shamefaced*.

Shelues, *sb.* sandbanks, reefs, 49 1. OE. *scylf*, ledge, shelf.

Shere, **sheyre**, *sb.* shire, province, 25. 23, 26. 1. OE. *scīr*.

Shiltreth, *v.* shelters, protects, 48. 22. From OE. *scildtruma*, shield-troop, guard; ME. *scheltrun*, *shiltroun*, a protection; hence Mod. Eng. *shelter*.

Shrewedely, *adv.* roughly, badly, 111. 13. From *Shrewd*, a.; ME. *schrewed*, past part. of *schrewen*, to curse.

Sickerlye, *adv.* surely, certainly, 42. 9. From ME. *siker*, a.; L. *sĕcūrus*, sure.

Simylitude, *sb.* simile, illustration, 42. 36. L. *similitūdo* (-*inem*), likeness; from *similis*, like.

Single, *a.* simple, alone, 22. 12. Late L. *singulus*, **singlo**, separate.

*****Siphogrant**. See *Syphogrant*.

*****Siphogranty** (= *ward*), 69. 36, 71. 15.

Sit, *past part.* sat, 47. 33. ME. *seten* (OE. *seten*), also *siten* after the infin., OE. *sittan*.

Skant, *adv.* scarcely, hardly, 139. 29. ME. *skant*, a. and adv. insufficient, -ly; Icel. *skamt*, neut. of *skammr*, short.

Skaselie, *adv.* See Scasely.

Skyrnyshe, *sb.* skirmish, 114. 8. From ME. *scarmish*, *skirmishe*, v.; OF. *eskermir* (*eskermissant*), to fence.

Slacly, *adv.* lazily, 23. 28. OE. *slæc*, *sleac*, a. slack, indolent.

Sleane, *ppl. a.* slain, 114. 13. From the infin., OE. *sléan*, to slay, past part. *geslagen*.

Sleping sicknes, *sb.* lethargy, 92. 16.

Sloughfullenes, *sb.* slothfulness, 60.35. From OE. *slāw*, a. slow, sluggish; ME. *slow*, *slough*.

Sloughishnes, *sb.* sluggishness, sloth, 94. 4. A formation from ME. *slough*, OE. *slāw*, as if with OE. suffix -*isc*. See prec.

Smacke, *sb.* flavour, taste, 116. 8. OE. *smæc*, taste.

So that, *conj.* provided that, 86. 30, 125. 37, 126. 23, 135. 25. OE. *swā*, so that + pron. *ðæt*.

Sodde, *ppl. a.* boiled, 52. 9. OE. *soden*, past part. of *séoðan*, to boil.

Sodeyne, *a.* Sudden, 51. 36, 120. 8. OF. *sodain*, *sudain*; late L. *subitānus*, sudden.

Som, *sb.* sum, amount, 38. 36. F. *somme*; L. *summa*.

GLOSSARIAL INDEX 279

Sophocles, 96. 29.
Sorte, *sb.* 'a lot,' a number, 53. 27. Cf. Puttenham, *Arte of Eng. Poesie*, 'a great sort of little children.' OF. *sorte*, L. *sors* (*sortem*), *properly* lot, destiny.
Spared, *ppl. a.* dispensed with, 26. 34. OE. *sparian*, to spare, abstain from.
Speces, *sb.* spices, 72. 16. ME. *spice*, *spece*; OF. *espice*, *spice*; L. *species* (*-iem*).
Spedelier, *adv.* more speedily, 64. 27. Compar. of *spedeli*, OE. *spēdlīce*; from *spēd*, success, speed.
Spende, *v.* make use of, consume, 64. 36. OE. *spendan*; from L. *dis-* or *ex-pendere*.
Spill, *v.* to spoil, ruin, 15. 20. OE. *spillan*, to destroy, waste.
Spite of there tethes, in despite of their utmost resistance, 119. 24. Cf. Shakesp. *Merry Wives*, v. 5. 133.
Stage, *sb.* her owne stage, 39. 36, her proper sphere. AF. *estage*, stage, dwelling-house; late L. **staticum*, dwelling-place.
Stand in, *v.* cost, 64. 9, 38. L. *constāre*, to stand one in, cost.
Staye, *sb.* pause, delay, 96. 5. In a good staye, 64. 16, stable, well-established. From the vb. *Stay*, (1) to support; (2) to remain. OF. *estaye*, sb. a prop.
Stomaked, *ppl. a.* tempered, hearted, 87. 22. From *Stomake*, sb.
Stomakes, *sb.* dispositions, hearts, 36. 38. OF. *estomac*, stomach.

Stoole, *v.* stole, 23. 16. ME. *stol*, *stool*, pret. of *stelen*, to steal.
Stoycall, *a.* stoical, unyielding, harsh, 20. 31. From *Stoic*, sb., L. *stoicus*, Gk. Στωϊκός, a Stoic.
Straunge, *a.* foreign, 76. 1. OF. *estrange*; L. *extrāneus*, belonging to the outside.
Strayte, streyte, *a.* and *adv.* strict, severe, 11. 36, 20. 28; strictly, 28. 27. OF. *estreit*; L. *strictus*.
Subtell, *a.* subtle, skilful, 40. 35. OF. *sotil*, *soutil*; L. *subtīlis*, fine, subtle. *b* inserted from L. in sixteenth cent., but not sounded.
Sueter, *sb.* suitor, those having a suit with any, 29. 38. From F. *suite*, pursuit, suit at law; late L. type **sequita*, for *secūta*, a following.
Sumwhether, *adv.* somewhere, 27. 38. OE. *sum*, some; *hwæder*, *hwider*, whither; ME. *wheder*, *whider*.
Surmount, *v.* increase, 48. 20. F. *surmonter*, to mount above.
Suyte, *sb.* suit, 44. 37. See Sueter.
Swychers, *sb.* the Swiss, 32. 6. Cf. MHG. *Switzer*, Swiss; Mod. G. *Schweizer*.
Symylitude, -lytude, *sb.* likeness, 20. 36, 45. 36. See Simylitude.
* *Syphogrant*, 57. 5, 58. 8, 60. 14. 63. 12, 19, 69. 1, 71. 8, 73. 8.
Syrians, 14. 34.

T

Tables, *sb. pl.* the game of tables, the modern backgammon, 18. 28. F. *table*; L. *tabula*, a table, also the game.

Take their houses, 43. 3; take to, &c.

Taprobane (Ceylon), 4. 25.

Temsice, George, provost of Cassel, 2. 1.

Terence, 42. 13.

Thadmynystratyon, *sb.* the administration, 22. 22. The elision of the *e* of the definite article before a word beginning with a vowel was common in ME.; cf. *thentente*, 98. 19.

Than, *adv.* then, 10. 3, 19. 14, 46. 16, 131. 8. OE. *ðænne*; ME. *than*, *then*.

The owne, its own, 80. 32, 92. 11, 126. 24.

Thefe stolen, *ppl. a.* stolen by a thief, robbed, 23. 19. Compound of *Thefe*, sb., OE. *þéof*, and *Stolen*, past part. of *to steal*; OE. *stelan*, past part. *gestolen*.

Their whear, *adv.* there where, 18. 5. OE. *ðǽr*, there, *hwǽr*, where; ME. *ther where*; *ther* confused in form with pron. *their*, *ther* = their, from ON. *þeggra*, gen. pl.

Them selfes, *pron.* themselves, 44. 21. OE. *hĕom*, dat. pron. + *self*, pron.; ME. *hem-*, *themself*. On the analogy of *miself*, *herself*, we have ME. *theirselves* with *self* treated as a sb. and made pl. Hence also, confusedly, *themselfes*.

Theodorus, 96. 24.

Theophrastus, 96. 18.

There awaye, *adv.* in these parts, 115. 32. Cf. *thereabouts*.

Thether, *adv.* thither, there, 67. 37, 98. 5. OE. *ðider*; ME. *thider*, *theder*; cf. *hider*, *heder* for hither. *d* changed to *th* before *r* as in *father*, OE. *fœder*, &c.

This notwithstanding, notwithstanding this, nevertheless, 61. 6. An absolute clause = L. *hoc non obstante*.

Thorough, *prep.* 27. 29; through, 27. 29. OE. *þurh*; ME. *thuruh*, *thoruh*, *thruh*.

Thronge, *ppl. a.* crowded, 69. 14. OE. *geþrungen*, past part. of *þringan*, to throng. ME. *thrungen*, *throngen*, thronged.

Throughlye, *adv.* thoroughly, 41. 24. OE. *þurh*, prep. through + adv. suffix *-līce*. See Thorough.

Thucydides, 96. 30.

To, *prep.* for, 45. 13. *adv.* too, 12. 10, 36, 62. 2, 65. 9. OE. *tō*, prep. and adv. Mod. Eng. distinguishes between the accented adv. and the unaccented prep.; cf. *of* and *off*.

Togethers, *adv.* together, 72. 22. 124. 30. OE. *tō-gœdre*, together; ME. *togedere* + *-es* from the adv. Gen. *d* becomes *th* before *r*; see Thether.

Torues, *sb. pl.* sods, turf, 5. 1. OE. *turf*; ME. *turf*, sod, turf; pl. *turues*, *torues*.

Towardnes, *sb.* inclination, 72. 7, 81. 29. From *Toward*, a.; ME. *tōward*, well-disposed; OE. *tōweard*, approaching.

Traine, trayne, *sb.* device, 40. 35, 42. 15. ME. *train*; OF. *trahin*, stratagem.

*Tranibore, 57. 8, 21, 58. 4, 63. 30, 73. 9.

Translatynge, *pres. part.* transferring, 49. 16. *Translate*, v., late L. *translātāre* from *translātus*, transferred.

* *Trapemernes*, 134. 4.

Trauaile, trauayle, *sb.* labour, toil, 45. 25, 46. 32. OF. *travail*, labour.

* *Tricius Apinatus*, 96. 31.

Trippe, *sb.* a stumble, fault. To be taken in a trip = to be caught tripping, 36. 5. ME. *trippen*, to step lightly.

Troughewyse, *adv.* in the manner of a trough, 6. 8, i. e. made with flat bottoms, resembling troughs. OE. *trŏg*, *trŏh*, trough; *wīse*, manner.

Tryffelynge, trifling, playing, 40. 5, pres. part. of ME. *triflen*, *truflen*; from OF. *trufle*, *sb.* jest, mockery.

Tunstall, Cuthbert, 1. 13.

Turfes, *sb. pl.* turf, sods, 130. 1. *See* Torues.

Twise, twyse, *adv.* twice, 2. 6, 87. 14. ME. *twies*. Mod. Eng. substitutes *ce* for final voiceless *s*; cf. *ones*, *once*.

U, V

Vacation, *sb.* holiday, exemption, 63. 17. L. *vacātio* (*-ōnem*), leisure, noun of action from *vacāre*, to be at leisure.

Valiaunt, *a.* strong, able, 62. 18. OF. *vaillant*, pres. part. of *valoir*, to profit; from L. *valēre*, to be strong.

Venetians, 31. 30.

Vespucci, Amerigo, 4. 4, 11, 22, 5. 4.

Vesputius. See *Vespucci*.

Ultraequinoctialles, *sb.* those living beyond the equator, 46. 26. From L. *ultra*, beyond; *aequinoctium*, time of equal day and night.

Ulysses, 3. 28.

Vnder, *prep.* below, inferior to, 76. 31. OE. *under*, beneath.

Unneadfull, *a.* unnecessary, 65. 25. OE. *un-* negative prefix; ME. *nēdful*, needful, from OE. *nied*, necessity.

Vnnumerable, *a.* unnumbered, countless, 15. 26. L. *numerābilis*, that can be numbered, with Eng. negative prefix *un-* for L. *in-*.

Vnsensybylyte, *sb.* For insensibility, 91. 18. L. *insensibilitas*, with E. *un-* for L. *in-*.

Vnsercheable, *a.* that cannot be sought out, 138. 5. From ME. *serchen*, to search; OF. *cercher*; L. *circāre*, to go round, explore.

Vnthyfty, *a.* An error for *Unthrifty*, 64. 4. From ME. *þrift*; Icel. *þrift* from *þrīfa*, to thrive.

Vntyed, *ppl. a.* unbound, unfettered, 23. 26. Negative *un-* + past part. of ME. *tiēn*; OE. *tīegan*, to tie, bind.

Vnweldye, *a.* unwieldy, clumsy, 27. 34. 120. 16. ME. *unweldi*, from ME. *welden*, to wield, rule, manage; cf. MLG. *unweldich*, unwieldy.

Void, *a.* empty, leisure, unoccupied, 60. 31. OF. *vuide*, *voide*, empty.

Vpholden, *ppl. a.* maintained, preserved, 64. 6. Prefix *ŭp-* + *holden*, pp. of ME. *holden*; OE. *healdan*, to keep, hold.

Vplandishe, -yshe, *a.* belonging to the rural districts, rustic, 15. 10; belonging to the land, up-lying, 49. 32. OE. *ŭplendisc*, from the uplands, rural.

Vprender, v. render up, surrender, 18. 34. OE. *ŭp*,

up + ME. *rendren*; F. *rendre*, L. *reddere*, to give back.

Vre, *sb.* use, practise, 98. 20; *v.* 15. 3. From OF. *ure, eure*, sb. work, operation. Cf. *inure, manure*.

Vse themselfes, *v.* behave, bear themselves, 66. 3. F. *user*; L. *ūsāre*.

Utopia, island of, 33. 9, 38. 27, 46. 28.

Utopians, 7. 17, 43. 23, *et passim*.

Utopus, King, 49. 24, 55. 30, 125. 26, 126. 8.

Vtter, *v.* reveal, disclose, 22. 9, 25. 1. From ME. *utter*, adv.; OE. *ūtor, uttor*, compar. of *ūt*, out.

Vyle, *a.* base, menial, 70. 10, 79. 31. L. *vīlis*, base, mean.

W

Waiward, *a.* wayward, perverse, 102. 21. ME. *aweiward*, wayward; OE. *on weg*, away, + suffix *-ward*.

Warrauntise, *sb.* warrant, guarantee, 75. 22. OF. *warentise, garantise*, from *warantir, garantir*, to warrant; cf. *warrandice* = warranty, in Scotch Law.

Wax, *v.* grow, become, 28. 8, 48. 15. OE. *weaxan*.

Way, *v.* weigh, 140. 32. OE. *wegan*, to bear, weigh; ME. *waien, weien*. Mod. spelling from contamination with the sb., OE. *ge-wiht*.

Weale publyque, *sb.* state, commonwealth, 5. 20, 7. 20, 9. 5, 23, 11. 16, 12. 34. OE. *wela*, weal, wealth; L. *publicus*, belonging to the people. A rendering of L. *respublica*.

Weldynge, *sb.* control, movement, 59. 24. Pres. part. of ME. *welden*; OE. *geweldan*, to control, wield.

Well a worthe, *int.* of sorrow, alas! 102. 13. Apparently a mixture of two phrases; wellaway, OE. *wā lā wā*, woe, lo, woe, and *woe worth the day*; *worth* = OE. *weorðan*, to become.

Well-sene, *ppl. a.* having seen much, 98. 7. Active use of past part. as in *well-read, -travelled*.

Welthes, *sb.* riches, possessions, 44. 4. Pl. of ME. *welðe*, an extension of *wele*, OE. *wela*, prosperity.

Whan, *conj.* when, 26. 20. OE. *hwænne*; ME. *whan, when*.

Whether, *pron.* which of two, whichever, 34. 2, 60. 10, 101. 5. OE. *hwæðer*, pron. and conj.

Whether, *adv.* whither, 18. 12, 74. 7, 24, 129. 2. OE. *hwæder, hwider*, whither; ME. *whider*, with change of *d* to *th* before *r*.

Whiles, whyles, *adv. and conj.* while, the while that, 22. 12, 36. 6, 45. 12; whyles that, 31. 23, 41. 5. OE. *hwīles*, adv. Gen. from *hwīl*, sb. time, while. Also as conj. alone or + *that*.

Whomewyth, with whom, 115. 25. The prep. is attached enclitically like the L. *cum*. Cf. G. *womit*.

Wiped beside their gooddes, 111. 25; cheated of their goods. Cf. Cooper, *Thesaurus*, 'I have wipte the fooles from their money.'

Witte, *sb.* understanding, intelligence, 46. 22. OE. *witt*, understanding; cf. *witan*, to know.

PRINTED IN GREAT BRITAIN
AT THE UNIVERSITY PRESS, OXFORD
BY VIVIAN RIDLER
PRINTER TO THE UNIVERSITY

Wolle, wulle, *sb.* wool, 59. 30, 64. 36, 75. 6, 80. 28. OE. *wull*; ME. *wolle, wulle*.

Wonders, *adv.* wondrously, 98. 10, 132. 8. Gen. of OE. *wundor*, sb. wonder, used adverbially.

Wonte, *a.* wonted, customary, 92. 4. From ME. *woned*; OE. *wunod*, past part. of *wunian*, to be accustomed to. Used as an adj. with change of *d* to *t* after *n*.

Wordely, *a.* worldly, 143. 36. From *Wordle*, sb. variant of *World*.

Wordle, *sb.* world, 22. 30, 82. 1, 6, 83. 1, 94. 29, *et passim*. A metathesis of *World*, common in ME.; OE. *weorold, worold, world*.

Wriede, *past part.* distorted, perverted, 42. 4. Past part. of ME. *wrien*, to twist; OE. *wrīgian*.

Wrythen, *ppl. a.* perverted, twisted, 86. 17. OE. *wriðen*, past part. of *wrīðan*, to twist.

Wul, wulle, *sb.* wool. *See* Wolle.

Wullen, *a.* of wool, 65. 3. A new formation from ME. *wull*, sb. Cf. OE. *wyllen* from *wull* + suffix *-īn*.

Wurse, *a.* worse, 22. 18. OE. *wyrsa*, worse; ME. *wurse, worse*.

Wyckers, *sb.* twigs, wickers. ME. *wiker*, a pliant twig.

Wyselyere, *adv.* more wisely, 47. 10. Compar. of ME. *wīsli*; OE. *wīslīc*, a. and adv.

Y

Ye, *int.* yea, 16. 9. ME. *ye*; OE. *géa*, yea.

Ymages, *sb.* statues, 105. 13. L. *imāgo (-inem)*, likeness.

Yocke, *sb.* yoke, 110. 15. OE. *geoc*; ME. *yok*.

Yong ones, young ones, 10. 3. ME. *yong*, young; OE. *geong* + ME. *ōnes*, pl. of *ōn*; OE. *ān*, one.

Z

* *Zapoletes, the,* 115. 5.